LORA BRODY
PLUGGED IN

LORA BRODY PLUGGED IN

LORA BRODY

WILLIAM MORROW AND COMPANY, INC.
NEW YORK

IT IS THE POLICY OF WILLIAM MORROW AND COMPANY, INC., AND ITS IMPRINTS AND AFFILIATES, RECOGNIZING THE IMPORTANCE OF PRESERVING WHAT HAS BEEN WRITTEN, TO PRINT THE BOOKS WE PUBLISH ON ACID-FREE PAPER, AND WE EXERT OUR BEST EFFORTS TO THAT END.

LIBRARY OF CONGRESS CATALOGING-IN-PUBLICATION DATA

BRODY, LORA, 1945-
LORA BRODY PLUGGED IN / LORA BRODY.—1ST ED.
P. CM.
INCLUDES INDEX.
ISBN 0-688-14961-8
1. KITCHEN UTENSILS. 2. HOUSEHOLD APPLIANCES, ELECTRIC.
I. TITLE.
TX656.B77 1998
683'.82—DC21
97-17682
CIP

PRINTED IN THE UNITED STATES OF AMERICA
FIRST EDITION
1   2   3   4   5   6   7   8   9   10

BOOK DESIGN BY DEBORAH KERNER
ILLUSTRATIONS BY RICHARD WAXBERG
WWW.WILLIAMMORROW.COM

To John,

Ellie,

Rose Mary,

Reggie and Jeff,

P.J.,

and Kevin

with love and gratitude

QUÖMODO ID CERNIT?

CONTENTS

ACKNOWLEDGMENTS

This book was created with the help of a team and, in part, with the help of one of my favorite *Plugged In* appliances—the computer's on-line service. At first we worked electronically—E-mail, telephone, fax—and then we spent three glorious and grueling weeks together in my kitchen testing appliances, translating manuals, creating and testing recipes, laughing, eating, and generally having one hell of a good time. We started out as strangers who love food and, through the joy that can come from cooking and creating together, have become friends forever.

My technical expert, John "the Rocket Scientist" Chovan, lives in Columbus, Ohio, where during the day he helps faculty at Ohio State University use technology for teaching and research and at night is a magnificent home cook and award-winning bread baker. John used his awesome scientific and culinary skills to explain the physics of the appliances in this book in laypeople language. When he wasn't dismantling machines to see what made them tick, he was creating and testing recipes.

Rose Mary Schaefer is the head houseware selling manager for the department store division of Dayton Hudson Corporation in Minneapolis, Minnesota. Rose Mary advised me on industry trends as well as gave me insight on what the consumer wants and was a steady hand when it came to overall organization. She is a recipe developer and tester of great skill and creativity and one of the most practical problem solvers I've ever met—every one should be lucky enough to have a Rose Mary in his or her life.

Professionally trained cook and freelance writer Elinor Nelson helped me from the very start of this project, first by assisting in the choosing of recipes to be tested, then with the actual testing (and retesting, in many cases). She was the first line of attack in the manuals department and the one who got all the hysterical calls that began, "Can you translate this into English?" Her calm manner, wonderfully competent skills, and inventive and creative plans of attack, as well as her attention to detail, made a huge job manageable.

Reggie and Jeff Dwork, from San Jose, California, run many important food lists on the Internet. They wrestled the data monster on this project. While the rest of us tossed incoherent thoughts and half-finished sentences at her, Reggie calmly and coolly caught every word and typed it (spelled and punctuated correctly) into her laptop computer. Hour after hour she sat at my kitchen table, tapping away, getting up only when she ran out of Tab or couldn't resist the urge to run yet one more test recipe in the bread machine (her favorite appliance). Jeff kept the computers up and running and the networks talking to each other as well as serving as the official appliance manual translator. Appliance junkies like the rest of us, Reggie and Jeff gave us sound advice when it came to making the hard choices about what did and didn't stay in the book. Reggie did the first edit of the recipes—in record time, I might add.

I don't think my computer-whiz, Kevin Ackert, realized quite what he was in for when I asked him to create a database that would not only allow me and six other people to input recipes in a certain way, but allow six people using six different operating systems talking to each other over different Internet servers to send those recipes to each other electronically. Thankfully Kevin has the patience of a saint and the genius of two Einsteins. My custom-made database made life easier for all of us . . . except Kevin. Thanks as well to Kevin's daughter, Angie, for her help in transcribing data.

God, in her wisdom, sent me P. J. Hamel, who has been my treasured right hand through my last several books and in my life in general. While it's become a bit more of a challenge to distract her from her real job of creating the world-class King Arthur Flour Baker's Catalog and the King Arthur Flour Baking Sheet, P.J.'s sage and sane advice is always available to me, be it cooking and recipes, food chemistry, practical advice, or just a gentle shove in the right direction whenever I need it.

Warm thanks to both Carol Fowler and Diane Phillips for their generous advice, suggestions, and recipes. And to Kathy Braden, Latin teacher at the Dublin School in Dublin, New Hampshire, for her skills at translating.

A girl is only as good as her agent, and when the agent is a good friend, then the girl is doubly blessed. Thank you, Susan Ginsburg, for your talent, support, and, above all, friendship. I treasure all three. I know Susan will join me in a tip of the hat to her assistant, John Hodgman—his even keel keeps both of us on a steady course.

A huge thank you goes to my wonderful editor, Pam Hoenig, who picked up this project somewhere in the middle and directed and shaped it into a finished book with enormous skill, good humor, and a kind and gentle touch. Pam's assistant, Naomi Glikman, was a godsend when it came to adding, subtracting, and moving around text.

I am grateful to members of the trade who gave me direction and advice, offered resources and contacts, as well as provided me with appliances to play with. They are: Paul Ackels and Sue Manory at Cuisinart; Susan Van Put at Krups; Christopher J. Hugan and Hillary Allard at Braun; Jeffrey Hamano at Zojirushi; Don Rao at Chandre; Mark Balsama at Panasonic; Lori Baker at Rival; Cherine G. Berg at Sanyo/Fisher; Joanne Turchany at West Bend; Becky Bunnwell at Black & Decker; Jackie Smalley at Sunbeam/Oster; Holly Smith-Berry at Toastmaster; Barb Westfield at Salton/Maxim; Priscilla Tuminello at Edgecraft; and Susan Bridges at T-Fal.

LORA BRODY
PLUGGED IN

INTRODUCTION

You may have started out with an inherited blender or a yard-sale microwave. Maybe your children gave you a bread machine so that your arthritic hands would be spared the kneading process. Perhaps you are newly married and find yourself surrounded by a bewildering sea of shiney white machines sporting plugs, digital readouts, and confusing operating manuals. Today's kitchen has at least one and perhaps as many as ten small electric appliances. Chances are they are underutilized (if they are used at all), when they could be helping you out.

Probably, like all of us, you are pressed for time and looking for a solution to the dinnertime crunch. In my house the answer lies in letting machines do the lion's share of the work. While I wouldn't dream of letting a SaladShooter (yuk!) touch my lettuce and cucumbers, I use the food processor to make coleslaw in seconds, the handheld blender to make perfect vinaigrette, the bread machine to make dough for rolls, the slow cooker to make chicken stew, and the rice cooker to make pilaf. I'll make applesauce in the microwave and then add it and some vanilla yogurt to the ice-cream machine to make frozen yogurt for dessert. For company, I'll use the blender for fresh strawberry daiquiris, the electric water smoker to make my own smoked salmon, and the deep fryer to make sweet potato fries.

The machines in this book are kitchen tools in much the way a good knife or measuring cup is. They can be employed in many ways, from helping you turn ingredients into the main part of a dish (the food processor, to make pasta dough) to cooking the entire dish as the slow cooker does. Not only do the following recipes put these machines through their paces in the expected ways, they encourage you to use them in nontraditional ways as well—making stock in the rice cooker or a cake in the electric skillet.

Machines will never replace your hands and head in the kitchen. There is no substitute for touch and taste when it comes to good cooking. But by allowing machines to help save time and energy, you gain the freedom to experiment with lots of new dishes or simply to put your feet up and relax.

While I couldn't include each and every electric kitchen appliance on the market, we have amassed a comprehensive list of every one we considered, just to demonstrate the amazing range and choice of small electrics on the market today. That they may not appear in the book (other than in this list) does not mean they are not useful kitchen tools. I own and use many of these appliances (excluding the cotton-candy machine, bagel machine, and hot-dog maker). While I don't use my chocolate-tempering machine (seductively called the Sinsation) or pizzelle iron (a fancy thin-waffle maker) every day—or even every month—my kitchen would be less fun without them. Obviously some of these gadgets are just plain silly and are probably given as gifts, used once, and put away until they are sold at garage sales. Others, such as a food processor, bread machine, and slow cooker, I wouldn't consider living without.

Survey of Electrical Appliances

1. BAGEL MACHINE
2. BLENDER
3. BLENDER, HANDHELD
4. BREAD MACHINE
5. CHEESE GRATER
6. CHOCOLATE-TEMPERING MACHINE
7. CITRUS JUICER
8. COFFEE GRINDER
9. COFFEEMAKER
10. COFFEE MILL
11. COMPUTER
12. CONVECTION OVEN
13. COOKIE PRESS
14. COTTON-CANDY MACHINE
15. CRISPER
16. DEEP FRYER
17. DEHYDRATOR
18. DONUT MAKER
19. DRINK MIXER
20. EGG COOKER
21. ELECTRIC KNIFE
22. ESPRESSO MACHINE
23. FONDUE POT
24. FOOD PROCESSOR
25. FOOD PROCESSOR, MINI
26. FROTHER
27. GRAIN MILL
28. GRIDDLE
29. GRILL, HORIZONTAL
30. GRILL, VERTICAL
31. HAND MIXER
32. HOT PLATE
33. HOT POT
34. HOT-DOG AND BUN COOKER
35. HOT-DOG COOKER

36. ICE-CREAM MAKER
37. ICE-CREAM SCOOP
38. ICE CRUSHER
39. IMMERSION HEATER
40. INSTANT HOT WATER FAUCET
41. JUICE EXTRACTOR
42. KNIFE SHARPENER
43. MEAT GRINDER
44. MEAT SLICER
45. MICROWAVE OVEN
46. MIXER, STAND
47. PASTA EXTRUDER
48. PASTA ROLLER
49. PEELER
50. PEPPER MILL
51. PIZZA BAKER
52. PIZZELLE IRON
53. POPCORN POPPER
54. POTATO STEAMER
55. RACLETTE GRILL
56. RICE COOKER
57. ROASTER
58. ROTISSERIE
59. SALADSHOOTER
60. SANDWICH MAKER
61. SCALE
62. SEAL-A-MEAL
63. SHRIMP SLICER AND DEVEINER
64. SIFTER
65. SKILLET
66. SLOW COOKER
67. SMOKER
68. STEAMER
69. TEAKETTLE
70. TEA MAKER
71. THERMOMETER
72. TIMER
73. TOASTER
74. TOASTER OVEN
75. TORTILLA PRESS
76. WAFFLE MAKER
77. WARMING BLANKET
78. WARMING TRAY
79. WOK
80. YOGURT MAKER

HOT PICKS

This book was written according to the Thumper Principle. Hopefully you remember the diplomatic little rabbit in *Bambi* who said, "If you can't say anything nice, then don't say anything at all." If you don't see it here, then it didn't make the cut. The team tested dozens of appliances, and the ones that made the top twenty are those they found the most useful, the most versatile, the sturdiest, the most time and energy saving, and the most apt to deliver good service in proportion to how much they cost. These are the appliances we would keep on our counters and use several times a week. I have generally avoided brand names except where I felt there was only one true star and the competition wasn't worth the money. The team has strongly held opinions about both appliances and brand names. Here's some feedback:

ELLIE

FAVORITE APPLIANCE: KitchenAid stand mixer and Cuisinart food processor. The hand mixers that convert to stand mixers don't have enough power. The steamer was a sleeper! She was surprised and delighted by its utility. Ellie loved the Vitantonio tortilla press and was extremely impressed with the first-class cookbook that came with it.

Bread machine: Zojirushi made the best bread and crust.

Ice-cream machine: Freezer canister models (Krups) made harder ice cream. Salt and ice machines make a softer product. Both of these are fun appliances, particularly for children, and they are very kid friendly, i.e., no blades, no hot surfaces.

Waffle maker: Very flexible and great for making French-toast waffles for the kids. Never leave burned remnants in the waffle maker. If the grill plates were removable so they could be washed in the sink, that would be fantastic.

REGGIE

FAVORITE APPLIANCES: Bread machine and slow cooker.

Bread machine: Zojirushi because it has a kneading element and is programmable.

Food processor: Has a Cuisinart and would only use a Cuisinart.

Microwave oven: Uses it mostly for reheating, but used to use it to render fat from beef to make low-fat meals.

Slow cooker: Wonderful for grains and beans. Has used it to bake cakes and breads with lots of success.

Stand mixer: Uses a KitchenAid and enjoys comparing and contrasting bread recipes made in it and in the bread machine.

ROSE MARY

FAVORITE APPLIANCE: Cuisinart food processor; she's used it to prep for everything (four-layer torte, bagel dough, purées, soup, and salad from start to finish). It's versatile and flexible. She advises getting the auxiliary flat lid.

Surprises:

> **HANDHELD BLENDER:** Perfect for making salad dressings; worth dirtying since it's so easy to clean.
>
> **KRUPS MINI FOOD PROCESSOR:** Didn't think it could hold its own against the Cuisinart, but it did beautifully.
>
> **RICE COOKER:** Cooks more than just rice.

Blender: Likes the KitchenAid, since it has a large-diameter container and can chop ice; others with wide mouths are just okay.

Ice-cream machine: Krups, since it has a freezer canister; or gelato machine by Williams-Sonoma.

Rice cooker: Loves the versatility, great for prepping; hidden cord storage of the Zojirushi is a nice feature.

Waffle maker: Versatile. She loves the 4x Belgian waffle maker by Vitantonio.

LORA

FAVORITE APPLIANCES: Couldn't live without my KitchenAid stand mixer (I actually own two!), my Cuisinart (get the new version with a flat lid—I hate messing with the damn feeding tube). I am also very impressed with the KitchenAid food processor—it seemed to have the same capabilities of its rival, but without the flash and high price. I couldn't live without my wonderful Zojirushi bread maker and its pal the Neuro Fuzzy Logic rice cooker and my three different sized Rival Crock-Pots. I use a coffee mill to grind wheat for bread; it is especially good if you are a one-loaf-at-a-timer (if you use it for grinding wheat, don't use it for anything else, especially coffee). I no longer use my stand mixer or food processor for kneading bread dough because I think the bread machine does a much better job.

Blender: Great for foamy milk shakes and frozen drinks. I love how the blender aerates liquids and purées soups; it will not make a mess. Do not pay extra for a gazillion buttons; all you need is a low, high, pulse, and off. Lexan versus a glass container is a real consideration; decide who is going to use it before you pick the type of container. The glass containers are too heavy for children to handle.

Hand mixer: Does not fit my cooking style. I typically use high-end, heavy-duty appliances since they are the sturdiest ones that will last, and the components are typically very sturdy, too.

Ice-cream maker: The Williams-Sonoma gelato maker worked very well and was so beautiful I kept it on the counter.

Microwave oven: I use it exclusively to heat things up; it's good for cooking grains, softening ice cream, and melting chocolate or butter, but I never cook a main course in it. Defrosting is too complicated to do. It's also too easy for things to boil over or explode and make a mess. It's too easy for food to get burned. Cooking is not even: Some spots are overcooked (in a matter of seconds) while others are still underdone; food is mainly just steamed.

Mini food processor: Krups worked better than all the others.

Smoker: I *love* the smoker! It's not an essential, but you can get a good deal on one, making it easier to justify the purchase. It's very easy to use a smoker; cleanup is easy; and it's easier than barbecuing since it is slow and does not require baby-sitting.

Steamer: A good idea but too small to prepare main courses or desserts. Plus it's too easy to get burned by the steam.

Tortilla press and waffle maker: The Vitantonio offerings were so much fun to use: Any batter or dough can be transformed into anything that is eminently edible.

Wok: I used it during my kitchen renovation as my only burner; made soups and chili in it.

My favorite off-the-wall appliance was the Sinsation chocolate-tempering machine. It's a must if you are into candy making and want to work with real chocolate that must be tempered.

I'd like to mention two other great appliances that I use daily in my kitchen: the Edgecraft knife sharpener (I use the professional model, but all of them work wonderfully well), and also by Edgecraft, the world's most beautiful and functional electric teakettle. If you need something to glamorize your kitchen counter, this stainless-steel beauty is the appliance for you.

JOHN

I love to bake, especially bread. If I cook meals, it has to be for six to ten people. Cooking for two is not amusing to me, and I look for ways to make it easier with very little cleanup.

Blender: Lookswise, I'd pick the bar model Waring blender available in the Williams-Sonoma catalog. I think the KitchenAid packs the most power. Make sure to pick a blender that has a removable bottom for easy cleanup.

Bread machine: The Zojirushi is my pick because it is so sturdy. I especially like the powerful motor for kneading whole-grain breads.

Food processor: I have used a KitchenAid model and a Cuisinart model. The KitchenAid is good for about 90 percent of the jobs I have asked it to do. The dual-size work bowls is a very nice feature, and it is very easy to clean. The Cuisinart does a superior job with dough and is very sturdy, but it is a pain to clean the big feed tube. So I use a flat lid and use the machine primarily to make French bread using Julia Child's recipe in *The Way to Cook*.

Handheld blender: The Cuisinart handheld blender felt good in my hand; it was well balanced and easy to maneuver without feeling awkward. The Hamilton Beach was the easiest to clean.

Hand mixer: I don't really use a hand mixer, except to make seven-minute frosting on the stove top. I want a very light model with few speeds, so the less-expensive models suit me just fine. I have an old General Electric mixer that is older than I can remember.

Ice-cream machine: I love frozen desserts, and these machines are simply wonderful. I do not like adding ice and salt to the canister models, so I pick the units with compressors. The Williams-Sonoma gelato maker is a gorgeous piece of machinery, and the smaller quantities it makes allow me to try out different recipes more frequently.

Mini food processor: For the few times that I need a small food processor, the small work bowl of the KitchenAid food processor works fine.

Rice cooker: I loved using the Zojirushi rice cooker with the "neural fuzzy" controls. It is a beautiful piece of equipment and is flexible enough to cook several different kinds of grains to perfection.

Skillet and wok: I use the Farberware stainless-steel models and really love them. They are large and hold their temperature very well.

Slow cooker: This was truly a surprise to me. My 1970s' image of the Crock-Pot has been shattered. It can be used for so many things that I never thought about, especially making cooked cereal.

Smoker: Very easy to assemble and to use. The food was out of this world. My favorite recipe using the smoker was a smoked-trout mousse served on matzo with balsamic capers. My mouth is still watering!

Stand mixer: I use a five-quart KitchenAid mixer when I bake. The large capacity allows me to make my giant bread recipes without straining my arms and shoulders. I really love the versatility of the attachments, especially the grain mill and rotary slicer/shredder.

KNOW YOUR MOTOR

To help you understand what can go wrong with an electric kitchen appliance, you should understand a little bit about how one works. An electric motor turns because the electricity entering the motor turns its coils of wiring into magnets. The poles of these magnets are aligned so the same poles are near each other. That is, the North Pole of one magnet is aligned with the North Pole of an opposing magnet. The magnetic fields push the magnets apart (like poles repel each other) and the magnetic coils located on the part that is free to rotate are pushed away from those that do not rotate. This turns the shaft of the motor. Due to the structure of the motor, as the coils turn, their polarity changes repeatedly and rapidly, causing the shaft to continue on its journey around and around.

If something physically prevents the motor from turning, like very heavy bread dough in a stand mixer or a chunk of carrot caught in the food processor, the motor can burn out. This happens because although the shaft is held in place, the electricity coursing through the motor's wires is still creating the large forces that want to turn it. The energy is not dissipated by moving the coils apart, and therefore the wires in the coils overload. The overload can blow a fuse or melt the wiring, and the motor will no longer operate. Once you smell the acrid odor of melted wiring, it is too late: The motor is a goner.

Some motors include a thermal circuit breaker that senses the temperature of the motor and stops it before it gets so hot that the wiring burns out. When these circuit breakers trip, they allow the motor to cool off before activating them again.

Preventive measures can save your motor from giving up the ghost. First, if a motor ever stalls, turn the power off *immediately*. Once whatever was preventing the motor from turning is unjammed, the motor should work properly. If your appliance is laboring heavily, feel the housing around the motor. If it is getting warm to the touch, turn it off and let it cool down before turning it back on. This, of course, could have a negative impact on your recipe, but a cupcake of prevention is worth a Sacher torte of cure.

GENERAL TIPS

- *Cooking is fun for the whole family, but electric kitchen appliances should be used by adults or by children with adult supervision.*

- *Read and heed the manufacturer's instructions and safety recommendations.*

- *Before purchasing any small appliance, talk to your friends and try out their appliances first. If possible, try them out at the store before buying. When considering a second-hand machine, plug it in and turn it on before deciding if it is appropriate for your use.*

- *Before you first use an appliance, wash the parts that come in contact with food according to the manufacturer's directions with warm, soapy water, then rinse well.*

- *Clean your appliances with a damp sponge sprinkled with baking soda; they will stay fresh and clean. Use a toothbrush or Q-Tips to clean hard-to-reach places.*

- *Leave tight-fitting tops and covers slightly ajar during storage so any moisture can have a chance to evaporate.*

- *Take care to clean appliances well—especially of flour and grains—before storing. Hidden food attracts insects—especially meal moths—and accumulated oil left on cooking surfaces attracts dirt and will become rancid, affecting the taste of the food.*

- *Stick to the brands that are sold by major manufacturers of small appliances to ensure top quality. Sources of information include corporate and consumer web pages, consumer magazines, on-line newsgroups and mailing lists, and cooking magazines that take no money from advertisers such as Cook's Illustrated. A knowledgeable department or gourmet store electrics buyer can be a gold mine of information. Go on a slow day and ask his or her opinion of brands and quality.*

- *Generally, do not use extension cords with your appliances and always make sure your cords are not draped so they can be tripped over. Heavy, hot, or steamy appliances can easily be pulled off the counter by accident if the cord is snagged.*

- *Turn the appliance off before unplugging it. Do not unplug an appliance to turn it off.*

- *Unplug any kitchen appliance before cleaning.*

- *Unplug the cord from the outlet before unplugging it from the appliance.*

- *Use the plug, not the cord, to pull from the outlet.*

- *Do not use electrical appliances during lightning storms; an electrical surge can damage the motor.*

- *Do not override any safety feature that was designed for your appliances.*

- *When buying a second-hand appliance, make sure all the parts are included and that they are not broken, cracked, chipped, or dented. Also make sure that nonstick coatings are not flaking or scratched and be sure to try the cord before you make your purchase. Make sure the appliance sits squarely on the work surface without rocking or tilting.*

- *Do not use an appliance wired for 220 voltage in a 110 outlet or vice versa.*

- *If keeping clear, plastic work bowls like those on food processors and blenders, clear and unscratched is important to you. Do not put them in* the dishwasher as the detergent will scratch them. You can extend the life of these bowls by washing them by hand in mild detergent.

- If an appliance is dropped and the plastic housing cracks, the impact is usually significant enough for internal damage to have occurred. Have the unit checked out by the manufacturer or an authorized repair service.

- Do not attempt a home repair on an appliance under warranty—you will invalidate the warranty.

- If the cord on an appliance is cracked or frayed, or if the plug is broken or missing a prong, do not use it. Take it to a manufacturer or authorized repair facility to have the cord and/or plug replaced with approved parts.

- To preserve nonstick coatings, use plastic or wooden utensils that will not scratch the coating. Wooden spatulas or chopsticks work very well.

- Make sure appliances have plenty of clear space around them on all sides, bottom, and top. If an appliance gives off heat or steam while it is being used, make sure it is not tucked under your cabinets or the heat and moisture may damage the cabinets and/or things inside.

- Most appliances with heating surfaces, such as waffle irons and griddles, are coated with a thin layer of nontoxic oil during shipment. This layer burns off the first time the appliance is turned on and may smell. Let the appliance heat up before using it the first time and throw away the first waffle or tortilla you cook on it, since it may absorb an odd taste from the appliance that first time around.

- Do not sit an electric appliance in a puddle of water since electricity and water do not mix. For most appliances to work properly, air must circulate correctly, and vents on the bottom of the appliance must be clear. Some appliances actually pull air into the vents on the bottom, so any water underneath could be pulled into the appliance as well, shorting out the electrical components.

- Select electrical appliances with features that match your individual cooking style.

If you plug in your appliance and it trips a circuit breaker or ground fault circuit interrupter (GFCI), there is an electrical short in your appliance. This can be a seriously dangerous situation and could lead to electrocution. Unplug the appliance immediately and take it back. The store should either give you a replacement or give you your money back. Under no circumstances should you try to use this defective appliance again.

Altitude affects the temperature at which water boils and how much doughs and batters rise. Cooking times will need to be adjusted to accommodate these differences. High-altitude baking usually requires less leavening, and water will boil at a lower temperature, requiring you to add more salt once the water is boiling or allow for longer cooking times. (Salt raises the boiling point of water, so liquids will be hotter before bubbling vigorously.) For instance, microwave oven cooking times will be longer at higher altitudes because water does not get as hot as it does at lower altitudes.

Do not use electric kitchen appliances in the garage. The chemicals in most garages can dissolve the insulation on power cords, making them unusable.

Cooking times in most instruction manuals are only suggested times. The first couple of times you make a recipe, you might want to stay close by, in the event that the actual cooking time is shorter than indicated.

The recipes in cookbooks and instruction manuals that accompany electric appliances are not always reliable. Test the recipes before serving them to your in-laws and keep careful notes of any corrections you have to make in the manual or booklet that comes with the machine.

Do not use any of the electric appliances outdoors unless the instructions specifically tell you that you can. Cords need to be grounded and protected from water.

Before using a new appliance, wash the cooking surfaces, then plug the appliance in to test. If it does not work properly, take it back for a replacement or a refund. Don't go the home-repair route.

Using the correct cord with each appliance is very important. Many cords look alike. Label cords as the appliances are first removed from the box.

You will be amazed at how easy it is to mistake one cord for another when they are not labeled.

- *Do not place appliances close to the edge of the counter since they can easily be knocked or pulled off, and rotating appliances can "walk off" the counter. Surfaces should be level, dry, and clean, and the appliance should have all of its rubber feet to help keep it in place.*

- *Do not overload your appliance past the recommended capacity in the instruction manual.*

- *Do not use parts or attachments from machines other than those that are intended for each machine. Only use genuine replacement parts.*

- *Keep hair, clothing, jewelry, and fingers away from all kitchen appliances. Use an apron to keep your tie from dangling loose, and always pull back long hair.*

- *Steam burns are a very real hazard when cooking with or without kitchen appliances. Use oven mitts whenever possible. Tilting the lid so the steam escapes away from your face is also recommended. Plastic wraps and bags hold steam in, so remove food carefully.*

- *Fill out and send in warranty cards, keeping a copy of the information for your files. Store appliance manuals and recipe booklets together with a copy of the warranty.*

- *Damaged or misplaced parts for appliances can be purchased from either an authorized repair facility or by mail order from third-party suppliers of genuine manufacturer's parts and accessories. We recommend the following two sources: Culinary Parts Unlimited (800) 543-7549 and European Kitchen Bazaar (800) 243-8540.*

BLENDER

I grew up in a 1950s suburban ranch house. Custom-designed and built by my father, it had some pretty advanced features: miniature stainless-steel doors that hid the toilet paper; a stereo (we called it a hi-fi) system that flooded each room (including the bathrooms) with whatever opera my father had selected so company could search for the toilet paper and listen to Maria Callas at the same time; a central control panel from which my parents could turn lights on and off (this came in handy when they thought it was time for my friends to go home); and a "rec" room in the basement. It wasn't until years later that I discovered that "rec" was short for recreation, not for wrecked, which was what my parents' friends got when they sat around the built-in, red Formica-covered bar eating red wine-veined Cheddar cheese spread on Triscuits and slugging down exotic frozen drinks that my father, not usually known for his reserve, served up in bathtub-sized glasses.

Blame it on the blender. Before the blender, drinks came in three flavors: scotch on the rocks, a dry martini, and rye and soda. The alcohol flavor in these basic models was pronounced enough that unless you had a drinking problem or were so wrapped up in conversation, it wasn't that much of a challenge to gauge just how much booze you were imbibing. The blender changed all that.

"Wait till you see this thing make milk shakes!" promised my father when he brought it home. We kids got to make exactly one chocolate milk shake before my parents and their friends whisked the blender away and set it up downstairs on bar-central. The next day the freezer section of the Philco was crammed with extra metal ice-cube trays. Suddenly, new bottles with bright, foreign-looking labels sprang up on the bar: rum (dark and light), tequila (the bottle with the worm—yuk!), and a delicately thin-necked bottle of grenadine that sported a label that looked like a pirate's treasure map. I watched in amazement as my father attacked a coconut with an ice pick and a hammer to supply my mother's request for fresh coconut milk for piña coladas. Drinks with slightly risqué movie-star names like Fuzzy Navel and Barnacle Bill replaced the ho-hum Tom Collins and gin and tonics. Names that reeked of disaster such as Mud Slide, Avalanche, Hurricane, and Tornado turned out to spell trouble only in the caloric sense as pint after pint of heavy cream splashed over ice cream, ice cubes, crème de cacao, and God knows what else, and emulsified and aerated into a sweetly frozen slush that tasted not so much like alcohol as it did a giant dessert you could quickly suck down through a straw. Actually, you couldn't taste the alcohol at all. "Hey, I'll have another glass of that!" echoed through the paneled basement.

The backlash occurred almost immediately. When the crowd around the bar woke up the morning after to confront the damage—megahangovers and ice-cream dimpled thighs and tummies—the new age of soda water with a twist of white wine was quickly ushered in. A genius invented Metrecal and the blender was whisked upstairs to blend diet drinks into instantly satisfying and hunger-pang quelling meals. The kids got back the new toy, and I perfected the art of the chocolate shake.

GENERAL DESCRIPTION

WHAT DOES IT DO? • Auntie Em! It's a twister! But the twisters found in the blender are totally under your command, and the results are miraculous, not disastrous. Within its covered container, a blender chops solid foods such as nuts, frozen fruit, or ice into small pieces; extracts liquids from foods that contain water or juice; and blends liquids and solids together in a tornadolike vortex. The vertical action of the vortex incorporates air into the mixture, making it frothy and, if you wish, downright foamy.

WHY DO I NEED THIS? • Blenders are best used for incorporating air into a mixture such as a frothy drink. They can process up to three to four cups of liquid—like sauces, soups, and cocktails. If processing a larger quantity, consider using a food processor or an electric stand mixer. For baking or for cocktails, making superfine sugar from granulated sugar is very easy in a blender, too.

HOW DOES IT WORK? • Blenders consist of a multispeed electric motor in a plastic or metal base that turns an assembly consisting of several short, sharp blades. The metal blades, typically configured to look like a bent airplane propeller, are at the base of a container and set at an angle such that the food in the bottom of the container comes in direct contact with them when they are turning at very high speed (typically several thousand times per minute). The food is either cut by the blades or is propelled into a cyclone within the container with the help of gravity to bring the food back to the blades, chopping and mixing the contents.

The container can be made out of plastic, glass, or stainless steel and has a plastic lid. The shape of the container is usually designed to enhance the blending action and to help you empty its contents and scrape the sides easily when blending is completed.

Plastic containers are light, less expensive, do not break easily, and are not sensitive to changes in temperature when adding hot foods to blend but can scratch in the dishwasher over time.

Glass containers are heavy and can be heat sensitive but are more durable in the dishwasher than plastic. Glass containers are not appropriate for use by children or anyone who does not have the strength to maneuver them.

Metal containers are best when blending frozen drinks. But the metal is not transparent, making it impossible to monitor what's going on inside without stopping the blender and taking off the lid.

Usually, the plastic lid on the container has a small opening with a secondary lid that enables ingredients to be added while the blender is on without allowing the contents to splash out (or allowing body parts to creep in) while the blades are spinning. It is important to scrape down the sides of the blender when combining dry and wet ingredients. Some manufacturers include a narrow, rigid plastic utensil for this job, or you can use a flexible rubber scraper. The secondary lid also allows steam to escape when blending hot foods. Some of these secondary lids are marked so they can be used to measure small amounts of food.

CARE AND MAINTENANCE • When cleaning a blender, it is very important to pay particular attention to the blade assembly since there are lots of pieces that need to be taken apart and thoroughly cleaned. Unplug the blender, then remove the container from the base unit. Wipe the base with a damp sponge to remove any food, *but do not immerse the base unit.* Remove the lid and any secondary lid from the container, then take apart the blade assembly. To do this, unscrew the retaining ring and separate the blade and the gasket from the container. The gasket and blade should not be put in the dishwasher, but rather washed by hand and left to air dry. Some blade assemblies should be dried by hand, so check the owner's manual for complete instructions. Plastic containers typically will scratch in the dishwasher, so they should be washed by hand as well. Once all parts are dried, reassemble the blender, but leave the plastic lid ajar. This will keep the container from smelling stale the next time you need to use it.

WHICH IS RIGHT FOR ME? • When purchasing a new blender, look for one that has a container that suits your cooking tasks. A flexible plastic lid is easier to use than a stiffer lid, although some are really hard to put on the container properly. Get the widest range of speeds you can afford; a pulse switch is great for chopping solid food. Metal couplings between the motor and the blade assembly will last longer than plastic ones.

Some blenders are noisier than others, and making a margarita can sound like a trip to the dentist office. Try it out before buying it and if the noise level is unacceptable, try another make or model.

COMMENTS • With some blenders, the container must be seated in a very precise way or the motor will not engage the blades properly. When using a blender, do not remove the container from the base unit with the motor running.

When chopping solid foods, make sure to cut or break the food into pieces small enough to allow them to fit down on the blades, or they will not be processed. If something gets stuck in the blades and they stop turning, turn the blender off immediately or the motor will burn out. You can tell if this has happened by the burning smell. Plastic parts in the assembly that connect the motor shaft to the blades are vulnerable to breakage.

BLENDER TIPS

Attach the blade and gasket (do not forget the gasket or your food will leak out) to the bottom of the blender container first. Then properly seat the container to the base unit. Add food to process and secure the lid and secondary lid. Only when these steps have been accomplished, should you then plug in the blender and turn it on to process food.

Place the cover firmly on the container before starting the motor and rest your hand on the container cover when starting the motor.

If the motor seems to labor when processing at a low speed, use the next higher speed to complete processing.

Always turn off the blender and allow the blade to come to a complete stop before removing the lid and the container.

When preparing drinks that use carbonated beverages, prepare the recipe using all but the carbonated ingredient. Pour the blended beverage into the serving containers and add the carbonated beverage last.

When making beverages that include frozen ingredients, use the pulse feature to produce a smoother texture.

Chill the jar before using it to make cold recipes. Metal and glass containers can be chilled in the freezer to retain cooler temperatures when blending frozen drinks. This won't work with plastic containers.

When blending a hot liquid, leave the feeder cap ajar to release the steam.

Make sure you leave enough room for the liquid to expand during blending.

Put the liquid portions of the recipes into the container first unless instructions in the recipe specify otherwise.

Push ingredients to be chopped down into the liquid portion of the recipe before you turn on the blender.

Do not put ice cubes in the blender without the addition of at least one cup of liquid.

- *The more uniform the pieces put into the blender, the more uniform the blended results will be. Most foods should be cut into ³/₄- to 1-inch cubes for more uniform results.*

- *Use your blender to grate hard cheese such as Cheddar or Swiss. First cut the cheese into cubes and refrigerate or freeze it before adding to the blender through the feeder cap while the motor is running.*

- *For hard bread crumbs use stale bread and for soft bread crumbs use fresh bread. Add pieces through the feeder cap while the motor is running.*

- *Use the blender to grind poppy seeds, grate coconut, reconstitute dry milk solids and frozen fruit juices, dissolve gelatin, and prepare instant puddings and milk shakes.*

- *Use it to grind coffee; whole spices; cereal grains; or nuts such as peanuts, cashews, and hazelnuts to make nut butters.*

- *Use it to purée cooked or uncooked foods for babies, toddlers, and special diets. Use it to whip cream or make fresh butter, by allowing the cream to continue whipping until the milk solids and buttermilk have separated.*

- *If your blender has a removable bottom, unscrew it to remove heavy dips and spreads, nut butters, mayonnaise, and products of a similar consistency by removing the processing assembly and pushing the mixture out through the bottom opening into a serving dish or storage container. Carefully remove the blade from the mixture.*

SCARLET LETTER SLUSH

Yield: 4 servings (about 5 cups, depending upon size and quantity of ice cubes)

Not just another pretty cocktail, this one combines the tartness of cranberries with the sweetness of triple sec. The color is gorgeous and the taste outrageous. Don't forget to make the cranberry ice cubes well ahead of serving time.

1 1/2 TO 2 CUPS CRANBERRY JUICE COCKTAIL, TO YOUR TASTE, FROZEN INTO ICE CUBES

1/2 CUP TRIPLE SEC

1/2 CUP GIN OR VODKA

1/2 CUP CRANBERRY JUICE COCKTAIL

1/2 CUP ORANGE JUICE

Use a food processor to shred the cranberry ice cubes for large, chunky slush. Insert the medium shredding or french fry disk into the work bowl. With machine running, drop the cranberry cubes through the feed tube and shred them.

Use a blender to finish the recipe. Pour the cranberry slush into a blender, add the other ingredients, cover, and pulse until smooth. Use any remaining cranberry ice in each glass for serving.

SPARKLING FRUIT SMOOTHIES

Yield: 2 servings

Personalize this by using your favorite yogurt and choice of fresh fruit. For a thicker drink, use frozen yogurt.

1 CUP PLAIN OR FRUIT-FLAVORED YOGURT

1 1/2 TO 2 CUPS CHOPPED FRESH FRUIT, TO YOUR TASTE

ABOUT 2/3 CUP ICE-COLD CHAMPAGNE, SPARKLING WATER, OR GINGER ALE

SPRIGS FRESH MINT OR FRUIT SLICES FOR GARNISH (OPTIONAL)

Combine the yogurt and fruit in a blender, cover, and process on high speed until smooth. Pour into glasses, filling one quarter full. Top off with the champagne. Gently stir to combine. Garnish with the sprigs of mint or the fruit slices, if desired.

Frozen Pineapple Daiquiri

Yield: 4 to 6 servings

Fresh pineapple gets star billing in this magnificent libation. Throw out those cheese and crackers and serve this as an aperitif, or skip the chocolate gâteau and treat your dinner guests to this as dessert. Either way, choose sweet, ripe pineapple for the best flavor.

1 LARGE FRESH RIPE PINEAPPLE, CORED AND
   CUT INTO CHUNKS

1 SMALL CAN FROZEN LEMONADE

6 OUNCES (³/₄ CUP) LIGHT RUM

8 TO 10 ICE CUBES

LIME SLICE AND SPRIG FRESH MINT FOR
   GARNISH

Place the pineapple chunks, frozen lemonade, and rum in a blender, cover, and blend on high speed just until smooth. With the motor running, add the ice cubes a few at a time and blend just until they are crushed and the mixture is thick. Serve immediately in wine glasses or goblets, garnished with a slice of lime and a sprig of mint.

Fruit-Rum-Cream Frappés

Yield: 2 servings

Tired of the same old margarita? Here's something just as smooth and just as good!

1 GENEROUS CUP PEELED AND DICED
   PINEAPPLE, PAPAYA, OR MANGO

2 TABLESPOONS SUGAR

¹/₂ CUP SWEETENED EVAPORATED MILK

¹/₂ CUP ORANGE JUICE

¹/₃ TO ¹/₂ CUP DARK RUM, TO YOUR TASTE

4 TO 6 ICE CUBES

Place everything except the ice in a blender, cover, and blend on high speed until smooth and thick. Add the ice, cover, and blend for an additional 20 seconds. Serve immediately.

Grasshopper

Yield: 2 servings

If this isn't the queen of fifties' drinks, I don't know what is.

3 OUNCES (¹/₃ CUP) WHITE CRÈME DE CACAO

2 OUNCES (¹/₄ CUP) GREEN CRÈME DE MENTHE

3 OUNCES (¹/₃ CUP) HEAVY CREAM

4 ICE CUBES

Place all the ingredients in the blender, cover, and blend on high speed until the mixture is thick and the ice crushed. Strain into cocktail glasses and serve immediately.

Basic Pancakes and Waffles

Yield: 12 large, 18 medium-size, or 24 silver-dollar pancakes, or about 8 waffles

This generic recipe for waffles and pancakes makes light, fluffy pancakes. The addition of fresh raspberries, fresh or dried blueberries, dried cranberries, or other fruit of your choice makes them even better. Try them with a pat of the Citrus Butter on page 33.

This batter can be made up to three days ahead of time and kept in a sealed container in the refrigerator.

4 CUPS ALL-PURPOSE FLOUR

2 TO 4 TABLESPOONS SUGAR, TO YOUR TASTE

1 TABLESPOON BAKING POWDER

1 TEASPOON SALT

1 TEASPOON BAKING SODA

4 LARGE EGGS

4 CUPS BUTTERMILK OR PLAIN YOGURT OR 4 CUPS MILK MIXED WITH ¹/₄ CUP VINEGAR OR FRESH LEMON JUICE

¹/₂ CUP (1 STICK) BUTTER OR MARGARINE, MELTED

UP TO 1 CUP BERRIES OR DICED FRESH OR DRIED FRUIT (OPTIONAL)

Place all the ingredients except the optional fruit in a blender, cover, and blend on medium speed for 30 seconds, then use a rubber scraper to push any dry ingredients down into the batter. Blend another 30 seconds. The batter should be smooth and thick but still pourable. Stir in the fruit by hand.

Oil a griddle or waffle iron and preheat it until a few drops of water sprinkled on the surface splatter immediately. Use a ¼-cup measure to pour out the batter onto the hot surface, leaving enough space for each pancake to expand. Turn the pancakes when the bubbles on the top surface pop and don't fill in. The flip side takes only half the amount of time needed to cook the first. Pancakes can be kept warm on a heavy-duty baking sheet in a warm oven. Leave them uncovered so they don't get soggy.

Check the waffles when the steam no longer comes out the sides of the pan. Check the underside to make sure it's browned before removing it from the iron.

BLENDER GAZPACHO

Yield: 6 to 8 servings (about 8 cups)

Sun-ripened "real" tomatoes fairly cry out for a dish that showcases their amazing flavor and color. Here it is—a classic summertime soup that can be made in minutes in the blender. This needs to be made at least two hours ahead and served very well chilled.

1 SMALL ONION, PEELED AND CHOPPED

1 LARGE CUCUMBER, PEELED, SEEDED, AND SLICED

1 SMALL BELL PEPPER, SEEDED AND DICED

4 LARGE RIPE FLAVORFUL TOMATOES, PEELED, SEEDED, AND DICED

½ CUP OLIVE OIL

⅓ CUP RED WINE VINEGAR

2 CUPS TOMATO JUICE

2 OR 3 CLOVES GARLIC, TO YOUR TASTE, PEELED

2 TABLESPOONS FRESH LEMON JUICE

2 TABLESPOONS FIRMLY PACKED DARK BROWN SUGAR

1 OR 2 LARGE DASHES OF TABASCO SAUCE, TO YOUR TASTE

¼ CUP PACKED SPRIGS FRESH DILL

¼ CUP PACKED FRESH CORIANDER (CILANTRO) LEAVES

SALT TO TASTE

PLAIN YOGURT FOR GARNISH

FINELY CHOPPED SCALLIONS FOR GARNISH

Whirl all of the vegetables together in a covered blender on medium speed with the oil, vinegar, and tomato juice until puréed. Add the remaining ingredients except the salt and garnishes and blend at high speed until combined. Season with salt, then pour into a tureen and chill.

Garnish with a dollop of yogurt and a sprinkling of scallions before serving.

SMOKED TOMATO SAUCE

Yield: About 4 cups

Simply the most divine tomato sauce you'll ever experience.

4 CUPS SMOKED TOMATOES (PAGE 365), WITH
   SKINS, SEEDS, AND PULP

$^1/_3$ CUP FIRMLY PACKED DARK BROWN SUGAR

$^1/_4$ CUP SHERRY VINEGAR

3 TABLESPOONS SOY SAUCE OR 1 TO 1$^1/_2$
   TEASPOONS SALT, TO YOUR TASTE

Slip the skins off the tomatoes and discard. Gently squeeze the juice and seeds into a blender. Chop the remaining pulp into coarse pieces and set aside. Cover and blend the juice and seeds together on medium speed into a thin purée. Pour this mixture into a skillet set over medium-high heat and simmer until reduced by half. Add the reserved pulp and the remaining ingredients and continue cooking over medium-high heat, stirring occasionally, until the sauce is thick and no longer watery.

Variation: For a more piquant sauce, add 1 tablespoon capers, drained, and $^1/_4$ cup packed chopped fresh Italian parsley leaves after the sauce has been removed from the heat.

POPOVERS

Yield: 10 popovers

I used to think popovers were some kind of magic food that regular folks couldn't make at home. Well, I still think they are some kind of magic—especially when eaten hot with an indecent amount of homemade Plugged-In Orange Marmalade (page 315)—but I also know that regular folks can and do make them at home—thanks to the blender.

2 LARGE EGGS

1 CUP WHOLE MILK

1 TABLESPOON BUTTER, MELTED

1 CUP ALL-PURPOSE FLOUR

$^1/_2$ TEASPOON SALT

The popovers will be placed in a cold oven. Place the rack in the center position and butter a muffin tin. Place the eggs, milk, and butter in a blender, cover, and blend on high speed for 10 seconds. Add the flour and salt, cover, and blend on medium speed only until smooth. Don't overmix.

Fill the muffin tins halfway with the batter and place in the cold oven. Turn the oven to 450°F and bake for 15 minutes. Reduce the temperature to 350°F and bake until the crust is deep brown and very crisp, 15 to 20 minutes. Serve immediately.

ORANGE CLAFOUTI

Yield: About 8 servings

Clafouti is a crustless tart much like a sweet quiche. Once you see how easy it is to make this pretty dessert, this recipe will become a staple. Try substituting dark sweet cherries for the orange (or use a combination of the two).

1 MEDIUM-SIZE ORANGE

$^1/_2$ CUP BLANCHED ALMONDS

1 $^1/_2$ CUP ALL-PURPOSE FLOUR

1 $^1/_2$ CUPS MILK

$^1/_3$ CUP SUGAR

$^1/_8$ TEASPOON SALT

3 LARGE EGGS

$^1/_2$ TEASPOON PURE ALMOND EXTRACT

Preheat the oven to 350°F. Grease a 10-inch skillet with a heat-safe handle. Use a small sharp knife to cut the peel from the orange, removing as much of the white pith as possible. Cut the orange crosswise into paper-thin slices, removing the seeds, if there are any; set aside.

In a covered blender on low speed, blend the almonds and flour together until finely ground. Add the milk, sugar, salt, eggs, and almond extract, cover, and blend on low speed until smooth. Pour the batter into the prepared skillet and arrange the orange slices over the batter in a single layer. Bake until the top is golden and a cake tester or toothpick inserted in the center comes out clean, 45 to 50 minutes. Serve hot or warm.

BLENDER GINGERBREAD

Yield: One 8-inch square cake (6 to 8 servings)

This batter is particularly well suited to the blender. Avoid overmixing, and you'll have a lovely soft cake. Please note when buying molasses that blackstrap has a much stronger taste than the regular kind.

1/2 CUP MILK

1 TABLESPOON FRESH LEMON JUICE

1 1/2 CUPS ALL-PURPOSE FLOUR, SIFTED
   BEFORE MEASURING

1/2 TEASPOON BAKING SODA

2 TEASPOONS GROUND GINGER

1 TEASPOON GROUND CINNAMON

1/2 TEASPOON GROUND CLOVES

1/2 TEASPOON SALT

FINELY GRATED ZEST OF 1 LEMON

1/2 CUP FIRMLY PACKED DARK BROWN SUGAR

2 LARGE EGGS

1/2 CUP MOLASSES

1/2 CUP (1 STICK) BUTTER, MELTED AND
   COOLED

Preheat the oven to 350°F with the rack in the center position. Butter an 8-inch square pan and dust it with flour, shaking out the excess. Mix the milk and lemon juice together (the mixture will curdle). Sift the flour, baking soda, spices, and salt together in a small bowl and set aside.

Place the curdled milk, lemon zest, brown sugar, eggs, molasses, and butter in a blender, cover, and mix on medium speed until smooth. With the motor off, add the dry ingredients, then cover and blend on medium speed for 30 seconds. Scrape down the sides of the container and blend until smooth, another 30 seconds.

Pour the batter into the prepared pan and bake until the top is dry and the cake has just started to pull away from the sides of the pan, 25 to 30 minutes. Cool the gingerbread in the pan before cutting into squares.

EASY RICOTTA DESSERT CREME

Yield: 1 serving

I like to think of this as instant, guilt-free mousse. Honey-and-almond-laced whipped ricotta makes the perfect topping for the berries of your choice. Try layering the berries and the ricotta in a parfait glass for an elegant and easy dessert.

1 CUP RICOTTA CHEESE

2 TABLESPOONS HONEY

FINELY GRATED ZEST OF 1 LEMON

2 TO 3 DROPS PURE ALMOND EXTRACT, TO YOUR TASTE

FRESH BERRIES OF YOUR CHOICE

Place all the ingredients except the berries in a blender, cover, and blend on medium speed until smooth. Refrigerate for 1 hour, then spoon over the berries and serve.

BLENDER ROCKY ROAD ICE CREAM

Yield: 4 cups

In this version of rocky road made without an ice-cream freezer, the marshmallows are melted and become part of the ice cream. This ice cream is best enjoyed within two days of making it.

¹/₂ CUP COLD MILK

1 ENVELOPE UNFLAVORED GELATIN

¹/₂ CUP MILK, SCALDED

1 CUP SEMISWEET CHOCOLATE CHIPS

2 CUPS MARSHMALLOWS (REGULAR OR MINI)

1 TEASPOON PURE VANILLA EXTRACT

1 CUP CHILLED HEAVY CREAM

Place the cold milk in the blender. Sprinkle on the gelatin and wait 5 minutes, then add the hot milk, cover, and blend on medium speed until the gelatin is dissolved. Remove the pouring cap and, with the blender on high, add the chocolate chips. When they are dissolved, with the blender still running, add the marshmallows one at a time, then add the vanilla.

Pour the mixture into a metal bowl and chill until cold. Return the mixture to the blender, add the heavy cream, cover, and process on high until thick and fluffy. Return to the metal bowl, cover, and freeze until firm before serving.

HOMEMADE FUDGESICLES

Yield: About 12 popsicles, depending on the size of your mold

These are so much better than store bought! If you don't have popsicle molds, pour the mixture into a 9-inch square pan, freeze, and cut into squares to serve.

1 CUP HEAVY CREAM

1/2 CUP HALF-AND-HALF

6 TABLESPOONS SUGAR

6 TO 8 TABLESPOONS HERSHEY'S INSTANT HOT COCOA MIX, TO YOUR TASTE

Put all the ingredients in a blender, cover, and blend on medium speed until smooth, 2 to 2½ minutes. Freeze in popsicle molds.

CREAMSICLE FRAPPÉ

Yield: 2 servings

You might call them milk shakes. In Rhode Island they're called cabinets. In Massachusetts we call them frappés. Call them what you like, this thick, creamy dessert you eat through a straw is a treat by any name. You can make this with vanilla ice cream or frozen nonfat yogurt, and for a real treat use fresh squeezed orange juice with the pulp.

1 PINT VANILLA ICE CREAM OR FROZEN YOGURT

2 CUPS ORANGE JUICE

ONE 12-OUNCE CAN ORANGE SODA

Place the ice cream or yogurt in a blender, add the orange juice, cover, and blend on high speed until smooth and thick. Divide between two tall glasses. Add the soda and stir gently (the harder you stir, the more the soda will fizz up). Drink immediately.

Espresso Milk Shake

Yield: 1 serving

There is a pizza shop/espresso bar in Provincetown, Massachusetts, called Spiritus. They make a mean espresso milk shake—I say mean because not only is it one of the more indulgent drinks around, with a megahit of caffeine to keep us highfliers flying high; it costs a whopping six bucks! My husband, St. David-sent-from-God, has only a few weaknesses in life; one (thank heavens) is me. The other is an occasional espresso milk shake. This one's for you, babe.

DOUBLE SHOT OF FRESHLY MADE ESPRESSO
   (DECAF FOR THE WIMPS), SLIGHTLY COOLED

1/2 PINT HÄAGEN-DAZS CHOCOLATE ICE
   CREAM, SLIGHTLY SOFTENED

1 CUP VERY COLD WHOLE MILK

WHIPPED CREAM FOR GARNISH (OPTIONAL)

Place all the ingredients except the garnish in a blender, cover, and blend on high speed until smooth and thick. Top with a generous dollop of whipped cream and serve immediately.

World's Best Chocolate Frappé

Yield: 2 servings

The world's best chocolate frappé starts with the world's best chocolate ice cream, a hit of chocolate ganache, and whole milk. Keep your low-fat frozen chocolate yogurt, your chocolate syrup, and low-fat milk. If I'm going to indulge, I want to do it all the way.

1/2 CUP CHOCOLATE GANACHE (PAGE 138)

1 PINT HÄAGEN-DAZS CHOCOLATE ICE CREAM,
   SLIGHTLY SOFTENED

2 CUPS VERY COLD WHOLE MILK

Soften the ganache in the microwave using 30-second bursts on high power or in the top of a double boiler over simmering water until it flows but is not hot. Place all the ingredients in a blender, cover, and process on high speed until smooth and foamy. Drink immediately.

Lassi

Yield: *4 servings*

Lassi is a cold, refreshing yogurt-based fresh fruit drink that comes from India. It can be made with whole-milk yogurt as well as low or nonfat. Make sure the fruit you use is ripe and sweet and flavorful as this is the secret to making this luscious drink so delicious.

If you have an electric yogurt maker, you might want to make homemade yogurt to use in this recipe.

1 ½ CUPS PEELED AND SLICED FRESH FRUIT
SUCH AS MANGO, BANANA, OR PEACHES

4 CUPS PLAIN YOGURT

2 TABLESPOONS HONEY

8 TO 10 ICE CUBES

Place all the ingredients in a blender, cover, and blend on high speed until the mixture is foamy and thick and most of the ice has disappeared. Serve immediately.

Raspberry Samba

Yield: *2 servings*

Tired of ice tea? Looking for something cool and easy to make on a hot summer day? Here's an instant air conditioner.

1 CUP FRESH OR FROZEN RASPBERRIES

2 TABLESPOONS SUGAR

4 TO 6 ICE CUBES

2 CUPS ORANGE JUICE

1 CUP RASPBERRY SHERBET

Place the raspberries, sugar, and ice in a blender, cover, and blend for 10 seconds on high speed. Add the orange juice and sherbet, cover, and blend on high speed until thoroughly smooth. Serve immediately.

BLENDER,

HANDHELD

I know how much you love whipped cream, so I bought you this gadget," said my friend Michael, handing me what looked like an electric knife fitted with a metal rod instead of a blade.

"Wow, thanks!" I said, immediately jamming the bottom of the rod into a bowl of cold heavy cream. Pressing a button on the handle I watched in amazement as the tiny blade at the end of the rod quickly whipped the cream into a soft cloud. "This is terrific," I shrieked in delight at the thought of whipped cream on demand. An instant later, the walls, counters, and Michael and I looked like Dalmatians. "You're supposed to turn the damn thing off before you lift it out of the bowl," he pointed out, a second too late. "Good thing I learned with something I love," I replied, licking whipped cream off my glasses.

GENERAL DESCRIPTION

WHAT DOES IT DO? • A handheld immersion blender—or wand—performs tasks similar to those of a countertop blender. The distinction is that instead of taking the food to the blender, you take the blender to the food. These are the

90s' descendants of the 50s' shake machines, but now you have the choice of aerating, puréeing, or mixing with them. Just sing "Help me, Wanda!" and life will be a Hamilton Beach.

WHY DO I NEED THIS? • Handheld blenders are best used for processing 1 to 1½ cups of liquid or semisolid foods, like salad dressing, small amounts of pancake batter, and milk shakes. For a larger quantity of food, use a blender or hand mixer. Since they work in open containers, chopping solid food can be risky unless the quantity is very small because pieces can be flung far and wide. They are great for puréering soups and vegetables right in the cooking pot and are used by many professional chefs in restaurant kitchens.

HOW DOES IT WORK? • Handheld blenders consist of a multispeed electric motor that turns a metal or plastic shaft. The speed is selected by means of a dial or knob, but the motor is only activated when a spring-loaded switch is held down. When this switch is let go, the motor stops, and the shaft stops spinning. The configuration of these devices is ambidextrous, so they work equally well for left- and right-handed cooks.

Some models come with a permanent all-purpose mixing blade, and some come with a variety of attachments that connect to the end of the shaft. Smooth plastic mixing attachments, metal corrugated whipping attachments, and metal chopping-blade attachments with honed edges are typical. The handheld blender fitted with the appropriate attachment is often put into a special container, made out of either plastic or metal, that holds the food to process. The motor is activated with the switch, and the spinning device is moved up and down in the food until the desired consistency is attained. A metal or plastic hood protects the world from the spinning attachment and the food being processed. It also serves as a kind of diving bell to take air down to the bottom of the container initially when beating or whipping.

The kind of food and how you want to process it determines which attachment, container, speed, and technique to use. Softer foods, such as cooked fruits and vegetables, usually require a gentle, smooth up-and-down motion to process them, but harder foods, like nuts or meats, require a more forceful approach. Foods that need lots of air incorporated into them, like egg whites and whipped cream, require the whipping attachment while mincing vegetables requires the metal chopping blade.

Making frozen drinks requires a higher speed to crush the ice than will mixing hot cocoa, although it seems somewhat dangerous to chop solid food with a handheld blender without some kind of eye protection. To chop solid food or to mix recipes that use flour as an ingredient, the handheld blender may not be the best choice. A regular blender or food processor may be safer, and a hand mixer will not activate the gluten in flour recipes as readily.

Make sure to keep a firm hold of the container with a free hand when using a handheld blender, or the container might run away. Also, when using the whipping attachment, hold it on the bottom of the container for several seconds until the liquid on the bottom begins to be processed and move the blender up and down to continue aerating. When using a handheld blender in something cooking on the stovetop, make sure the cord stays clear of the burner or flame and that you hold on to the pot handle.

CARE AND MAINTENANCE • Handheld blenders are simple to clean and usually come with a storage device of some sort to hang the blender and attachments to dry after they are washed. The blender is unplugged from the wall and placed under warm running water. When connecting or disconnecting attachments, be sure to hold them by their shafts and not their sharp blades. The blades are made to cut things, so do not place them in a sinkful of soapy water where they will become invisible. Wash and dry them immediately after use and put them away. Do not submerge the motor and make sure the attachments are dry before storing them.

WHICH IS RIGHT FOR ME? • If using your handheld blender for several tasks, more than one or two speeds are necessary. The more speeds, the greater the variety of tasks possible. The same is true for the variety of attachments: More attachments usually means greater versatility. Plastic containers help you to see if the food on the bottom has been blended thoroughly, but metal containers are sturdier and better for making chilled food. Metal construction, such as the shaft and the housing, will usually last longer than plastic, but it will make the device heavier to lift. A storage device will help to keep track of the attachments and will let the handheld blender be at the ready-and-waiting.

COMMENTS • When using the handheld blender in a flat container, be prepared for it to splatter a bit. You will need to judge for yourself what amount of splatter is acceptable.

HANDHELD BLENDER TIPS

- Use either the deep container that comes with the handheld blender or select a deep bowl so the mixture doesn't splatter all over your kitchen.

- A gentle up-and-down motion will help to incorporate all of the ingredients uniformly throughout the mixture.

- Always make sure the blade has stopped before lifting the blender out of the mixture you are processing.

- If you plan to blend something cold, prerefrigerate or freeze the metal container that comes with the handheld blender or a deep metal bowl.

- When incorporating air into mixtures, make sure you have enough room in your mixing container for the recipe to expand.

- To incorporate the most air in the quickest way, use the higher speeds.

- When whipping air into a mixture, hold the blade just under the surface.

- Use to froth hot milk for cappuccino or latte coffee drinks.

- When making compound butters, take the butter out of the refrigerator first and let it soften while you assemble the remaining ingredients. Add the liquid gradually and beat the mixture constantly so the mixture doesn't separate.

- When blending dips, do not completely pulverize every ingredient. Leave some texture for interest.

- Many savory dips can be reused as fillings for canapés, sauces for meat or fish with the addition of a little more liquid, or can be mixed in with mashed potatoes for a new taste.

- Use the handheld blender to purée small amounts of cooked foods to make baby food, to reconstitute frozen juice, or to reconstitute powdered milk.

- When puréeing, use an up-and-down motion to move the blade through the mixture.

SMOKY JOE BLOODY MARY

Yield: 1 serving

The ultimate Bloody Mary—this one's smokin'!

1 CUP SMOKED TOMATOES (PAGE 365), WITH SKINS, SEEDS, AND PULP, PURÉED

1 TABLESPOON PREPARED HORSERADISH, OR LESS IF DESIRED

1/4 TEASPOON CELERY SALT

1 JIGGER TEQUILA

2 TO 3 DROPS OF TABASCO SAUCE, TO YOUR TASTE

JUICE AND FINELY GRATED ZEST OF 1 LIME

DILL PICKLE SPEAR

Use a handheld blender on high speed to mix all the ingredients, except the pickle, together. Serve over ice with a spear of dill pickle for garnish.

CHOCOLATE MALTED MILK

Yield: 2 servings

An old-time classic.

1/3 CUP MALTED DRINK POWDER (AVAILABLE IN MANY SUPERMARKETS AND GOURMET FOOD SHOPS)

1 TABLESPOON UNSWEETENED COCOA POWDER

2 TABLESPOONS HONEY

1 TEASPOON PURE VANILLA EXTRACT

1 CUP MILK

1 CUP CHOCOLATE ICE CREAM, SOFTENED

Place the malted drink powder, cocoa, honey, and vanilla in a tall glass or pitcher and process with a handheld mixer on high speed until combined. Add the milk and ice cream and blend again until smooth.

FRUIT CREAM FRAPPÉS

Yield: 1 serving

Not your usual milk shake—try this thick, cool tropical thirst quencher when you're looking for a change from the ordinary frappé.

1 CUP DICED RIPE PINEAPPLE, PAPAYA, OR
  MANGO

2 TABLESPOONS HONEY

1/2 CUP EVAPORATED MILK

1/2 CUP CRACKED ICE CUBES

Place the fruit, honey, and milk in a tall glass or pitcher and blend on high speed with a handheld blender. Add the ice and process until smooth, thick, and foamy. Pour into a glass or goblet.

PUFFED PANCAKE

Yield: 6 servings

We loved watching this pancake puff up dramatically in the oven. First cousin to Yorkshire pudding, it looks like a fallen soufflé and tastes just great for breakfast or an easy supper.

1 CUP MILK

2 CUPS ALL-PURPOSE FLOUR

1/2 TEASPOON SALT

4 LARGE EGGS

1 CUP HALF-AND-HALF

2 TABLESPOONS BUTTER

CONFECTIONERS' SUGAR, TO YOUR TASTE

2 TABLESPOONS FRESH LEMON JUICE

Pour the milk into a medium-size bowl. Sift together the flour and salt using a strainer set over the milk. Mix together until smooth with a handheld blender on high speed. Add the eggs, one at a time, and blend for 4 or 5 seconds after each addition. Add the half-and-half and mix just until well blended. Cover the batter and refrigerate for at least 2 hours.

Preheat the oven to 450°F with the rack in the upper third of the oven but not in the highest position. Place the butter in a 10-inch glass pie plate and set it in the oven just long enough to melt the butter, 2 to 3 minutes. Remix the batter using

the handheld blender to ensure a smooth batter. Pour the batter into the hot butter to a depth of ½ inch. Bake until the pancake rises, about 15 minutes, then reduce the oven temperature to 375°F and bake until the pancake top puffs and turns crispy brown, 10 to 15 minutes longer. There may still be liquefied butter in the middle of the pancake, but that's okay. Sprinkle with the confectioners' sugar and lemon juice before cutting into wedges. Serve with syrup for breakfast or sliced fruit if desired.

Variation: Add 1 teaspoon ground cinnamon to the batter.

CITRUS BUTTER

Yield: 1 generous cup

The sweet flavor of orange butter, heightened with vanilla and nutmeg, is great atop hot pancakes and waffles.

³⁄₄ CUP (1½ STICKS) UNSALTED BUTTER, AT ROOM TEMPERATURE

2 TABLESPOONS SUGAR

FINELY GRATED ZEST AND JUICE OF 1 LIME

FINELY GRATED ZEST AND JUICE OF 1 LEMON

2 TABLESPOONS FRESH ORANGE JUICE

2 TABLESPOONS ORANGE-FLAVORED LIQUEUR

Combine the butter, sugar, zests, and juices in a narrow container and blend on high speed with a handheld blender until light and fluffy. Add the liqueur and blend until smooth. Store in a covered container in the refrigerator for up to two months.

CURRIED PUMPKIN SOUP

Yield: 6 servings (about 8 cups)

Use freshly cooked or canned pumpkin to whip up this made-for-autumn soup. It also makes a lovely cold summer soup.

continued

¼ CUP (½ STICK) BUTTER

1 LARGE ONION, PEELED AND CHOPPED

1 LARGE CLOVE GARLIC, PEELED AND MINCED

1 TEASPOON CURRY POWDER

½ TEASPOON SALT

¼ TEASPOON GROUND CORIANDER

¼ TEASPOON CAYENNE PEPPER

4 CUPS CHICKEN BROTH

2 CUPS FRESHLY COOKED OR CANNED PUMPKIN
(NOT PUMPKIN PIE FILLING)

ONE 12-OUNCE CAN EVAPORATED MILK

SOUR CREAM OR PLAIN YOGURT AND CHOPPED
FRESH CHIVES FOR GARNISH

Melt the butter in a saucepan over medium heat, add the onion and garlic, and cook, stirring, until softened, about 10 minutes. Do not allow the garlic to brown or burn. Add the curry powder, salt, coriander, and cayenne and cook for 1 minute. Add the broth and simmer, uncovered, for 20 minutes.

Stir in the pumpkin and evaporated milk and cook for 5 minutes. Purée the soup with a handheld blender on high speed and serve hot or cold garnished with a dollop of sour cream and a sprinkling of chives.

Avocado Soup

Yield: 6 servings (about 8 cups)

Great hot or cold, this velvety soup is a one-pot recipe. It can be served either hot or chilled and can be made up to 24 hours ahead and stored in a covered container in the refrigerator.

3 LARGE RIPE AVOCADOS, PEELED, PITTED,
AND DICED

1 TO 1½ TEASPOONS CURRY POWDER, TO
YOUR TASTE

SALT AND FRESHLY GROUND BLACK PEPPER TO
TASTE

1 CUP HEAVY CREAM

4 CUP CHICKEN OR VEGETABLE BROTH

1 TABLESPOON FRESH LEMON JUICE

FINELY CHOPPED FRESH CHIVES OR ITALIAN
PARSLEY LEAVES

Place all the ingredients except the lemon juice and parsley in a 2-quart saucepan over medium heat. Bring to a simmer and cook for 5 to 10 minutes. Use a handheld blender on high speed to purée the soup, add the lemon juice, and taste for salt and pepper. Serve hot or cold, garnished with chopped chives or parsley.

Carol Fowler's Unclassic Caesar Salad

Yield: 4 servings

Carol says, "I love the way the immersion blender does salad dressings with softened/cooked vegetables as ingredients. They really get creamy and cling nicely to the greens. I also prefer not using a raw or coddled egg in this kind of dressing."

If you don't have a smoker, you can use caramelized garlic and onions. These can be made in the slow cooker (see the recipe on page 297). Add several cloves of garlic to the slow cooker while you are making the onions and allow them to cook until deep golden brown and very soft.

For the dressing:

2 CLOVES GARLIC OR MORE TO YOUR TASTE

1 ONION

1/3 CUP EXTRA VIRGIN OLIVE OIL

2 TABLESPOONS RICE WINE VINEGAR

4 ANCHOVIES

1 TABLESPOON DIJON MUSTARD

TABASCO OR WORCESTERSHIRE SAUCE (OPTIONAL), TO YOUR TASTE

1 TABLESPOON ANCHOVY PASTE (OPTIONAL)

For the salad:

16 ROMAINE LETTUCE LEAVES, ROUGHLY TORN

16 SEASONED CROUTONS

OPTIONAL INGREDIENTS:

FRESHLY GRATED PARMESAN OR ROMANO CHEESE

GRINDS OF BLACK PEPPER

SMALL CUBES OF BLUE CHEESE AND ANCHOVIES

Remove the peel from the smoked garlic and onion and combine all the dressing ingredients in a tall narrow container, using a handheld blender on high speed to mix. The solid ingredients will disintegrate; the liquids will emulsify and become thick and creamy. Combine the salad ingredients in a serving bowl and toss with the dressing. Garnish before serving.

Store any leftover dressing in an airtight container up to 1 week.

Celery Root and Potato Purée

Yield: 6 to 8 servings

The winning team of the microwave oven and the handheld blender turn any vegetable into a smooth puréed side dish. Celery root makes its appearance in farm stands and supermarkets in the late fall. Its brown, wrinkled exterior masks a sweet lovely inside. Use a sharp vegetable peeler and lots of energy to remove the outer skin.

By adding additional stock or milk, this becomes a soup that can be served either hot or cold.

¼ CUP CHOPPED ONIONS	½ TEASPOON SALT
¼ CUP (½ STICK) BUTTER	½ TEASPOON FRESHLY GROUND WHITE PEPPER
1¼ POUNDS IDAHO POTATOES (ABOUT 2 LARGE), PEELED AND CUBED	1 CUP CHICKEN STOCK
1 MEDIUM-SIZE CELERY ROOT, PEELED AND CUBED	1 TEASPOON SUGAR
	¼ CUP LIGHT CREAM
1 TABLESPOON FRESH LEMON JUICE	

Place the onions and butter in a large microwavable bowl, cover, and cook on high power until the onions have wilted, about 5 minutes. Add the remaining ingredients except the cream, cover, and microwave on high power until the vegetables are extremely tender, 8 to 9 minutes. Add the cream and purée with a handheld blender on high speed until completely smooth. Serve hot.

Variation: To make soup, add 2 cups more stock or milk, adjust the salt and pepper, and serve hot or cold.

White Bean and Garlic Purée

Yield: 6 servings (about 6 cups)

If you're looking for something a little different to serve with drinks, here's a velvety smooth bean purée infused with garlic and herbs. It can be used hot or cold as a dip or spread on crackers or toast. You can use any kind of dried white bean to make this.

2 CUPS DRIED WHITE BEANS

5 CUPS CHICKEN OR VEGETABLE BROTH

5 LARGE CLOVES GARLIC, PEELED AND MASHED

1 BAY LEAF

1 TABLESPOON CHOPPED FRESH THYME
LEAVES, OR 1 TEASPOON DRIED

1 TABLESPOON CHOPPED FRESH ROSEMARY
LEAVES, OR 1 TEASPOON DRIED

$^1/_3$ CUP EXTRA VIRGIN OLIVE OIL

FINELY GRATED ZEST AND JUICE OF 1 LEMON

$^1/_4$ CUP HEAVY CREAM OR SUBSTITUTE $^1/_4$ CUP
ADDITIONAL CHICKEN OR VEGETABLE BROTH

1 TO 2 TEASPOONS SALT, TO YOUR TASTE

FRESHLY GROUND WHITE PEPPER TO TASTE

Rinse the beans and place them in the slow cooker with the broth, garlic, and herbs. Cover and cook until the beans are very tender, on low for 4 hours or on high for 3 hours. Remove the bay leaf. Add the olive oil, zest, and lemon juice. Use a handheld blender on high speed to purée the mixture, adding the cream or additional broth until the mixture is spreading or dipping consistency. Season with salt and pepper and serve hot, cold, or at room temperature.

PEANUT SATE MARINADE FOR CHICKEN, PORK, OR BEEF

Yield: 1 cup

If you are looking for a nontraditional approach to barbecue, consider this peanut-based sauce, which will give your chicken or meat a Thai flavor.

$^1/_4$ CUP PEANUT BUTTER (SMOOTH OR
CHUNKY)

1 MEDIUM-SIZE ONION, PEELED AND CHOPPED

2 CLOVES GARLIC, PEELED AND MINCED

$^1/_4$ CUP FRESH LEMON JUICE

$^1/_4$ CUP SOY SAUCE

2 TABLESPOONS FIRMLY PACKED DARK BROWN
SUGAR

1 TEASPOON TABASCO SAUCE

2 TABLESPOONS VEGETABLE OIL

Combine the ingredients in a small bowl. Using a handheld blender, blend on high speed until smooth. Use the sauce as a marinade 15 minutes before grilling. It will keep for up to three months in a tightly covered container in the refrigerator.

PEAR AND ALMOND CLAFOUTI

Yield: One 9-inch dessert (6 to 8 servings)

A *clafouti* is a crustless quiche. It should be served warm, either plain or with a scoop of vanilla ice cream or frozen yogurt.

1 POUND RIPE, FLAVORFUL PEARS

JUICE OF 1 LIME

4 EXTRA LARGE EGGS

1/3 CUP SUGAR

2 TABLESPOONS BUTTER, MELTED

1 CUP HEAVY CREAM

1 TEASPOON PURE ALMOND EXTRACT

FINELY GRATED ZEST OF 1 LIME

1/3 CUP HONEY

Preheat the oven to 350°F with the rack in the center position. Generously butter a 9-inch glass or pottery quiche pan. Place the pan on a rimmed baking sheet (to protect your oven from spills).

Peel and core the pears and cut them into thin slices. Toss the slices together with the lime juice to coat. Use a handheld blender on high speed to beat the eggs with the sugar, butter, cream, and extract in a medium-size bowl until smooth. Add the lime zest and mix to combine. Pour a thin layer of the batter over the bottom of the pan. Layer the slices of pear in an overlapping pattern on top, then add the remaining batter. Drizzle the honey on top. Bake the *clafouti* until the top is puffed and the filling is set, 25 to 30 minutes. Serve warm with ice cream.

ZABAGLIONE

Yield: 4 servings

This hot, frothy, sinfully rich custard is the ultimate nonchocolate indulgence. Italian restaurants used to have it on the menu, then came the cholesterol thing, and diners were shunning anything with eggs—especially something so blatantly egg-driven. Now that we've all run some marathons, done the Nordic Track, and swum those laps, can't we bring back zabaglione—especially since the handheld blender makes it with such grace and ease?

The only challenging part of this recipe is being careful not to overcook and scramble the egg yolks. The mixture should not boil. It is finished when it reaches 165°F on a candy or instant-read thermometer. Remember that it will continue to cook in the pan briefly even after it is removed from the heat. Allow for this small factor when deciding if the zabaglione is done.

Zabaglione can be served cold, but I can't imagine why anyone in their right mind would give up the pleasure of inhaling the hot Marsala before digging in.

1 PINT VERY RIPE, SWEET STRAWBERRIES,
    HULLED, RINSED, AND SLICED

2 TABLESPOONS PLUS ½ CUP SUGAR

8 EXTRA LARGE EGG YOLKS

FINELY GRATED ZEST OF 1 LARGE LEMON

¾ CUP PLUS 2 TABLESPOONS SWEET MARSALA

Toss the strawberries together with the 2 tablespoons sugar to coat and allow them to come to room temperature. Select 4 wine glasses and place them on the work space. Divide the strawberries and any liquid between the wine glasses.

Place the eggs, the remaining ½ cup sugar, and the lemon zest in the top of a double boiler or in a metal mixing bowl set over a pan of gently simmering water. Using a handheld blender, beat the mixture together on high speed until light and creamy. Blend in the Marsala and continue to froth the mixture with the handheld blender. The zabaglione will first become foamy, then it will expand to almost double its original volume. Finally, it will subside slightly into a light creamy mass. Take care not to allow the mixture to boil (see discussion above). When the custard coats a spoon or reaches 165°F on an instant-read thermometer, immediately pour it into the wine glasses and serve.

WHIPPED JELL-O

Yield: 4 servings (about 4 cups)

I was going to give this a fancy name like Strawberry Seafoam, but then anyone who loved this dessert as a kid might miss the boat, as it were. If you've never tasted whipped Jell-O, then you're in for a real treat. It ain't fancy, that's for sure, but it's cookin' like Mom's (unless Mom never got beyond TV dinners).

continued

A very fancy version of this dessert can be made with coffee-flavored Jell-O. You can actually pass this off as a pretty swell grown-up dessert at a dinner party. Serve it in wine glasses instead of that Tupperware bowl.

1 SMALL PACKAGE RED JELL-O (STRAWBERRY, RASPBERRY, OR CHERRY)

1 CUP BOILING WATER

4 ICE CUBES

1 CUP HEAVY CREAM, WHIPPED TO SOFT PEAKS

In a deep mixing bowl, dissolve the Jell-O in the boiling water. Add the ice cubes and beat with a handheld blender on high speed, holding the blade just under the surface, until the mixture is very foamy. Fold in the whipped cream and chill until soft but set, about 1 hour.

PASTRY CREAM

Yield: 2 cups

Forget everything you remember about gluey pastry creams. This one is positively ethereal! Use it with the Strawberry Tart (page 131).

3 LARGE OR EXTRA LARGE EGG YOLKS

1/2 CUP SUGAR

1/2 TEASPOON PURE VANILLA EXTRACT

1/2 CUP ALL-PURPOSE FLOUR

1 CUP MILK

3/4 CUP HEAVY CREAM

Combine the egg yolks, sugar, and vanilla in a medium-size saucepan and, using a handheld blender, beat on high speed until light and lemon colored. Add the flour and beat it in thoroughly with the blender.

In another saucepan, bring the milk to a boil, then slowly add it to the yolk mixture, blending thoroughly with the handheld blender. Continue blending and cook the mixture over medium heat until well thickened. Cook only briefly to prevent curdling. Remove from the heat.

Place the pastry cream in a bowl and cover it with plastic wrap, taking care to press the wrap down into the bowl directly onto the cream (so that a skin won't form on the top). Refrigerate until cool.

In another bowl, whip the cream until stiff. You may use the handheld blender or the hand mixer. I have found, however, that the hand mixer (with the beaters chilled) whips the cream up stiffer than the handheld blender. Fold the whipped cream into the pastry cream and use immediately.

INSTANT PASTRY CREAM

Yield: About 4 cups

This is really a children's dessert . . . that's what I told the crew as I was testing it. Funny thing is there wasn't a child in sight, and the contents of the mixing bowl disappeared before I could spoon it into serving dishes. We needed to invent a grown-up use for it, and pastry cream was the universal choice. So, next time you are faced with cream puffs to fill, look no further than that box of instant chocolate pudding and your handheld blender.

1 SMALL PACKAGE INSTANT CHOCOLATE
   PUDDING MIX

1 CUP HEAVY CREAM

In a deep mixing bowl, prepare the chocolate pudding according to the package directions using the heavy cream in place of the milk. Use a handheld blender to beat the mixture on high speed until it is smooth and thick. Chill for 30 minutes, then spoon into either your mouth or a pastry bag fitted with a small round tip and pipe into Profiteroles (page 214).

EASY CHOCOLATE WHIPPED CREAM

Yield: About 2 cups

While whipped cream is a pretty serious indulgence, the idea of chocolate whipped cream is the ultimate one. It's so easy to make with the handheld blender—try it on hot cocoa instead of marshmallows, or use it to fill the Devil's Food Crepes on page 345.

continued

3 TABLESPOONS CONFECTIONERS' SUGAR   1 CUP VERY COLD HEAVY CREAM

$^1/_4$ CUP UNSWEETENED COCOA POWDER

About 1 hour before you plan to make the chocolate whipped cream, place the metal blender jar or a deep, narrow metal bowl in the freezer. Sift together the confectioners' sugar and cocoa. Add the cream to the chilled container or bowl and use a handheld blender fitted with the whipped disk (if your machine has one) or the standard blade to beat the cream on high speed until it holds firm peaks. Add the sugar and cocoa and blend until very smooth. Use immediately or spoon into a fine mesh strainer set over a bowl. Cover with plastic wrap and refrigerate. The cream will lose some of its volume but will be usable for about 6 hours.

RASPBERRY—WHITE CHOCOLATE SAUCE

Yield: 2 cups

This lovely sauce is the perfect match for a slice of rich chocolate cake or lemon bread. It's also terrific drizzled over fresh fruit, especially berries. Be sure to use real white chocolate. Check the label and make sure that it contains cocoa butter, not palm kernel or coconut oil. If you don't wish to use alcohol, use one of the fruit syrups found in espresso bars to make flavored coffee.

1 CUP HEAVY CREAM

10 OUNCES BEST QUALITY WHITE CHOCOLATE,
   BROKEN OR CHOPPED

$^1/_4$ CUP FRAMBOISE (RASPBERRY LIQUEUR)
   OR RASPBERRY SYRUP

Place the cream in a $1^1/_2$-quart saucepan over medium heat. Bring it to a simmer and add the chocolate. Reduce the heat to low and blend with a handheld blender on high speed until very smooth. Off the heat, blend in the framboise or syrup. Cool before serving.

     If the sauce is stored in the refrigerator, it will firm up. To soften, microwave for 30 to 40 seconds on high power and stir until smooth.

BREAD

MACHINE

My mother and I bought our first bread machines over ten years ago. They were those R2D2 models with rounded glass tops that occasionally walked off the counter during a particularly challenging knead cycle. Over the course of writing three bread machine books together, Mom and I have come to the conclusion that the best way to use the bread machine is to knead, proof, and let the dough rise in the machine; then take it out, form it by hand, and bake the loaf in the oven. Daily homemade bread is now a staple in both our houses, and we're delighted to share the company of several million other enlightened home cooks who have been won over.

Besides the usual suspects (folks like us who want homemade bread without a lot of fuss and bother), bread machine devotees range from men who are attracted to its digital panel, doctors who have done the wine thing and are ready to move on, senior citizens and physically challenged people who are no longer able to knead dough by hand, and even a small but stellar group of famous folks. P. J. Hamel of the King Arthur Flour Baker's catalog reports that J. D. Salinger is a convert.

My very favorite bread machine luminary is Yo-Yo Ma. Jill Molinari, the manager of our local Williams-Sonoma Grand Cuisine, alerted me to the fact that the famous cellist had been in looking for a copy of the new edition of my bread machine book. There wasn't a copy left in the store, and she hated to turn him away empty-handed. "Couldn't you send him a copy?" she asked me. Could I! In a fevered pitch of excitement I wrapped up a book and stuck in a fan letter thanking Mr. Ma profusely for the countless hours of joy that had been afforded our family listening to him play. I sent off the package ecstatic at the thought that my book would actually be sharing space in the same dwelling as a talent so tremendous and so adored by me as Yo-Yo Ma. Several weeks later a small package arrived at our house. Inside was a CD: Emanuel Ax, Pamela Frank, and Yo-Yo playing Chopin's Trio for Violin, Cello, and Piano in G Minor, Opus 8. The "G Minor" was crossed off, and written across it was "Sour Do Major"; it was inscribed, "To Lora Brody with Warmest Wishes, Yo-Yo Ma." Needless to say, I was in heaven.

Chopin is my music of choice when I make bread these days. I truly believe that the music has elevated my skill, turned me into a more sensitive, more artistic baker—the results are rhapsodic, especially when I make Sour Do.

GENERAL DESCRIPTION

WHAT DOES IT DO? • A bread machine is a cybernetic personal bakery for your kitchen counter. In fact, one very early model resembles a robot from a science fiction movie. Bread machines automatically mix bread doughs and take them through a series of kneading and rising periods. They can also bake the bread right in the machine for fresh, delicious bread, perfect every time.

WHY DO I NEED THIS? • Bread machines are much easier to clean than food processors and neater to use than an electric stand mixer. While the manufacturers' intended purpose for bread machines is to make a variety of freshly baked breads, they are unbelievable for making yeasted doughs to finish shaping by hand to make pizza, dinner rolls, focaccia, cinnamon rolls, or a myriad of other creations. Also, bread machines will not oxygenate flour like stand mixers do; thus the pH of the recipe will not change, and results will be more consistent and reliable.

HOW DOES IT WORK? • A bread machine consists of a metal pan that is placed inside a metal or plastic chamber that heats up by way of a heating element. The metal pan has a nonstick coating, a paddle attached to a shaft, and features that protrude into the pan to help with kneading. The metal pan is removed from the bread machine, and the bread ingredients are placed in it. When the filled pan is placed in the bread machine baking chamber, the shaft engages with a drive mechanism in the bottom of the machine. The lid, which might be solid or clear plastic or might have a glass window in it, is closed and one of several cycles that is appropriate for your recipe is selected by means of a touch pad. The bread machine must be situated on the counter so that air will flow unobstructed into the air vents that are cut into the plastic housing and the heat generated by the bread machine will not damage anything that is sitting nearby. A keypress on the touch pad starts the machine.

The bread machine will do several things in sequence. Which elements of the sequence are used, their order, and their duration are all determined by the brains of the bread machine, the electronic controller. Actually, the real brain is that of the cook.

The electronic controller is a computer chip that tells the motor in the machine when to turn the shaft that turns the paddle in the pan, usually alternating between clockwise and counterclockwise rotation, allowing the features that protrude inside the pan to snag the dough and knead it. It also tells a heating element when to warm the ingredients or to bake the bread and tells a fan when to pump warm air into the baking chamber to speed rising and to remove the excess moisture when the bread is done baking. Audible alarms are told when to signal that it is time to add extra ingredients and that the machine has finished either making the dough or baking the bread.

If dough is the end result, the machine will stop at the end of the dough cycle. After the machine is unplugged, the pan is removed from the baking chamber, and the dough is removed from it. If the protruding features are removable, they are removed from the pan first to help the dough slide out. If the paddle is embedded in the dough when the dough is removed from the machine, it can easily be removed before the next step. The dough is shaped into the desired form, and the remaining steps of the recipe are followed.

If bread is made completely through the baking cycle, the signal will sound to indicate the end of the cycle. When the machine is unplugged, the pan should be removed using potholders, since it will be very hot. The kneading element is removed from the pan, if there is one, and the bread is slid out of the pan and onto a cooling rack. Make sure the paddle has not been baked into the bottom of the bread. If it has, carefully use a toothpick to pull it out.

CARE AND MAINTENANCE • Nonstick surfaces can be scratched very easily with a knife or other sharp objects, so do not clean the pan with anything other than a hot soapy dishcloth or sponge. If the paddle sticks to the shaft and cannot be removed for cleaning, put hot soapy water in the pan and run the machine through the first knead cycle or let it soak for a couple of hours. Do not put the pan or paddle in the dishwasher.

From time to time, dump any crumbs or excess flour that has accumulated inside the baking chamber or use a shop vac to clean it when the machine is cool. These little leftovers tend to attract meal moths, so an ounce of prevention will be worth much more than a pound of cure. The outside of most bread machines can be wiped clean with a soft damp cloth.

It's a good idea to put the paddle and any kneading features back in the pan once it is cleaned and store the pan in the bread machine.

WHICH IS RIGHT FOR ME? • Bread machines come with a variety of features and cycles. Machines are sized by the maximum size loaf of bread that they make. They come in 1-, 1½-, and 2-pound sizes. The 1½- and 2-pound loaf machines are reasonable sizes to purchase. The 1-pound machines will have you running back to the store to buy a larger machine. But bigger is not always better unless you use the bread machine strictly as a dough maker. With very large machines, like the 3-pound machines that are emerging on the market, the weight of the dough tends to collapse back onto itself when baking in the machine, resulting in a frustrated baker.

Programmable cycles increase the flexibility and control the baker has over what happens in the bread machine. This feature is necessary if baking a wide variety of breads. The number and kind of cycles is the distinguishing feature for bread machines. All bread machines have a basic white bread cycle that is used for most recipes. A dough cycle is necessary since it is not practical to watch the machine to tell when to take out the dough before the machine bakes it, and all bread machines will do the trick. If you like to make whole wheat bread, then look for a machine that offers this setting, which gives longer knead and rise cycles. Raisin bread cycles will beep to indicate the appropriate time to add fruit or nuts that are better left whole rather than pulverized if put into the dough too early. Some machines will make butter or jam, too. Stick to the brands that are sold by major manufacturers of small appliances to ensure top quality.

COMMENTS • In our experience the bread machine is a marvelous dough maker, but a rather second-rate place in which to bake a loaf of bread. Moisture, the thing that makes bread in testing, is also the thing that can cause machine-baked bread to sink during baking. In order to make a loaf of bread that rises and bakes successfully in the bread machine, the liquid-to-dry ingredients ratio is one that invariably creates a dry, rather boring loaf. We urge you to experiment with the Manual or Dough cycles on your machines. The difference will amaze you.

Most bread machines make odd-shaped loaves; round, square, or long rectangles. To slice taller loaves, turn them on their sides to cut them. Bread machines that have convection features, in our experience, dry the surface of the dough too much, causing unfavorable results. The pan on some older models of bread machines does not have a sealed bottom, so ingredients must be added while it is situated in the machine. This feature has definite disadvantages, since ingredients can spill into the baking chamber, and if you make a mistake, the pan cannot simply be pulled out of the machine to be emptied to start over.

BREAD MACHINE TIPS

● *Use top, fresh, quality ingredients such as unbleached, nonchemically treated flour made from hard wheat that contains at least 12 grams of protein per cup. Check the nutritional panel on the bag. Remember this is given in $^1/_4$ cups, so multiply by 4.*

● *Use fresh instant active dry yeast. We do not recommend the rapid-rising variety. SafInstant and Red Star are excellent brands.*

● *If you are using a delayed cycle, do not use fresh eggs or any other perishable ingredient that will sit for hours in the bread machine. Either use powdered eggs or save these recipes for when you do not have to use the delayed cycle.*

● *For the very best results, open the machine and check the dough during the first 5 to 10 minutes of the first kneading cycle. Flour acts like a sponge and will absorb moisture to varying degrees, depending on the humidity and barometric pressure, so you may need to add more flour or liquid to achieve a smooth, supple, soft ball of dough. If the dough in the* machine is either a wet, messy glob or a dry desert and it has not yet begun the bake cycle, press Stop, add a small amount of liquid or flour, and press Start. Or cancel the cycle and restart from the beginning. This will not affect the bread.

- If you are partial to whole-grain breads and are winding up with lower loaves than you wish, try a double knead cycle: Place the ingredients in the machine and program for the Dough cycle (or its equivalent). At the end of the final knead, reprogram the machine for Bread or Whole Wheat and press Start. The dough has been given an extra workout to develop the gluten, which will result in a higher loaf. Or try Lora Brody's Bread Dough Enhancer (available at gourmet food stores).

- Sweet doughs will also benefit from an extra rise in a cool place. Place the dough in a gallon-size heavy-duty zippered plastic bag in the refrigerator for 2 to 24 hours.

- To convert any bread recipe to a bread machine recipe, cut down the ingredients so the amount of flour matches the capacity of your machine. That is, if you have a 1-, 1^1/$_2$-, or 2-pound machine, you should be using about 2, 3, or 4 cups of flour, respectively. Then reduce the other ingredients accordingly.

- Very hot water or other liquids or ingredients (above 115°F) will kill the yeast, and your bread will not rise. If you have toasted nuts or melted butter, allow to cool before adding them to the dough.

- Try using your bread machine as a dough kneader and proofing box, then forming the dough and baking it in a conventional oven. Most 1^1/$_2$- to 2-pound breads can be baked at 375°F until the bottom sounds hollow when tapped or the loaf registers an internal temperature of 190°F on an instant-read thermometer, about 40 minutes.

- If the paddle sticks to the shaft inside, try applying a little nonstick vegetable spray next time before you add your ingredients to the pan.

- When you take a loaf of bread out of the bread pan, always account for the paddle and put it right back in the pan where it belongs or it might end up in the garbage disposal.

- *Some ingredients such as crystallized ginger and wheat berries, if too hard, may scratch the nonstick surface of the bread machine pan. Soak them first to soften before adding to the dough or knead in by hand.*

- *If you can, remove the metal pan from the bread machine before you place the ingredients in it to avoid spilling things into the baking chamber or on the heating element.*

- *Use the Whole Wheat cycle for breads containing not only whole wheat flour, but other heavy flours, such as rye, cornmeal, and buckwheat.*

- *Use the French Bread cycle for breads low in fat and sugar. These cycles have a shorter knead time and a longer rise time to produce crisp crusts and soft interiors.*

- *Use the Sweet Bread cycle for breads that are high in sugars and fat as well as ingredients that might burn easily, or use it if you are having trouble with thick, overbaked crusts.*

- *If possible, remove the pan from the machine and the bread from the pan before the cool down cycle starts. This will prevent soggy crusts. Cool for at least 20 minutes on a wire rack before slicing or the inside will be gooey and raw looking.*

- *Unless you are using the machine in a very cold space, it will not ruin your bread to open the lid to check or touch the dough during the kneading and rising cycles. Try not to leave the lid open for more than 30 seconds each time as you don't want the interior to cool off.*

- *If you lose electricity and the dough has not begun to bake, remove it to a heavy-duty zippered plastic bag, and set it in a cool place until the power is restored, then return it to the machine, starting with the first cycle. This will not affect the dough.*

- *For high-altitude baking, reduce the yeast by a third and increase the salt by 25 percent and the water by a few tablespoons. Check the dough during the first kneading cycle, adding additional water to make the dough soft, smooth, and supple. For more high-altitude baking tips, E-mail to: blanche007@aol.com.*

- *Avoid the Rapid Bake cycle if possible as well as rapid rise yeast. Both speed the process of bread baking without allowing the dough to develop the proper texture and flavor.*

- *Two primary factors will result in superior yeasted bread products. A wet, slack dough will provide less resistance to the yeast's action and will make the crumb softer and moister. After the first rise, remove the pan from the machine, punch down the dough, cover the dough in the pan with plastic wrap, and let it rise in the refrigerator until it doubles in bulk. This long slow rise allows the flavor to develop more fully and builds character into the dough.*

- *Take care not to add excessive amounts of salt or sugar. Both will inhibit the action of the yeast. Dried fruits (which are very high in sugar) should be added during the last few minutes of the final knead cycle or kneaded in by hand. Two other ingredients that can inhibit the yeast's activity are fresh garlic and cinnamon.*

- *Often loaves with collapsed tops are the result of a very wet dough or one that has heavy ingredients such as cheese, eggs, nuts, or fruit. The loaf rises, but the tall loaf shape cannot sustain itself during baking. Try adding less liquid, or set the machine for Dough cycle and remove the dough after the final knead and form smaller loaves to bake in the conventional oven.*

- *Raw tops are the result of bread that has risen too high, hit the top of the machine, and sunk back down. Try adding less yeast next time. Be sure to add salt—this will slow the rise as well.*

- *Pale loaves can be darkened by adding sugar or dairy products such as fresh or nonfat dry milk.*

- *The addition of fats (oil, butter, margarine, cheese, egg yolks, and most dairy products) will make a rich, tender crumb and a soft crust.*

- *An entire community of bakers is truly plugged in and electronically communicate their questions, tips, and recipes through the Bread Baker's Digest. To subscribe, send an electronic message to: bread-bakers-request@lists.best.com and include in the body of the message only the word "Subscribe." Tell them Lora sent you!*

THE BEST WHITE BREAD

Yield: 1 loaf

When white bread went out of fashion I didn't stop eating it, and I certainly didn't stop baking it. Otherwise, my kids would have had nothing to bring for school lunch. Yes, overprocessed, air-filled, tasteless white bread is awful, but the home-made kind is still pretty swell.

You can either bake this loaf right in the machine or, if you wish to form it into a braid or free-form loaf, add Lora Brody's Bread Dough Relaxer along with the flour for better behaved dough and a large, softer loaf that stays fresh longer.

1 TABLESPOON ACTIVE DRY YEAST (NOT RAPID RISE)

3 CUPS UNBLEACHED ALL-PURPOSE FLOUR

1 1/2 TEASPOONS SALT

1 TABLESPOON SUGAR OR HONEY

3 TABLESPOONS LORA BRODY'S BREAD DOUGH RELAXER (AVAILABLE AT GOURMET FOOD STORES) FOR HAND-FORMED, OVEN-BAKED DOUGH OR 3 TABLESPOONS NONFAT DRY MILK

2 TABLESPOONS BUTTER OR VEGETABLE OIL

1 CUP WARM WATER (110 TO 115°F), OR AS NEEDED

1 LARGE EGG MIXED WITH 3 TABLESPOONS MILK

Place all the ingredients in the pan of a bread machine. Program your machine for the Dough setting (or equivalent) and remove the dough after the final cycle is complete. Check the dough after the first few minutes of kneading, adding additional water if necessary to make a smooth, supple, soft ball. At the end of the final cycle, remove the dough and place it on a very lightly floured or lightly oiled work surface.

Spray or grease a heavy-duty baking sheet. Roll the dough into an 18 × 6-inch rectangle. Use a pizza cutter, knife, or bench knife to cut the dough lengthwise into 3 long strips, leaving the pieces connected at one end. Braid the strips without stretching them and secure the end by pinching it and tucking it under the loaf. Place the braid on the prepared pan and brush with the egg glaze. Allow to rise, uncovered, in a warm, draft-free place until almost doubled in bulk.

Meanwhile, preheat the oven to 450°F with the rack in the center position.

continued

Brush again with the egg glaze. Bake for 15 minutes, then reduce the oven temperature to 375°F and bake until the top is deep golden brown and the bottom sounds hollow when tapped, or until an instant-read thermometer inserted in the center measures 190°F, another 20 minutes.

WHOLE WHEAT SOURDOUGH BEER BREAD

Yield: 1 large loaf, 2 small loaves, or 24 dinner rolls

Here's the queen of all sourdough whole wheat loaves. Use the bread machine to make the dough and bake it if you wish. I prefer doing my baking in the oven.

For the dough:

1 TABLESPOON ACTIVE DRY YEAST (NOT RAPID RISE)

2 TEASPOONS SALT

2 TABLESPOONS LORA BRODY'S SOURDOUGH BREAD ENHANCER (AVAILABLE AT GOURMET FOOD STORES)

1 1/2 CUPS UNBLEACHED ALL-PURPOSE FLOUR

2 TABLESPOONS PURE MAPLE SYRUP OR HONEY

2 CUPS WHOLE WHEAT FLOUR

8 OUNCES (1 1/3 CUPS) FLAT BEER, OR AS NEEDED (TO MAKE BEER FLAT, HEAT IT, THEN COOL TO ROOM TEMPERATURE)

For the topping:

1 LARGE EGG BEATEN WITH 1/4 CUP MILK

SESAME OR POPPY SEEDS

Put all the dough ingredients in the pan of a bread machine, program for Whole Wheat, and press Start if you wish to bake the bread in the machine. Otherwise, program for the Dough setting (or equivalent). Check the dough after the first few minutes of kneading, adding additional beer if necessary to make a smooth, supple, soft ball. At the end of the last cycle, remove the dough and form it into either 1 large loaf, 2 smaller loaves, or 24 rolls and set on a heavy-duty baking sheet lightly coated with nonstick vegetable spray. Brush the top(s) with the egg glaze, cover with a clean kitchen cloth, and set in a warm, draft-free place to rise till doubled in bulk.

Bake in a preheated 400°F oven 40 to 50 minutes for the large loaf, 30 to 40 minutes for the smaller loaves, and 20 minutes for the rolls. Check with an instant-read thermometer to make sure the internal temperature is 190 to 200°F. Cool on a wire rack before slicing.

LIGHT WHOLE WHEAT BREAD

Yield: 1 loaf

The sweet, nutty taste of this bread comes from the whole wheat flour. Whole wheat bread will not rise as high as white bread since there is not as much gluten (protein) in it. The white wheat flour called for in this recipe makes a loaf with just as much of the nutritional benefits of regular whole wheat, but with a lighter consistency and taste. King Arthur White wheat flour is available in supermarkets or by calling (800) 827-6836. If you prefer a taller loaf, try adding 1 tablespoon of Lora Brody's Bread Dough Enhancer along with the flour.

1 TABLESPOON ACTIVE DRY YEAST (NOT RAPID RISE)

3 CUPS WHITE WHEAT FLOUR

1 1/2 TEASPOONS SALT

2 TABLESPOONS HONEY OR MOLASSES

3 TABLESPOONS CANOLA OIL

1 1/4 CUPS WATER, OR AS NEEDED

1/4 CUP SESAME SEEDS (OPTIONAL)

Place all the ingredients in the pan of a bread machine, program for Whole Wheat, and press Start. Check the consistency of the dough during the first 5 minutes of the first knead cycle, adding additional water, if necessary, to make a smooth, supple soft ball. Try to remove the dough immediately after the bake cycle to prevent the crust from getting soggy.

To bake in a conventional oven, oil one 8-cup bread pan or two smaller pans. Form the dough into either 1 large or 2 smaller loaves, cover with a clean kitchen cloth or plastic wrap, and allow to rise in a warm, draft-free place until almost doubled in bulk.

Preheat the oven to 375°F with the rack in the center position. Bake the large loaf for 45 minutes and the small loaves for 30 minutes. Test for doneness by inserting an instant-read thermometer; the bread should have an internal temperature of 190 to 200°F. Cool for at least 15 minutes before slicing.

PUMPERNICKEL BREAD

Yield: 1 large loaf

Deep and dark and looking for some tuna salad and a slice of onion, this deli-style pumpernickel is made either completely in the bread machine or can be hand formed and baked in the oven.

1 TABLESPOON ACTIVE DRY YEAST
  (NOT RAPID RISE)

2 TABLESPOONS LORA BRODY'S SOURDOUGH
  BREAD ENHANCER (AVAILABLE AT GOURMET
  FOOD STORES)

3 TABLESPOONS HERSHEY'S UNSWEETENED
  COCOA POWDER (NOT DUTCH PROCESSED)

2 CUPS UNBLEACHED ALL-PURPOSE FLOUR, OR
  AS NEEDED

1 CUP DARK RYE FLOUR (AVAILABLE IN HEALTH
  FOOD STORES)

2 TEASPOONS SALT

1 $^1/_3$ CUPS WARM WATER, OR AS NEEDED

$^1/_4$ CUP CORNMEAL

$^1/_3$ CUP VEGETABLE OIL

2 TABLESPOONS BLACKSTRAP MOLASSES

1 LARGE EGG WHITE BEATEN WITH 2
  TABLESPOONS WATER

BLACK CARAWAY SEEDS

Place all the ingredients except the egg white glaze and caraway seeds in the pan of a bread machine, program for Whole Wheat, and press Start. Watch the dough forming during the first few minutes of the kneading cycle and add additional water or all-purpose flour as needed to form a smooth, supple, soft ball. Try to remove the loaf from the machine as soon as it finishes baking so it won't get too soggy.

Alternately, program the machine for the Dough setting (or equivalent). Sprinkle a heavy-duty baking sheet with cornmeal. At the end of the final cycle, remove the dough to a lightly floured work surface and mold it into a round, free-form loaf, cover with a damp cloth, and allow it to rise in a warm, draft-free place until doubled in bulk.

Preheat the oven to 375°F with the rack in the center position. Brush the bread with the egg glaze and sprinkle with the seeds. Bake until the bottom sounds hollow when tapped and the top crust is quite firm, until an instant-read thermometer inserted in the center registers 190 to 200°F, 35 to 45 minutes.

DOUBLE SUN-DRIED TOMATO BAGUETTES

Yield: 4 baguettes

These are gorgeous loaves of bread, rich with a double whammy of tomato flavor from the combination of tomato powder and sun-dried tomato bits. The Parmesan cheese and pumpkin seeds give it additional flavor as well as crunch. This recipe calls for some special ingredients that have to be mail-ordered, but the result is worth the effort. Both tomato powder and semolina are available through the King Arthur Flour Baker's catalog.

For the dough:

1 TABLESPOON ACTIVE DRY YEAST (NOT RAPID RISE)

2 TEASPOONS SALT

2²/₃ CUPS UNBLEACHED ALL-PURPOSE FLOUR

2 TABLESPOONS KING ARTHUR TOMATO POWDER

¹/₄ CUP SUN-DRIED TOMATO OIL OR OLIVE OIL

¹/₃ CUP FRESHLY GRATED REGGIANO PARMESAN CHEESE

1 TABLESPOON DRIED BASIL

¹/₃ CUP SEMOLINA FLOUR

1 TABLESPOON LORA BRODY'S SOURDOUGH BREAD ENHANCER (AVAILABLE AT GOURMET FOOD STORES)

SNIPPED OIL-PACKED SUN-DRIED TOMATOES

1 CUP WATER, OR AS NEEDED

For the pan:

CORNMEAL

For the topping:

1 LARGE EGG WHITE BEATEN WITH 2 TABLESPOONS WATER

FRESHLY GRATED REGGIANO PARMESAN CHEESE

Place all the ingredients for the dough except the pumpkin seeds and sun-dried tomatoes in the pan of a bread machine and program for the Dough setting (or equivalent). Check the dough after the first few minutes of kneading, adding additional water if necessary to make a moist, smooth, supple, soft ball. Two minutes before the end of the final knead cycle, add the pumpkin seeds and tomatoes (these can also be kneaded in by hand, if you wish). Remove the dough to a lightly floured work surface and divide it into 4 equal pieces.

Sprinkle 2 baguette pans (to make 4 baquettes) with cornmeal. Form four 12- to 14-inch baguettes and place 2 of them in each of the baguette pans. Brush the tops with the egg glaze and sprinkle with Parmesan cheese. Cover with a clean kitchen cloth or plastic wrap and set in a warm, draft-free place to rise until almost doubled in bulk.

Preheat the oven to 475°F with the rack in the center position. Bake the baguettes for 12 minutes, then reduce the oven temperature to 375°F and cook until the tops are deep golden brown and the bottoms sound hollow when tapped, another 15 to 18 minutes. Cool on a wire rack before slicing.

English Muffin/Toast

Yield: 8 muffins

Terrance S. Goodman, an Internet friend and marvelous baker, generously shared his recipe for making superlative English muffins in the bread machine.

For the dough:

1 1/4 CUPS WARM WATER (110 TO 115°F)

2 TABLESPOONS VEGETABLE OIL

1 TABLESPOON SUGAR

1 TEASPOON SALT

1/8 TEASPOON BAKING POWDER

3 CUPS UNBLEACHED ALL-PURPOSE FLOUR

2 1/4 TEASPOONS ACTIVE DRY YEAST
(NOT RAPID RISE)

To knead:

CORNMEAL

Put all the dough ingredients in the pan of a bread machine and program for the Dough setting (or equivalent). After the machine has completed the second rising, remove the dough to a work surface sprinkled with cornmeal. Roll the dough to a 1/4-inch thickness, sprinkling with flour, if necessary, to avoid sticking. Use a biscuit or cookie cutter to cut out 3- to 4-inch circles. Place 1/2 inch apart on an ungreased baking sheet, cover with a clean kitchen cloth or plastic wrap, and let rise in a warm, draft-free place until doubled in bulk, about 30 minutes.

Bake on a lightly oiled electric skillet set on medium-low (325°F) or in a skillet until deep golden brown, about 8 minutes on each side. Let cool. To serve, split and toast.

GLUTEN-FREE RICE BREAD

Yield: 1 loaf

The bread machine has made it possible for people with gluten allergies to enjoy home-baked bread. Most of the ingredients listed here can be found in health food stores or natural food markets.

½ CUP WARM WATER (110 TO 115°F)

3 TABLESPOONS GRANULATED SUGAR, DIVIDED

1½ TEASPOONS ACTIVE DRY YEAST
(NOT RAPID RISE)

1 CUP BROWN RICE FLOUR

⅔ CUP WHITE RICE FLOUR

⅔ CUP POTATO FLOUR

1 TABLESPOON NONFAT DRY MILK

1 TABLESPOON BUTTER OR MARGARINE

1 TEASPOON SALT

1 TEASPOON PURE VANILLA EXTRACT

1 LARGE EGG BEATEN IN A MEASURING CUP
WITH ENOUGH WATER ADDED TO EQUAL
½ CUP LIQUID

Place all the ingredients in the pan of a bread machine, program for the Rapid cycle, and press Start. At the end of the baking cycle and before the cooling cycle, remove the bread from the pan and allow it to cool on a wire rack at least a half hour before slicing.

HERBED ONION FOCACCIA

Yield: 8 to 10 servings

Focaccia is a chewy, flattish usually round loaf that looks a lot like overrisen pizza with dimples. This is classic focaccia at its best—sweet onions and the country scent of fresh rosemary—in short, perfection.

While focaccia is best eaten the day it is made, it's fine toasted the next day. The trick is to keep it at room temperature, not in the refrigerator. If you wish to freeze it, cool first, then wrap it airtight in plastic wrap. Defrost still wrapped. You can freeze focaccia for six months.

This dough can be made up to 48 hours ahead of time. Place it in a large, well-oiled bowl, cover with oiled plastic wrap, and refrigerator until ready to roll out and bake. Or you can roll out the dough, cover it with oiled plastic wrap, and refrigerate it for its final rise, or even overnight.

1 LARGE SPANISH ONION, PEELED AND CUT
INTO EIGHTHS

2 TABLESPOONS PLUS $\frac{1}{3}$ CUP OLIVE OIL,
DIVIDED

1 TABLESPOON ACTIVE DRY YEAST (NOT RAPID
RISE)

$\frac{1}{2}$ CUP CORNMEAL

3 CUPS UNBLEACHED ALL-PURPOSE FLOUR

2 TEASPOONS SALT

1 $\frac{1}{4}$ CUPS WARM WATER (110 TO 115 °F)

2 TABLESPOONS MIXED DRIED HERBS SUCH AS
BASIL, THYME, ROSEMARY, TARRAGON,
AND DILL

1 TO 2 TABLESPOONS GARLIC OR OLIVE OIL, TO
YOUR TASTE

COARSE SALT AND FRESHLY GROUND BLACK
PEPPER TO TASTE

You can prepare the onion either in the microwave or on the stove top. For the microwave, place the onion and 2 tablespoons of the oil in a microwaveable bowl. Cover and microwave on high power until the onion is very soft and has just started to turn golden, 8 to 12 minutes. Let the onion stay in the covered dish to cool.

On the stove top, heat 2 tablespoons of the oil in a skillet. Add the onion and cook over medium heat, stirring occasionally until the onion is very soft and just starting to turn golden, about 20 minutes. Allow the onion to cool in the pan.

When the onion is cooled, strain off the cooking liquid into a small bowl, pressing down on the onion to release as much as possible.

Place the remaining $\frac{1}{3}$ cup of olive oil, the yeast, cornmeal, flour, salt, and dried herbs in the pan of a bread machine. Program for the Dough setting (or equivalent) and, at the end of the final knead, add the onion (but not the liquid) to the machine. Restart and knead only until the onion is roughly mixed in. The dough will be wet, and the onion will remain in clumps, sticking out of the dough.

Oil a pizza pan or heavy-duty baking sheet. Place the dough on the pan and pat it into a 12-inch disk. Coat the top of the focaccia with the onion juices. Cover with plastic wrap and let rise either at room temperature until doubled in bulk or in the refrigerator overnight.

Preheat the oven to 450°F with the rack in the center position. Just before baking the focaccia, use your fingertips to poke indentations on its surface. Drizzle on the garlic oil, then sprinkle with coarse salt and pepper. Bake for 10 minutes, reduce the oven temperature to 350°F, and bake until the focaccia is golden brown, another 12 to 15 minutes. Serve hot or at room temperature or slice and use for sandwiches.

VERSATILE PIZZA DOUGH

Yield: One 16-inch pizza or two 10-inch pizzas

Whether you make pizza, calzones, breadsticks, rolls, or tortilla bread, you'll marvel at the many shapes and forms you can stretch, cut, and mold this dough into. A recipe for Grissini (thin breadsticks) made with this dough follows (page 64).

For the dough:

2 TEASPOONS ACTIVE DRY YEAST (NOT RAPID RISE)

3 CUPS UNBLEACHED ALL-PURPOSE FLOUR

1 1/2 TEASPOONS SALT

1/4 CUP OLIVE OIL (OPTIONAL)

1 CUP WATER, OR AS NEEDED

To make the pizza:

CORNMEAL

1 CUP SAUCE OF YOUR CHOICE

GRATED CHEESE (OPTIONAL)

Place all the dough ingredients in the pan of a bread machine and program for the Dough setting (or equivalent). At the end of the final cycle, remove the dough to a lightly oiled work surface.

Preheat the oven to 450°F with the rack or a pizza stone in the upper third but not the highest position in the oven. Oil a heavy-duty baking sheet or dust a pizza pan with cornmeal. Roll or pat the dough out to fit the pan. For a thick crust pizza, roll it 1/2 inch thick and allow it to rise, covered with a clean kitchen cloth, in a warm, draft-free place, for about 20 minutes before saucing. For a thin crust, roll it 1/4 inch thick, top with a thin coating of sauce, sprinkle with cheese, and bake it immediately. Bake until the crust is browned and the top is bubbling and any cheese has melted, 15 to 18 minutes.

BROCCOLI AND CHEESE CALZONES

Yield: 6 calzones

These half-moon pockets of pizza dough are baked with the filling of your choice. The following recipe calls for a simple filling of broccoli and cheese; you can substitute ham, cooked sausage, roasted peppers, and/or any type of vegetable, meat, and cheese that appeals to you. Calzones make a great on-the-run lunch.

continued

5 TABLESPOONS OLIVE OIL

1 MEDIUM-SIZE ONION, PEELED AND THINLY
   SLICED

4 CUPS (¾ POUND) BROCCOLI FLORETS

SALT AND FRESHLY GROUND BLACK PEPPER TO
   TASTE

1 RECIPE VERSATILE PIZZA DOUGH
   (PAGE 63)

2 CUPS GRATED CHEESE (MOZZARELLA OR
   MONTEREY JACK ARE FINE)

Heat the olive oil over medium heat in a large skillet, then add the onion and cook, stirring, until light golden brown. Add the broccoli and continue to cook, stirring occasionally, until tender. Season with the salt and pepper. Let the broccoli mixture cool.

Place the dough on a lightly floured work surface. Cut the dough into 6 even pieces and roll them into balls. Let rest for 5 minutes. Roll out each piece of dough into a 6-inch circle. Distribute the broccoli filling evenly over the 6 circles and top the filling with the grated cheese. Brush the rim of the dough with water and fold in half; it should look like a half moon. Twist the edges together, or press them with the tines of a fork, so the filling does not spill out during baking. Brush olive oil over the surface of the calzones and, with a sharp knife or scissors, cut a slit in the top of each one. Bake until the tops are golden brown, 20 to 25 minutes. Serve hot from the oven, warm, or at room temperature.

GRISSINI

Yield: About 40 breadsticks

These thin breadsticks are served in bread baskets in fine Italian restaurants. You can make your own with the Versatile Pizza Dough recipe found on page 63.

1 RECIPE VERSATILE PIZZA DOUGH (PAGE 63)

OLIVE OIL

COARSE SALT (OPTIONAL)

Preheat the oven to 400°F with the rack in the center position. Line a heavy-duty baking sheet with parchment paper or aluminum foil, coating the foil with nonstick vegetable spray. Divide the pizza dough into 4 pieces. On a lightly oiled work surface, roll each piece out to a 10 × 12-inch rectangle. Use a pizza wheel or knife to cut the rectangle into ten 12-inch-long strips. Repeat with the remaining 3 pieces of dough. Transfer the strips to the prepared pans, leaving 1 inch of space between them. Brush the strips with oil, sprinkle on the salt, if desired, and bake until golden brown, 5 to 7 minutes. Immediately remove to a rack to cool completely before storing at room temperature.

RYE CRACKER SEED BREAD

Yield: Varies with the size of the crackers

Making your own crackers is terrific fun, and the bread machine makes the dough part a snap! Take care to use really fresh seeds and herbs as this is where the real flavor of the crackers come from. This may take a bit of practice before you get the hang of it, but it's worth it, and soon you'll find yourself turning out world-class flatbreads. You'll find semolina and rye flours in health food stores and in the baking aisle of many supermarkets.

2 CUPS UNBLEACHED ALL-PURPOSE FLOUR

$^1/_2$ CUP RYE FLOUR

$^1/_2$ CUP SEMOLINA

2 TEASPOONS SALT

1 CUP WATER, OR AS NEEDED

$^2/_3$ CUP ASSORTED SEEDS SUCH AS SESAME,
    POPPY, FENNEL, CARAWAY, AND/OR ANISE

$^1/_4$ CUP MIXED DRIED HERBS SUCH AS
    ROSEMARY, BASIL, DILL, TARRAGON,
    AND/OR THYME

1 TEASPOON FRESHLY GROUND BLACK PEPPER

1 TABLESPOON COARSE SALT (OPTIONAL IF
    YOU LIKE A SALTY, CRUNCHY CRACKER)

Place the flours, salt, and water in the pan of a bread machine and program for the Dough setting (or equivalent). Check the consistency after the first few minutes of kneading, adding additional water if necessary to make a smooth, supple, soft ball of dough. Allow the dough to knead through the first knead cycle and the first rest cycle, then remove it to a lightly floured work surface.

Preheat the oven to 450°F with the rack in the center position. Select several heavy-duty baking sheets and spray them with nonstick vegetable spray or coat them lightly with vegetable oil.

Combine the seeds, herbs, pepper, and salt in a small bowl. Divide the dough into 8 pieces. Working with 1 piece at a time (keep the others covered with a cloth or plastic wrap), scatter about 1 tablespoon of the seed mixture on the work surface. Press the dough into it and begin to roll it out as thin as possible. If it sticks, flip it over, apply more seeds, and continue rolling. The goal is to get the dough as thin as possible and impregnated with lots of seeds. You may find it easier to finish the rolling right on the baking sheet. Repeat with the remaining dough and seed mixture. (The sheets will be baked one at a time; you may be able to fit more than 1 cracker bread on a sheet. These don't rise as they contain no leavening.)

Bake the cracker breads until the top side is quite brown, 4 to 5 minutes, then flip them over to get the other side equally brown. At this point you can even slide them off the sheet and bake them right on the oven rack. Cool completely on a wire rack before serving. Store, uncovered, in a dry place.

If the cracker breads get soggy (which they will during humid weather), they are easily recrisped by placing them in a preheated 250°F oven for 10 minutes.

Irish Soda Bread

Yield: One 8- or 9-inch loaf

This recipe uses the bread machine for one knead cycle. If you cannot program for this, simply press Stop or Cancel after the first knead cycle.

To freeze, cool completely, then store in a heavy-duty zippered plastic bag. Defrost, still wrapped, at room temperature, then slice and toast.

1 1/2 TEASPOONS SALT	1 CUP DRIED CURRANTS
1 TEASPOON BAKING POWDER	1 ROUNDED TABLESPOON CARAWAY SEEDS
3/4 TEASPOON BAKING SODA, FREE OF LUMPS	1 CUP BUTTERMILK
1/4 CUP SUGAR	1/4 CUP (1/2 STICK) BUTTER, MELTED AND SLIGHTLY COOLED
4 CUPS SIFTED UNBLEACHED ALL-PURPOSE FLOUR, OR AS NEEDED	2 LARGE EGGS

Select an 8-inch round cake pan, an 8- or 9-inch metal pie tin, or a heavy-duty baking sheet and coat it generously with vegetable shortening or softened butter.

Place all the ingredients in the pan of a bread machine and program for the

Dough setting (or equivalent). The dough will be sticky at first, but will firm up as it kneads. If it has not formed a ball after 7 minutes of kneading, add a bit more flour until a ball forms.

At the end of the first kneading cycle, stop the machine. Preheat the oven to 375°F with the rack in the center position. Remove the dough to a lightly floured work surface and pat it into an 8-inch round shape with a domed top and place on the cake pan, pie tin, or baking sheet. Use a sharp knife dipped in flour to score a 1-inch-deep by 4-inch-long cross on top of the dough. This will expand during baking to give the bread its characteristic marking. Bake until a cake tester or toothpick inserted in the center comes out clean, 35 to 40 minutes. If the top seems to be turning too brown before the baking time is up, cover it loosely with aluminum foil. Cool on a wire rack, then slice thinly and serve with butter, cream cheese, and/or jam.

My Mother's Challah

Yield: 1 large challah braid

My mother, Millie Apter, is famous for her challah. When you try her recipe for this tender-crumbed, slightly sweet, fresh-tasting egg bread, you'll no doubt agree. Whole wheat pastry flour is available in health food stores. It is not the same as regular whole wheat flour. If you cannot find it, then use three cups all-purpose white flour instead.

1 TABLESPOON ACTIVE DRY YEAST (NOT RAPID RISE)

2 CUPS UNBLEACHED ALL-PURPOSE FLOUR, OR AS NEEDED

1 CUP WHOLE WHEAT PASTRY FLOUR

1 1/2 TEASPOONS SALT

3 TABLESPOONS HONEY

1/4 CUP VEGETABLE OIL

2 EXTRA LARGE EGGS

3/4 CUP WATER, OR AS NEEDED

1 LARGE EGG BEATEN WITH 2 TABLESPOONS WATER

Place all the ingredients except the egg glaze in the pan of a bread machine and program for the Dough setting (or equivalent). Check the dough after the first few minutes of kneading and add flour or water as necessary to make a smooth, supple, soft ball. At the end of the final cycle, remove the dough to a lightly floured work surface, cover with a clean kitchen cloth or plastic wrap, and allow it to rest for 15 minutes. At this point you can also refrigerate the dough in a freezer-strength heavy-duty zippered plastic bag for up to 24 hours.

To form the loaf, grease or spray a heavy-duty baking sheet with vegetable oil. Without working it too much, gently work the dough into a 10-inch-long rectangle. Place it on the prepared baking sheet and, leaving the strips attached at one end, divide the dough into 3 equal strips. Braid the strips, securing the other ends firmly together. Brush with the egg glaze and allow to rise, uncovered, in a warm, draft-free place until almost doubled in bulk.

Preheat the oven to 400°F with the rack in the center position. Glaze the loaf again just before baking. Bake for 15 minutes at 400°F, then reduce the oven temperature to 375°F and continue baking until the loaf sounds hollow when tapped on the bottom or an instant-read thermometer inserted in the center registers 190°F, an additional 20 to 30 minutes. If the top of the bread is browning too quickly, cover it loosely with aluminum foil. Remove to a wire rack to cool completely before slicing.

Soy Vey

Yield: One 1- to 1½-pound loaf

This unusual version of traditional Jewish challah was created by Lynda Mackey of Columbus, Ohio, and won first place in a special competition at the Ohio State Fair in 1994. You can either let the bread machine run completely through its cycle or take the dough out and shape it by hand.

For the dough:

¾ CUP SOY MILK (AVAILABLE IN HEALTH FOOD STORES)

2 TABLESPOONS HONEY

2¼ TEASPOONS ACTIVE DRY YEAST (NOT RAPID RISE)

3 CUPS UNBLEACHED ALL-PURPOSE FLOUR

½ CUP SOY FLOUR (AVAILABLE IN HEALTH FOOD STORES)

¼ CUP SOYBEAN OIL (AVAILABLE IN HEALTH FOOD STORES)

3 LARGE EGGS, OR EQUIVALENT EGG SUBSTITUTE

1 LARGE EGG YOLK, OR EQUIVALENT EGG SUBSTITUTE

For the topping:

1 LARGE EGG WHITE BEATEN WITH
  2 TABLESPOONS WATER

2 TABLESPOONS POPPY SEEDS

Place the dough ingredients in the pan of a bread machine. Using the White Bread setting, program it for Bake, if you wish to use the machine as your oven, or program for the Dough setting (or equivalent) and remove the dough after the final rise to a lightly floured work surface. Shape the dough into a 14-inch oval and cut it lengthwise into 3 strips, leaving one end connected. Braid the strips, securing the other end. Transfer the braid to a greased heavy-duty baking sheet and cover with a clean kitchen cloth or plastic wrap. Allow the braid to rise in a warm, draft-free place until doubled in bulk, then brush the top with the egg glaze. Sprinkle with the poppy seeds.

Preheat the oven to 375°F. Bake the braid until the top is well browned and the bottom sounds hollow when tapped or the bread registers an internal temperature of 190°F on an instant-read thermometer, about 40 minutes. Cool on a wire rack before slicing.

Variation: You can substitute water for the soy milk and another kind of oil for the soybean oil to tone down the soy taste.

BRIOCHE

Yield: 1 large loaf

I've made hundreds of loaves of brioche, that buttery rich French yeast bread. I've made it by hand, in the stand mixer, in the food processor, and in the dough mixer. I think the bread machine does far and away the best job.

The temptation to add more flour to this sticky, slack dough should be avoided at all costs. The dough won't really form a typical ball during the kneading process, and it might appear somewhat oily as well. This is fine. After its refrigerated long rise, it will be the most wonderful dough you've ever worked with. Orange oil is available in gourmet stores and through the King Arthur Flour Baker's catalog.

continued

6 9

For the dough:

1 CUP (2 STICKS) UNSALTED BUTTER,
VERY SOFT

3 EXTRA LARGE EGGS

¹/₄ CUP WATER, OR AS NEEDED

1 TEASPOON ORANGE OIL OR FINELY GRATED
ZEST OF 1 LARGE ORANGE

1¹/₄ TEASPOONS SALT

2 TABLESPOONS SUGAR

3 TABLESPOONS NONFAT DRY MILK

3 CUPS UNBLEACHED ALL-PURPOSE FLOUR, OR
AS NEEDED

1 TABLESPOON ACTIVE DRY YEAST (NOT RAPID
RISE)

For the topping:

1 LARGE EGG YOLK BEATEN WITH 3
TABLESPOONS MILK OR HEAVY CREAM

COARSE SUGAR (OPTIONAL)

Place all the dough ingredients in the pan of a bread machine, program for the Dough setting (or equivalent), and remove the dough after the final cycle is complete. Check the dough after the first few minutes of the first knead cycle. It should be quite wet, but should still form a very soft, slack ball (add more water or flour as necessary to achieve the right consistency). At the end of the final cycle, remove the dough to a large, heavy-duty zippered plastic bag and refrigerate at least 12 hours or overnight.

Butter an 8-cup loaf pan or brioche mold. Place the cold dough on a lightly floured work surface and shape it either into one loaf or a number of rolls. Cover with an oiled piece of plastic wrap and allow to rise in a warm, draft-free place until almost doubled in bulk.

Preheat the oven to 425°F with the rack in the center position. Brush the tops of the loaf or rolls with the egg glaze and sprinkle with the sugar. Bake for 15 minutes, then reduce the oven temperature to 350°F and bake until it registers an internal temperature of 190°F on an instant-read thermometer, another 10 to 12 minutes for rolls, 30 minutes for a loaf. Remove from the pan(s) and cool on a wire rack before slicing.

KILLER STICKY BUNS

Yield: 14 sticky buns

You know those sticky-bun takeout places that have sprouted up in malls everywhere? Well, I thought their buns were pretty swell until I started fooling around with some sweet dough and some leftover caramelized pecans. Making these ten megaton babies is much easier than you'd expect—and a hell of a lot of fun as well. If you're in a big hurry, you can use store-bought frozen white dough. Thaw according to the manufacturer's instructions.

For the filling:

1 1/2 CUPS RAISINS

1/2 CUP ORANGE JUICE

1/4 CUP BRANDY

For the dough:

1 TABLESPOON ACTIVE DRY YEAST (NOT RAPID RISE)

3 CUPS UNBLEACHED ALL-PURPOSE FLOUR

2 TABLESPOONS SUGAR

1 1/2 TEASPOONS SALT

3 TABLESPOONS LORA BRODY'S BREAD DOUGH RELAXER (OPTIONAL, FOR A RICHER, MORE WORKABLE DOUGH; AVAILABLE AT GOURMET FOOD STORES)

2 EXTRA LARGE EGGS

1/3 CUP VEGETABLE OIL

2/3 CUP WATER, OR AS NEEDED

For the topping:

6 TABLESPOONS (3/4 STICK) BUTTER

1/2 CUP HONEY

1/2 CUP FIRMLY PACKED DARK BROWN SUGAR

2 CUPS PECAN HALVES

For brushing:

3 TABLESPOONS BUTTER, MELTED

Ahead of time, make the filling by placing the raisins, orange juice, and brandy in a microwavable bowl. Cover and microwave on high power for 5 minutes. Allow to cool to room temperature, still covered. Drain the raisins, reserving any remaining liquid.

For the dough, place all the dough ingredients in the pan of a bread machine and program for the Dough setting (or equivalent). Five minutes into the first knead cycle, check the dough. Add as much additional water as needed to achieve a smooth, supple, soft ball. At the end of the final cycle, remove the dough to an oiled bowl or heavy-duty zippered plastic bag and refrigerate for 2 to 3 hours.

For the topping, place all the ingredients in a skillet over medium heat or an electric skillet set at 250°F. Stir until the mixture boils, then allow to simmer for 5 minutes.

To assemble the sticky buns, select a 12-inch springform pan with 3-inch-high sides; Teflon is best for this recipe. Coat the sides of the pan generously with butter. Pour the hot topping into the pan and tilt from side to side or use a mixing spoon to evenly distribute the filling over the bottom of the pan.

On a lightly floured work surface, roll the dough into a rectangle that measures about 20 × 8 inches. Brush the surface with the melted butter, reserving a little to brush the formed buns, then scatter the raisins over the dough, leaving a 1-inch clean border around the edges. If there is any liquid left over from soaking the raisins, pour it over the pecan topping.

Starting with the long edge away from you, roll the dough jelly roll style to form a tight 20-inch-long roll. Use a knife or dough scraper to cut the roll into 14 slices and place each slice about 1 inch apart on top of the pecan mixture. Brush the tops with the reserved butter, then cover with plastic wrap and allow to rise in a warm, draft-free place until almost doubled in bulk.

Preheat the oven to 350°F with the rack in the center position. Bake the rolls until the crust is well browned and the sugar is bubbling up around the dough, about 40 minutes. The buns should register an internal temperature of 200°F on an instant-read thermometer.

Remove the pan from the oven and immediately invert onto a slope-sided heatproof platter. The nut-covered surface is the top. Scoop any topping still in the pan onto the buns. Cool for 15 to 20 minutes before serving.

Variation: Substitute slivered almonds for the pecans and dried cherries or cranberries for the raisins.

KOLACHES

Yield: 2 dozen

Kolaches, fruit-filled pastry rolls, are one of (the former) Czechoslovakia's national pastries. Here is a sweet dough that contains a rich, satisfying prune and apricot filling.

For the dough:

1½ CUPS WARM WATER (110 TO 115°F)

⅓ CUP VEGETABLE OIL

¼ CUP SUGAR

1 LARGE EGG

1 TEASPOON SALT

3 TABLESPOONS NONFAT DRY MILK

2 TEASPOONS ACTIVE DRY YEAST (NOT RAPID RISE)

3½ CUPS UNBLEACHED ALL-PURPOSE FLOUR, OR AS NEEDED

For the filling:

1/2 POUND PITTED PRUNES

1/2 CUP APPLESAUCE

1/2 TEASPOON GROUND CINNAMON, DIVIDED

ONE 8-OUNCE PACKAGE DRIED APRICOTS

3/4 CUP WATER

1/3 CUP SUGAR

MELTED BUTTER

Place all the dough ingredients in the pan of a bread machine and program for the Dough setting (or equivalent). Check the dough during the first few minutes of the knead cycle to make sure it has a soft, slightly sticky consistency. Adjust the water or flour as necessary.

Meanwhile, prepare the fillings. In the work bowl of a food processor fitted with the metal blade, process the prunes, applesauce, and 1/4 teaspoon of the cinnamon together until smooth. Remove and set aside. In a microwavable 4-cup glass measure, bring the apricots and water to a low boil in the microwave on high power, about 4 minutes. Cover, reduce the power to medium-low, and let simmer for 10 minutes. Remove from the microwave and let stand until almost all the water has been absorbed by the apricots, about 15 minutes. In the work bowl of a food processor fitted with the metal or plastic blade, process the apricots with the sugar and the remaining 1/4 teaspoon of cinnamon until smooth. Set aside.

Punch down the dough and roll it out onto a lightly floured work surface into a large square, 1/4 inch thick. Cut into 3-inch squares. Place a heaping teaspoon of either filling in the center of each dough square. Fold the top left corner of the dough over the filling. Next, fold the bottom right corner of the dough over the filling at the center. Stretch the upper right corner of the dough and fold it over the center. Take the last corner, stretch it slightly, and fold it over, completing a dough square. Continue making kolaches with the remaining dough and filling.

Place in greased muffin tins, cover with plastic wrap, and let rise in a warm, draft-free place for about 45 minutes. Bake in a preheated 375°F oven until light golden brown, about 25 minutes. Brush the tops with melted butter when removed from the oven. Allow to cool before serving.

Variation: Fill with other fruit fillings as desired. If you like, bake in the bread machine as you normally would for a loaf of sweet bread.

ORANGE AND CINNAMON BISCOTTI

Yield: 24 cookies

These crunchy Italian cookies are not too sweet or too rich and are perfect served with sliced pears, espresso, or an Italian dessert wine for a real treat. Thanks to the bread machine they're a snap to make.

1 CUP SUGAR

1/2 CUP (1 STICK) UNSALTED BUTTER, AT ROOM TEMPERATURE

2 LARGE EGGS

2 TEASPOONS GRATED ORANGE ZEST

1 TEASPOON PURE VANILLA EXTRACT

2 CUPS UNBLEACHED ALL-PURPOSE FLOUR

1 1/2 TEASPOONS BAKING POWDER

1 TEASPOON GROUND CINNAMON

1/4 TEASPOON SALT

Preheat the oven to 325°F. Line two heavy-duty baking sheets with parchment paper or aluminum foil and either grease or coat with nonstick vegetable spray.

Place all the ingredients in the pan of a bread machine and program for the Dough setting (or equivalent). Knead until all the ingredients are well combined and a smooth ball of dough forms.

Divide the dough in half. With lightly floured hands, form each half into a 12 × 3 × 3/4-inch log. Position the logs on the prepared baking sheets and bake until firm to the touch, about 35 minutes.

Remove from the oven and cool for 10 minutes. Using a serrated knife, cut on the diagonal into 1-inch-thick slices. Arrange the slices cut side down on the baking sheets. Bake until their bottoms are golden, about 12 minutes. Turn the biscotti over and bake until the bottoms are golden, another 12 minutes. Transfer to wire racks and cool.

QUICK CHEESE BISCUITS

Yield: 10 to 12 biscuits

Looking for an almost instant breakfast or something to serve for lunch in a rush? Try adding these five ingredients to your bread machine. You only have to knead until the dough forms a ball.

2 CUPS BISQUICK baking mix

2/3 CUP MILK

2 OUNCES CHEDDAR cheese, shredded
   (1/2 CUP)

1/4 CUP (1/2 STICK) BUTTER OR MARGARINE,
   MELTED

Preheat the oven to 425°F with the rack in the center position. Place all the ingredients except the melted butter in the pan of a bread machine and select the Dough setting (or equivalent). Allow to knead only until a ball is formed. Press and drop the dough by spoonfuls onto an ungreased heavy-duty baking sheet, leaving about 1½ inches between the biscuits. Bake until golden, 8 to 10 minutes. Brush the melted butter over the warm biscuits before removing from the sheet. Serve warm.

ROQUEFORT CHEESE BREAD

Yield: 1 large loaf

This bread keeps especially well because of its high fat content. The Roquefort flavor is subtle enough that it is difficult to identify. People who claim to dislike blue cheeses love this. The aroma is amazing. Any fine blue cheese can be substituted for the Roquefort.

1 TABLESPOON ACTIVE DRY YEAST (NOT RAPID
   RISE)

3 CUPS UNBLEACHED ALL-PURPOSE FLOUR

3 TABLESPOONS NONFAT DRY MILK

1/3 CUP CORNMEAL

1 TEASPOON SALT

1 TABLESPOON UNSALTED BUTTER, AT ROOM
   TEMPERATURE

1 LARGE EGG

1/3 CUP CRUMBLED ROQUEFORT CHEESE

1 CUP WATER, OR AS NEEDED

Place all the ingredients in the pan of a bread machine, program for White Bread, and press Start. Check the dough after the first 5 minutes of the first knead cycle, adding more water if necessary to form a smooth, supple, soft ball. This is a heavy dough, and the top may sink during the baking cycle—this will not affect the taste of the finished bread.

Hot Buttered Pretzels

Yield: 8 pretzels

I learned how to make these soft pretzels from my friend and Czarina of bakers, P. J. Hamel. You, too, can be a pretzel maker, thanks to your bread machine. Make sure your oven is clean before you start; these pretzels bake at 500°F and any stray spills will start to burn and smoke. The baking soda glaze gives the pretzels a wonderful shiny crust.

For the dough:

2 1/2 CUPS UNBLEACHED ALL-PURPOSE FLOUR

1/2 TEASPOON SALT

1 TEASPOON SUGAR

2 1/4 TEASPOONS ACTIVE DRY YEAST (NOT RAPID RISE)

7/8 CUP WARM WATER (110 TO 115°F), OR AS NEEDED

For the topping:

1/2 CUP WARM WATER

2 TABLESPOONS BAKING SODA

COARSE OR KOSHER SALT

3 TABLESPOONS BUTTER, MELTED

Place all the dough ingredients in the pan of a bread machine and program for the Dough setting (or equivalent). Five minutes into the first knead cycle, check the dough. Add as much additional water as needed to achieve a smooth, soft, slack dough. At the end of the second knead cycle, press Cancel and remove the dough to a large (gallon-size) heavy-duty zippered plastic bag. Seal the bag and allow the dough to rest at room temperature for 30 minutes.

Preheat the oven to 500°F. Prepare two heavy-duty baking sheets by spraying them with nonstick vegetable spray or lining them with parchment paper. Transfer the dough to a lightly oiled work surface and divide into 8 equal pieces. Allow the pieces to rest, uncovered, for 5 minutes. While the dough is resting, combine the 1/2 cup water and baking soda in a shallow bowl. Make sure the baking soda is thoroughly dissolved or your pretzels will look splotchy.

Roll each piece of dough into a long, thin rope about 26 inches long and twist each rope into a pretzel. Dip each pretzel in the baking soda solution and place on one of the prepared baking sheets. Sprinkle the tops lightly with salt and allow them to rest, uncovered, for 10 minutes.

Bake the pretzels until golden brown, 8 to 9 minutes. Remove from the oven and brush each several times with the melted butter. Use up all the butter, giving each pretzel multiple coatings. Eat the pretzels warm or reheat them in the microwave.

SOBA NOODLES

Yield: ½ pound

I had my doubts about making homemade soba noodles. But those lovely buckwheat noodles, which are the basis of some great Japanese dishes, were not nearly as illusive as I thought they'd be. The bread machine, it turns out, handled the dough with ease, and I cranked out the noodles on my pasta roller. It's great fun to make these, and your miso soup will applaud your efforts.

1 ¼ CUPS BUCKWHEAT FLOUR (AVAILABLE IN
    HEALTH FOOD STORES)

1 CUP HIGH-GLUTEN BREAD FLOUR

1 ¼ TEASPOONS SALT

⅔ CUP WATER, OR AS NEEDED

Place all the ingredients in the pan of a bread machine and program for the Dough setting (or equivalent). The dough will be very crumbly at first. Allow it to knead for several minutes before dribbling in more water. Add only enough water to form a dryish ball. Knead for only one cycle, then press Cancel and remove the dough to a heavy-duty zippered plastic bag and seal. Allow it to rest at room temperature for 1 to 3 hours.

Cut the dough in half and, keeping the half you are using covered, pat one piece into a rectangle about ¼ inch thick. Dust with flour and pass it through a pasta roller positioned at the widest setting. Fold the dough into thirds like a letter and feed the unfolded end through the rollers again. Repeat the folding and rolling twice more. Set the rollers on the next smaller setting, lightly flour the dough again, fold, and pass it through the rollers twice. Decrease the setting another notch, flour the dough, fold, and roll, then decrease the setting a final time, flour the dough, fold, and roll.

Place a floured tray under the rollers and insert the thinnest cutting blade. Roll the dough through and allow the noodles to fall onto the tray. Sprinkle with flour and toss to coat well. The noodles are quite fragile and shouldn't be manipulated more than is necessary. Repeat with the remaining dough.

Allow the noodles to dry, uncovered, for 20 minutes before cooking in rapidly boiling water for 1 minute, or freezing, for up to 2 months, to cook at a later time.

DESIGNER MASHED POTATOES

Yield: 8 servings (3 to 4 cups)

In our search for the best and the brightest mashed potatoes, we decided to perform the old John Henry test. Which appliance, we wondered, could produce mashed potatoes that elicit rave reviews? We didn't bother with the food processor or the blender, because we know those turn potatoes to glue. We figured the hand mixer would declare victory, but wanted to also try the handheld blender. We added the bread machine on a lark (if we didn't, who would?). Imagine our surprise when the bread machine emerged the hands-down winner! The others weren't terrible, but they did leave a trace of glue. Not the bread machine . . . fluffy and perfect! Okay, we know this isn't rocket science, but it is cutting edge.

We like traces of lumps in our mashed potatoes, but you can regulate the lumpiness by turning off the machine when it reaches your desired level of smoothness. And yes, these potatoes are worth the calories.

2 POUNDS SMALL RED POTATOES, SCRUBBED AND CUT INTO PIECES (WE LIKE THE SKINS IN OUR MASHED POTATOES, BUT YOU CAN PEEL THEM IF YOU LIKE)

1 TO 2 CLOVES GARLIC, TO YOUR TASTE, PEELED AND MINCED

1/4 CUP (1/2 STICK) BUTTER

6 TABLESPOONS LIGHT CREAM

1/2 CUP FRESHLY GRATED PARMESAN CHEESE

1 TEASPOON SALT

FRESHLY GROUND BLACK PEPPER TO TASTE

Place the potatoes with water to cover in a microwavable bowl. Cover and microwave on high power until the potatoes feel quite soft when pierced with a fork, 10 to 15 minutes. Drain the water and place the potatoes with the rest of the ingredients in the pan of a bread machine, program for the Dough setting (or equivalent), and remove the mixture after the final cycle is complete.

The first time you make these potatoes, keep an eye on the kneading action so that you know when to turn off the machine. We found that it took about 10 minutes in our Zojirushi, but your machine may take a different amount of time, and you may prefer your potatoes more or less mashed than we do.

Variation: Substitute Brie or blue cheese for the Parmesan or omit the cheese and add 1 to 2 tablespoons of prepared horseradish or ¹/₂ cup of Caramelized Onions (page 297).

POTATO GNOCCHI

Yield: 4 servings

Gnocchi are tender potato dumplings that can be used as a first course (much as you would use pasta) or a side dish with fish or chicken.

2 LARGE IDAHO POTATOES (ABOUT 1³/₄ POUNDS), PEELED AND CUT INTO 1-INCH-THICK SLICES

3 TEASPOONS SALT, DIVIDED

2 LARGE EGG YOLKS

1³/₄ CUPS ALL-PURPOSE FLOUR

1 TEASPOON FRESHLY GROUND BLACK PEPPER

1 TEASPOON VEGETABLE OIL

¹/₂ CUP (1 STICK) BUTTER, MELTED

FRESHLY GRATED PARMESAN CHEESE

SNIPPED FRESH CHIVES

Place the potatoes in a medium-size saucepan, cover with cold water, and add 1 teaspoon of the salt. Bring the water to a boil, reduce the heat to medium-low, and simmer until the potatoes are tender, about 40 minutes. Drain the potatoes and return them to the pan. Shake the pan gently over low heat to dry them. Place the potatoes in the pan of a bread machine and program for the Dough setting (or equivalent). With the machine running, add the egg yolk, the flour, and 1 teaspoon of the salt and the pepper. Let the machine knead until the mixture forms a smooth, slightly sticky dough.

Remove the dough from the machine and divide it into fourths. On a lightly floured work surface, roll each piece into a 15-inch-long rope about ³/₄ inch in diameter. Using a floured knife, cut each rope into 30 pieces.

continued 79

Bring a large pot of water to a boil. Add the remaining salt and the oil, then drop the gnocchi into the boiling water. When gnocchi rise to the surface, cook 30 seconds more. Drain in a colander.

Melt the butter in a large skillet over medium-low heat and add the gnocchi. Toss gently and season with salt, pepper, and a generous grating of Parmesan cheese. Sprinkle with chives and serve.

BREAD MACHINE STRAWBERRY JAM

Yield: 4 cups

Many bread machines feature a jam cycle. No one resisted the idea of making jam in my bread machine more vigorously than I did. But when faced with a bumper crop of sweet native berries and the jelly jar approaching empty, I figured, what the hell. Boy, was I surprised, and delighted!

Powdered fruit pectin can be found in most supermarkets and in all health food and natural food stores.

4 CUPS RIPE, VERY SWEET FRESH
    STRAWBERRIES, HULLED AND RINSED
1 CUP SUGAR

2 TABLESPOONS FRESH LEMON JUICE
$^1/_4$ CUP POWDERED FRUIT PECTIN

Place the berries and sugar in a large bowl and use a potato masher to crush them into a chunky purée. Mix in the lemon juice and pectin, then pour and scrape the mixture into the pan of a bread machine, with the paddle in place, program for Jam Cycle, and press Start.

At the end of the cycle, use oven mitts to remove the pan, which will be very hot because of the boiling sugar syrup. Pour the jam into sterilized glass jars or plastic containers with sterilized lids and store in the refrigerator for up to 3 months or freeze for up to one year.

D E E P

F R Y E R

Do you love crispy, crunchy, golden brown batter-coated, eat-it-with-your-hands-then-use-your-shirt-as-a-napkin, good-as-Mama-made, deep-fried-till-it-crackles chicken? On the other hand, do you suffer from the post-1980s' "Fear of Frying" syndrome? Thwarted by this conflict, have you considered resorting to other ways of fixing chicken, such as steaming, boiling, stewing, and sautéing it in broth, but just couldn't force yourself to do it? Well, I say, if at first you don't fricassee, fry fry a hen.

Fantasize this worst case scenario: The nutrition police swoop down and confiscate all the deep-fat fryers. They take most of the oil as well. Could you live without french fries, fried clams, cannoli, shrimp toast, scallion pancakes, zeppoli, donuts, apple fritters, tempura, beignets, and chicken-fried steak, to name just a few items that would never make the transition to alternative cooking techniques? Pressure-cooker fried clams? I don't think so.

So I won't look like the Mickey Mouse in the Macy's Thanksgiving Parade, I am judicious in my choice of fried food, as well as in the frequency with which I eat it. I admit it, my deep-fat fryer is not an appliance that has a permanent place on my kitchen counter. It gets hauled out for very special cooking occasions. On Mardi Gras I make beignets, and on the Fourth of July when the rest of the world is poaching salmon, I make real fried chicken. I make apple fritters every autumn from newly harvested, Massachusetts-grown McIntosh apples, and I am slowly perfecting the world's best beer-batter-fried onion rings. If I'm going to eat fried clams, I want great fried clams. Why should I settle for fried cheese sticks when I can make *mozzarella en carroza*, a deep-fried ham-and-cheese sandwich served in a puddle of anchovy lemon parsley sauce?

How did I conquer my fear of frying? I use a "parachute" in the form of a three-mile run before the fact. After the fact, I want to sit and lick my chops and ruminate over just how good, good fried food can be.

GENERAL DESCRIPTION

WHAT DOES IT DO? • Deep fryers are primarily used to cook food in hot liquids, usually fat. They are safer and cleaner than frying in an open vessel on the stove top. Most modern deep fryers allow you to move the food into and out of the hot fat while the lid is closed, thus reducing the mess of hot oil spattering on your kitchen counter and the danger of it burning the cook. These models also filter the oil and particles from the vapor that escape from the fat during cooking, keeping your kitchen clean and helping to control odors.

WHY DO I NEED THIS? • If you are tired of your kitchen cabinets getting soaked with sooty grease and you'd rather not have hot oil spatter when deep-frying, then this is the appliance to buy. And if deep-fried foods are appealing, but you want to control the type of oil used as well as the exact temperature and duration of cooking, then a deep fryer will help to achieve these goals.

HOW DOES IT WORK? • To fry foods, place fat in the fryer and plug the appliance into an electrical outlet. A heating element located between the inside of the fryer and the outside plastic housing heats up the oil to a temperature set by a dial or slide on the outside of the appliance. Once the desired temperature is achieved, a signal light typically comes on.

Food is placed in the stainless-steel frying basket, and the lid of the fryer is closed. Either a knob is turned or a lever pulled to lower the basket and the food into the bath of hot fat. On some models, the basket rotates constantly to move the food around, allowing it to cook more evenly. The signal light will turn off and on indicating that the heating element is keeping the fryer at the desired temperature.

The greasy and sooty steam from the cooking food passes through a filter and only clean water vapor escapes from the unit during cooking. At the appointed time, the knob is turned or the lever is pulled, and the basket raises the cooked food out of the deep fryer. By pushing a button to release the lid, the food can be removed from the fryer using tongs or a slotted spoon.

CARE AND MAINTENANCE • When finished cooking, the basket is removed from the fryer and washed as is any other stainless steel utensil. Most of them are dishwasher safe. The cooled oil is carefully poured through a paper filter, such as a coffee filter, and is saved to reuse.

When the unit has cooled to room temperature, wipe out the inside with a paper towel with a little dish detergent on it, then rewipe it to remove the soap, but do not immerse it.

From time to time, according to the manufacturer's directions, change the filter. These can be purchased from manufacturer-authorized service centers or wherever new fryers are sold.

WHICH IS RIGHT FOR ME? • When buying a brand new deep fryer, pick the type that has a replaceable filter in the lid and one that allows the hot basket to be removed from the appliance to empty the cooked food onto paper towels to drain.

COMMENTS • Do not open the cover while frying or the purpose of the filter will be defeated. If you open the lid, the greasy steam escapes into your kitchen to find its way to your cabinets, cookware, and countertops.

DEEP FRYER TIPS

- *Cut the food to be fried into uniformly sized pieces so they will cook more evenly.*

- *Foods of different densities have different cooking times. Cook like-density foods together.*

- *Do not overcrowd the deep fryer because it will decrease the temperature below the optimal level and food will stick together.*

- *Foods fried at the right temperature absorb far less oil than those cooked in oil that is not hot enough. Most foods fry best between 365° and 375°F.*

- *Once oil is used to cook fish, do not reuse it.*

- *When oil gets dark or excessively foamy and fails to brown food properly, it is time to throw it out.*

- *To filter used oil, try the following steps: 1) Let the fryer cool to room temperature; 2) Pour the cooled oil into a large bowl; 3) Wipe out the inside of the fryer with paper towels; 4) Clean the basket with hot soapy water and dry it very well; 5) Put the basket back in the fryer, but keep it in the up position; 6) Place a couple of layers of paper towels in the basket; 7) Pour the oil slowly through the paper towels and into the fryer; 8) Discard the towels, close the fryer, and store it in the refrigerator. Unfortunately, this takes up a lot of room, but if you have the space, it is a great way to recycle the oil.*

- *Be aware that a fryer requires a rather large quantity of oil. The model we tested used a little more than 3 quarts.*

- *Operate the fryer out from under the kitchen cabinets and make sure appropriate clearances around and under it are maintained.*

- *A fryer can be used to make soups, chowders, stews, braised dishes, steamed puddings, and many of the same recipes listed for the rice cooker, steamer, and slow cooker. To slow cook, braise, or simmer, remove the basket and place the food directly into the container. As a steamer, use the basket with a small amount of liquid in the bottom of the container. Set the thermostat so that the liquid is at a bare simmer and proceed according to the recipe. You can also bake potatoes in the fryer: Wash the potatoes and place only as many as can fit in one layer in the basket (it's better if they don't touch as this might cause them to steam). Do not put any water in the fryer. Place the basket in the container and cover. Turn the control to 400°F and cook for 1 hour. During the last 15 minutes of cooking, set the cover slightly ajar so any steam can escape.*

- *To use the fryer to warm buns, rolls, moo shu pancakes, and tortillas, place the basket in the container, add a few tablespoons water, cover, and set the control at 175°F. When the indicator light goes on, position the basket, cover, and heat for 5 to 7 minutes.*

> You can use your fryer to pop corn by placing $1/2$ cup of oil in the container. Turn the control to 350°F. When the light indicates the oil is ready, add 1 cup popping corn, stirring with a long-handled spoon to coat the kernels with the oil. Cover, and when almost all the corn is popped, tilt the cover slightly and stir to make sure all the kernels have popped.

RECIPES

RAINBOW CHIPS

Yield: Each pound of sliced raw vegetables yields about 40 chips

Tired of spending so much money on the fancy store-bought variety of vegetable chips? Try making your own. The trick to perfect chips is not to crowd the fryer.

CANOLA OR CORN OIL TO FILL THE ELECTRIC
   FRYER

1 LARGE SWEET POTATO OR YAM, PEELED

1 LARGE BEET, PEELED

2 THICK CARROTS, PEELED

2 THICK PARSNIPS, PEELED

1 LARGE TURNIP, PEELED

COARSE SALT AND FRESHLY GROUND PEPPER
   (RED, WHITE, OR BLACK) TO TASTE

Heat the oil in an electric fryer to 370°F.

Meanwhile, fit the 4mm slicing disk into the work bowl of a food processor. Trim the vegetables so they just fit in the feed tube, leaving them as large as possible. Slice, then pat dry thoroughly with paper towels.

Depending on the size of the slice and the capacity of your fryer, place 5 to 10 slices at a time in the fry basket, lower into the hot oil, and fry until crisp and warped looking, 2 to 4 minutes. Don't mix the vegetables as they take different amounts of time to cook. Drain on paper towels and season with salt and pepper. Repeat with the remaining vegetable slices.

Store, uncovered, at room temperature for up to 2 days. If the chips get soggy, recrisp by placing them in a single layer on a heavy-duty baking sheet in a preheated 300°F oven for 10 minutes. Don't let them brown.

Variation: Try sprinkling the cooked chips with ground cumin, chili powder, or garlic salt.

CHIPS GALORE

Wait until you see how easy and how much fun it is to make your own chips. Forget potatoes! You'll be delighted with the results of the nifty snacks. This is also a good use for leftover stale bagels and pita bread.

BAGELS

CORN TORTILLAS

PITAS

WONTON SKINS

CANOLA OR CORN OIL TO FILL THE ELECTRIC FRYER

SALT, GARLIC POWDER, PEPPER, SPICES, DRIED HERBS OF YOUR CHOICE

For bagel chips, start out with partially frozen bagels. An easy way to do this is to take frozen bagels, microwave each for 12 to 15 seconds on high power, then slice in the work bowl of a food processor fitted with the 4mm slicing disk.

For tortillas and pitas, split open and slice by hand into wedges. For wonton skins, cut into desired size pieces.

Heat the oil to 375°F in an electric fryer. Place about 10 pieces at a time (you'll determine the optimum amount by trial and error) in the fry basket, lower into the hot oil, and fry until golden, about 1 minute. Drain on a baking sheet covered with paper towels. Sprinkle with salt and spices or herbs to taste. Store in a brown paper bag to further degrease.

SOPAIPILLAS

Yield: 12 wedges

These crispy, puffed wedges absorb surprisingly little oil when fried and taste wonderfully crunchy. Although they are traditionally part of Mexican or Southwestern cuisine, they'll beautifully complement any type of meal. They can be served with honey or syrup or, for a different twist, try guacamole or salsa. I have a friend who swears they're best with chicken salad!

CANOLA OR CORN OIL TO FILL THE ELECTRIC FRYER

1 CUP ALL-PURPOSE FLOUR

1/2 TEASPOON SALT

1/2 TEASPOON BAKING POWDER

1 1/2 TEASPOONS NONFAT DRY MILK

1 TEASPOON VEGETABLE SHORTENING

1/2 CUP COLD WATER

Heat the oil in an electric fryer to 370 to 380°F.

Meanwhile, fit the metal blade into the work bowl of a food processor. Place the flour, salt, baking powder, dry milk, and shortening in the work bowl and pulse 3 to 4 times to blend. With the machine running, pour the water into the feed tube and process until the ingredients start to come together, about 15 seconds. Turn off the food processor and place the contents on a lightly floured work surface. Mix the ingredients by hand, adding more flour if necessary to make a soft dough.

Roll the dough out on a lightly floured work surface into a circle about 1/8 inch thick. Cut each circle into 12 pie-shaped wedges.

Place the sopaipillas two or three at a time into the fry basket, lower into the hot oil, and fry, turning several times, until golden brown, 5 to 7 minutes. Drain on paper towels. Repeat with the remaining wedges.

The cooked sopaipillas can be stored in a heavy-duty zippered plastic bag at room temperature.

RADIATORS

Yield: 10 cups

Until I made these I couldn't for the life of me figure out how they got this name— but as my kids say, "Duh, Mom." The perfect Super Bowl or picnic fare.

CANOLA OR CORN OIL TO FILL THE ELECTRIC
FRYER

1 POUND COOKED RADIATORI PASTA (YOU CAN
SUBSTITUTE RIGATONI OR ANY OTHER
PASTA SHAPE OF YOUR CHOICE)

2/3 CUP CORNMEAL

SALT TO TASTE

Heat the oil in an electric fryer to 370 to 380°F.

Sprinkle the cooked pasta with the cornmeal, shaking off any excess. In batches of about two handfuls at a time, place in the fry basket, lower into the hot oil, and fry until the pasta begins to color, 2 to 3 minutes. Drain on paper towels and season with salt. Repeat with the remaining pasta. Serve immediately.

FRIED ZUCCHINI

Yield: 4 servings

This is an easy way to use up a bumper zucchini crop. They make a great addition to an appetizer tray or a tasty first course.

2 TO 4 ZUCCHINI, ABOUT 1 POUND

1 CUP ALL-PURPOSE FLOUR

SALT AND FRESHLY GROUND BLACK PEPPER
   TO TASTE

PEANUT, VEGETABLE, OR CORN OIL TO FILL THE
   ELECTRIC FRYER

FRESH LEMON JUICE, TO YOUR TASTE

Cut the zucchini into small sticks. To do this, cut off the ends of each zucchini; do not peel. Cut the zucchini into 2-inch pieces. Cut each piece into lengthwise slices about ½ inch thick. Cut each slice into strips about ½ inch wide. There should be about 4 cups.

Season the flour with salt and pepper. Dredge the zucchini sticks in the flour and shake off the excess.

Heat the oil in an electric fryer to 375°F. Place half the batch in the fry basket, lower into the hot oil, and stir, until golden and crisp-tender, 3 to 4 minutes. Remove and drain on paper towels. Repeat with the remaining sticks. Serve immediately, sprinkled with salt and pepper and lemon juice.

PESTO CHEESE PILLOWS

Yield: About 2 dozen

These yummy snacks can be fried or baked. Use store-bought pesto or make your own (page 117). This recipe uses store-bought dough (available in the freezer section of the supermarket), or you can make your own using your favorite white bread recipe.

CANOLA OR CORN OIL TO FILL THE ELECTRIC
   FRYER

1 POUND WHITE BREAD DOUGH, THAWED IF
   FROZEN

½ CUP PREPARED PESTO

¾ POUND MOZZARELLA CHEESE, CUT INTO 24
   CHUNKS

¾ POUND SLICED SMOKED TURKEY, DIVIDED
   INTO 24 PORTIONS

Heat the oil in an electric fryer to 370 to 380°F.

While the oil is heating, divide the dough into 2 equal pieces to form the tops and bottoms of the pillows. On a lightly floured work surface, roll out each piece of dough to a rectangle 9 × 12 inches and ¼ inch thick. Brush each piece of dough with the pesto.

Wrap each piece of cheese in a portion of smoked turkey and place the smoked turkey/cheese bundles on one of the dough rectangles, evenly spaced about 1½ inches apart, leaving a ½- to ¾-inch perimeter along the outside edge of the dough rectangle. Brush water along the perimeter and in between the bundles. Place the second dough rectangle on top and press down with your fingers in between the bundles. Use a ravioli cutter or pizza wheel to cut apart the bundles. If necessary, press together the edges of the bundles with your fingers.

In batches of 3 to 4 pieces, place in the fry basket, lower into the hot oil, and fry until golden on both sides, about 5 minutes. Drain on paper towels, then repeat with the remaining bundles. Serve immediately.

Variation: Substitute smoked mozzarella or ham.

APPLE DUMPLINGS

Yield: 10 large dumplings

Ellie had the bright idea to use wonton wrappers to enclose her apple dumplings. I think they make the best crust I've ever tasted. Wonton wrappers are sold near the Asian vegetables in the supermarket.

¼ CUP (½ STICK) BUTTER

6 GRANNY SMITH OR CORTLAND APPLES, CORED, PEELED, AND CUT INTO BITE-SIZE PIECES

¼ CUP FIRMLY PACKED DARK BROWN SUGAR

1 TEASPOON GROUND CINNAMON

1 TEASPOON GRATED LEMON ZEST

10 WONTON WRAPPERS

CANOLA OR CORN OIL TO FILL THE ELECTRIC FRYER

CONFECTIONERS' SUGAR

Melt the butter in a large skillet over medium heat. Add the apples, sugar, cinnamon, and lemon zest and cook, stirring, until softened slightly. Remove to a bowl and chill well.

continued

Place about ¼ cup of the mixture in the center of each wonton wrapper. Moisten the edges of the wrapper with water. Bring the four corners to a point on top and bring the edges together, pressing firmly. Repeat with the remaining wrappers and filling.

Heat the oil in an electric fryer to 375°F. Add the dumplings to the fry basket two at a time, lower into the hot oil, and fry until golden brown. Drain on paper towels, dust with confectioners' sugar, and serve hot. Repeat with the remaining wontons.

Variation: Substitute pears for the apples, omitting the cinnamon, or peaches or nectarines, using nutmeg instead of the cinnamon.

CORN FRITTERS

Yield: 2 to 2½ dozen fritters

Crispy outside, sweet and succulently tender inside, these corn fritters can be an appetizer dipped in salsa or a side dish to a turkey dinner. They're also wonderful served up as a breakfast dish, topped with real maple syrup.

3 LARGE EGGS

½ CUP (1 STICK) BUTTER, MELTED

½ CUP MILK

⅔ CUP ALL-PURPOSE FLOUR

5 TEASPOONS BAKING POWDER

½ CUP FIRMLY PACKED DARK BROWN SUGAR

¼ TEASPOON SALT

ONE 16-OUNCE CAN WHOLE KERNEL CORN, WELL DRAINED

ONE 7-OUNCE CAN CREAMED CORN

CANOLA, CORN, OR PEANUT OIL TO FILL THE ELECTRIC FRYER

Using a hand mixer on medium speed, beat the eggs with the melted butter and milk. Add the dry ingredients and mix well. Beat in both corns.

Heat the oil in an electric fryer to 370°F. Carefully drop large ladlefuls (about ¼ cup each) into the fryer, no more than 5 at a time. Fry till golden, turning to fry the other side. Remove the cooked fritters to a baking sheet or large platter covered with a double layer of paper towels to drain. Repeat with the remaining batter. Serve immediately.

MOZZARELLA EN CARROZZA

Yield: 4 servings

This recipe, which translates from the Italian as mozzarella in a carriage, is the ultimate toasted cheese sandwich. Serve it hot with the tangy caper, lemon, and anchovy sauce as a first course preceeding a light dinner—it's filling! The preparation can be done up to the frying step up to six hours ahead. Refrigerate the carrozzas until ready to cook. Prepare the simple sauce just before you cook the carrozzas.

For the sauce:

¹/₂ CUP (1 STICK) BUTTER

¹/₄ CUP OLIVE OIL

8 FLAT ANCHOVY FILLETS, DRAINED

2 TABLESPOONS CAPERS, DRAINED

JUICE OF 1 LARGE LEMON

1 CUP FRESH ITALIAN PARSLEY LEAVES,
    CHOPPED

1 WIDE LOAF ITALIAN BREAD

4 VERY THIN SLICES PROSCIUTTO OR SMOKED
    TURKEY

8 OUNCES FRESH WHOLE-MILK MOZZARELLA
    CHEESE, CUT INTO 4 EQUAL SLICES

¹/₄ CUP MILK

2 LARGE EGGS

VEGETALBE OIL FOR DEEP FRYING

Heat the butter and olive oil in a skillet. When melted, add the anchovies and cook, stirring constantly, over medium heat until dissolved. Stir in the capers, lemon juice, and parsley and cook 2 to 3 more minutes to heat thoroughly. Keep at room temperature until ready to use.

Cut the bread into 8 equal slices, trimming off the crust. Grind the crust and any remaining bread in a food processor or blender to make coarse crumbs. Use your hands to slightly flatten the slices of bread. Wrap a slice of prosciutto or turkey around each slice of mozzarella and place it on a slice of bread. Top with another slice to make a small sandwich. Pinch the edges together. Stir the milk together with the eggs, then dip the sandwich briefly in the mixture without allowing it to get soggy. Roll the sandwich in the bread crumbs, then dip in the milk/egg mixture one more time. Use your fingers to seal the seams. Heat the oil in a deep fryer according to manufacturer's directions and fry the carrozzas 2 at a time (or 1 at a time if your fryer is small) until very deep golden brown. To serve, place a carrozza on a small plate and top with sauce. Serve hot.

F O O D

PROCESSOR/MINI

Back in the early 1970s when food processors first made the scene, most American chefs turned their noses up at the idea of using a machine to prepare food. Many American home cooks blanched at the thought of spending several hundred dollars on an appliance that had the potential to reduce both celery and fingers to mush in seconds.

It took a visionary in the person of Carl Sontheimer to convince Americans that the food processor had a place in every restaurant and home kitchen. Once Mr. Sontheimer made the trademark Cuisinart, the Kleenex and Xerox of food processors, other companies soon got on the bandwagon. Some think it took the French robot coup to convince any American holdouts that if it was fine for French cooks to purée, mince, chop, slice, and dice by machine, then it was okay for us as well.

In the end the Cuisinart has weathered the storms of competition and remained the premier food processor. Imagine your kitchen without it—I couldn't.

GENERAL DESCRIPTION

WHAT DOES IT DO? • A food processor is a multipurpose appliance, the Clydesdale of the kitchen. It can be used to slice, shred, or chop solid foods; blend or emulsify liquids; mix and knead dough; and purée soft foods.

WHY DO I NEED THIS? • Food processors will help with just about any job in the kitchen, except washing the dishes. But even this task will be made simpler by using a food processor, since there will be fewer bowls and utensils to clean up when the cooking is done.

HOW DOES IT WORK? • A food processor consists of a single-speed electric motor in a base unit that turns a shaft. The shaft transfers the rotary motion to an attachment within a detachable plastic work bowl. The motor is controlled by an on/off switch for continuous processing or by a pulse switch for intermittent processing.

The work bowl comes in a variety of capacities, from 3 to 20 cups, and has a handle for easy emptying and a lid. The lid offers protection from the spinning blades and disks and provides control of the food through its feed tube and pusher. Every food processor has an interlock with the lid to prevent the motor from coming on when the lid is off. Usually, the very large capacity food processors have heavier duty features, such as a metal base, larger motor, and a steel shaft instead of a plastic one.

Standard attachments include a metal blade with sharp edges designed to chop foods and mix batters; a plastic dough blade that does not have sharp edges, but can mix and knead pasta, bread, and pie crust doughs; metal slicing disks with sharp blade features that turn whole foods into slices of varying thickness; and shredding disks that grate solid food to a variety of degrees of coarseness.

The blade attachments are located at the bottom of the work bowl when they are operating. Food is placed in the work bowl with the appropriate attachment; the lid is locked into place, and when the motor is turned on, the shaft turns the blade to either chop, blend, mix, or knead the contents of the work bowl. As the motor turns, it also generates heat. Pay attention to this since it can become an issue when making heat-sensitive food such as pie crust dough. Pulsing the motor instead of letting it run continuously will help control the amount of heat generated in the work bowl. Also, try chilling the attachment and bowl in the freezer for 10 to 15 minutes before using. When running the food processor, if heat-sensitive food starts to melt, stick the entire work bowl with the food in it in the freezer for several minutes to slow down the melting.

The feed tube can vary in size, some food processors have dual-size feed tubes. If you have more than one food processor, make sure to use the correct

F O O D

PROCESSOR/MINI

pusher for each machine. If you try to push food through the feed tube with a pusher that is too long, you risk having the appliance take a chunk of plastic out of the pusher, damaging the plunger and the disk, and introducing plastic shrapnel into your gazpacho.

Some food processors also come with a whisk attachment that consists of metal or plastic beaters that rotate and spin in the work bowl powered by the rotating shaft, making the food lighter and fluffier. Whisks typically do not reach 100 percent of the food in the work bowl, since food tends to hide along the bottom outside edge. Stop the motor and use a spatula to scrape the food toward the center of the work bowl, then continue processing. The whisk attachment is okay for rather small amounts of food, but it does not incorporate as much air as does a mixer.

CARE AND MAINTENANCE • Even though food processors are work-horses, do not be tempted to push the outside of the envelope. Trying to grind very hard grains such as dried corn with your food processor will chew up your metal blade attachment and increase the risk that metal shavings will end up in your corn-meal. At best it will dull the blade. And trying to knead a dough that is too heavy will cause the motor to stall and possibly burn out. Pay careful attention to the manu-facturer's directions.

Also, when working with sharp attachments, treat them as you would any sharp knife. Pay special attention where you put them before and after you wash them. Do not submerge them in a sink full of sudsy water. Once they are washed and rinsed, dry them immediately and put them away.

The work bowl and lid can be washed by hand or in the upper rack of a dish-washer, according to the manufacturer's directions, although dishwashing detergent will dull Lexan's shiny finish. Pay particular attention to feed tubes, since many food processors will not allow you to disassemble them completely for a thorough cleaning. The base of the food processor should be wiped with a damp towel but never immersed in water. Check nooks, crannies, and the back side of the base for drips and splatters. Leave the top askew so the innards dry and stay fresh for the next use.

WHICH IS RIGHT FOR ME? • Carefully select the correct food processor size, especially if planning to use it to process liquid foods. Bigger is not necessarily better. (There is a wide selection and variety of price, quality, size, and function. So it pays to talk to your friends; try out their food processors and those at the store before buying.) If more food is put in a food processor than it is designed for, the motor could burn out, or an incredible mess will be created in the kitchen when it overflows. Some motors are more powerful than others, so if you intend to knead lots of whole-grain bread doughs or chop ice, choose a food processor with a heavy-duty motor.

COMMENTS • Optional attachments can include slicers of additional thicknesses, citrus juicer, julienne disks, crinkle-cut disks, and a flat lid without a tall feed tube, which can be useful when using the blades and storing the processor in a smaller space. You will not have to wash the complicated feed tube every time you use the machine.

Storage devices for the attachments can either be included or purchased as a separate option, as well as continuous feed chutes to increase the virtual work bowl capacity.

FOOD PROCESSOR/MINI FOOD PROCESSOR TIPS

- *If you own more than one food processor, make sure you use the correct plunger with each machine. Otherwise, the disks might break or chip the plastic plunger.*

- *Do not substitute anything for the plunger, like a wooden spoon, a finger, or a chopstick. You can ruin the machine, cause splinters to get into your food, or worse.*

- *Placing the metal blade in the dishwasher will eventually dull the edges.*

- *Do not use the lid interlock switch to turn the machine on and off.*

- *Do not allow the processor to run unattended. If you are processing unusually hard ingredients (such as Parmesan cheese), keep one hand firmly on the lid, as the machine may jump.*

- *To prevent the attachment from falling out of the work bowl and into your prepared cake pans, slip a finger up through the hole in the bottom of the work bowl. Hold the attachment in place while you pour and scrape the liquid out of the bowl.*

- *When removing the blade or disk from the work bowl, set the cover upside* down on the counter with the feed tube down to balance it. When removing the slicing or shredding disks, they can safely sit right inside the cover, saving your counter space for other things and keeping your counter clean.

- If a dough is too stiff to knead by hand, then do not attempt to knead it in the food processor.

- To help you clean your appliance, leave the metal blade in the bowl and add hot water and a little soap and pulse.

- When processing foods that are not very heavy, like herbs, garlic, and soft cheeses, use the pulse action to give the food a chance to fall back into the blades.

- Our experience has taught us not to use the food processor to process cooked potatoes. If you do, they will turn into a gluey mass.

- Do not overload the food processor with liquid. It will leak at the shaft and could run over the top of the work bowl.

- When making a recipe in the food processor and it leaks out of the bottom, next time rearrange ingredients so the wet ingredients go in last.

- To easily mince garlic and shallots, run the machine and drop them through the feed tube, processing to mince. The same can be done with Parmesan and Romano cheeses.

FOOD PROCESSOR RECIPES

SMOKED TOMATO KETCHUP

Yield: About 4½ cups

If you want to give a whole new life to burgers, fries, and hot dogs, try a little of this.

4 CUPS SMOKED TOMATOES (PAGE 365), WITH SKINS, SEEDS, AND PULP

3 TABLESPOONS BOURBON

2 TEASPOONS GREEN TABASCO SAUCE

2 TEASPOONS BALSAMIC VINEGAR

4 TEASPOONS FIRMLY PACKED DARK BROWN SUGAR

2 TEASPOONS BLACKSTRAP MOLASSES

⅓ CUP HONEY

2 TABLESPOONS SOY SAUCE

In the work bowl of a food processor fitted with the metal blade, process all the ingredients together until completely smooth. Place the mixture in either a regular or electric skillet and cook, uncovered, over low heat (225°F), stirring occasionally, until the mixture is reduced by about a third and quite thickened. This will keep refrigerated in a tightly closed container for two months.

SPICED NUT BUTTER

Yield: 1¹/₄ cups

Served as a snack, in a sandwich, or as an addition to your brunch table, this spicy spread will liven up toast, bread, muffins, even pancakes. When you make Spicy Nuts (page 186), double everything so you can make this great recipe.

1 CUP SPICY PECANS

1 CUP (2 STICKS) UNSALTED BUTTER, SOFTENED

1 TEASPOON HONEY

Place the nuts in the work bowl of a food processor fitted with the metal blade and pulse 8 to 10 times to finely chop. Add the butter and honey and process until smooth and well mixed. Place in an airtight container and refrigerate for up to 4 weeks.

Variaton: Substitute cream cheese for the butter.

ROASTED RED PEPPER SALSA

Yield: 8 servings

My favorite time to make homemade salsa is when the first crop of homegrown tomatoes shows up in the market. If you are lacking homegrown and are faced with the hothouse variety, use Italian plum tomatoes instead as they have more flavor.

continued

If you want to try something a little different, substitute basil for the coriander.

4 LARGE, RIPE TOMATOES OR 8 PLUM
    TOMATOES, CHOPPED (ABOUT 4 CUPS), OR
    TWO 16-OUNCE CANS CHOPPED TOMATOES
    (IF YOU CAN'T FIND CHOPPED, WHOLE ARE
    FINE—YOU'LL HAVE TO CHOP THEM
    YOURSELF)

1 MEDIUM-SIZE RED ONION, COARSELY
    CHOPPED

ONE 6-OUNCE JAR ROASTED SWEET RED
    PEPPERS, DRAINED AND COARSELY
    CHOPPED

1 LARGE CLOVE GARLIC, MINCED

1/3 CUP CHOPPED FRESH CORIANDER
    (CILANTRO) LEAVES

2 TABLESPOONS RED WINE VINEGAR, PLUS
    ADDITIONAL TO YOUR TASTE

3 TABLESPOONS OLIVE OIL

1/2 TEASPOON SALT, PLUS ADDITIONAL TO
    YOUR TASTE

5 TO 7 DROPS TABASCO SAUCE (OPTIONAL),
    TO YOUR TASTE

Place all the ingredients except the Tabasco in the work bowl of a food processor fitted with the metal blade and process in a pulsing motion until the mixture is just combined but not smooth. By hand, stir in additional vinegar or salt, as well as the optional Tabasco. Serve at room temperature or chill until serving time. Pass with a basket of tortilla chips, pita triangles, or vegetable crudités.

TROUBLE IN TAHITI

Yield: About 4 cups

Salsa isn't just tomatoes—it can be any mixture of fresh fruits, vegetables, and spices. Here's a tropically inspired version that can be served with any sort of grilled meat or fish.

1/3 CUP FRESH MINT LEAVES

1 RIPE PINEAPPLE, PEELED, CORED, AND CUT
    INTO 8 WEDGES

2 LARGE, RIPE MANGOES, PEELED, PIT
    REMOVED, AND CUT INTO LARGE CHUNKS

2 ORANGE BELL PEPPERS, SEEDED AND
    COARSELY CHOPPED

2 LIMES, ZEST AND WHITE PITH

1/2 CUP SALTED PEANUTS, CHOPPED

Insert the 4mm (or smaller, depending on how coarse you prefer) slicing disk. Slice the pineapple wedges. Set the pineapple aside and remove the slicing disk. Insert the metal blade, add the mangoes, bell peppers, pineapple, and limes and pulse 3 or 4 times to combine. Add the mint leaves and peanuts and pulse 2 or 3 times to combine. Chill 2 to 3 hours so the flavors can combine before serving.

GUACAMOLE

Yield: 1¹/₂ cups

The trick to making good guacamole is selecting ripe, flavorful avocados and resisting the temptation to process them into mush. This is where the pulse option of the food processor comes in handy.

1 SMALL PURPLE ONION, QUARTERED

2 RIPE AVOCADOS, PEELED, PITTED, AND CUT INTO 2-INCH CHUNKS

JUICE OF 2 LIMES

1 LARGE, RIPE PLUM TOMATO, SEEDED AND CUT INTO ¹/₄-INCH DICE

SALT AND FRESHLY GROUND BLACK PEPPER TO TASTE

DASH OF TABASCO OR HOT PEPPER SAUCE

Place the onion in the work bowl of a food processor fitted with the metal blade and process until chopped but not mushy. Add the remaining ingredients and pulse only until mixed. Serve immediately or store in an airtight container until ready to use. Serve with taco chips or vegetable sticks.

GEFILTE FISH

Yield: 20 medium-size gefilte fish

If the words "ground poached fish" don't light your culinary candle, just remember that grown men have been brought to tears by the memory of their mother's gefilte fish (actually, perhaps it was the memory of the homemade horseradish). Before the food processor revolutionized our lives, this recipe was so labor intensive it was saved only for holidays. Now that grinding has been made easy, the only drawback is the expense—these ingredients are not cheap, so brace yourself as you place the order with your fish market. If you've ever had homemade gefilte fish, you know the end result is worth it.

ABOUT 2 POUNDS EACH CARP, PIKE, AND
  WHITE FISH, FILLETED TO GIVE ABOUT
  3¹/₂ POUNDS SKINNED FISH; DISCARD
  THE GILLS BUT RESERVE THE HEADS,
  BONES, AND SKINS

3 MEDIUM-SIZE ONIONS, SLICED

4 MEDIUM-SIZE CARROTS, SLICED

LARGE SPRIG FRESH ITALIAN PARSLEY

SALT AND FRESHLY GROUND BLACK PEPPER
  TO TASTE

8¹/₂ CUPS WATER

4 LARGE EGGS, LIGHTLY BEATEN

Rinse the fish heads, bones, and skins, place them in a large saucepan with one of the onions, two of the carrots, and the parsley, and season with salt and pepper. Cover with 8 cups of the water. Bring to a boil, cover, reduce the heat to medium-low, and simmer for 1 hour or longer. Pour the broth through a fine mesh strainer, discarding the bones and cooked vegetables.

Place half of the fish fillets in the work bowl of a food processor fitted with the metal blade and process until the mixture is completely smooth, taking care not to heat it by overprocessing. Remove the mixture to a large bowl and repeat with the remaining fillets. Process the 2 remaining onions until very finely chopped. In a large bowl, mix together the ground fish with the onions, eggs, and the remaining ¹/₂ cup of water and season with salt and pepper.

Use a soup spoon dipped in cold water to shape the fish mixture into about 20 medium-size balls. Heat the reserved strained broth in a large skillet or sauté pan. Gently drop the balls of fish into the simmering but not boiling liquid. Partially cover and simmer very gently for 1¹/₂ to 2 hours. Add the remaining carrot slices during the last 30 minutes of cooking.

Drain and place the fish balls on a platter, cool slightly, cover, and refrigerate. Remove the carrot pieces and reserve for garnish. Strain the broth into a bowl, cool, and chill overnight. Serve the gefilte fish garnished with the carrot pieces, the jelled broth or aspic, and plenty of homemade horseradish (page 102).

Salmon Croquettes

Yield: 10 croquettes

Croquettes are an easy way to combine cooked meats and fish with vegetables (often found lurking in the form of leftovers in your refrigerator). Croquette literally means crunchy on the outside. These are crunchy, indeed, but with a creamy interior—no one will complain about leftovers if they come in this form.

Instead of coating the croquettes with the usual bread crumbs, this recipe calls for stuffing—you can make your own or buy it prepared.

1 MEDIUM-SIZE ONION, PEELED
    AND QUARTERED

1 LARGE CARROT, CUT INTO CHUNKS

1 STALK CELERY, CUT INTO CHUNKS

2 TABLESPOONS CHOPPED FRESH DILL, OR
    1/2 TEASPOON DRIED

ONE 15-OUNCE CAN SALMON, UNDRAINED,
    SKIN, BONES, AND CARTILAGE REMOVED,
    OR 2 CUPS FINELY CHOPPED LEFTOVER

COOKED FISH, CHICKEN, TURKEY, HAM, OR
    SHELLFISH

1 LARGE EGG

1/2 CUP MAYONNAISE

1 TABLESPOON DIJON MUSTARD

2 TABLESPOONS STEAK SAUCE

3 CUPS GROUND SEASONED STUFFING, DIVIDED

VEGETABLE OIL FOR FRYING

Place the onion, carrot, and celery in the work bowl of a food processor fitted with the metal blade and pulse several times, until they are in small pieces. Add the dill, salmon, egg, mayonnaise, mustard, steak sauce, and 1½ cups of the stuffing (reserve the rest in a heavy-duty zippered plastic bag). Run the processor until the mixture is uniformly ground. Cover and chill the mixture for several hours or overnight.

With wet hands, form the chilled mixture into 10 patties, place them in the bag with the stuffing, and coat evenly. Heat ½ inch of the oil in an electric skillet set on medium-high heat (375°F), or until a stuffing crumb sizzles in the oil. Fry the patties, 4 or 5 at a time, until golden brown on both sides, adding more oil if necessary. Drain on paper towels and serve immediately.

HORSERADISH

Yield: About ¾ cup, depending on the size of the root

My mother still makes her horseradish by hand. She says her tears, activated by its powerful aroma, are a key ingredient. I myself can do without the bloody knuckles I always get when I use a hand grater, blinded by tears and tending a furiously running nose. No matter how you make your horseradish, trust me, fresh is incomparable to the kind you buy in the store.

1 LARGE HORSERADISH ROOT, PEELED

1 COOKED BEET (FRESHLY COOKED OR CANNED)

2 TABLESPOONS RED WINE VINEGAR

1 TEASPOON SUGAR

In the work bowl of a food processor fitted with the fine grating disk, grate the horseradish and beet together. Stir in the vinegar and sugar. Store in a tightly covered glass jar in the refrigerator until ready to serve. Will keep, refrigerated, for several months.

PUCCINIS

Yield: 48 pieces

Rugelach, those tender snail cookies found in many delis and in the homes of old-time cookie bakers, inspired this savory pastry. Not only are they a terrific cocktail pickup; they make a lovely teatime snack as well as an elegant garnish for a plate of soup or bowl of stew. These are best eaten within two hours of baking. Don't refrigerate or freeze them. They can be assembled and refrigerated unbaked for 24 hours, or even frozen unbaked for two months.

This is a hands-on job, but even the rank beginner will soon get the hang of filling and rolling the triangles of dough. Don't worry if the first few aren't picture-perfect, or if they aren't all the same size—the outtakes become the cook's samples.

Oh, about the name—when we pulled these out of the oven and our music buff took the first bite, he sighed and pronounced them "positively operatic."

1 CUP (2 STICKS) UNSALTED BUTTER, AT ROOM
   TEMPERATURE

8 OUNCES CREAM CHEESE (DO NOT USE
   WHIPPED CREAM CHEESE), AT ROOM
   TEMPERATURE

2 CUPS ALL-PURPOSE FLOUR

1 TO 1 1/2 POUNDS SMOKED TURKEY

1/2 POUND MOZZARELLA CHEESE, SHREDDED

2 LARGE EGGS BEATEN WITH 2
   TABLESPOONS MILK

In the work bowl of a food processor fitted with the metal blade, cream the butter and cream cheese together until smooth. Add the flour and process until a soft dough forms. Divide the dough into 4 portions, wrap each with plastic wrap, and refrigerate until the dough is firm, an hour or longer. Remove the dough from the refrigerator and allow it to rest on the counter for 15 minutes before proceeding.

Preheat the oven to 350°F. Line 3 heavy-duty baking sheets with parchment paper or heavy-duty aluminum foil, or butter each sheet and dust it with flour, shaking off the excess. One at a time, roll out each dough portion on a lightly floured work surface into a 9-inch circle 1/8 inch thick. Cut the dough into 12 triangles or pieces of pie. With a thin knife, loosen the triangles and coat one side with a thin layer of smoked turkey and cheese. Starting with the wide end, roll the triangle up and bend the ends around to form a slightly crescent shape. Place the Puccinis about 1 1/2 inches apart on the prepared baking sheets. Brush with the egg glaze and bake until lightly browned, 16 to 18 minutes. Serve immediately.

Variation: For a vegetarian version, leave out the turkey. Be bold and experiment with your favorite savory fillings. We loved the versions filled with pesto, as well as those with sun-dried tomatoes, tapenade, and goat cheese.

SMOKED SALMON PÂTÉ

Yield: 1 1/2 cups

This is not anything like the salmon cream cheese spread you can buy at the deli. Fresh, rich, and chock-full of smoked salmon, it's an elegant pre-dinner offering.

continued

3 SCALLIONS, SLICED

1/2 POUND SMOKED SALMON

8 OUNCES CREAM CHEESE (DO NOT USE
WHIPPED CREAM CHEESE), CUT INTO
CHUNKS

2 TABLESPOON FRESH LEMON JUICE

FRESHLY GROUND BLACK PEPPER TO TASTE

1/4 TEASPOON SALT

3 TO 4 DASHES TABASCO SAUCE, TO YOUR
TASTE

1/3 CUP CHOPPED FRESH DILL

In the work bowl of a food processor fitted with the metal blade, pulse the scallions 3 to 4 times to chop them finely. Add the salmon and pulse 3 to 4 times. Add the remaining ingredients except the dill and process until completely smooth. Finally, add the dill and process just to distribute it through the pâté. Spoon into ramekins, cover, and chill until ready to serve spread on crackers or toast.

Duck Liver Mousse

Yield: 2 1/2 cups

This is so addictive, so sinfully rich, and so amazingly simple to make—once you try it, you'll never resort to store-bought pâté again. Duck livers are not as hard to come by as you may think—next time you buy a whole duck, look in the little paper bag (unless your butcher has removed it for his own use). You can easily substitute chicken livers in this recipe.

1 POUND DUCK OR CHICKEN LIVERS, RINSED
AND TRIMMED OF FAT AND MEMBRANES

1 CUP CHICKEN BROTH

2 TO 3 SPRIGS FRESH ITALIAN PARSLEY, TO
YOUR TASTE

1/2 CUP DRY SHERRY

2 SHALLOTS, SLICED

3 CLOVES GARLIC, MASHED

1 BAY LEAF

1 CUP (2 STICKS) UNSALTED BUTTER, AT ROOM
TEMPERATURE

1/4 CUP BRANDY OR COGNAC (OPTIONAL)

1 TEASPOON FRESH LEMON JUICE

1 TEASPOON DRY MUSTARD

1/2 TEASPOON GROUND NUTMEG

1 1/2 TO 2 TEASPOONS SALT, TO YOUR TASTE

FRESHLY GROUND BLACK PEPPER TO TASTE

1/4 CUP (1/2 STICK) BUTTER, MELTED

Place the livers, broth, parsley, sherry, shallots, garlic, and bay leaf in a medium-size saucepan over medium heat. Bring the liquid to a boil, then reduce the heat to medium-low and simmer for 15 minutes. Discard the liquid and bay leaf.

Place the remaining solids in the work bowl of a food processor fitted with the metal blade and process until completely smooth. With the processor on, add the softened butter through the feed tube a tablespoon at a time, waiting until it is combined before adding more. The mixture should be creamy and smooth. Add the brandy, lemon juice, and seasonings. Adjust the salt and pepper and scrape the mousse into one large or several smaller ramekins. Pour the melted butter on top to cover and refrigerate until ready to serve. Pass around with toast or crackers.

AMPS

Yield: About 3 cups

AMPS started out as a joke when John Chovan won the Blue Ribbon at the Ohio State Fair in the cooking with Spam category. I said, "Hey, we have to have an upscale version of Spam in our book, something really great that you could only make with a plugged-in appliance." John came up with the name, which is not only an anagram of Spam and an electrical play on words, but also stands for Another Meat Product Simulation. It was up to me to come up with a recipe that was worthy of all these mental aerobics. Here is it is . . . try it and let me know what you think. My E-mail address is in the back of the book.

Dried mixed herbs of Provence are available in gourmet shops, or you can make your own with a pinch each of dried tarragon, basil, rosemary, chervil, thyme, and untreated lavender.

2 CUPS UNSALTED CHICKEN BROTH

2 TEASPOONS HERBES DE PROVENCE

2 CLOVES GARLIC, PEELED AND CRUSHED

1 MEDIUM-SIZE ONION, PEELED AND CHOPPED

1 POUND SMOKED TURKEY, CUT INTO
   1-INCH CUBES

1 TABLESPOON DIJON MUSTARD

2 TO 3 TABLESPOONS DRY SHERRY
   (OPTIONAL), TO YOUR TASTE

1 TEASPOON GREEN PEPPERCORNS, DRAINED

FRESHLY GROUND BLACK PEPPER TO TASTE

continued

Place the chicken broth, herbs, garlic, and onion in a saucepan over medium heat. Bring the mixture to a rapid simmer and continue cooking until it has reduced to a little more than ½ cup. Strain through a fine mesh strainer or piece of cheesecloth and set aside to cool slightly. You should have ¼ to ⅓ cup liquid.

Place the turkey, mustard, and sherry in the work bowl of a food processor fitted with the metal blade and process until the turkey is ground, scraping down the sides of the work bowl as necessary. Then, with the machine running, add the reduced stock and process until the mixture is very smooth. Add the peppercorns and process for 20 seconds, just to combine them. Season with pepper (try not to overprocess the mixture at this point; the peppercorns should not be completely ground up).

Spoon and scrape the mixture into ramekins, cover with plastic wrap that touches the mixture, and refrigerate until ready to serve. To serve, cut thin slices and serve as you would a pâté, with toast, mustard, and cornichons (small, crisp pickles).

CHILI CHEESECAKE

Yield: One 10-inch cake (12 servings)

Cheesecake is usually just considered a dessert. However, this combination of smooth cream cheese laced with the zing of chili makes for a sparkling new take on a first course or appetizer.

To prepare the pan:

ENOUGH CORN CHIPS TO EQUAL 1½ CUPS VERY FINE CRUMBS

⅓ CUP BUTTER

For the cheesecake:

2 POUNDS CREAM CHEESE (DON'T USE WHIPPED CREAM CHEESE), AT ROOM TEMPERATURE

⅓ CUP HEAVY CREAM

4 EXTRA LARGE EGGS

2 TEASPOONS MILD CHILI POWDER

1 OR 2 CANNED CHIPOTLE PEPPERS, (TO YOUR TASTE), MINCED

1 CUP SHREDDED OR GRATED SMOKED GOUDA CHEESE

1 MEDIUM-SIZE ONION, PEELED, CHOPPED, AND SAUTÉED UNTIL SOFTENED IN 3 TABLESPOONS BUTTER

½ CUP FRESH CORIANDER (CILANTRO) LEAVES, MINCED

⅓ CUP SMOKED HAM, TRIMMED VERY LEAN AND MINCED

Preheat the oven to 300°F with the rack in the center position. Butter a 10-inch cake pan with 3-inch-high sides. Grind the chips in the work bowl of a food processor fitted with the metal blade until very fine. Add the butter and process for 20 seconds. Use this mixture to coat the bottom and halfway up the sides of the pan.

Place the cream cheese, cream, eggs, chili powder, and chipotles in the processor and process until completely mixed. Add the remaining ingredients and process just to blend, not to a smooth consistency.

Pour the batter into the prepared pan, shake to level the top, and set the pan in a large roasting pan. Add hot water to a depth of 2 inches up the sides of the cake pan. Bake the cake for 1 hour and 45 minutes. At the end of this time, turn off the oven, but let the cake remain inside with the door closed for 1 more hour.

Remove the pan to a counter and let rest until completely cool, at least another hour. Do not refrigerate. Cover the top with plastic wrap and unmold onto a baking sheet. Invert onto a large cake plate. To serve, rim the cheesecake with salsa. Slice or serve with chips.

CHAROSET

Yield: 3 to 4 cups, depending on the size of the apples

This traditional dish is part of the Passover seder. It represents the mortar used by the Jewish slaves to build pharaoh's pyramids. This delectable mixture of tart apples, nuts, raisins, and wine is a natural for the food processor—just be careful not to overprocess it and make a purée. It should be fairly chunky. I always make extra so that we can enjoy it on matzo during the whole eight days of Passover.

3 LARGE TART APPLES, SUCH AS GRANNY SMITH, CORED, PEELED, AND COARSELY CHOPPED

2 TEASPOONS GROUND CINNAMON, OR TO YOUR TASTE

$^1/_2$ CUP WALNUTS OR ALMONDS

2 TEASPOONS GROUND GINGER, OR TO YOUR TASTE

$^1/_3$ CUP RAISINS

ABOUT $^1/_4$ CUP SWEET RED PASSOVER WINE

Place all the ingredients in the work bowl of a food processor fitted with the metal blade and pulse on and off until the mixture is chopped but not puréed. Serve on matzo.

CARROT-GINGER SOUP

Yield: 6 to 8 servings

Hot or cold, this soup is a great starter or almost a meal in itself. It's thickened with potatoes—not cream—but tastes indulgent just the same.

ONE 2-INCH PIECE FRESH GINGER, PEELED

4 LARGE SHALLOTS, CUT IN HALF

GRATED ZEST OF 1 LARGE ORANGE

2 POUNDS CARROTS, SLICED INTO 1-INCH
   PIECES

3 LARGE IDAHO POTATOES, PEELED AND CUT
   INTO CHUNKS

6 CUPS CHICKEN OR VEGETABLE BROTH

1 CUP ORANGE JUICE

5 TO 10 DROPS TABASCO SAUCE, TO YOUR
   TASTE

2 TO 3 TABLESPOONS SOY SAUCE, TO YOUR
   TASTE

Place the ginger, shallots, and orange zest in the work bowl of a food processor fitted with the metal blade and process until fine, about 10 seconds. Place this, along with all the remaining ingredients except the Tabasco and soy sauce, in a slow cooker set on high, a rice cooker, or a large, covered heavy-bottomed pot over medium heat and cook until the vegetables are very soft, about 2 hours for the slow cooker and 30 minutes for the rice cooker and on the stove top.

Use a slotted spoon to transfer the solids, then one quarter of the liquid back to the food processor. Process for 15 seconds, scrape down the work bowl, and continue to process until smooth, about 10 seconds more. Combine with the reserved cooking liquid, season with the Tabasco and soy sauce, and serve hot or cold garnished with a dollop of plain yogurt or sour cream.

BORSCHT

Yield: 8 to 10 servings

An icy cold cup of borscht topped with a dollop of low-fat yogurt or sour cream is my favorite summer soup. Served piping hot, it makes a marvelous winter's chill-chaser. While you can cook the potato with the beets, my preference is to cook it separately so it will keep its color.

½ CUP FRESH DILL, OR 1 TABLESPOON DRIED

2 LARGE BUNCHES BEETS (ABOUT 3 POUNDS), PEELED

1 MEDIUM-SIZE ONION, PEELED AND QUARTERED

2 STALKS CELERY

10 CUPS WATER

2 TABLESPOONS SALT

2 TEASPOONS SOUR SALT (AVAILABLE IN THE SPICE SECTION OF THE SUPERMARKET), OR THE JUICE OF 1 MEDIUM-SIZE LEMON

¾ CUP SUGAR, OR TO TASTE

FRESHLY GROUND BLACK PEPPER TO TASTE

SLICED BOILED POTATO, SOUR CREAM, OR PLAIN YOGURT FOR GARNISH

F O O D

PROCESSOR/MINI

Place the dill in the work bowl of a food processor fitted with the metal blade and pulse 2 to 3 times to chop it. Leaving the dill in the work bowl, change to the shredding disk and shred the beets. Keeping the beets in the work bowl (unless you have a small food processor that won't fit any more, in which case you can remove the beets and dill to your slow cooker or rice cooker), change the shredding disk to the 4mm slicing disk and slice the onion and celery.

Place the vegetables with the rest of the ingredients in your slow cooker, rice cooker, or a large, heavy-bottomed pot set over medium heat. If you are using a slow cooker, cook it on low for 6 to 8 hours or on high for 2 to 3 hours. If you are using a rice cooker, cook until the beets are soft, about 30 minutes. If you are cooking on the stove top, cover the pot, bring the water to a gentle simmer, then reduce the heat to low and cook until the beets are soft, about 30 minutes.

Serve hot or cold with the boiled potato or a dollop of the sour cream or yogurt.

Variation: For Creamy Borscht, once the soup is cooked according to the above directions, beat 3 large eggs together with 2 cups of sour cream or plain yogurt in a large bowl. Whisking constantly, very gradually mix in 2 cups of the hot borscht. Stir this egg mixture into the remaining soup. Serve with a dollop of sour cream or plain yogurt.

Seafood Gazpacho

Yield: 10 servings

The trick to making really great gazpacho in the food processor is not to overblend it. You want the vegetables to retain their personalities, you don't want the soup to look like mush. Depending on the size of your food processor, you might have to do this in batches.

1 CLOVE GARLIC, PEELED

5 RIPE TOMATOES, PEELED, SEEDED, AND
    QUARTERED

1 LARGE CUCUMBER, PEELED, SEEDED, AND
    CUT INTO PIECES

1 GREEN BELL PEPPER, SEEDED AND CUT INTO
    CHUNKS

1 LARGE YELLOW ONION, PEELED AND
    QUARTERED

1 FRESH JALAPEÑO PEPPER (OPTIONAL),
    SEEDED AND MINCED

5 CUPS TOMATO JUICE

1/3 CUP OLIVE OIL

1/3 CUP RED WINE VINEGAR

TABASCO SAUCE, TO YOUR TASTE

1 TEASPOON SALT, OR TO YOUR TASTE

1 CUP PEELED AND DEVEINED COOKED SHRIMP,
    CUT INTO 1/2-INCH PIECES

CROUTONS (OPTIONAL)

FRESH ITALIAN PARSLEY OR CORIANDER
    (CILANTRO) LEAVES (OPTIONAL) FOR
    GARNISH

In the work bowl of a food processor fitted with the metal blade, coarsely chop the garlic, tomatoes, cucumber, bell pepper, and onion, working in batches if necessary. Transfer the vegetables to a large bowl and stir in the jalapeño, tomato juice, olive oil, vinegar, Tabasco, and salt. Mix well. Add the shrimp, cover, and chill thoroughly for several hours.

Ladle the gazpacho into chilled bowls and garnish with croutons and parsley. Serve immediately.

Millie's Herring Salad

Yield: 8 servings

Your family and friends will find this easy-to-make appetizer completely irresistible. Take care not to overblend; you don't want the mixture to lose its personality. Look for herring snacks (marinated herring pieces) in jars in the refrigerated case of food stores and delicatessens. The salad can be made up to 3 days in advance and refrigerated in a tightly covered container. Bring to room temperature before serving.

ONE 32-OUNCE JAR HERRING SNACKS

1 DAY-OLD ROLL OR SLICE WHITE BREAD

¼ CUP CIDER VINEGAR

1 LARGE YELLOW ONION, CUT INTO LARGE CHUNKS

1 LARGE STALK CELERY, CUT INTO 1-INCH PIECES

1 GRANNY SMITH OR OTHER FIRM, TART APPLE, CORED, PEELED, AND QUARTERED

1 HARD-COOKED EGG, QUARTERED

1 TABLESPOON SUGAR

CRACKERS OR THINLY SLICED PUMPERNICKEL BREAD

Empty the herring into a sieve to drain; discard the juice. Break the roll or bread into several pieces, place in a small bowl, and sprinkle with the vinegar. Set aside.

In the work bowl of a food processor fitted with the metal blade, combine the onion, celery, and apple. Pulse on and off for 2 or 3 seconds, until coarsely chopped. Add the egg and process another 5 seconds. Add the herring, roll (and any unabsorbed vinegar), and sugar and pulse to a coarse consistency.

Transfer to a serving bowl and serve immediately with crackers or pumpernickel bread.

FRESH GARDEN SALAD

Yield: 10 servings

Here's a recipe for someone who owns all the food processor blades and attachments and wonders what to do with them. This one-bowl salad can accommodate your tastes as well as whatever fresh produce is available. Pick and choose the vegetables that appeal, adding those that are fresh and in season. If you have a large food processor, you can make this without emptying the work bowl. If you run out of room, empty the processed ingredients into a serving bowl and continue.

continued

For the vinaigrette:

¹/₄ CUP PACKED FRESH ITALIAN PARSLEY
  LEAVES

¹/₄ CUP BALSAMIC VINEGAR

2 TEASPOONS DIJON MUSTARD

¹/₂ CUP SALAD OIL

¹/₂ TEASPOON SALT

FRESHLY GROUND BLACK PEPPER TO TASTE

For the salad:

2 SMALL, FIRM, RIPE TOMATOES

¹/₂ CUP PITTED BLACK OLIVES

1 CUCUMBER, PEELED AND CUT TO FIT THE
  FEED TUBE

1 SMALL RED ONION, PEELED AND HALVED

3 MEDIUM-SIZE CARROTS

1 MEDIUM-SIZE ZUCCHINI

10 LARGE RADISHES

1 MEDIUM-SIZE TO LARGE HEAD ROMAINE
  LETTUCE, WASHED, DRIED, AND CUT INTO
  SECTIONS TO FIT THE FEED TUBE

In the work bowl of a food processor fitted with the metal blade, add the parsley and pulse 3 to 4 times. With the machine running, add the remaining vinaigrette ingredients. Process until smooth and blended.

Remove the metal blade, but not the dressing. Insert the thick, 6mm slicing disk and slice the tomatoes. Add the olives to the feed tube and slice. Insert the 4mm slicing disk and slice the cucumber and onion. Insert the medium shredding disk and shred the carrots and zucchini. Insert the 3 × 3 julienne blade and julienne the radishes. Insert the 8mm slicing disk and slice the romaine. Cover the work bowl with plastic wrap and refrigerate until ready to serve. Turn the salad out into a large serving bowl and toss to distribute the vegetables and dressing.

Variations: Add sliced cooked ham or chicken to create a chef's salad.

PICKLED BEET SLAW

Yield: 6 cups

Here's a welcome change from your everyday coleslaw. Take care not to press hard on the beets as you pass them through the shredding blade of the food processor; you don't want them mushy.

1 CUP PICKLED BEETS, DRAINED, WITH JUICE
    RESERVED

1 LARGE SWEET ONION, PEELED, AND CUT IN
    HALF HORIZONTALLY

1 SMALL RED CABBAGE (ABOUT 1 1/2 POUNDS),
    CORED, WITH OUTER LEAVES REMOVED

For the dressing:

1/2 CUP MAYONNAISE OR PLAIN YOGURT

1/4 CUP FIRMLY PACKED DARK BROWN SUGAR

1/4 CUP PLUS 2 TABLESPOONS RESERVED BEET
    JUICE

2 TABLESPOONS SOY SAUCE

1/3 CUP PLAIN YOGURT

2 TABLESPOONS CARAWAY SEEDS (OPTIONAL)

F O O D

PROCESSOR/MINI

In the work bowl of a food processor fitted with the 4mm medium shredding disk, shred the beets, onion, and cabbage together. In a bowl, whisk together the mayonnaise, brown sugar, beet juice, and soy sauce. Mix in the yogurt and caraway seeds.

    Place the dressing in a large serving bowl or dish. Add the shredded vegetables and toss well. Chill for at least 1 hour before serving.

ASIAN COLESLAW

Yield: 5 cups

This zesty and colorful variation on a theme features contrasting colors and textures of red onion, mandarin oranges, jicama, and cabbage. An orange sesame dressing complements the fresh garden taste.

For the dressing:

1 CUP MAYONNAISE

1 TEASPOON RED WINE VINEGAR

GRATED ZEST OF 1 ORANGE

2 TABLESPOONS ORANGE JUICE

1/4 TEASPOON MILD SESAME OIL

2 TABLESPOONS SOY SAUCE

SALT TO TASTE

For the coleslaw:

1 MEDIUM-SIZE HEAD CABBAGE, CORED, WITH
    OUTER LEAVES REMOVED, QUARTERED, AND
    CUT TO FIT THE FEED TUBE

1 JICAMA, PEELED AND CUT TO FIT THE
    FEED TUBE

1 ORANGE, PEELED, SEEDED, AND SECTIONED

1 MEDIUM-SIZE RED ONION, PEELED AND
    QUARTERED

continued

Place the dressing ingredients in the work bowl of a food processor fitted with the metal blade and process until smooth, 10 to 12 seconds, then pour into a large bowl. Set side.

Without washing the work bowl, remove the metal blade and insert the medium shredding disk. Shred the cabbage, jicama, and orange. Add these to the dressing. Remove the shredding disk and insert the fine or medium slicing disk. Using the large feed tube, slice the red onion. Add the onion slices to the bowl and toss gently to coat with the dressing. Serve immediately or cover and refrigerate for several hours or overnight.

Latkes

Yield: 20 pancakes

Potato pancakes used to be reserved for Hanukkah, but now that the food processor has eliminated the need for the hand grater, there's no excuse not to have them more often. If you are careful to select organic potatoes, there's no need to peel them, just make sure to scrub them well.

1 MEDIUM-SIZE ONION, PEELED

2 LARGE IDAHO POTATOES, SCRUBBED

1 LARGE EGG

1 TEASPOON SALT

$^1/_4$ CUP ALL-PURPOSE FLOUR

$^1/_2$ TEASPOON BAKING POWDER

VEGETABLE OIL FOR FRYING

Shred the onion and potatoes separately in the work bowl of a food processor fitted with the medium shredding disk. Place the grated potatoes in a large bowl and cover them with cold water.

Meanwhile, in another large bowl, mix together the egg, salt, flour, and baking powder. Empty the potatoes into a strainer and press out the liquid. Add the onions and potatoes to the egg mixture and stir to combine.

Heat about $^1/_4$ inch of oil in an electric skillet set on medium-high (375°F). When the oil sizzles, drop in small amounts of the mixture, using a tablespoon to form 3- to 4-inch pancakes, turning when golden. Drain on paper towels and serve hot with applesauce (page 191).

Carrot–Sweet Potato Pancakes

Yield: 20 to 30 pancakes

Adding carrots and sweet potatoes gives these savory pancakes a beautiful color and a lovely sweetness.

1 SMALL ONION, PEELED AND HALVED

1 LARGE SWEET POTATO, PEELED AND
  QUARTERED

1 MEDIUM-SIZE CARROT, PEELED

1/2 TEASPOON GROUND CINNAMON

1/2 TEASPOON SALT

1/2 TEASPOON BAKING POWDER

1/4 CUP ALL-PURPOSE FLOUR

1 LARGE EGG

VEGETABLE OIL FOR FRYING

Shred the onion, potato, and carrot together in the work bowl of a food processor fitted with the medium shredding disk. Remove the vegetables to a mixing bowl and stir in the remaining ingredients.

In a large skillet over medium heat, add enough oil to cover the bottom of the pan and heat it to 375°F or until a small drop of the batter sizzles instantly when added to the pan. Drop the batter by the tablespoonful in the hot oil to form 3- to 4-inch round pancakes, flattening them slightly, and cook until the underside is golden, 3 to 4 minutes. Turn and cook the other side to golden, then drain on paper towels and serve hot with the traditional applesauce (page 191) or salsa.

Vegetable Purées

Yield: 6 to 8 servings as a side dish (3 to 4 cups of purée)

"I don't eat baby food," my husband claimed.

"You will when you try this," I told him.

"Famous last words," he insisted.

He ate his words.

Baby food to one person, heavenly vegetable purées to the rest of us. Root vegetables such as potatoes, parsnips, turnips, carrots, and celery root lend themselves particularly well to purées. Cooked greens such as spinach and watercress, as well as things like broccoli and cauliflower, are also great. You can add caramelized onions or garlic to all of these to bring out a sweet, earthy taste, or you can combine several vegetables as long as the tastes are copacetic.

Here is a master recipe that you can use to turn your favorite vegetable, or vegetables and fruit combination, into delectable purées, followed by two specific recipes.

2 POUNDS VEGETABLES AND FRUITS OF YOUR CHOICE (ABOUT 6 CUPS OF CHUNKS)

$^1/_2$ TO $^3/_4$ CUP LIQUID, AS NEEDED

SALT AND FRESHLY GROUND BLACK PEPPER TO TASTE

Variation 1:

2 SWEET POTATOES OR YAMS (ABOUT 1 POUND), PEELED AND CUT INTO CHUNKS

2 PARSNIPS (ABOUT $^1/_2$ POUND), PEELED AND CUT INTO CHUNKS

8 CANNED PINEAPPLE SLICES (ABOUT $^1/_2$ POUND), CUT INTO CHUNKS (RESERVE THE JUICE)

$^1/_2$ TO $^3/_4$ CUP PINEAPPLE JUICE FROM THE CANNED PINEAPPLE, AS NEEDED

$^1/_4$ TEASPOON FRESHLY GROUND BLACK PEPPER

$1^1/_2$ TEASPOONS SALT

1 TABLESPOON FIRMLY PACKED DARK BROWN SUGAR

GRATED ZEST OF 1 LEMON

Variation 2:

1 LARGE SWEET POTATO OR YAM (ABOUT $^3/_4$ POUND), PEELED AND CUT INTO CHUNKS

4 CANNED PEAR HALVES (ABOUT $^1/_2$ POUND), CUT INTO CHUNKS (RESERVE THE JUICE)

3 LARGE CARROTS (ABOUT $^3/_4$ POUND), CUT INTO CHUNKS

$^1/_2$ TO $^3/_4$ CUP PEAR JUICE FROM THE CANNED PEARS, AS NEEDED

$^1/_4$ TEASPOON FRESHLY GROUND BLACK PEPPER

1 TEASPOON SALT

$^1/_2$ TEASPOON GROUND CINNAMON

GRATED ZEST OF 1 LEMON

Place the ingredients (including only $^1/_2$ cup of the liquid) in a microwavable bowl. Cover and microwave on high power until the fruits and vegetables feel soft when punctured with a fork, about 10 minutes.

Place the mixture in the work bowl of a food processor fitted with the metal blade and process until smooth, 1 to 2 minutes. Add more liquid if necessary to reach the desired consistency.

The best way to warm purées is in a covered dish in the microwave.

PESTO

Yield: About 1½ cups

Summer, when the garden is overflowing with a bumper basil crop, is the time to make pesto. Make extra and store it in small plastic containers in the freezer. Use the best-quality Parmesan cheese you can find, such as Reggiano. The extra cost is worth the extra-fine flavor; and grate it yourself.

2 CUPS LOOSELY PACKED FRESH BASIL LEAVES	½ CUP PINE NUTS
4 CLOVES GARLIC, PEELED	¾ CUP OLIVE OIL
¼ TEASPOON SALT	½ CUP FINELY GRATED PARMESAN CHEESE

In the work bowl of a food processor fitted with the metal blade, place all of the ingredients except the oil and cheese and process until smooth. Scrape down the bowl once or twice to ensure even blending. Add the oil through the feed tube with the machine running. Add the cheese and pulse 5 to 6 times to combine. Taste and add salt if necessary.

Pesto will keep for several weeks stored in a tightly covered container in the refrigerator, or it can be frozen for up to 6 months.

TOMATO PESTO

Yield: 2½ cups

While you can buy sun-dried tomato paste in the tube, it isn't nearly as tasty and price-effective as making your own. Try this spread on toasted rounds of bread, or instead of mustard in a sandwich. Add a tablespoon to a cup of mayonnaise for a tangy-sweet spread for sandwiches and dressing for salads.

Sun-dried tomatoes that come without the oil need to be soaked in white vinegar to remove some of the salt that is used in the curing process. While this step is not quite as easy as opening a jar of oil-packed tomatoes, you will find the price difference such that this small step is worth the time and effort.

continued

1 CUP SUN-DRIED (NOT OIL PACKED)
TOMATOES

2 CUPS WHITE VINEGAR

$1/2$ CUP PINE NUTS

2 TO 3 CLOVES GARLIC, TO YOUR TASTE,
PEELED

$1/4$ TEASPOON FRESHLY GROUND BLACK
PEPPER

$1/2$ TEASPOON SALT

$1/4$ CUP PACKED FRESH BASIL LEAVES

$2/3$ CUP FRESHLY GRATED PARMESAN CHEESE

3 TEASPOONS CAPERS, DRAINED

2 TABLESPOONS SHERRY VINEGAR

$1/2$ TO $2/3$ CUP OLIVE OIL, AS NEEDED

Place the tomatoes in a sieve set into a mixing bowl. Add the vinegar to cover and allow the tomatoes to soak for 15 minutes. Drain off the vinegar and discard. Rinse the tomatoes in hot water. Place them in the work bowl of a food processor fitted with the metal blade and process until finely diced, scraping down the work bowl once or twice. Add all the other ingredients except the oil and process until blended. With the motor running, add the oil to the work bowl through the feed tube, to the desired consistency.

Tomato pesto will keep for several weeks stored in a tightly covered container in the refrigerator, or it can be frozen up to 6 months.

THE DISH FORMERLY KNOWN AS MEAT LOAF

Yield: 1 large meat loaf (6 to 8 servings)

Here is a meat loaf like your mother never made! Mellow from the hint of herbs, earthy from the porcini mushrooms, spicy from the sun-dried tomatoes, tart from the dry sherry, and nutty from the bulgur. The combination is (and this word *can* be used for meat loaf!) sublime. We like it with the Designer Mashed Potatoes (page 78) for dinner, or made into the best meat loaf sandwich ever for lunch.

1 CUP WATER

$1/2$ CUP UNCOOKED BULGUR

1 OUNCE SUN-DRIED (NOT OIL PACKED)
TOMATOES (ABOUT 10 OF THEM)

$1/8$ OUNCE DRIED PORCINI MUSHROOMS

3 LARGE CLOVES GARLIC, PEELED

1 MEDIUM-SIZE ONION, PEELED AND CUT INTO
CHUNKS

$1/2$ CUP LOOSELY PACKED FRESH ITALIAN
PARSLEY LEAVES

½ CUP LOOSELY PACKED FRESH HERB LEAVES SUCH AS BASIL, THYME, SAGE, TARRAGON, OR ROSEMARY, OR 2 TABLESPOONS MIXED DRIED HERBS

1 LARGE OR EXTRA LARGE EGG

1 TABLESPOON BALSAMIC VINEGAR

1 TABLESPOON SOY SAUCE

½ CUP DRY SHERRY

2 TABLESPOONS TOMATO PASTE

2 TABLESPOONS FIRMLY PACKED DARK BROWN SUGAR

2 TEASPOONS SALT

½ TEASPOON FRESHLY GROUND BLACK PEPPER

1 POUND GROUND BEEF

1 POUND GROUND VEAL, OR ANOTHER POUND GROUND BEEF

Preheat the oven to 375°F with the rack in the lower third of the oven. Grease an 8-cup loaf pan.

To prepare the bulgur, bring the water to a boil in a small saucepan, add the bulgur, and simmer over low heat until the water is absorbed. Depending upon the coarseness of the bulgur, this can take from 5 to 20 minutes.

Combine the sun-dried tomatoes and porcini mushrooms in a small bowl and cover with boiling water until softened, about 10 minutes. Drain the water and set aside.

In a food processor fitted with the metal blade, drop the garlic cloves through the feed tube with the machine running and process for a few seconds until minced. Turn off the machine and remove the lid. Add the rest of the nonmeat ingredients, including the bulgur and softened tomatoes and mushrooms. Replace the lid and process for about 60 seconds, stopping once to scrape down the sides of the bowl. The mixture will be smooth but not puréed.

If you have a very large food processor, at this point you can add the meats (in 10 to 12 chunks) and process for another 1 to 2 minutes, until finely ground.

If your food processor is not large enough to add all of the meat, you can remove about half of the nonmeat ingredients, add the meats, and process until finely ground. Then place the contents of the work bowl, along with the reserved half of the nonmeat ingredients, in a large bowl and mix together by hand.

Another way to mix all of the ingredients if you don't have an oversized food processor is to combine the processed nonmeat ingredients with the meats in the bowl of a stand mixer using the paddle attachment on medium speed until well combined.

Form the mixture into an oval or rectangular mound in the greased pan and bake until an instant-read thermometer inserted in the center reads 170°F, 60 to 70 minutes.

THE DISH FORMERLY KNOWN
AS MEAT LOAF (VEGETARIAN)

Yield: 1 large loaf (8 to 10 servings)

This is Ellie's pride and joy. I challenged her to come up with a dish worthy of this name—and boy did she ever rise to the occasion.

2 CUPS UNCOOKED COUSCOUS

4 CUPS BOILING WATER

4 LARGE CLOVES GARLIC, PEELED

1/2 CUP LOOSELY PACKED FRESH ITALIAN
    PARSLEY LEAVES

1/2 CUP LOOSELY PACKED FRESH HERB LEAVES
    SUCH AS BASIL, THYME, SAGE, OR
    TARRAGON, OR 2 TABLESPOONS MIXED
    DRIED HERBS

2 SMALL ONIONS, PEELED AND CUT INTO
    CHUNKS

1 RED BELL PEPPER, SEEDED AND CUT INTO
    CHUNKS

6 OUNCES MUSHROOMS

3 CARROTS, CUT INTO CHUNKS

1 SMALL TURNIP, PEELED AND CUT IN HALF

2 SMALL PARSNIPS, PEELED AND CUT INTO
    CHUNKS

2 TABLESPOONS OLIVE OIL OR GARLIC OIL

1 LARGE OR EXTRA LARGE EGG

1 LARGE EGG WHITE

1 TABLESPOON BALSAMIC VINEGAR

1/3 CUP PINE NUTS

1 TABLESPOON SALT

1 TEASPOON FRESHLY GROUND BLACK PEPPER

JUICE OF 1/2 LEMON

1 1/4 CUPS ALL-PURPOSE FLOUR (FOR PATTIES
    ONLY)

VEGETABLE OIL (FOR PATTIES ONLY)

To prepare the couscous, combine it with the water, cover, and let sit until the liquid is absorbed, about 5 minutes. Set aside.

Drop the garlic cloves through the feed tube of a running food processor fitted with the metal blade and process for a few seconds, until the garlic is minced. Add the parsley and herbs and process until finely chopped. Without cleaning the bowl, remove the metal blade and insert the shredding disk. Drop the vegetable chunks through the feed tube and shred. Because of the volume, you may have to empty the work bowl once or twice during the shredding.

Heat the oil in a large skillet or an electric skillet set on medium-high heat (350°F) and cook the shredded vegetables until softened, about 15 minutes, stirring frequently.

Mix the vegetables in a very large bowl with 5 cups of the couscous and the remainder of the ingredients (except the flour if making the loaf). Use a large spoon or your hands.

Preheat the oven to 375°F. For the loaf, grease a 9 × 13-inch baking pan. Form the mixture into an oval or rectangular shape in the pan. Bake until a knife or cake tester inserted in the center comes out hot, about 1 hour.

For the patties, add the flour to the mixture and combine. Form the mixture into 4-inch patties. Coat each patty with some of the remaining couscous, carefully pressing it into the patty. Using an electric skillet or another large skillet, cook the patties in about ¼ inch of hot vegetable oil over medium-high heat (350°F), turning once, until golden brown on both sides, about 10 minutes total.

PARMESAN CHEESE SCONES

Yield: 8 scones

Scones have found their tasty way into every corner coffee shop. While the usual variety is sweet, this savory version offers the zesty flavor of Parmesan with a hint of onion and oregano. For really great results, use freshly grated Reggiano Parmesan. Serve these with scrambled eggs in place of the usual toast or bagel.

2 CUPS UNBLEACHED ALL-PURPOSE FLOUR	¹/₂ CUP WHOLE MILK
¹/₄ TEASPOON SALT	2 LARGE EGGS, LIGHTLY BEATEN
2 TEASPOONS BAKING POWDER	SCANT TEASPOON TABASCO SAUCE
³/₄ CUP FRESHLY GRATED PARMESAN CHEESE	³/₄ CUP CHOPPED ONIONS
1 TEASPOON DRIED OREGANO, CRUMBLED	2 TABLESPOONS BUTTER, MELTED
¹/₄ CUP (¹/₂ STICK) BUTTER, CHILLED AND CUT INTO PIECES	

Preheat the oven to 400°F with the rack in the upper third of the oven but not in the highest position. Lightly grease a heavy-duty baking sheet.

Place the flour, salt, baking powder, cheese, and oregano in the work bowl of a food processor fitted with the plastic blade and process for 15 seconds. Add the chilled butter and process until the mixture resembles coarse crumbs.

In a small bowl, stir together the milk, eggs, Tabasco, and onions. With the processor running, pour this mixture through the feed tube and continue processing until a sticky dough forms. Scrape the dough out onto a lightly floured work surface and, with lightly floured hands, pat it into a 9-inch disk. Divide it into 8 wedges and transfer them to the baking sheet, setting them 1½ inches apart. Brush the tops with the melted butter and bake until lightly browned, 20 to 25 minutes.

DOTTIE'S BLINTZES

Yield: 12 to 14 blintzes

My dear friend Dottie Sternburg makes the world's best blintzes. Plump pillows of sweet cheese filling, nestled in tender crepes, covered with blueberry sauce—they are world class! Here's her recipe with the option of using the tortilla press to make the crepes. You can find farmer cheese in the dairy section of many supermarkets and in some gourmet stores.

For the crepes:

1 CUP UNBLEACHED ALL-PURPOSE FLOUR, MEASURED AFTER SIFTING

1 CUP WHOLE MILK

3 EXTRA LARGE EGGS

1 TABLESPOON VEGETABLE OIL

½ TEASPOON SALT

1 TABLESPOON SUGAR

For the filling:

1 POUND CREAM CHEESE (DO NOT USE WHIPPED CREAM CHEESE)

8 OUNCES FARMER CHEESE

2 LARGE EGG YOLKS

1 TABLESPOON BUTTER, MELTED

2½ TABLESPOONS SUGAR

For the sauce:

1 QUART FRESH OR FROZEN BLUEBERRIES

⅓ CUP SUGAR

1 TABLESPOON INSTANT TAPIOCA

JUICE OF 1 LEMON

To assemble and cook the blintzes:

2 TO 3 TABLESPOONS BUTTER

SOUR CREAM

To make the crepes, place the ingredients in the work bowl of a food processor fitted with the plastic blade and process or blend until smooth, then transfer to a pitcher or container with a spout. Heat a tortilla maker according to the manufacturer's directions and pour enough batter to make a puddle in the center slightly larger than a silver dollar. Gently close the lid—but not all the way—to spread the batter. Use an open-and-close motion to cook the crepe, turning if necessary to complete the other side. Keep the crepes moist by layering them in waxed paper or plastic wrap.

For the filling, place the ingredients in the work bowl of a food processor fitted with the plastic or metal blade and process just until smooth. Don't over-process as it will make the filling runny.

For the sauce, place the blueberries in a medium-size nonreactive saucepan and sprinkle the sugar over them. Sprinkle in the tapioca and lemon juice and toss to combine. Allow the mixture to sit for 15 minutes, then cook over low heat, stirring constantly, until the berries give up their juices and begin to thicken. Cool slightly before serving.

To assemble and cook the blintzes, place 2 teaspoons of the filling in the lower third of the underside (the less brown side) of the crepe. Roll it up and tuck the ends underneath to make a neat package. Continue with the remaining crepes and filling. Heat 1 tablespoon of the butter in an electric skillet set on medium-high heat (350°F). Cook the crepe packets, several at a time, taking care not to crowd them in the pan and adding more butter as necessary, until they are brown and the edges are crisp, 5 to 6 minutes on each side. Serve hot with blueberry sauce and a dab of sour cream.

NECTARINE-ALMOND BREAD

Yield: 2 loaves

Tangy, tart, sweet, and crunchy are the flavors and textures in this easy-to-prepare quick bread. Quick breads are relatively fast to assemble and bake because they are made with leavenings other than yeast and don't require a preliminary rising. These breads have a tender, moist, and light texture. The crumb is slightly coarse and crumbly.

If you can't find fresh nectarines, you may substitute ripe peaches.

continued

2 1/2 CUPS UNBLEACHED ALL-PURPOSE FLOUR

4 TEASPOONS BAKING POWDER

1/2 TEASPOON BAKING SODA

1 TEASPOON SALT

1/2 CUP SUGAR

1 1/2 POUNDS RIPE NECTARINES

2/3 CUP CANOLA OIL

4 LARGE EGGS

1 TEASPOON PURE ALMOND EXTRACT

1 2/3 CUPS ALMOND PASTE (PAGE 141),
   CUT INTO PIECES

1 CUP SLICED ALMONDS

Preheat the oven to 350°F with the rack in the center position. Grease two loaf pans and dust them with flour, shaking out the excess. Sift the dry ingredients together in a small bowl and set aside.

Cut the nectarines in half and remove the pits. Insert the metal blade in the work bowl of a food processor. Add the nectarines, oil, eggs, extract, and almond paste and process until combined, about 30 seconds. Add the dry ingredients and almonds and pulse 6 to 8 times to combine. Spoon the batter into the prepared pans and smooth the tops. Bake until a cake tester or toothpick inserted in the center comes out clean, 55 to 60 minutes. Cool the cakes in the pans for 10 minutes before inverting onto a wire rack to cool completely.

GINGER CHEESECAKE

Yield: One 8-inch cheesecake (10 to 12 servings)

If you love the combination of ginger and chocolate, then this cheesecake is the one for you. Unabashedly sophisticated and gorgeous to boot, it has an ethereally smooth and creamy texture studded with sparks of candied ginger. A chocolate crumb crust completes the extravaganza. This is a rich dessert that feeds a crowd. While it doesn't do well in the refrigerator, it can be frozen up to 3 months if wrapped airtight. Defrost at room temperature while still wrapped. Please note that this recipe calls for an 8 × 3-inch round layer pan—this is not a springform pan.

1 TO 2 TABLESPOONS BUTTER FOR GREASING
   THE PAN

1/2 CUP CRUSHED GINGERSNAPS

1/2 CUP CRUSHED CHOCOLATE WAFERS

1/2 CUP (1 STICK) UNSALTED BUTTER,
   MELTED

2 POUNDS BEST QUALITY CREAM CHEESE
    (DON'T USE WHIPPED CREAM CHEESE), AT
    ROOM TEMPERATURE

$\frac{1}{2}$ CUP HEAVY CREAM

4 EXTRA LARGE EGGS

$1\frac{1}{2}$ CUPS SUGAR

2 TEASPOONS PURE VANILLA EXTRACT

2 TABLESPOONS PEELED AND FINELY GRATED
    FRESH GINGER

1 CUP FINELY CHOPPED CANDIED GINGER
    (STORE BOUGHT OR SEE RECIPE
    ON PAGE 312)

Preheat the oven to 300°F with the rack in the center position. Butter the sides and bottom of an 8 × 3-inch cheesecake pan and line the bottom with parchment paper. Butter the parchment.

Combine the gingersnaps, chocolate wafers, and melted butter in a small bowl. Toss to coat the crumbs with the butter. Press the crumbs into the bottom and halfway up the sides of the cheesecake pan. It's fine if the edges are uneven.

Place the cream cheese, heavy cream, eggs, sugar, vanilla, and grated ginger in the work bowl of a food processor fitted with the metal blade and process until thoroughly mixed and very smooth. Add the candied ginger and process for another 10 seconds, just to distribute it evenly.

Pour the batter into the prepared pan and shake gently to level the top. Set the pan in a large roasting pan and add hot water 2 inches deep in the roasting pan. Bake the cake for 1 hour and 45 minutes. At the end of this time, turn off the oven, but let the cake remain in the oven with the door closed for one more hour. Remove the pan to a counter and let it rest until completely cool, at least another hour. Do not refrigerate. Cover the top with plastic wrap and unmold onto a baking sheet. Invert onto a cake plate to serve.

BÊTE NOIRE

Yield: One 9-inch cake (8 to 10 servings)

This delicious and unusual chocolate dessert is a snap to make in a food processor. Eaten hot out of the oven, it's a perfect marriage between a soufflé and a truffle. At room temperature it ranks right up there with the world's best chocolate experience. Whichever way you serve it, don't forget to add a generous dollop of the white chocolate cream—the perfect partner.

continued

8 OUNCES UNSWEETENED CHOCOLATE, CHOPPED

4 OUNCES BITTERSWEET OR SEMISWEET CHOCOLATE, CHOPPED

5 EXTRA LARGE EGGS, AT ROOM TEMPERATURE

$^1/_2$ CUP WATER

1 $^1/_3$ CUPS SUGAR

1 CUP (2 STICKS) UNSALTED BUTTER, AT ROOM TEMPERATURE, CUT INTO TABLESPOONS

Preheat the oven to 350°F with the rack in the center position. Lightly grease a 9-inch layer cake pan and line the bottom with a 9-inch circle of parchment paper. Lightly grease the parchment with butter. Set the cake pan in a jelly roll pan or roasting pan.

Place the chocolates in the work bowl of a food processor fitted with the metal blade. Crack the eggs into a spouted cup. Combine the water and sugar in a small saucepan and, stirring occasionally, cook over medium-high heat until the sugar dissolves and the mixture comes to a vigorous boil. Pour the boiling syrup over the chocolate, cover the processor with the feed tube in place, and process until the chocolate is completely melted and the mixture smooth, about 12 seconds. With the machine on, add the butter a tablespoon at a time, then add the eggs. Process for an additional 15 seconds.

Pour and scrape the batter into the prepared pan, leveling the top with a rubber scraper. Place the cake pan and jelly roll pan in the oven and add hot water about one inch deep in the larger pan. Bake the cake for exactly 30 minutes. The top will have a thin, dry crust, but the inside will be very moist. Carefully remove the cake pan from the oven (leave the water bath until it cools). Cover the top of the cake with a piece of plastic wrap, then invert it onto a flat plate or baking sheet. Peel off the parchment. Cover with a light, flat plate and immediately invert again.

WHITE CHOCOLATE CREAM

This topping, which has the consistency of soft cream cheese, must be made at least a day in advance. It will keep for a week in the refrigerator or can be frozen.

12 OUNCES BEST QUALITY WHITE CHOCOLATE, BROKEN INTO SMALL PIECES

$^1/_2$ CUP HEAVY CREAM

$^1/_2$ TO $^2/_3$ CUP CRÈME DE CACAO OR LIGHT RUM

Place the pieces of white chocolate in the work bowl of a food processor fitted with the metal blade or in a blender. In a small saucepan heat the cream to just below boiling, then pour it over the chocolate and process or blend until completely smooth. Add the liqueur to taste. Chill completely.

ESPRESSO–WHITE CHOCOLATE TORTE

Yield: One 9-inch pie (10 servings)

A dark layer of semifrozen mousse hides a delicious surprise. This dessert, a must for lovers of white chocolate, is a taste sensation that is worth the calories.

For the white chocolate layer:

10 OUNCES WHITE CHOCOLATE, CHOPPED

1 $^1/_4$ CUPS HEAVY CREAM

1 TABLESPOON CORNSTARCH

$^2/_3$ CUP COLD MILK

For the crust:

ONE 9-INCH CHOCOLATE CRUMB CRUST
   (RECIPE FOLLOWS)

For the dark chocolate layer:

10 OUNCES SEMISWEET CHOCOLATE, CHOPPED

$^1/_4$ CUP FREEZE-DRIED "INSTANT" ESPRESSO
   POWDER

1 $^1/_4$ CUPS HEAVY CREAM

3 TABLESPOONS CORNSTARCH

$^2/_3$ CUP COLD WHOLE MILK

For garnish:

3 OUNCES WHITE CHOCOLATE

Place the white chocolate in the work bowl of a food processor fitted with the metal blade and let the machine run until the chocolate is finely chopped, about 30 seconds.

In a medium-size saucepan over medium-high heat, bring the cream to a simmer. With the food processor running, pour the hot cream through the feed tube and mix well with the white chocolate, about 15 seconds.

In a small bowl, mix the cornstarch with the milk, add it to the food processor, and process for 5 seconds to combine. Return the mixture to the saucepan and cook over low heat until it thickens, about 6 minutes. Pour into the crust and freeze.

With a clean work bowl and metal blade, pulse-chop the semisweet chocolate and espresso powder together to break up the chocolate, then let the machine run until the chocolate is finely chopped, about 30 seconds.

Heat the heavy cream in a medium-size saucepan over medium-high heat until it simmers. With the food processor running, pour the hot cream through the feed tube and mix well with the semisweet chocolate, about 15 seconds.

continued

In a small bowl, mix the cornstarch with the milk, add it to the food processor, and process for 5 seconds to combine. Return the mixture to the saucepan and heat until it thickens, about 6 minutes.

Spread the dark chocolate mixture evenly on top of the frozen white chocolate mixture. Freeze until firm, about 3 hours. Defrost in the refrigerator 1 hour prior to serving. Use a clean, dry vegetable peeler to shave white chocolate on top for decoration.

CHOCOLATE CRUMB CRUST

25 FAMOUS CHOCOLATE WAFERS

$^1/_4$ CUP ($^1/_2$ STICK) UNSALTED BUTTER, MELTED

Preheat the oven to 375°F with the rack in the center position. Generously butter a 10-inch pie plate. Break the wafers in half and place them in the work bowl of a food processor fitted with the metal blade. Process to crumbs. Add the butter and process until well mixed. Press the mixture evenly over the bottom and up the sides of the prepared pie plate. Bake for 15 minutes, then cool completely before using.

PEAR AND GINGER TART

Yield: One 12-inch tart (8 to 10 servings)

This autumn dessert blends together pears and ginger in a sweet open-faced tart. Comice and Anjou are hardy pear varieties that hold their shape when poached or baked.

1 RECIPE SWEET PASTRY CRUST (PAGE 130), CHILLED

1 LARGE EGG WHITE, SLIGHTLY BEATEN WITH A FORK

8 RIPE BUT FIRM COMICE OR ANJOU PEARS (ABOUT 3 POUNDS)

²/₃ CUP SUGAR

³/₄ TEASPOON GROUND GINGER

¹/₂ CUP WATER

6 TABLESPOONS APRICOT PRESERVES

WHIPPED CREAM (OPTIONAL)

Preheat the oven to 425°F with the rack in the center position. Roll out the chilled pastry about ⅛ inch thick to fit a 12-inch tart pan. Line the pan with the pastry, prick the bottom with a fork, and brush with the egg white (this keeps the pastry from getting soggy as it bakes with the pear filling). Bake the crust for 10 minutes and remove from the oven. Let cool thoroughly.

Meanwhile, peel 6 of the pears and cut each of them into eighths. Cut away and discard the cores. Place the pear wedges in a large, nonreactive saucepan and add the sugar, ginger, and water. Cover and cook over medium heat until tender but still firm, 8 to 10 minutes. Don't let the pears overcook and turn mushy. Use a slotted spoon to turn the pear wedges occasionally so the pieces cook evenly. Drain but reserve ¼ cup of the pear liquid. Arrange the pear wedges close together in the pastry shell.

Peel and quarter the remaining 2 pears. Cut away and discard the cores. Cut the quarters into thin slices. Arrange the slices symmetrically over the cooked pears.

Combine the apricot preserves with the reserved pear liquid. Bring to a boil and strain through a metal strainer to remove any lumps. Brush the pears with the apricot mixture, reserving about half of it, and bake until the top is well browned, about 30 minutes.

Remove from the oven and brush with the remaining apricot mixture. Let stand until warm. Serve with whipped cream.

SWEET PASTRY CRUST

Yield: 1½ pounds dough (enough to make three 8-inch tart crusts)

The food processor makes pastry crust without overworking it. Process only until the dough is uniformly moistened and begins to mass together in clumps. Do not overprocess by letting the dough form into a ball; this will result in a tough pastry.

2½ CUPS UNBLEACHED ALL-PURPOSE FLOUR	1 TEASPOON PURE VANILLA EXTRACT
½ CUP SUGAR	1 CUP (2 STICKS) UNSALTED BUTTER, CHILLED
⅛ TEASPOON SALT	
1 LARGE EGG	

Place the flour, sugar, and salt in the work bowl of a food processor fitted with the metal blade and process with 2 or 3 short pulses to blend. Combine the egg and vanilla in a small bowl.

Cut the chilled firm butter into 12 to 16 pieces and scatter them over the flour-sugar mixture. Using 8 to 10 rapid pulses, process until the mixture resembles coarse crumbs. Then, with the machine running, pour the egg mixture down the feed tube in a steady stream and continue to process just until the ingredients come together.

Remove the dough from the bowl and place it on a clean, dry work surface. With the heel of your hand, smear a small amount of the dough on your work surface by pushing it away from you. Repeat with small amounts of the remaining dough. When you've worked all the dough in this manner, give it a couple more strokes to bring it together into a smooth, homogeneous unit. Press the dough into a ball. Wrap well in plastic wrap and refrigerate until firm, about 2 hours.

Preheat the oven to 400°F with the rack in the center position. Lightly butter either one large (14-inch) tart pan or two smaller (8-inch) pans. Roll the dough out on a lightly floured work surface and press it into the bottom and up the sides of the pan(s), cutting off the excess dough. Prick the bottom and sides with the tines of a fork and place the tart pan(s), on a baking sheet.

To prebake the crust, bake for 10 minutes at 400°F, then lower the oven temperature to 350°F and bake until the crust is golden brown and no raw dough areas remain, another 8 to 10 minutes. Cool completely to room temperature before proceeding.

STRAWBERRY TART

Yield: One 9- or 10-inch tart (8 to 10 servings)

A wonderful spring or summer recipe when strawberries are at their peak of flavor. This is a great combination of cookie dough crust with light pastry cream and fresh, ripe strawberries.

1 RECIPE SWEET PASTRY CRUST (PAGE 130)

1 RECIPE PASTRY CREAM (PAGE 44)

3 PINTS FIRM, FRESH, RED, RIPE STRAWBERRIES, HULLED, RINSED, AND DRAINED

1 CUP ORANGE MARMALADE

1 TABLESPOON WATER

$^1\!/_3$ CUP ALMOND SLIVERS, TOASTED (SEE NOTE BELOW)

Roll out the dough on a cold, lightly floured work surface. Line a 9- or 10-inch pie plate, preferably a flan ring, with the pastry. Prick the bottom all over with the tines of a fork. Freeze for 15 minutes while you preheat the oven to 375°F. Bake the crust for 15 minutes, then reduce the oven temperature to 350°F. Bake until the center is dry and the edges are lightly browned, another 10 to 15 minutes. Cool completely on a wire rack.

Spoon the pastry cream into the pie shell and smooth it with a rubber scraper. Arrange the strawberries cut sides down, close together, and symmetrically over the pastry cream.

Spoon the marmalade into a small nonreactive saucepan and add the water. Cook, stirring, over medium heat until the marmalade is thinned. Pour the mixture through a metal strainer into a small bowl and cool slightly. When the marmalade is cooled but still liquid, brush the berries with it. Sprinkle the almonds over the top. Cover and chill until ready to serve.

Note: Preheat the oven to 375°F with the rack in the upper position. Spread the nuts in a single layer on a heavy-duty rimmed baking sheet or jelly roll pan. Taste the nuts, stirring or shaking the pan once or twice for 7 to 10 minutes or until they are golden brown.

FROZEN KEY LIME PIE

Yield: One 10-inch pie (8 servings)

While you can certainly buy a premade chocolate crumb crust in the supermarket, it's (almost) just as easy to make your own. Famous Chocolate Wafers can be found in the cookie aisle of the supermarket.

25 FAMOUS CHOCOLATE WAFERS

1/4 CUP (1/2 STICK) UNSALTED BUTTER, MELTED

1 recipe FROZEN KEY LIME ICE CREAM (PAGE 168), SLIGHTLY SOFTENED

1 CUP HEAVY CREAM, WHIPPED TO SOFT PEAKS

THINLY SLICED LIME FOR GARNISH

Preheat the oven to 375°F with the rack in the center position. Generously butter a 10-inch pie plate. Break the wafers in half and place them in the work bowl of a food processor fitted with the metal blade and process until they are crumbs. Add the butter and process until well mixed. Press the mixture evenly over the bottom and up the sides of the prepared pie plate. Bake for 15 minutes, then cool completely.

Pour and scrape the ice cream into the pie shell, smoothing the top. Freeze until solid. To serve, either garnish with whipped cream rosettes or spread a layer of whipped cream over the top. Place a lime wedge on each piece.

ESPRESSO MOCHA BARS

Yield: 48 bars

If you love chocolate with your coffee, then you will love these sinfully rich and very grown-up tasting cookies. Mocha beans are the coffee-flavored, coffee bean-shaped candies found in espresso shops and gourmet stores. They are not chocolate-covered coffee beans.

For the crust:

3/4 CUP (1 1/2 STICKS) BUTTER, CUT INTO 1-INCH PIECES

1 1/2 CUPS UNBLEACHED ALL-PURPOSE FLOUR

1/4 CUP CONFECTIONERS' SUGAR

For the topping:

1/4 CUP (1/2 STICK) BUTTER, CUT INTO 1-INCH PIECES

1/2 CUP FIRMLY PACKED DARK BROWN SUGAR

3 LARGE EGGS

2 TABLESPOONS FREEZE-DRIED "INSTANT" ESPRESSO POWDER

1 TABLESPOON PURE VANILLA EXTRACT

1 1/2 CUPS WALNUT PIECES

8 OUNCES MOCHA BEANS

F O O D

PROCESSOR/MINI

Preheat the oven to 350°F with the rack in the center position. Generously grease or butter a 9 × 13-inch baking pan. In the work bowl of a food processor fitted with the metal blade, process the butter, flour, and confectioners' sugar until the dough forms a ball, about 45 seconds. Remove the dough from the work bowl and press it evenly into the bottom of the prepared pan. Bake until set, 15 to 18 minutes.

While the crust bakes, prepare the topping ingredients. Process the butter and brown sugar together until smooth, about 15 seconds. Add the eggs, espresso powder, and vanilla and process until combined, about 10 seconds. Add the walnuts and pulse 2 to 3 times to chop if the pieces are large. Use a rubber scraper to stir in the nuts and mocha beans. Spread the mixture evenly over the baked crust and bake until set, another 25 to 30 minutes, then cool completely on a wire rack before cutting into squares.

Variations: Use white chocolate chips instead of the mocha beans or eliminate the espresso powder and add mint lentils in place of the mocha beans.

CHOCOLATE-PECAN SHORTBREAD

Yield: About 24 bars

1 CUP (2 STICKS) BUTTER, SOFTENED

1/4 CUP SUGAR

1/4 CUP FIRMLY PACKED LIGHT BROWN SUGAR

1/2 TEASPOON PURE VANILLA EXTRACT

2 CUPS ALL-PURPOSE FLOUR

1/3 TEASPOON SALT

1/2 CUP COARSELY CHOPPED MACADAMIA NUTS

ONE 12-OUNCE PACKAGE CHOCOLATE CHIPS

For the chocolate glaze:

THE REMAINING CHOCOLATE CHIPS

1 TO 2 TABLESPOONS MILK, AS NEEDED

continued

Preheat the oven to 375°F with the rack in the center position. Butter a 13 × 19-inch baking pan. In the work bowl of a food processor fitted with the metal blade, cream together the butter and sugars until the mixture is light and fluffy; blend in the vanilla. Add the flour and salt and mix only until blended; the dough will be quite stiff. Pulse in the nuts and 1¾ cups of the chocolate chips.

Press the dough into the prepared pan and sprinkle the top with the remaining ¼ cup chocolate chips; press lightly into the dough. Bake until light golden brown, 18 to 20 minutes. Cool completely in the pan.

Meanwhile, make the chocolate glaze. Place the remaining chocolate chips in a microwavable dish and add 1 tablespoon of the milk. Heat for 1 minute on high power; stir until the chocolate is completely melted and the texture is smooth. Blend in the additional milk, 1 teaspoonful at a time, until the mixture flows, but is not completely liquid. Pour the mixture into a heavy-duty zippered plastic bag and close the bag tightly, removing all the air. Snip a tiny piece off one corner of the bag (not more than ⅛ inch). Holding the top of the bag tightly, drizzle the glaze in the desired pattern on the shortbread. Cut into bars to serve.

LINZER HEART COOKIES

Yield: 48 filled cookies

Great flavor and thin, crisp, melt-in-your-mouth texture distinguish these wonderful raspberry jam-filled sandwich cookies. The easy-to-roll dough is readily cut into pretty heart shapes.

1 CUP HAZELNUTS, TOASTED (SEE NOTE, PAGE 131)

1 CUP GRANULATED SUGAR

2½ CUPS ALL-PURPOSE FLOUR, MEASURED AFTER SIFTING

1 TEASPOON BAKING POWDER

1 TEASPOON SALT

¾ CUP (1½ STICKS) BUTTER, VERY COLD

2 LARGE EGGS

1 TEASPOON PURE VANILLA EXTRACT

1 CUP SEEDLESS RASPBERRY JAM

½ CUP CONFECTIONERS' SUGAR

Place the hazelnuts and sugar in the work bowl of a food processor fitted with the metal blade and process until the nuts are finely chopped, about 30 seconds. Add the flour, baking powder, and salt and process to blend, about 20 seconds, stopping once to scrape down the sides of the work bowl.

Cut the butter into 1-inch pieces, add to the work bowl, and process to the consistency of coarse meal, 15 to 20 seconds. Add the eggs and vanilla and process until the mixture starts to combine, about 15 seconds. Flatten the dough to a 1-inch-thick disk. Chill in plastic wrap until firm, about 2 hours.

Preheat the oven to 400°F with the rack in the center position. Select two heavy-duty baking sheets and line them with parchment paper or aluminum foil. If using foil, spray it with nonstick vegetable spray.

Divide the dough into quarters. On a well-floured work surface, roll each quarter out to a thickness of ⅛ inch. Using a 3-inch, heart-shaped cookie cutter, cut out an even number of hearts. Transfer with a rubber scraper onto the baking sheets. If desired, cut 1-inch-diameter holes from the center of half the cookies; a plain round pastry tip works well for this.

Bake the cookies, one sheet at a time, until lightly colored and firm, about 8 minutes. Cool the cookies on wire racks. When completely cool, spread 1 rounded teaspoon of jam on each of the whole hearts. Sprinkle the cutout cookies with confectioners' sugar and press them gently onto the jam. The jam will show through the holes.

RASPBERRY SURPRISE

Yield: 48 pieces

Rose Mary had to talk me into this one, but I'm glad she did. It's definitely a throw-back to the fifties, a dessert made with a pretzel crust, cream cheese, and Jell-O. Yes, we've covered all the food groups here. Trust me, next time you want a funky but fun ending to a family meal (or you're looking for something to serve your bridge group), this is the baby.

continued

2½ CUPS CRUSHED PRETZELS

3 TABLESPOONS PLUS ¾ CUP SUGAR

¾ CUP (1½ STICKS) BUTTER, MELTED

1 CUP HEAVY CREAM

8 OUNCES CREAM CHEESE (DO NOT USE
WHIPPED CREAM CHEESE), AT ROOM
TEMPERATURE

ONE 6-OUNCE PACKAGE RASPBERRY JELL-O

2 CUPS BOILING WATER

TWO 10-OUNCE PACKAGES FROZEN
RASPBERRIES

Preheat the oven to 350°F with the rack set in the upper third of the oven but not in the highest position. Butter a 9 × 13-inch baking pan. In the work bowl of a food processor fitted with the metal blade, pulse the pretzels until finely crushed. Add the 3 tablespoons sugar and pulse once or twice to combine. With the machine running, pour the melted butter into the work bowl through the feed tube and pulse 2 or 3 times to combine. Spread the crust over the bottom of the prepared pan and bake for 10 minutes. Remove from the oven and set aside to cool completely.

In a medium-size bowl, whip the heavy cream with a hand mixer fitted with the beater attachment on high speed until stiff peaks form. Do not overbeat. Set aside until ready to use.

In another bowl, using the washed mixer, cream together the cream cheese and the remaining ¾ cup sugar on medium speed until smooth. Fold in the whipped cream and spread evenly over the cooled crust.

In another medium-size bowl, combine the Jell-O and boiling water until dissolved. Stir in the frozen raspberries; they will thaw as you stir them. Refrigerate until thickened, 8 to 10 minutes. Watch the mixture closely; it should not be allowed to set in the bowl. Spread the thickened mixture evenly over the cream cheese layer and chill for 2 hours before serving by cutting into squares.

Variation: Substitute strawberries, blueberries, or blackberries and the corresponding Jell-O flavor.

STRAWBERRY ICE CREAM

Yield: 2³/₄ cups

Here's an almost instant dessert! While this recipe calls for strawberries, you can use almost any frozen fruit. If you wish, substitute 1 cup plain yogurt for the heavy cream; the result will be just as creamy and a bit on the tangy side.

ONE 16-OUNCE PACKAGE FROZEN WHOLE
   STRAWBERRIES

1 CUP HEAVY CREAM

2 TABLESPOONS FRESH LEMON JUICE

3 TABLESPOONS SUPERFINE SUGAR

FINELY GRATED ZEST OF 1 LEMON

In the work bowl of a food processor fitted with the metal blade, drop the frozen fruit through the feed tube with the machine running, one or two pieces at a time until all the berries are puréed. Add the remaining ingredients and process until smooth, about 10 seconds. The sherbet should be smooth and well blended without any trace of solid pieces of fruit. Serve immediately or place in an airtight container and freeze up to 1 month.

Variations: Use fresh or frozen raspberries with 2 tablespoons of orange juice and orange zest instead of the lemon juice and zest. Or pineapple and mango enhanced with 1 tablespoon of orange liqueur and the finely grated zest of 1 lime.

TROPICAL SORBET

Yield: 6 cups

Fresh and light and welcome on a summer's day, this is better than the store-bought kind, any time.

¹/₂ CUP WATER

¹/₂ CUP SUGAR

1 LARGE, RIPE MANGO, PEELED, PITTED,
   AND CUBED

1 LARGE, RIPE PAPAYA, PEELED, SEEDED,
   AND CUBED

ONE 20-OUNCE CAN PINEAPPLE CHUNKS
   IN UNSWEETENED JUICE

JUICE FROM 2 LIMES

1 CUP FRESH ORANGE JUICE

continued 1 3 7

Place the water and sugar in a small saucepan over high heat and bring to a simmer. Boil, stirring, only until the sugar dissolves, about 2 minutes, then chill until cold.

In the work bowl of a food processor fitted with the metal blade, place the mango, papaya, and the pineapple and its juice and process until puréed. Place the mixture in a bowl and stir in the sugar syrup and lime and orange juices. Freeze the mixture in an ice-cream machine according to the manufacturer's directions.

GANACHE

Yield: 2¼ cups

Use this versatile recipe to make chocolate sauce, glaze, frosting, filling, or truffles. Use the best quality semi-or bittersweet chocolate you can afford to guarantee the best taste.

1 CUP HEAVY CREAM

10 OUNCES SEMISWEET OR BITTERSWEET CHOCOLATE, COARSELY CHOPPED

Simmer the heavy cream in a small saucepan over medium-low heat. Place the chocolate in the work bowl of a food processor fitted with the metal blade and process until finely ground, 1 to 2 minutes. With the machine running, pour the hot cream through the feed tube until the mixture is smooth, another 30 seconds.

Chocolate sauce: Use hot as a topping for ice cream or the dessert of your choice.

Chocolate glaze: Allow the ganache to cool just until it thickens but still flows. Pour over a cake or other dessert and smooth the top with a metal scrapper.

Chocolate frosting: Chill the ganache until it is almost firm, then apply it in swirls to a cake.

Chocolate filling: Allow the ganache to cool to room temperature. Pour it into a mixing bowl and, using either the stand or hand mixer fitted with the whipping attachment, beat the ganache until it turns lighter in color and has doubled in volume. Immediately spoon it into a pastry bag and use it to fill cream puffs, cupcakes, etc.

Chocolate truffles: Allow the ganache to chill until it is solid, then use a teaspoon to scoop out small pieces. Roll them in unsweetened cocoa powder and place them in small paper cups.

Hot Fudge Sauce

The hot fudge sauce can be made ahead up to 2 weeks. Refrigerate in a covered container and warm in the microwave, or freeze up to 6 months. Defrost either at room temperature or in the microwave.

8 OUNCES BITTERSWEET CHOCOLATE, CHOPPED

4 OUNCES UNSWEETENED CHOCOLATE, CHOPPED

3 TABLESPOONS UNSALTED BUTTER, CUT INTO SMALL PIECES

½ CUP FIRMLY PACKED DARK BROWN SUGAR

2 CUPS HEAVY CREAM

Place the chocolates, butter, and brown sugar in the work bowl of a food processor fitted with the plastic blade.

Heat the cream in a 2-quart saucepan over medium heat. As soon as small bubbles appear around the edge of the pan, reduce the heat to medium-low and allow the cream to come to a boil. If the cream threatens to overflow the pan, lower the heat even more and stir vigorously with a wire whisk. Allow the cream to simmer for 15 minutes, stirring occasionally.

With the machine off, pour the hot cream through the feed tube and process until smooth, about 20 seconds. (This can also be done with the handheld blender; be sure to use a deep bowl to avoid splattering.) Use immediately or store in a covered container in the refrigerator or freezer.

Vanilla Sugar

Real vanilla-scented sugar is a treat that can be used in a variety of ways. My favorite is to sprinkle it in a thick layer on top of pound cake or cookies as they come out of the oven. Dipping the rim of a dessert glass in egg white and then in the sugar gives a perfect finish to the dessert inside. Those who favor flavored coffees may want to stir in a spoonful for added taste.

Vanilla sugar is simple to make. You can either stick the fresh bean right into the container of sugar or actually grind the bean and sugar together for a really deep and aromatic result. Vanilla-scented sugar in a pretty jar, tied with a ribbon, makes a lovely holiday or hostess gift.

continued

½ CUP PLUS MORE (UP TO 3 POUNDS) SUGAR   3 TO 5 VANILLA BEANS, TO YOUR TASTE, EACH
CUT INTO 4 LENGTHS

In the work bowl of a food processor fitted with the metal blade, grind the ½ cup sugar with the vanilla beans. Stop frequently to combine the beans and sugar. Pour the mixture into a large airtight jar and add more sugar, shaking to combine. This mixture only gets better with age—after about 3 weeks it's ready to use.

To use, sift the required amount of sugar. Return the vanilla pieces from the sieve to the jar of sugar. More sugar can be added to the jar as sugar is used. Tiny specks of vanilla beans will remain in the sifted sugar.

ALMOND BAKED APPLES

Yield: 6 servings

Here's a simple recipe that shows off that homemade almond paste on page 141.

6 CORTLAND OR OTHER BAKING APPLES,
PEELED AND CORED ALMOST TO THE
BOTTOM

2 TABLESPOONS BUTTER, MELTED

½ CUP DRIED BREAD CRUMBS

1 CUP ALMOND PASTE (BELOW)

Preheat the oven to 350°F with the rack set in the upper third of the oven but not the highest position. Brush the apples with the melted butter and roll in the bread crumbs. Use a teaspoon to stuff the almond paste into the center of each apple. If any butter, bread crumbs, or almond paste remain, spread them on top of the apples. Place the apples touching in a pie pan. Bake until the apples are soft, but still intact, 30 to 40 minutes. Serve warm or at room temperature with a scoop of vanilla ice cream or frozen yogurt.

ALMOND PASTE

Yield: 1²/₃ cups

This task is made easy by the food processor. Freshly made almond paste is a whole world away from the oversweetened store-bought kind.

1¹/₂ CUPS BLANCHED SLIVERED OR WHOLE
   SKINNED ALMONDS

1 CUP SUGAR

2 TEASPOONS PURE ALMOND EXTRACT

3 TABLESPOONS COLD WATER

In the work bowl of a food processor fitted with the metal blade, process the almonds and sugar together until finely ground, about 60 seconds. Scrape down the sides of the work bowl to ensure even mixing. With the machine running, add the extract and water through feed tube and process until smooth, about 60 seconds. Remove, tightly wrap in plastic wrap, and place in a heavy-duty zippered plastic bag. Store in the refrigerator for up to 2 months.

MINI FOOD PROCESSOR RECIPES

TOFU SALSA DIP

Yield: 8 servings

Here's an almost instant dip to serve your vegetarian pals.

ONE 10¹/₂-OUNCE PACKAGE SOFT TOFU,
   DRAINED

1 CUP MEDIUM-HOT SALSA

In the work bowl of a mini food processor, blend the tofu and salsa until smooth. Chill before serving.

Chili-Spiced Pretzels

Yield: 1 pound pretzels

For a very different snack, try this. If you're expecting a crowd, double the recipe.

1 POUND SOURDOUGH PRETZELS	1 TABLESPOON DIJON MUSTARD
¹/₂ CUP MILD SESAME OIL	2 TABLESPOONS RED OR WHITE VINEGAR
1 TEASPOON CHILI POWDER	5 DROPS TABASCO SAUCE

Place the pretzels in a shallow mixing bowl and break them into 2-inch pieces with your hands.

Place the oil, chili powder, mustard, vinegar, and hot sauce in the work bowl of a mini food processor and blend to mix completely. Pour the mixture over the broken pretzels, toss to evenly coat, and let soak for 2 hours, stirring occasionally.

Preheat the oven to 220°F with the rack in the center position. Arrange the pretzel pieces in a single layer on an aluminum foil-lined, heavy-duty baking sheet. Bake for 1 hour, stirring every 15 minutes. Allow to cool completely before serving or storing in an airtight container.

Indonesian Chicken Wings

Yield: 2 pounds

Chicken wings or chicken legs or a combination of both are marinated in a sesame-scented marinade, then rolled in sesame seeds and baked. These can be served hot or cold.

For the marinade:

3 TABLESPOONS SESAME OIL

JUICE OF 1 LEMON

1 MEDIUM-SIZE CLOVE GARLIC, PEELED AND
    MINCED

2 TABLESPOONS SOY SAUCE

1 TABLESPOON MOLASSES

1 TEASPOON GROUND CORIANDER

¹/₂ TEASPOON GROUND CUMIN

PINCH OF CAYENNE PEPPER

To complete the dish:

2 POUNDS CHICKEN WINGS

¹/₃ CUP SESAME SEEDS FOR COATING THE
    CHICKEN

Place the marinade ingredients in the work bowl of a mini food processor and process until smooth. Pour over the wings or legs in a shallow baking dish and mix well. Cover with plastic wrap and marinate in the refrigerator for 1 to 2 hours.

Just before cooking, drain off the marinade and roll the chicken pieces in the sesame seeds. Preheat the oven to 375°F. Line a heavy-duty baking pan with aluminum foil and arrange the chicken pieces on it in a single layer. Bake until the skins are well browned and the chicken is crispy, about 25 minutes. Serve hot or cold.

FOOD

PROCESSOR/MINI

TAMARI–ROASTED CASHEW BUTTER

Yield: 1¹/₂ cups

This is a grown-up alternative to peanut butter. Tamari sauce (a kind of soy sauce) is available in the Asian food section of the supermarket. You can make this spread smooth or crunchy by the amount of blending you do.

3 TABLESPOONS TAMARI SAUCE

1 CUP CASHEWS, SALTED OR NOT, TO YOUR
TASTE

¹/₂ CUP (1 STICK) BUTTER, AT ROOM
TEMPERATURE

Preheat the oven or toaster oven to 350°F. In a small bowl toss together the tamari and nuts. Place them on a heavy-duty baking sheet (or small pan for the toaster oven) and toast for 4 minutes. Allow the nuts to cool, then place them in the work bowl of a mini food processor, add the butter, and process until smooth. Store in a tightly covered container in the refrigerator for up to 4 months.

BROCCOLI PESTO

Yield: 1 cup

Hankering for pesto? Fresh out of basil? Here's a magnificent alternative.

continued

1 CUP CHOPPED BROCCOLI FLORETS

2 CLOVES GARLIC, PEELED

$^1/_4$ CUP OLIVE OIL

$^1/_2$ CUP WALNUT PIECES, PINE NUTS, OR
    BLANCHED ALMONDS

2 TABLESPOONS FRESH LEMON JUICE

$^1/_4$ CUP FRESHLY GRATED PARMESAN CHEESE

SALT AND FRESHLY GROUND BLACK PEPPER TO
TASTE

Place all the ingredients in the work bowl of a mini food processor and process until smooth, scraping down the sides of the bowl frequently. Serve over pasta, on toasted Italian bread, as a garnish for soups, and as a sauce for chicken or fish dishes.

LIME-CHILI GRILLED FISH

Yield: 4 to 5 servings

This grilled fish presentation will remind you of summer with its fresh seasonings and zingy taste. You can, if you wish, substitute Italian parsley for the cilantro.

For the marinade:

$^3/_4$ CUP OLIVE OIL

3 TABLESPOONS RED WINE VINEGAR

3 TABLESPOONS FRESH LIME JUICE

1 SMALL JALAPEÑO PEPPER, SEEDED AND
    MINCED

1 TEASPOON MINCED GARLIC

$^1/_4$ CUP PACKED, FINELY CHOPPED FRESH
    CORIANDER (CILANTRO) LEAVES

SALT AND FRESHLY CRACKED BLACK PEPPER TO
TASTE

For the fish:

3 POUNDS FISH FILLETS, SUCH AS SNAPPER OR
    STRIPED BASS, WITH SKIN

Place all the marinade ingredients in the work bowl of a mini food processor and blend until completely combined. Place the fish fillets either in a shallow baking pan or a large, heavy-duty zippered plastic bag. Add the marinade and cover or close the bag. Let marinate in the refrigerator for at least 1 hour or as long as 4 hours.

    Remove the fillets from the marinade and grill, skin side up, about 6 minutes, basting once or twice with the marinade, then turn and grill until the flesh flakes easily and the center is cooked through, another 4 to 6 minutes. Different grills will take more or less time, depending on the proximity of the fish to the heat source and the intensity of the heat.

Spicy Yogurt Marinade

Yield: 1 scant cup

Chicken or fish marinated in this yogurt mixture remains tender and moist after cooking. It's a wonderful way to prepare foods for the grill, including vegetables.

$^1/_2$ CUP PLAIN YOGURT

2 TABLESPOONS FRESH LEMON JUICE

1 TABLESPOON CANOLA OR OTHER
   VEGETABLE OIL

$^1/_4$ CUP CHOPPED ONIONS

1 CLOVE GARLIC, PEELED AND MINCED

1 TEASPOON CUMIN SEEDS OR $^1/_2$ TEASPOON
   GROUND, OR TO YOUR TASTE

1 TEASPOON DIJON MUSTARD, OR TO YOUR
   TASTE

$^1/_2$ TEASPOON GROUND CORIANDER

SALT TO TASTE

Place all the ingredients in the work bowl of a mini food processor, process until smooth, and taste for balance of seasonings.

Marinate poultry or meat in the mixture for a couple of hours or as long as overnight, covered and refrigerated.

Sun-Dried Tomato Mayonnaise

Yield: 1 cup

This is the most amazing stuff! It will enhance your lasagne and spaghetti sauce, top off your hors d'oeuvres, and, yes, it will even help you make friends and influence people.

1 CLOVE GARLIC, PEELED

4 OIL-PACKED, SUN-DRIED TOMATOES,
   DRAINED

2 TABLESPOONS CHOPPED FRESH ITALIAN
   PARSLEY LEAVES

2 TABLESPOONS CAPERS, DRAINED

2 TABLESPOONS CHOPPED FRESH BASIL
   LEAVES

$^3/_4$ CUP MAYONNAISE

1 TABLESPOON FRESH LEMON JUICE

Combine all the ingredients in the work bowl of a mini food processor and process until smooth. Store in a tightly covered container in the refrigerator for up to 2 weeks.

SOUTHWESTERN GRILLING SAUCE

Yield: 1 cup

We put this on swordfish steaks and grilled them. What a hit! There were no left-overs. The mayonnaise keeps the fish moist and tender and keeps it from sticking to the grilling rack. You can use this sauce on shellfish, chicken, or vegetables as well.

1 CUP MAYONNAISE

2 TABLESPOONS CHOPPED FRESH CORIANDER (CILANTRO) LEAVES

2 TABLESPOONS ROASTED GREEN CHILES (CANNED ARE FINE)

1/8 TEASPOON CHILI POWDER

2 TABLESPOONS FRESH LIME JUICE

1 TEASPOON GROUND CUMIN

Place all the ingredients in the work bowl of a mini food processor and blend until creamy. Store in a tightly covered container in the refrigerator for up to 2 weeks.

ORANGE–SPICED CHILI PASTE

Yield: 1/3 cup

This zesty spice rub gives chicken, fish, or vegetable dishes a zip and zing that will wake up your taste buds. If you cannot find elephant garlic, use two cloves regular garlic instead.

1 TEASPOON GROUND CUMIN

1 TEASPOONS MILD CHILI POWDER

1 CLOVE ELEPHANT GARLIC, PEELED

FINELY GRATED ZEST OF 1 ORANGE

1 TABLESPOON FRESH LIME JUICE

1 TABLESPOON SESAME OIL

2 TO 3 DROPS HOT SESAME OIL, TO YOUR TASTE

1 SMALL ONION, PEELED AND CHOPPED

1/2 TEASPOON GROUND GINGER

2 TABLESPOONS SOY SAUCE

Place all the ingredients in the work bowl of a mini food processor and process to a thick paste. Store in a tightly covered container in the refrigerator for up to 1 month.

SWEET AND SOUR CURRY SPICE RUB

Yield: ³/₄ *cup*

The mini food processor is perfect for mixing up this thick paste. Rub it on chicken or meats up to 1 hour ahead (or as long as overnight). Then grill, roast, or sauté.

1 TABLESPOON GROUND CUMIN

1 TABLESPOON CURRY POWDER

1 TABLESPOON GROUND CORIANDER

1 TABLESPOON SWEET PAPRIKA

1 TABLESPOON FIRMLY PACKED DARK BROWN SUGAR

1 TABLESPOON MOLASSES

2 MEDIUM-SIZE CLOVES GARLIC, PEELED AND MINCED

¹/₂ CUP RED WINE VINEGAR

¹/₄ CUP SESAME OIL

Place all the ingredients in the work bowl of a mini food processor and process until smooth. Store in a tightly covered container in the refrigerator for up to 1 month.

DRY SPICE FISH RUB

Yield: Scant ¹/₂ *cup*

The mini food processor is the perfect appliance in which to make dry rubs for all your cooking needs. Here are four recipes for rubs: one for fish, one for meat, one for chicken, and one for foods to be barbecued. The key to a great rub is to use fresh herbs and spices—not the ones that have been lurking in the back of your pantry for over a year—they won't have any taste left at all.

¹/₄ CUP CARAWAY SEEDS

2 TABLESPOONS GROUND CUMIN

1 TABLESPOON GROUND CORIANDER

1 TABLESPOON SALT

1 TABLESPOON FRESHLY GROUND BLACK PEPPER

Combine all the ingredients in the work bowl of a mini food processor and process until completely blended.

Rub over the fish before grilling, roasting, baking, or steaming. Feel free to increase or decrease the amount of each spice as you wish. The rub will keep for several months if covered and stored in a cool, dry place.

LIGHTNING RUB

Yield: 1 cup

While you may not see lightning when you apply this savory mixture of herbs and spices to chicken, fish, or meat, you'll find the flavors illuminating in a way that will spark your taste buds. This will keep for several months if stored in an airtight container away from heat and light. Try it on rice and grilled vegetables as well.

1 TABLESPOON MUSTARD SEEDS

1 TO 2 TABLESPOONS CHILI POWDER, TO YOUR TASTE

1/4 CUP FREEZE-DRIED CHIVES

2 TABLESPOONS ONION POWDER

2 TABLESPOONS GARLIC POWDER

2 TABLESPOONS KOSHER SALT

1 TABLESPOON GROUND CORIANDER

1 TABLESPOON GROUND GINGER

2 TEASPOONS FRESHLY GROUND BLACK PEPPER

2 TEASPOONS GROUND ALLSPICE

1 TEASPOON GROUND CINNAMON

1/2 TEASPOON GROUND CLOVES

1/2 TEASPOON FRESHLY GRATED NUTMEG

In the work bowl of a mini food processor, combine all the ingredients and grind to a fine powder.

DRY SPICE MEAT RUB

Yield: Scant 1/2 cup

1/4 CUP FRESHLY GROUND BLACK PEPPER

1 TABLESPOON GROUND CORIANDER

1 TABLESPOON GROUND CUMIN

1 TEASPOON RED PEPPER FLAKES

1 TEASPOON GROUND CINNAMON

Combine all the ingredients in the work bowl of a mini food processor and process until completely blended.

Rub over the meat before grilling, roasting, or braising. Feel free to increase or decrease the amount of each spice as you wish. The rub will keep for several months if covered and stored in a cool, dry place.

DRY SPICE CHICKEN RUB

Yield: Scant ³/₄ cup

3 TABLESPOONS GROUND GINGER

2 TABLESPOONS GROUND TURMERIC

1 TABLESPOON GROUND ALLSPICE

2 TABLESPOON FRESHLY GROUND BLACK
   PEPPER

1 TEASPOON GROUND CLOVES

3 TABLESPOONS GROUND CARDAMOM
   (OPTIONAL)

Combine all the ingredients in the work bowl of a mini food processor and process until completely blended.

     Rub over the chicken before grilling, baking, or roasting. Feel free to increase or decrease the amount of each spice as you wish. The rub will keep for several months if covered and stored in a cool, dry place.

ALL-PURPOSE BARBECUE-STYLE SPICE DRY RUB

Yield: Scant ¹/₃ cup

Try this on ribs or chicken the next time you're craving that down-home barbecue taste.

¹/₄ CUP SWEET PAPRIKA

1 TABLESPOON GROUND CUMIN

1 TABLESPOON FIRMLY PACKED DARK BROWN
   SUGAR

1 TABLESPOON CHILI POWDER

1 TABLESPOON KOSHER SALT

1 TABLESPOON FRESHLY GROUND BLACK
   PEPPER

1 TEASPOON CAYENNE PEPPER

¹/₄ TEASPOON GROUND CLOVES

Combine all the ingredients in the work bowl of a mini food processor and process until completely blended.

continued 149

Rub over the food at least 1 hour or as long as 12 hours before grilling. Feel free to increase or decrease each spice as you wish, but try to maintain the balance between aromatic spices like cloves and earthy spices like paprika. The rub will keep its pungency for several months if covered and stored in a cool, dry place.

GRAINY MUSTARD

Yield: About 2³/₄ cups

The mini food processor is perfect for making homemade mustard. When you see how easy it is to do, you might be inspired to go into business like my friend Mr. Heinz.

Both mustard seeds and powdered mustard are available in gourmet shops as well as the spice section of many supermarkets, but when buying the seeds in bulk, your best bet, economically, is an Indian food store, if you have one nearby.

1³/₄ CUPS WHITE WINE VINEGAR

1 MEDIUM-SIZE ONION, PEELED AND QUARTERED

2 TABLESPOONS FRESH THYME LEAVES

¹/₂ CUP WATER

¹/₂ CUP WHITE MUSTARD SEEDS

3 TABLESPOONS MUSTARD POWDER

1 TEASPOON FRESHLY GROUND WHITE PEPPER

1 TABLESPOON FIRMLY PACKED DARK BROWN SUGAR

1 TABLESPOON SOY SAUCE

Combine the vinegar, onion, thyme, and water in a microwavable bowl. Cover and microwave on high power until the mixture begins to simmer, about 3 minutes. Allow the mixture to cool completely to room temperature, then strain out the herbs and retain the liquid.

Place the mustard seeds in the work bowl of a mini food processor and grind them to a grainy powder. Add the remaining ingredients and then the liquid and process to combine. Spoon and scrape the mustard into sterilized jars, cover, and store in the refrigerator for up to 3 months.

GRILL,

ELECTRIC

I wait until the second minus-thirty-degree week of winter to put our outdoor grill away, and then it's begrudgingly. I once kept it out with the expectation that grilled lamb chops would be enough to drive me outdoors to cook in February. I forgot that I would have to dig the grill out from a frozen snow bank before I could start cooking. Yuk.

While the electric grill will never have quite the same ambience or deliver the same result as outdoor cooking, it does make a rather acceptable substitute when you're dying for a grilled burger or want to char some veggies in mid-winter. While it might help to dress in shorts and drink beer out of a can while you're standing around the indoor grill, my guess is that the taste of the food is enough to make you happy you invested in this handy appliance.

GENERAL DESCRIPTION

WHAT DOES IT DO? • Electric grills cook shish kebabs, chops, potatoes, or anything else that could benefit from cooking with direct heat that is only an inch or so away.

WHY DO I NEED THIS? • When the weather dictates that you cannot grill outdoors, stay inside and make grilled foods in your kitchen. Electric grills reduce the amount of smoke generated by allowing the drippings to fall into a small pool of water under the heating elements so they do not burn. And cleanup is easy since drippings do not burn onto the grill.

HOW DOES IT WORK? • A metal or ceramic tray serves as the base of the unit, and a heating element sits inside of it. A wire grill sits on top of the base unit about an inch above the heating element. Water is poured into the base, and the power cord is plugged into the wall. The heating element starts to glow and gets hot. Food is placed on the wire grill or on a rotisserie above the grill, and the heat cooks the food.

CARE AND MAINTENANCE • Since water is in the bottom of the base unit, cleanup is a snap. Using a nonstick vegetable spray on the wire grill before grilling also eases cleaning. Unplug the cord and let the unit cool. Remove the wire grill and wash it with hot, soapy water. Carefully remove the heating element and set it aside. Then pour the water out of the base unit and wash it with a soapy sponge. Rinse and dry the grill and the base unit, then reassemble all the pieces to store the appliance.

WHICH IS RIGHT FOR ME? • Pick the features that will be most useful for the foods you want to grill. Roasting whole chickens means a rotisserie is something to buy. If you only want to grill chicken breasts, chops, hamburgers, or shish kebabs, a simple grill will do the trick.

ELECTRIC GRILL TIPS

- *Depending on the kind of foods you are grilling, there will be more or less fat spraying. Make sure to monitor children around the grill. Position the grill away from surfaces that could be ruined by popping fat.*

- *Grilling foods will give off some smoke, so be sure to use the grill in a well-ventilated area.*

- *Bring foods to be grilled to room temperature if possible before starting to cook.*

- *Allow the grill to cool completely before dismantling it to clean.*

- *There is usually a safety switch that will not allow the unit to operate unless the drip pan and control panel are securely in place. If your grill won't start, check these out.*

- *Always preheat the grill before placing the food on it.*
- *Avoid placing the food on or near the heating coil.*
- *Monitor the amount of water in the drip pan, adding more if necessary only after turning off the grill.*
- *Don't move the grill while it is still hot.*
- *Don't cover any part of the grill with aluminum foil as this will throw the thermostat off.*

RECIPES

GRILLED ONION, SHALLOT, AND GARLIC RELISH

Yield: About 3 cups

There is something irresistible about the flavor and texture of root herbs when they are grilled to a crunchy brownness. The sugar caramelizes and creates a golden sweetness that, when combined with the mellow acid of good red wine vinegar, is a marriage made in heaven. This relish can be used with so many kinds of main courses that it's a good idea to make extra—it will disappear in no time. This recipe also makes a fabulous gift; store it in a pretty glass jar and make yourself an extremely popular house guest.

$^1/_3$ CUP OLIVE OR VEGETABLE OIL

$^1/_4$ CUP RED WINE VINEGAR

$^1/_4$ CUP SOY SAUCE

2 TABLESPOONS DIJON MUSTARD

3 TABLESPOONS MOLASSES

1 LARGE BERMUDA ONION (ABOUT 8 OUNCES), CUT INTO 1-INCH-THICK SLICES

8 LARGE SHALLOTS (ABOUT 1 CUP), SLICED IN HALF THE LONG WAY

1 LARGE SPANISH ONION (ABOUT 10 OUNCES) OR SEVERAL VIDALIA ONIONS, CUT INTO 1-INCH-THICK SLICES

20 CLOVES GARLIC (ABOUT 1 CUP), PEELED, OR 8 CLOVES ELEPHANT GARLIC (FOR A MILDER RELISH), CUT INTO 1-INCH-THICK SLICES

FINELY GRATED ZEST AND JUICE OF 1 LIME

2 TABLESPOONS BRANDY-SOAKED RAISINS (OPTIONAL)

continued   153

Place the oil, vinegar, soy sauce, mustard, and molasses in a nonreactive 1-quart bowl and stir with a fork to combine. Add the onions, shallots, and garlic and toss to cover all the pieces with the marinade. Allow the mixture to sit for the time that it takes to preheat an electric grill according to the manufacturer's directions (the pieces may stay in the marinade, refrigerated, for up to 24 hours before grilling).

Use a slotted spoon to remove the pieces and scatter them in a single layer over a mesh grilling rack (the pieces are too small to sit right on the conventional rack). Reserve the marinade in the mixing bowl. Grill, turning once, until the onions are cooked, charred in some places, 12 to 15 minutes. Try not to incinerate the garlic; remove it as soon as it is golden. All the pieces will cook unevenly, with some very black parts and some that don't look cooked at all; don't worry, this is fine.

Transfer the cooked pieces back to the marinade. Toss together and add the lime zest and juice. Place the mixture in the work bowl of a food processor fitted with the metal blade and, using the pulse button, process only until the mixture is blended and the pieces are $1/8$ inch. Do not purée the mixture; it should not be smooth. Return to the mixing bowl and stir in the raisins, if desired. Store in a tightly covered container in the refrigerator until ready to serve. It will keep for several months.

Variation: You can substitute orange zest and juice for the lime, if you wish a sweeter taste, as well as a tablespoon of brandy-soaked dried cranberries for the raisins.

GRILLED SWEET CORN

Yield: 8 ears of corn

This grilled corn is spiked with a spicy-sweet flavored butter. Be sure to select sweet young corn that has been picked within a short time of grilling.

$1/2$ CUP (1 STICK) BUTTER OR MARGARINE, SOFTENED

2 TABLESPOONS FIRMLY PACKED DARK BROWN SUGAR

1 TABLESPOON SOY SAUCE

1 TEASPOON TABASCO SAUCE

1 TEASPOON DIJON MUSTARD

8 EARS FRESH SWEET CORN, HUSKS AND SILKS REMOVED

Preheat an electric grill according to the manufacturer's directions. Place the butter, brown sugar, soy sauce, Tabasco sauce, and mustard in the work bowl of a mini food processor and process until completely blended or cream everything together in a small bowl.

Rub each ear of corn generously with the butter mixture. Arrange the corn directly on the grill, turning a quarter turn every 5 minutes, basting with the remaining butter mixture, cooking for a total of 15 minutes, until the corn is unevenly browned on all sides. Remove the foil and serve hot.

RANGOON GRILLED EGGPLANT

Yield: 2 servings

Select smallish eggplant for this dish as the larger ones can be tough and bitter. The Asian ingredients can be found in most supermarkets as well as Asian groceries and gourmet stores.

3 TABLESPOONS SZECHUAN CHILI PASTE

1 TABLESPOON DARK SOY SAUCE

2 TABLESPOONS DRY SHERRY OR CHINESE RICE WINE

3 TABLESPOONS RED WINE VINEGAR

2 TABLESPOONS SUGAR

$^1/_4$ CUP PLUS 2 TABLESPOONS SESAME OIL

1 TABLESPOON CHOPPED GARLIC

SALT TO TASTE

4 SMALL EGGPLANT ($^1/_2$ TO 1 POUND TOTAL WEIGHT), ENDS TRIMMED AND CUT IN HALF LENGTHWISE

Combine all the ingredients except the eggplant in a large nonreactive bowl and mix well. Add the eggplant, toss well to coat, and let marinate at room temperature for at least 1 hour or up to 4 hours.

Preheat an electric grill according to the manufacturer's directions. Remove the eggplant from the marinade and grill 5 to 7 minutes, until lightly browned. Turn the pieces and grill another 5 to 6 minutes, basting frequently with the marinade. Slice into 1-inch pieces and serve hot or at room temperature.

RED POTATOES AND ONIONS

Yield: 4 servings

Grilling gives these sweet potatoes a lovely crisp outside. The flavor and texture are complemented by the onions and parsley.

20 SMALL RED NEW POTATOES, SCRUBBED AND BOILED IN WATER TO COVER UNTIL SLIGHTLY TENDER BUT NOT SOFT, 5 OR 6 MINUTES, AND DRAINED

$^1/_4$ CUP OLIVE OIL

3 LARGE SPANISH OR VIDALIA ONIONS, CUT INTO $^1/_2$-INCH-THICK SLICES

2 TABLESPOONS RED WINE VINEGAR

COARSE (KOSHER) SALT TO TASTE

FRESHLY GROUND BLACK PEPPER TO TASTE

$^1/_3$ CUP FRESH ITALIAN PARSLEY LEAVES

Preheat an electric grill according to the manufacturer's directions.

Coat the potatoes with 1 tablespoon of the olive oil and grill, turning once, until browned and tender, about 15 minutes.

Brush one side of the onion slices with another tablespoon of the olive oil and place, oiled side down, on the grill. Cook until brown and just tender, 5 to 7 minutes. Do not overcook.

Cut the potatoes in half, place them in a bowl, and carefully toss with the remaining 2 tablespoons of olive oil, the vinegar, salt, pepper, and parsley.

Arrange the grilled onion slices in the center of a platter and top with the potatoes. Serve at room temperature.

MIXED GRILLED VEGETABLES

Yield: 8 servings

Miniature vegetables can be found in many supermarkets and at farm stands. Take care not to overcook these so as not to overpower their tenderness and delicate taste.

1 1/2 CUPS OLIVE OIL

1 CUP DRY WHITE WINE

4 CLOVES GARLIC, CRUSHED

1 CUP COARSELY CHOPPED FRESH ITALIAN
 PARSLEY LEAVES

1/2 CUP COARSELY CHOPPED FRESH BASIL
 LEAVES

1 TEASPOON SALT

1 TEASPOON FRESHLY GROUND BLACK PEPPER

12 TINY BEETS

12 TINY ARTICHOKES, STEMS TRIMMED

12 TINY EGGPLANT

3 SMALL HEADS RADICCHIO, RINSED AND
 PATTED DRY

GRILL,

ELECTRIC

Combine the oil, wine, garlic, 1/2 cup of the parsley, basil, salt, and pepper in a large bowl. Cover and let stand for at least 1 hour.

Clean the beets well, leaving 1 inch of stem and trimming the roots. Place them in a saucepan, cover with water, and bring to a boil. Reduce the heat to medium-low, cover, and simmer until just tender, about 15 minutes. Drain and let cool in a bowl of cold water. Drain again and slip off the skins.

Spread the beets, artichokes, and eggplant in a shallow roasting pan. Cut the heads of the radicchio into quarters and place them in a bowl. Pour 1 1/2 cups of the marinade over the beets, artichokes, and eggplant and 1 cup over the radicchio. Cover both dishes and let them stand at room temperature, turning the vegetables occasionally, for 4 hours.

Preheat the oven to 400°F. Uncover the roasting pan, place it in the oven, and bake, basting frequently with the marinade, until the vegetables are tender, 35 minutes. Allow them to cool slightly. Preheat an electric grill according to the manufacturer's directions.

Thread the beets, artichokes, eggplant, and radicchio separately onto 16- to 18-inch-long skewers. Grill them, turning and basting frequently with the marinade, until lightly browned, about 12 minutes. Remove the vegetables from the skewers and arrange them on a large serving platter. Garnish with the remaining 1/2 cup of parsley and serve.

Grilled Pizza with Artichokes, Tomatoes, and Feta

Yield: 6 small pizzas

Grilling pizza brings out a whole new world of flavors. For this Greek-style pizza, artichoke hearts are chopped and tossed with fresh tomatoes, feta, and mint and spread on the pizza.

1 RECIPE VERSATILE PIZZA DOUGH (PAGE 63)

ONE 10-OUNCE CAN ARTICHOKE HEARTS, DRAINED AND CUT INTO QUARTERS

2 TABLESPOONS OLIVE OIL

SALT AND FRESHLY GROUND BLACK PEPPER TO TASTE

2 LARGE, VINE-RIPENED TOMATOES, SEEDED AND ROUGHLY CHOPPED (ABOUT 2 CUPS)

2 OUNCES FETA CHEESE, CRUMBLED (¹/₃ CUP)

¹/₄ CUP CHOPPED FRESH MINT LEAVES

Preheat an electric grill according to the manufacturer's directions. Divide the pizza dough into 6 even pieces and gently pat and stretch each one into a rough 8- to 10-inch circle on a lightly floured work surface.

In a large bowl, combine the topping ingredients; it's best if they are at room temperature.

Grill the underside of each pizza until dry and easily removable from the grill, 2 to 3 minutes. Turn it over and sprinkle with an equal amount of the topping. Grill another 2 to 3 minutes and serve immediately.

Tex-Mex Burgers

Yield: 6 servings

All the familiar flavors of chili—in a different form. Serve this topped with red beans, guacamole, salsa, and a dab of sour cream for a south-of-the-border meal from the grill.

NONSTICK COOKING SPRAY

2 POUNDS EXTRA-LEAN GROUND BEEF

1/2 CUP FINELY CRUSHED TORTILLA CHIPS

1 MEDIUM-SIZE ONION, FINELY CHOPPED

1 TABLESPOON CHILI POWDER

1 TABLESPOON WORCESTERSHIRE SAUCE

1 TEASPOON GARLIC SALT

1 CUP PREPARED BARBECUE SAUCE

6 LARGE FLOUR TORTILLAS

SALSA, RED BEANS, GUACAMOLE, SOUR CREAM, AND FRESH CORIANDER (CILANTRO) LEAVES (OPTIONAL)

Preheat an electric grill according to the manufacturer's directions.

In a medium-size bowl, combine the beef, tortilla chips, onion, chili powder, Worcestershire sauce, garlic salt, and 1/2 cup of the barbecue sauce. Mix lightly and form into 6 patties, flattening them slightly.

Grill until the patties are no longer pink in the center, about 8 minutes on each side (the cooking time will depend on the grill, the food's distance from the heat, and the thickness of the burgers). Serve the burgers wrapped in tortillas (warmed on the grill, if desired) with the remaining salsa, the remaining 1/2 cup of barbecue sauce, the red beans, guacamole, sour cream, and coriander.

ASIAN STEAK SALAD

Yield: 4 servings

Grilled steak takes on an Asian flavor in this substantial salad entrée, which is equally delicious served hot or cold.

1 POUND BONELESS BEEF TOP SIRLOIN STEAK, CUT 1 INCH THICK

2 TABLESPOONS FRESH LIME JUICE

2 TABLESPOONS SOY SAUCE

1 TABLESPOON SUGAR

2 TEASPOONS DARK SESAME OIL

1 SERRANO PEPPER, SEEDED AND FINELY CHOPPED

1 LARGE CLOVE GARLIC, CRUSHED

1 LARGE RED ONION, SLICED

3 TABLESPOONS CHOPPED FRESH CORIANDER (CILANTRO) LEAVES

4 CUPS TORN MIXED SALAD GREENS OR THINLY SLICED NAPA CABBAGE

2 TABLESPOONS COARSELY CHOPPED PEANUTS (OPTIONAL)

Preheat an electric grill according to the manufacturer's directions. Broil the steak on the grill only until it is rare in the center. Remove from the grill and allow to stand for 10 minutes. Trim off the fat and carve crosswise into thin slices.

continued

In a medium-size bowl, whisk together the lime juice, soy sauce, sugar, sesame oil, serrano pepper, and garlic, then add the onion and cilantro. Pour over the beef mixture and toss to coat.

Arrange the salad greens on a serving platter; top with the beef mixture. Sprinkle with the peanuts and serve immediately.

GRILLED LAMB AND GREEN TOMATOES

Yield: 6 servings

Green tomatoes are plentiful in a summer garden. Their tart taste perfectly complements the other ingredients in this grilled dish.

1 ½ CUP RASPBERRY VINEGAR

⅓ CUP OLIVE OIL

¼ CUP MOLASSES

½ CUP CHOPPED FRESH MINT LEAVES

½ TEASPOON COARSELY GROUND BLACK PEPPER

¼ TEASPOON SALT

16 LARGE MUSHROOM CAPS, WIPED CLEAN

16 SMALL GREEN TOMATOES

4 POUNDS BONELESS LEG OF LAMB, TRIMMED OF FAT AND CUT INTO 1 ½-INCH CUBES

Mix the vinegar, oil, molasses, mint, pepper, and salt together in a large nonreactive bowl. Add the mushrooms, tomatoes, and lamb and toss to combine. Cover with plastic wrap and marinate in the refrigerator for 3 to 4 hours, stirring occasionally.

Preheat an electric grill according to the manufacturer's directions.

Thread the mushrooms, tomatoes, and meat alternately on 8 long thin metal skewers. Reserve the marinade. Place the skewers on the grill 4 inches above the heat. Grill until the lamb is well browned, but still pink on the inside, 10 to 12 minutes, turning and basting with the marinade frequently. Serve immediately.

CURRIED CHICKEN ON THE GRILL

Yield: 8 servings

This unusual Indonesian-inspired dressing adds a crusty coating to the outside of the chicken after it is removed from the grill. Chicken tenders (also called fingers) are available in most supermarket meat aisles.

1 CUP SALTED ROASTED PEANUTS	2 TEASPOONS CURRY POWDER
1 CUP BITTER ORANGE MARMALADE	1 TEASPOON SALT
$^1/_2$ CUP OLIVE OIL	$3^1/_2$ POUNDS BONELESS CHICKEN TENDERS
$^1/_2$ CUP FRESH ORANGE JUICE (FROM 1 LARGE ORANGE)	1 CUP UNSWEETENED SHREDDED COCONUT FOR GARNISH
ONE 6-OUNCE JAR DIJON MUSTARD	1 CUP DRIED CURRANTS OR RAISINS FOR GARNISH
$^1/_4$ CUP FRESH TARRAGON LEAVES, OR 2 TABLESPOONS DRIED	

Combine everything but the chicken and garnishes in the work bowl of a food processor fitted with the metal blade and process until blended. Coat the chicken pieces thoroughly with this marinade in a shallow nonreactive roasting pan. Cover with plastic wrap and let marinate in the refrigerator for 4 to 6 hours, turning the pieces occasionally.

Preheat the oven to 350°F. Bake the chicken with the marinade for 20 minutes. After 10 minutes, preheat an electric grill according to the manufacturer's directions. Remove the chicken from the marinade and grill 3 to 4 inches from the heat for 4 to 5 minutes on each side, basting frequently with the marinade. Remove the chicken to a large serving platter, sprinkle with the coconut and currants, and serve.

GRILLED SHRIMP KEBABS

Yield: 12 appetizer servings; 6 main-course servings

You can easily substitute scallops or swordfish chunks if you wish in this recipe.

$^1/_3$ CUP WORCESTERSHIRE SAUCE

$^1/_2$ CUP MAYONNAISE

$^1/_2$ CUP FRESH LEMON JUICE

2 CUPS BOTTLED CLAM JUICE OR CHICKEN
BROTH

1 TABLESPOON FIRMLY PACKED DARK BROWN
SUGAR

$^1/_4$ CUP CHOPPED FRESH CORIANDER
(CILANTRO), DILL, BASIL, OR OTHER HERBS,
OR 4 TEASPOONS DRIED

1 $^1/_2$ POUNDS LARGE SHRIMP, PEELED AND
DEVEINED, OR LARGE SCALLOPS

2 GREEN BELL PEPPERS, SEEDED AND CUT
INTO 1-INCH SQUARES

2 RED BELL PEPPERS, SEEDED AND CUT INTO
1-INCH SQUARES

1 LARGE SPANISH ONION, CUT INTO WEDGES

12 MUSHROOMS

In a rectangular baking dish large enough to hold the skewers, combine the Worcestershire sauce, mayonnaise, lemon juice, clam juice, brown sugar, and herbs. On 6 long or 12 small skewers, arrange the shrimp, swordfish, or scallops alternately with the vegetables, ending with a mushroom to anchor. Place the skewers in the pan with the marinade, rolling them around to coat evenly. Cover with plastic wrap and refrigerate for at least 2 hours or up to 12 hours, turning once or twice during this time.

Preheat an electric grill according to the manufacturer's directions. Remove the kebabs from the marinade and drain. Pour the reserved marinade into a small saucepan. Grill the kebabs until the seafood is cooked but still tender and the vegetables are lightly browned, about 4 minutes, then turn and cook about another 4 minutes.

Boil the remaining marinade briefly and spoon over the skewers before serving.

HONEY BARBECUED SALMON

Yield: 6 servings

The quick marinade for this recipe comes from ingredients you should have on hand. Any extra sauce (that hasn't come in contact with the fish) can be refrigerated and used with another grilling dish.

For the marinade:

¹/₃ CUP KETCHUP

2 TABLESPOONS HONEY

1 TABLESPOON COARSE-GRAINED MUSTARD

1 TABLESPOON VINEGAR OR FRESH LEMON JUICE

4 TO 5 DROPS TABASCO SAUCE, TO YOUR TASTE

1 TEASPOON SOY SAUCE

1 CLOVE GARLIC, CRUSHED (NO NEED TO PEEL)

1 TEASPOON VEGETABLE OIL

¹/₄ TEASPOON FRESHLY GROUND BLACK PEPPER

For the grill:

SIX 4-OUNCE SALMON FILLETS

Combine all the marinade ingredients and mix well. Pour over the salmon in a shallow nonreactive dish and refrigerate at least 1 hour or up to 3 hours.

Preheat an electric grill according to the manufacturer's directions. Grill the salmon just until it flakes and is no longer translucent in the center, 4 to 5 minutes on each side.

ICE-CREAM

MAKER

Iscream, you scream, we all scream for nonfat frozen yogurt sweetened with Nutrasweet—I don't think so. Come on, admit it, given the choice (all calories being equal), you'd head straight for the genuine article: the super-rich, high-test, high taste, creamy smooth, flavor-packed, premium-grade, triple scoop, lick-fast-so-it-won't-drip-down-your-wrist ice cream. If you haven't experienced the heavenly high that comes from stirring summer-ripened strawberries or peaches, or the world's best chocolate, or freshly toasted pistachios into heavy cream, adding some sugar and perhaps an egg yolk or two, pouring it into an ice-cream maker and within an hour tasting you own homemade ice cream, then there is a reason you're settling for nonfat frozen yogurt. Allow yourself to be seduced—you'll never look at frozen yogurt in quite the same way again.

GENERAL DESCRIPTION

WHAT DOES IT DO? • Who needs the Good Humor man when you can make incredible frozen desserts right in your own kitchen? Ice-cream makers stir and chill a variety of syrup- or cream-based mixtures to make ice cream, gelato, sorbet, and other frozen treats with ingredients you select.

WHY DO I NEED THIS? • Connoisseurs of frozen desserts will find this appliance indispensable. You select the freshest ingredients, and only those ingredients that you want to eat are combined to make very tasty and refreshing desserts.

HOW DOES IT WORK? • Electric ice-cream makers have two basic configurations. A most familiar form is an electric version of the hand-cranked ice-cream freezer. The mixture is poured into a freezing container that is either chilled in the freezer hours ahead of time or the container is surrounded by ice and salt. The salt raises the freezing temperature of the ice so cold is transferred from the melting ice to the mixture in the container. The container turns by means of an electric motor, thus allowing a plastic paddle inside the container to stir the mixture as it freezes.

The second configuration is that of a sophisticated electric freezer. A compressor cools a fluid that is circulated by a pump. The chilled fluid is directed past a metal work bowl. In the work bowl is the mixture and a paddle. A motor turns the paddle to stir the mixture while it freezes.

In both configurations, the mixture is constantly stirred to ensure a texture that is free from large ice crystals and smooth in your mouth.

CARE AND MAINTENANCE • The work bowl or freezing container can be used to store the frozen dessert and can be cleaned with warm soapy water as can the paddle. For a machine that uses ice, pour the salty ice water down the drain, then rinse the chamber with water and dry thoroughly. The housing can be wiped with a damp cloth.

If the ice-cream maker uses some sort of coolant, do not tip the machine on its side or upside down. The coolant is in a sealed container, but you do not want to risk it escaping onto your kitchen floor because it can be poisonous.

WHICH IS RIGHT FOR ME? • The freezer-type machines are very expensive, but you do not have to keep tending to them by adding ice and salt. They make smaller quantities at a time, and you have to decide if that is appropriate for your particular use.

The machines that have a canister that you freeze ahead of time tend to make softer ice cream than the ones that use ice and salt. You have to plan ahead to make sure the canister is frozen in time to make the dessert. And the canister takes up room in the freezer that might not be available. But they are the least expensive type of ice-cream machine to buy.

COMMENTS • If the mixture freezes too hard, the paddle will get stuck and the motor will stall out or possibly burn out. Also, take care not to spill salt water into the ice cream, which is easier to do than you might think. If it happens, throw away the inedible mixture and start over.

ICE-CREAM MAKER TIPS

) *While ice cream can be consumed immediately after it is processed in the machine, its flavor and texture will be better if it is allowed to "ripen" in the freezer for several hours before serving.*

) *Always chill the ice-cream base before adding it to the machine.*

) *If you are using an ice-cream maker that requires brine (salt solution), be extra careful to cover the inner container before removing it to prevent salt contamination.*

) *Homemade ice cream should be consumed within one week of making it.*

) *Store ice cream in sturdy plastic containers with tight-fitting lids.*

) *Overrun is the process of whipping air into ice cream. The more overrun, the less dense the ice cream. Gelato and sorbet have very little overrun while inexpensive commercial brands have so much air beaten into them during the freezing process that when they melt they become foam.*

) *The addition of ingredients such as whole milk, cream, eggs, sour cream, and sweetened condensed and evaporated milk will make rich, creamy ice cream while fruit juice, skim milk, and low-fat yogurt-based ice creams will be thinner and contain more ice crystals.*

) *When making fruit- and fruit juice-based ice creams, substitute an equal amount of light corn syrup for granulated sugar for a lighter, smoother texture.*

) *The addition of unflavored gelatin or foods that contain gelatin (marshmallows, for example) will result in a smoother, creamier ice cream.*

) *When making any frozen dessert, be sure to use pure vanilla extract since artificial vanilla loses its flavor when frozen.*

- Unless you are absolutely sure of the safety of your eggs, always cook custard-based ice creams to just below the boiling point to kill any salmonella bacteria. Take care not to allow the mixture to boil or it will curdle.

- One quart (4 cups) of ice cream will serve six people. When using it as an accompaniment to pie, cake, or other desserts, plan on 8 medium-size or 10 small scoops.

- Freezing tends to dampen flavors, so keep this in mind when you are making the ice cream and boost the flavors accordingly.

RECIPES

CINNAMON ICE CREAM

Yield: 4 cups

Here's the perfect accompaniment to apple pie, gingerbread, or chocolate crepes.

3 CUPS HEAVY CREAM

1 CINNAMON STICK

1 VANILLA BEAN OR 2 TEASPOONS PURE
   VANILLA EXTRACT

3 LARGE EGG YOLKS

1 1/4 CUPS SUGAR

Pour the heavy cream into a 1-quart saucepan over medium heat and bring to a simmer. Remove from the heat and add the cinnamon stick and vanilla bean or extract. Allow the mixture to stand at room temperature for 1 hour, then remove both the bean and stick. Bring the cream back to a simmer.

In a large bowl, either with a handheld blender or mixer or whisk, beat the eggs yolks and sugar together until the mixture is thick and light yellow. Slowly add the hot cream, beating constantly. Return the mixture to the saucepan and cook over low heat, stirring constantly, just until the mixture coats the back of a spoon. Immediately pour the mixture through a fine mesh strainer into a large bowl and chill completely.

Pour the mixture into the container of an ice-cream maker and freeze according to the manufacturer's directions.

KEY LIME ICE CREAM

Yield: About 3 cups

While fresh Key limes are scarce as hen's teeth, bottled Key lime juice can be found in gourmet shops. It gives a tropical flavor to this smooth, sweet-tart ice cream. You'll be closer to a South Florida sunset with every lick. A recipe for Frozen Key Lime Pie is on page 132.

ONE 14-OUNCE CAN SWEETENED CONDENSED
    MILK

1 CUP HEAVY CREAM

1$^{1}/_{8}$ CUP KEY LIME JUICE

GRATED ZEST OF 1 LIME

$^{1}/_{2}$ CUP BUTTERMILK

Combine all the ingredients, pour into the container of an ice-cream maker, and freeze according to the manufacturer's directions.

WHITE CHOCOLATE ICE CREAM WITH BITTERSWEET CHOCOLATE SAUCE

Yield: About 6 cups

It's very important to use the best quality real white chocolate for this fabulous ice cream. Read the wrapper to make sure the chocolate is made with cocoa butter, not palm kernel or coconut oil.

For the ice cream:

3$^{1}/_{2}$ CUPS LIGHT CREAM

1 VANILLA BEAN

6 EXTRA LARGE EGG YOLKS

$^{1}/_{4}$ CUP GRANULATED SUGAR

8 OUNCES WHITE CHOCOLATE, CHOPPED

For the sauce:

$^{1}/_{2}$ CUP HEAVY CREAM

$^{1}/_{2}$ CUP (1 STICK) UNSALTED BUTTER, CUT
    INTO PIECES

$^{1}/_{3}$ CUP LIGHT CORN SYRUP

$^{1}/_{3}$ CUP CONFECTIONERS' SUGAR, SIFTED

10 OUNCES BITTERSWEET CHOCOLATE,
    CHOPPED

For the ice cream, pour the cream into a 2-quart saucepan over high heat. Add the vanilla bean and bring to a simmer. Remove from the heat and remove the vanilla bean. (It can be rinsed and reused.)

In a large metal bowl, use the handheld blender or whisk to beat the eggs together with the sugar until the mixture is light and thickened. Dribble in the hot cream and blend or whisk. Return the mixture to the pan and cook over medium-high heat, mixing constantly with a wooden spoon or rubber scraper, until the mixture just begins to thicken and coats the back of the spoon. Immediately strain the custard through a fine mesh strainer back into the metal bowl, add the chopped white chocolate, and stir until it melts. Cover and chill completely.

Pour the mixture into the container of an ice-cream maker and freeze according to the manufacturer's directions.

For the bittersweet chocolate sauce, place the cream, butter, corn syrup, and sugar in a 1-quart saucepan over medium-high heat. Stir until the butter melts and the mixture is smooth, 3 to 4 minutes. Add the chocolate and stir until it melts and the mixture is smooth. Cool slightly before using or storing in a closed container in the refrigerator. Reheat in the microwave. This sauce can be refrigerated for up to 3 weeks, or frozen for up to 3 months.

To serve, scoop the ice cream into individual bowls, top with the warm sauce, and serve immediately.

CHOCOLATE MINT CHIP ICE CREAM

Yield: 4¹/₂ cups

There is something magical about the combination of mint and chocolate. This is the ice cream you (hopefully) remember from your childhood with the addition of some mint-flavored chocolate.

²/₃ CUP HARD RED AND WHITE PEPPERMINT
   CANDIES

8 SMALL SQUARES (4 OUNCES) GHIRARDELLI
   MINT CHOCOLATE

3 CUPS LIGHT CREAM

¹/₄ CUP LIGHT CORN SYRUP

6 EXTRA LARGE EGG YOLKS

¹/₃ CUP SUGAR

continued

Unwrap the peppermint candies and place them in a heavy-duty zippered plastic bag. Use a heavy rolling pin or hammer to crush but not pulverize them. Unwrap the chocolate and break or chop each square into 5 to 6 pieces.

Place the cream and corn syrup in a 1-quart saucepan over medium-high heat. Bring the mixture to a simmer, then remove it from the heat.

In a metal bowl, use a handheld blender to beat the egg yolks together with the sugar until thick and smooth. Gradually add the hot cream, blending constantly. Return the mixture to the saucepan and cook over medium-high heat, stirring with a wooden spoon or rubber scraper until the mixture just begins to thicken and leaves a path on the back of the spoon when a finger is drawn through it. Do not allow the mixture to boil.

Pour the mixture through a fine mesh strainer into a metal bowl, then add half the peppermint candies, stirring, until they melt. Reserve the other half. Refrigerate the mixture until it is cold.

Stir in the remaining candies and the chocolate, pour into the container of an ice-cream maker, and freeze according to manufacturer's directions.

DEBBY EPSTEIN'S AMAZING CHOCOLATE GELATO

Yield: About 3½ cups

My friend Debby Epstein is the queen—no, make that the goddess—of ice-cream makers. She is the artist in residence at Ciao Bella Gelato Company in San Francisco. If you are lucky enough to live nearby, or love chocolate enough to travel some distance to taste the best ice cream in the world, then you're luckier than most of us. For all those who aren't close enough to taste Debby's dark, velvet-smooth chocolate creations, she's generously shared this recipe. Thanks, Debby!

4 OUNCES SEMISWEET CHOCOLATE, CUT INTO CHUNKS

2/3 CUP SUGAR

1/2 CUP WATER

1/2 CUP LIGHT CORN SYRUP

3/4 CUP UNSWEETENED COCOA POWDER

1/2 TEASPOON PURE VANILLA EXTRACT

2 CUPS WATER

Place the chocolate in a 2-quart bowl. Place the sugar, water, and corn syrup in a small saucepan over medium-high heat. Bring to a boil and allow to boil for 2 minutes. Pour the syrup over the chocolate and stir until it has melted and the mixture is smooth. Sift in the cocoa and stir until the mixture is smooth. Add the vanilla and stir in the water. Chill in the refrigerator until cold.

Pour into the container of an ice-cream maker and freeze according to the manufacturer's directions.

Tiramisù Biscotti Gelato

Yield: 5 cups

Now that the ubiquitous tiramisù has appeared on every dessert list in the nation, it's time to take the dessert to the next plateau—and here it is! Creamy, smooth, rich tiramisù ice cream, studded with crunchy chunks for chocolate-dipped biscotti. Forget dinner and go right for dessert.

4 LARGE EGGS

1 CUP SUGAR

2 CUPS HEAVY CREAM

8 OUNCES BITTERSWEET CHOCOLATE, CHOPPED

1 CUP MASCARPONE

$1/4$ CUP PLUS 2 TABLESPOONS KAHLÚA OR OTHER COFFEE LIQUEUR

ABOUT 4 CHOCOLATE-DIPPED BISCOTTI, CHOPPED BY HAND INTO ROUGHLY 1-INCH CHUNKS TO EQUAL 2 CUPS

Before starting, set up a large stainless-steel bowl with a strainer over it.

Blend the eggs and sugar together in a medium-size saucepan with a hand-held blender or mixer until frothy and thick, about 5 minutes, occasionally stopping to scrape down the sides of the pan (you may have to tilt the pan to reach all of the mixture). It should be very foamy, with the consistency of a milk shake.

Heat the heavy cream in a small saucepan over high heat until it begins to simmer. Over low heat, add the hot cream to the egg mixture, blending with a hand-held blender or a whisk until it just thickens (about 180°F on an instant-read thermometer). Be careful not to let the cord of the blender get into the flame and also be careful not to let the mixture boil as it will curdle.

continued

Immediately pour the mixture through a fine mesh strainer into the stainless-steel bowl. Add the chocolate and continue to mix with the blender or whisk only until the chocolate has melted and the mixture appears smooth. Add the mascarpone and mix with the blender or whisk until well blended. Stir in the Kahlúa. Chill until cold.

Pour the mixture into the container of an ice-cream maker and freeze according to the manufacturer's directions. During the last few minutes of the freezing process, add the broken-up biscotti so that the action of the machine combines them into the ice cream. Freeze until solid before serving.

BURNED SUGAR GELATO

Yield: About 4 cups

If you are a caramel freak, then this is the dessert for you! Make no mistake, this is BIG caramel flavor delivered in the smoothest, creamiest frozen state. Actually, because of the amount of sugar in it, this gelato does not freeze to a completely solid state in the ice-cream maker. It must be scraped into a container to spend some time in the refrigerator freezer before it is served; it will still be a very soft ice cream.

1 ½ CUPS SUGAR

½ CUP WATER

3 CUPS HEAVY CREAM

Line a heavy-duty baking sheet with aluminum foil sprayed with nonstick vegetable spray. Place the sugar and water in a large, heavy-bottomed saucepan. The mixture will look lost sitting there at the bottom, but you will need the room when you add the cream to the hot syrup. Cook the mixture over high heat, stirring, just until the sugar melts. Then allow it to boil without stirring until it begins to turn amber. Do not leave the stove! This can go from fine to burned in a twinkling.

Watch carefully as the sugar gets deeper mahogany in color. As soon as it is deep golden brown, remove the pan from the stove and carefully pour the cream into the syrup. It will splatter, so watch out! Mix to combine, then chill until cold.

Pour into the container of an ice-cream maker and freeze according to the manufacturer's directions. Transfer to another container to freeze to a more solid state in the refrigerator's freezer.

EARL GREY GINGER SORBET

Yield: About 1 quart

We invented this extraordinary sorbet one sweltering hot summer day when yet another glass of ice tea just would not do. You'll be delighted with the refreshingly sophisticated flavor and the lovely color.

1 1/2 CUPS GINGER SYRUP (PAGE 312)

2 CUPS VERY STRONG EARL GREY TEA MADE
   BY STEEPING 2 1/2 CUPS HOT WATER WITH
   3 EARL GREY TEA BAGS

FINELY GRATED ZEST AND JUICE OF 1 LEMON

Combine the ingredients, pour into the container of an ice-cream machine, and freeze according to the manufacturer's directions.

CANTALOUPE-CIDER SORBET

Yield: 7 to 8 cups

Select very sweet, flavorful cantaloupes for this recipe. This creates a tart/sweet palate-cleansing sorbet.

4 CUPS CANTALOUPE PURÉE (THE SEEDED
   PULP FROM ABOUT 1 1/2 LARGE
   CANTALOUPES PUT THROUGH A FOOD
   PROCESSOR OR BLENDER)

1/3 TO 1/2 CUP SUGAR, TO YOUR TASTE

GRATED ZEST AND JUICE OF 3 LIMES

2 ENVELOPES UNFLAVORED GELATIN

1 1/2 CUPS APPLE CIDER

continued 173

Combine the cantaloupe purée, sugar, and lime zest and juice in a large bowl and stir to dissolve the sugar.

Soften the gelatin in the cider for 5 minutes, then heat to dissolve the gelatin (either by placing in a small saucepan set over low heat and stirring constantly, or in a microwavable glass measure in the microwave on high for 1 minute). Stir into the cantaloupe mixture.

Pour the mixture into the container of an ice-cream machine so that it is only three quarters full. Freeze according to the manufacturer's directions.

Note: This recipe will work in an ice-cream machine with a half-gallon container. If your machine is smaller, freeze in two batches.

MANGO SORBET

Yield: 3 cups

There is nothing as sweetly seductive as a ripe mango, unless it's the frozen version found in this luscious sorbet. Choose soft, ripe mangoes for the fullest flavor.

3 LARGE, RIPE MANGOES, PEELED, PITTED, AND CUBED

1/2 CUP SUGAR

1/4 CUP LIGHT CORN SYRUP

FINELY GRATED ZEST AND JUICE OF 1 LIME

Place the mangoes in the work bowl of a food processor fitted with the metal blade and purée until smooth. Add the remaining ingredients and process to combine. Refrigerate the mixture until cold.

Pour the mixture into the container of an ice-cream maker and freeze according to the manufacturer's directions.

GRAPEFRUIT SHERBET

Yield: 2 quarts

Try this with Texas ruby red grapefruit for a singularly stunning taste and color.

2 CUPS SUGAR

4 CUPS WATER

2 CUPS FRESH GRAPEFRUIT JUICE

CRÈME DE CASSIS AND VODKA (OPTIONAL)

Combine the sugar and water in a medium-size nonreactive saucepan and bring to a boil. Add the grapefruit juice and cool. Chill thoroughly.

Pour the mixture into the container of an ice-cream maker and freeze according to the manufacturer's directions. Serve individual portions, if desired, with crème de cassis and a touch of cold vodka poured over the top.

STRAWBERRY SORBET

Yield: 4 servings

So, you're looking for a no-fat recipe—well, here it is. This recipe, while quite simple, packs big flavor, especially if you can get very sweet ripe local berries while they are in season. Please note that the strawberries are crushed rather than puréed; this gives more texture to the finished sorbet.

3 CUPS FRESH STRAWBERRIES, HULLED

1 CUP SUGAR

1 CUP WATER

JUICE OF 1 LEMON

Combine the strawberries and sugar in a large bowl. Use a fork or potato masher to crush the berries. Mix in the water and lemon juice, pour the mixture into the container of an ice-cream maker, and freeze according to the manufacturer's directions.

Raspberry Granita

Yield: About 4 cups

A granita is the grown-up version of slush, and this granita, with the addition of framboise (raspberry liqueur), is most definitely a grown-up dessert. Or use it as a palate cleanser between courses.

1 CUP SUGAR

1 CUP WATER

2 CUPS FROZEN RASPBERRIES

1 TABLESPOON FRESH LEMON JUICE

3 TABLESPOONS FRAMBOISE OR OTHER RASPBERRY LIQUEUR

In a small saucepan, bring the sugar and water to a boil over high heat, stirring until the sugar is dissolved. Reduce the heat to low and simmer for 3 minutes. Chill until completely cold.

Place the chilled syrup and remaining ingredients in a blender or the work bowl of a food processor fitted with the metal blade and process until the berries are puréed and the mixture smooth.

Pour the mixture into the container of an ice-cream maker and freeze according to the manufacturer's directions until completely slushy (the liqueur will prevent the granita from freezing solid). The granita is best served within 6 hours.

MICROWAVE

O V E N

Julia Child E-mailed me a wonderful microwave story. Here it is along with my reply:

Dear Lora,

I just had a melt-down with my quite new micro-wave! I was defrosting some buffalo steaks (not nearly as good as good beef steaks, in my opinion!). They were to be in only 2 minutes, so I turned them on low, went upstairs, and paid them no mind, since they were to be in so short a time. I forgot about them, actually. In about half an hour I smelt something burning, but saw no smoke anywhere, and concluded our upstairs tenants had been burning the bacon. Then I really smelt smoke, started downstairs, and the house was choking in a black fog. Really scared, I called 911—within 2 minutes a couple of fire trucks with lights flashing and sirens screaming drew up, 8 helmeted firemen rushed into the house, rushed all over the house, and produced 4 blackened buffalo steaks—the machine had caught fire! Why? I shall never know

I now have a new machine, the simplest I could find, but it is so complicated I have to look at the directions any time I do anything more unusual than just turning it on. I have a new oven, too, after some 15 years. Same thing—infinitely complicated. How to be successful with "timed bake," or to set the clock?

Love to you all, Julia

Dear Julia,

Thanks for the wonderful story for Plugged In. *Some enterprising young chef could turn those incinerated buffalo steaks into a trendy new dish. I envision something in the "constructed" mode—with the fire theme running through it: a plate carved from smoldered timbers from Mt. St. Helena set atop a hand-forged flame tamer; a pool of sauce made with off-the-Scoville-Chart-Chilies; the steaks, sliced paper thin with a laser, layered with some charming asbestos chips and garnished with tiny extension ladders made with puff pastry. The whole dish could be flambéed in some virgin kerosene. Naturally it would be served by a hard-bodied, young fireman dressed only in his hose.*

Love, Lora

GENERAL DESCRIPTION

WHAT DOES IT DO? • Microwave ovens cause molecules in food to rub against each other, heating up the food. This heat causes food to cook. Some microwave ovens have additional features that can be used to monitor the food as it cooks or to brown it.

WHY DO I NEED THIS? • Microwave ovens are fast and do not heat up the kitchen like conventional ovens do. If you are a busy cook, you can make extra servings, freeze them, then heat them up quickly in the microwave as you need them. Heating up frozen entrées, making popcorn, partially cooking chicken before putting it on the barbecue, proofing bread dough, and melting chocolate are just several of the conveniences that a microwave can provide.

HOW DOES IT WORK? • Conventional ovens cook food by surrounding it with very hot air. The hot air around the food raises the temperature of the surface of the food and transfers heat to the inside of the food, causing the food to cook. Microwave ovens do not work this way. Microwaves cause the molecules inside the food to vibrate. When the vibrating molecules rub against other molecules in the food, the friction causes the food to heat up. The heat that is generated then cooks the food from the inside out, and the oven cavity only gets hot as a result of whatever heat is generated in the food.

To use a microwave oven, food is placed inside, the door closed, the timer set, and the Start button pressed. When the timer is started, a device called a magnetron turns on and emits waves of electrons at a selectable intensity, set by the power setting adjustment. These electrons travel into the plastic- or metal-walled cavity of the microwave oven in which food is placed. Microwaves travel only in a straight line, so either they need to be reflected into several directions by a metal fanlike stirrer, or the food needs to move about the oven cavity on a turntable. Some recipes instruct to turn the food part way through the cooking time. This is especially important if you do not have a turntable in the oven cavity. Because cooking time is a function of the amount of microwaves absorbed, the more food in the oven, the longer it takes to cook it.

Generally, do not use metal or ceramic containers with metallic paint on them in the microwave oven. The microwaves cannot penetrate metal, so your food will not cook evenly. In addition, if two metal surfaces in the microwave oven are sufficiently close to one another, the microwave energy will cause a spark to develop, which could short out the brains in your oven controller or cause a fire.

By the way, if the food inside the microwave oven should catch fire, do not open the door. Opening the door gives the fire a giant blast of fresh oxygen, which could cause it to erupt into a larger fire. If the power cord is accessible, unplug your oven first, but otherwise simply let the fire go out on its own. Of course, if it gets out of control, you should call the fire department and then evacuate your house.

Recent studies have shown evidence of some plastics breaking down into toxic substances when microwaved. If in doubt about the safety of your utensils, do not use them. Instead, try switching to glass or ceramic. You can have your utensils tested at a county agricultural extension agency to be sure.

The cooking food is monitored by watching it through the glass window on the door. The microwaves are stopped from traveling through the window by a metallic screen. The holes in the screen are too small and are too far apart for the microwaves to pass through, so they are reflected back into the oven cavity. Thus it is safe to stand in front of a microwave oven that is working properly.

The cooking process continues until one of several things happen. The most common is that the timer runs to zero and the magnetron is switched off. On some models, the power of the microwaves is adjusted automatically to the lowest setting to keep the food warm for a preset amount of time. A few models come equipped with a temperature probe that is stuck into the center of the food. In these cases, the magnetron turns on when the Start button is pressed and turns off when the temperature probe reaches the temperature that you select.

One important factor to remember is that when the magnetron turns off, cooking does not immediately stop. The heat that is in the food continues to cook it for a time. This is why most microwave oven recipes include a time for the dish to rest once it is removed from the oven.

To help avoid messy cleanup, cover food that is microwaved with either a glass or ceramic dish or cellophane. When using cellophane, leave one corner loose to let steam escape during cooking. When any covering is removed, hot steam will escape, so lift off the cover with the dish pointing away from your face.

When cooking thick liquids like a stew or hot cereal, stop the microwave oven part way through the cooking time and stir the food. This helps distribute the heat and ensures even cooking. Otherwise, hot spots will develop and will either overcook the food, causing cementlike lumps, or will release a pocket of steam that could cause the food to explode all over the inside of your oven.

Because microwave cooking does not involve direct heat from a heating element, dishes tend not to brown as they would using other methods. We all know that browned food looks and tastes better, so microwave oven manufacturers have come up with several ingenious mechanisms to help fill this gap.

Searing pans are typically ceramic dishes that fit in the microwave oven cavity and have special properties that allow the microwaves to heat them up. Once they are hot, they tend to heat directly the food that comes in contact with the pan, thus browning it. A new version of the searing pan is the crisper pan, which has a dense plastic pad on its bottom that absorbs microwaves very fast, thus heating up the pan.

Another mechanism to help with browning are convection oven features that circulate hot air while the microwaves cook the food. Hot air directly in contact with food allows it to brown. A new model of microwave oven has a halogen heating element that turns on to heat the food directly and thus brown it.

Newer microwave ovens have a modicum of programmability. For example, it is possible to set a microwave oven to cook for a time on high power, then switch to a lower setting with a browning feature, and finally switch to a warming cycle. Some come preprogrammed with various power setting and time combinations based on the type and amount of food you are cooking. The more flexibility, the better you can tailor the cycle to meet your cooking needs.

CARE AND MAINTENANCE • With minimal care, your microwave oven should last many years. Wipe out the interior with a damp cloth and clean up any spills as they occur. Over time, strong smells can build up; sprinkling baking soda on a damp sponge and wiping down the interior will help to eliminate them.

MICROWAVE

O V E N

The common things that can go wrong are that the controller breaks or the mechanisms for the stirrer or carousel give up the ghost. As microwave ovens get older, the seal between the door and the oven cavity can tend to break down, and any abuse, such as setting hot dishes on it, cutting it with a knife, or letting food deposits build up on it, can hasten the process. In these cases the microwave energy leaks out of the oven and can find its way into your body, which can have harmful effects, particularly if you are wearing a pacemaker. If you spill something on the seal, wipe it off immediately. Microwave oven leakage detectors can be purchased, or you can take your oven to a county extension agent or an authorized repair shop to have it checked for leaks.

WHICH IS RIGHT FOR ME? • If baking is your passion, a microwave oven is probably not the best choice of appliance. Baked goods prepared in a microwave oven do not brown and tend to cook unevenly, even with a carousel and close supervision.

When evaluating microwave ovens for purchase, select a model with features that match your individual cooking style. If flexibility is a priority, choose one that can be programmed. If simply reheating food or preparing frozen entrées, pick a simpler model that has a timer and adjustable power settings. Larger oven cavities can handle bigger foods or larger quantities of different foods, but remember that larger amounts of food take longer to cook.

Oven cavity walls that are plastic tend to stain over time, so metal cavities are easier to keep clean. To monitor the food while it is cooking, it is a good idea for the oven to have a light inside. Most modern microwave ovens turn on the light whenever the door is open or whenever the oven is on. Some older models have lights that you must turn on and off by means of a switch on the oven control panel.

Smaller and older microwave ovens have timers that are set physically by turning a dial or knob. Newer and more expensive models have a touch pad for setting the time and selecting various features.

MICROWAVE OVEN TIPS

⬗ Generally, do not use metal containers, plastic bag ties, or ceramic containers with metallic paint or metal-based glazes in your microwave. If the container gets hot before the food, assume that it isn't microwave safe.

⬗ Let your food rest while the residual heat in the food continues to cook it.

⬗ When any covering is removed, hot steam will escape. Lift the cover off away from you.

⬗ Bowls that are not microwavable get hot in the microwave oven. To test a bowl, fill a 1-cup measure with water and place it in the bowl. Put both in the microwave oven and run for 1 minute on high power. If the water gets hot and the bowl stays cool, then the bowl is microwave safe. If the bowl gets hot, then do not use it in the microwave.

⬗ Styrofoam will melt in the microwave and will infuse into the food in the container. Do not use Styrofoam in the microwave oven.

⬗ Some foods "explode" in the microwave due to trapped steam. Eggs, butter, and margarine have internal water that, when microwaved, turns to steam and splatters the food all over the oven cavity. For this reason it is imperative to cover these foods well when microwaving them.

⬗ If food cooks onto the side of the microwave, put a cup of water inside the oven and run it until the water boils. Let the steam permeate the food, and it will be easier to clean off.

⬗ Put wet cellulose sponges in the microwave oven for 30 seconds to disinfect.

⬗ Food quantities affect cooking times. If you double the recipe, plan on doubling the cooking time.

⬗ The denser the food, the longer the cooking time. When cooking foods of various shapes and thicknesses, place the thicker part closest to the outside of the dish and the thinner part toward the center.

⬗ The smaller the area of the food, the faster it will cook. Like-sized foods will cook at the same time.

● *Most foods will cook, reheat, or defrost better when covered or wrapped. Pierce plastic wrap with the tip of a sharp knife to vent the steam.*

● *The microwave is a great place to melt cheese. The higher the fat content, the faster the cheese will melt. Overcooked, however, it will become tough and stringy. Hard or dry cheeses tend to crisp rather than melt to a smooth consistency.*

● *To melt chocolate in the microwave, chop it into small pieces, then microwave, uncovered, on high power for 30-second intervals, stirring between each with a rubber scraper. It's better to heat the chocolate to the point at which it is almost, but not completely melted, then stir to combine any unmelted bits.*

● *If a recipe calls for melting chocolate and butter or margarine or vegetable shortening together, this can be done in the microwave. Chop the chocolate into small pieces, add the fat, and microwave uncovered on high for 20 seconds, then stir and microwave at 15-second intervals until the fat has melted. Continue to stir; the heat of the melted fat will melt the remaining chocolate.*

● *To soften chocolate to make chocolate curls, place a solid block of chocolate on a paper towel. Microwave on high power for 15 to 20 seconds, just until the top is slightly soft. Run a vegetable peeler or chef's knife held at a soft angle over the top to make the curls. Reheat as necessary to make more curls.*

● *To dissolve gelatin, place at least 3 tablespoons liquid in a small glass dish. Sprinkle 1 tablespoon gelatin over the liquid and allow it to soften for 3 to 4 minutes. Microwave, uncovered, on high power for 1 to 1 ½ minutes, until the gelatin has melted and the mixture is clear.*

● *When heating milk or cream in the microwave, take care to use a much larger container than the amount would usually indicate. This will prevent overflows if the milk or cream boils up.*

● *Use the microwave to bring cold butter and cream cheese to room temperature before beating them. Use it to soften ice cream as well.*

- *Soften preserves to make glazes for cakes, pies, and tarts. Use 1 cup red currant jelly mixed with 1 tablespoon lemon juice. Microwave, covered, on high power for 1 to 2 minutes, until the jelly has liquefied. Stir and spoon over the dessert.*

- *You can reliquefy crystallized honey and maple syrup in the microwave, as well as softening brown sugar; sprinkle it with a few drops of water and place it in an open plastic bag. Microwave for 10-second intervals on high power until softened.*

- *Make simple syrup by placing 2 cups granulated sugar and 1 cup water in a 6-cup Pyrex measure. Microwave, uncovered, on high power for 3 to 4 minutes, until the mixture boils and the sugar has dissolved.*

- *Blanch fresh fruit such as peaches or apricots, or vegetables such as tomatoes, by placing them in a large bowl of hot water and microwaving, uncovered, on high power, until the skins split. Rinse under cool water and slip off the skins.*

- *Poach fresh fruit in the microwave by placing it in a large bowl of wine or fruit juice and cooking, uncovered, on high power until the fruit is soft.*

- *Plump or refresh dried fruit by placing it in a bowl with orange, cranberry, or apple juice, or wine or water. Cover and microwave on high power until the fruit is soft. Allow to cool in the juice.*

- *Rehydrate dried beans, peas, and lentils by placing them in a large bowl. Cover with hot water and microwave, uncovered, on high power for 10 to 12 minutes, until the water boils. Boil 2 minutes, then allow to cool 30 minutes before changing the water and continuing to cook according to recipe directions.*

- *Dry fresh herbs by placing them between layers of paper towels and microwaving on high power until the herbs are dry. Crumble and store in tightly sealed jars or plastic bags.*

- *Refresh stale bread and rolls by wrapping them in slightly damp paper towels and microwaving on high power for 15 to 20 seconds.*

- *Warm alcohol for flambéed desserts by placing it in a Pyrex measure and microwaving on high for 20 to 30 seconds, until it feels warm, then remove the alcohol from the microwave and pour it into a flameproof cup or bowl before igniting with a match.*

- *Heat mugs, bowls, and dishes by filling them or rinsing them with hot water and microwaving for several minutes.*

RECIPES

SUGAR NUTS

Yield: 1 cup

Choose your favorite nuts to include in this mixture. These make great party fare—think of them around Thanksgiving or Super Bowl time.

3 CUPS NUTS OF YOUR CHOICE—WALNUTS, PECANS, OR ALMONDS

⅓ CUP SUPERFINE SUGAR

2 TABLESPOONS WATER

2 TABLESPOONS SESAME SEEDS

Place the nuts, sugar, and water in a large microwavable dish and toss together. Microwave, uncovered, on high power for 3 minutes. Remove and stir to coat all the pieces. Let stand for 3 minutes, then spread the nuts in a single layer on a parchment-paper-covered baking sheet and sprinkle with the sesame seeds. Cool before placing in an airtight container.

Variations: You can change the flavor by adding ¼ teaspoon ground cinnamon, fennel seeds, or ground cumin to this recipe.

SPICY NUTS

Yield: 1 pound

Use this as something to nibble on, to pass at a party, or as an ingredient in quick breads, scones, and muffins.

³/₄ CUP BOURBON

¹/₂ CUP SUPERFINE SUGAR

2 TABLESPOONS FIRMLY PACKED DARK BROWN
    SUGAR

1 TABLESPOON WORCESTERSHIRE SAUCE

1 TABLESPOON CORN OIL

1 POUND PECANS OR WALNUTS

1 TEASPOON CAYENNE PEPPER

1 TEASPOON GROUND CUMIN

¹/₂ TEASPOON SALT

¹/₄ TEASPOON FINELY GROUND BLACK PEPPER

In a medium-size microwavable bowl, combine the bourbon, sugars, Worcestershire sauce, and oil. Microwave on high power until the sugar is dissolved, about 2 minutes. Stir in the nuts. Spread the mixture on a parchment-paper-covered microwavable plate and microwave on high power for 3 minutes. Meanwhile, mix together the spices. Toss the hot nuts in the spice mix to coat. Spread on a parchment-paper-covered baking sheet until cool and dry. Store in a tightly sealed container.

BREAD AND BUTTER PICKLES

Yield: 6 cups

When the garden is overflowing with end-of-the-summer bounty and you're looking for a good use for pickling cucumbers, think of this almost instant way to make world-class pickles.

2 POUNDS PICKLING CUCUMBERS, ENDS
    TRIMMED AND SLICED INTO ¹/₈-INCH-THICK
    ROUNDS

1 MEDIUM-SIZE ONION, QUARTERED, THEN CUT

INTO ¹/₈-INCH-THICK SLICES (CUCUMBERS
AND ONIONS CAN BE SLICED IN FOOD
PROCESSOR WITH 4MM SLICING DISK)

1 1/2 TEASPOONS SALT

2 TABLESPOONS MUSTARD SEEDS

2 TEASPOONS CELERY SEEDS

2 TEASPOONS GROUND TURMERIC

1 TEASPOON CLOVES

1 1/2 CUPS FIRMLY PACKED DARK BROWN
SUGAR

2 CUPS CIDER VINEGAR

Place the cucumbers and onion in a 3-quart microwavable dish. Add the salt and toss to coat all the pieces. Cover and microwave on high power until the cucumbers start to sweat, about 2 minutes. Transfer to a colander, rinse with cool water, and set aside to drain for 5 minutes.

Using the same dish, mix together the rest of the ingredients and stir to dissolve the sugar a bit. Add the cucumbers and onion and toss to coat. Cover and microwave on high power until the liquid is hot but not quite boiling, about 8 minutes. Remove and let cool.

Cover and refrigerate overnight before serving. They will keep in the refrigerator for several months.

CAPONATA

Yield: 8 to 10 servings (about 6 cups)

Caponata is an Italian ratatouille, made subtly different from the French ratatouille by the addition of celery, olives, and capers. Caponata is best when the flavors have been allowed to mellow 24 hours before serving.

1 LARGE EGGPLANT (ABOUT 2 POUNDS)

2 MEDIUM-SIZE ONIONS, CHOPPED

1 YELLOW BELL PEPPER, SEEDED AND
CHOPPED

2 TO 3 CLOVES GARLIC, TO YOUR TASTE,
MASHED

1 STALK CELERY, CHOPPED

1/2 CUP TOMATO PASTE

3 TABLESPOONS FIRMLY PACKED DARK BROWN
SUGAR

1 1/2 TABLESPOONS RED WINE VINEGAR

1 TEASPOON BALSAMIC VINEGAR

2 TABLESPOONS CAPERS, DRAINED

1 CUP PITTED AND CHOPPED BRINE-CURED
BLACK OLIVES

SALT AND FRESHLY GROUND BLACK PEPPER
TO TASTE

continued

Dice the eggplant into ½-inch cubes and soak in salted water to cover for 1 hour. Place the pieces in a large sieve or colander set in a large bowl and position a heavy plate so that it rests on top of the eggplant. Weight the plate with something heavy such as a can. Let the liquid drain off for about 20 minutes.

Combine the eggplant, onions, bell pepper, garlic, and celery in a microwavable 3-quart glass bowl or casserole. Microwave, uncovered, on high power for 10 minutes, stirring once halfway through the cooking; the vegetables should be soft but not mushy. Stir in the tomato paste, brown sugar, and vinegars. Microwave, uncovered, on high power for 5 minutes. Stir in the capers and olives and season with salt and pepper. Transfer to a serving bowl and serve warm or room temperature.

INDIAN PEA SOUP

Yield: 8 servings

Thick and rich—and low in fat—this soup is a great way to warm a cold autumn night. You can make a vegetarian version by using vegetable stock for the cooking liquid (see the recipe on page 255).

2 TABLESPOONS VEGETABLE OIL

1 LARGE ONION, FINELY CHOPPED

2 CLOVES GARLIC, MINCED OR PRESSED

3 LARGE CARROTS, CUT INTO ½-INCH-THICK SLICES

½ TEASPOON GROUND CUMIN

½ TEASPOON GROUND GINGER

¼ TEASPOON GROUND TURMERIC

1½ CUPS DRIED SPLIT PEAS, RINSED AND PICKED OVER FOR PEBBLES

5 CUPS CHICKEN, BEEF, OR VEGETABLE BROTH

5 TO 10 DROPS HOT SAUCE, TO YOUR TASTE

SALT AND FRESHLY GROUND BLACK PEPPER TO TASTE

Place the oil in a large microwavable bowl. Add the onion, garlic, and carrots, cover, and microwave on high power for 4 minutes. Add the cumin, ginger, turmeric, peas, and broth, cover again, and microwave on high power for 15 minutes. Stir and add additional broth or water if the mixture is very thick. Microwave on high power until the peas are soft all the way through but still hold their shape, an additional 10 to 15 minutes. Season with hot sauce, salt, and pepper and serve hot.

For a smoother consistency, purée the soup with a handheld blender on high speed or in several batches in the blender or a food processor fitted with the metal blade.

Chilled Zucchini Soup

Yield: 6 servings

This soup, thickened with potato, seems creamy and rich, but is quite low in calories. Using vegetable broth makes this perfect for a vegetarian menu. It can be served hot or cold.

1 CLOVE GARLIC, PEELED

1 LARGE IDAHO POTATO, PEELED AND
   QUARTERED

1 LARGE ONION, CUT INTO CHUNKS

5 MEDIUM-SIZE ZUCCHINI, TRIMMED

3½ CUPS VEGETABLE OR CHICKEN BROTH

½ TEASPOON SALT

⅓ CUP FRESH BASIL LEAVES, OR
   1 TABLESPOON DRIED

½ TEASPOON TABASCO SAUCE

1 CUP LOW-FAT PLAIN YOGURT FOR GARNISH

To prepare the vegetables, in the work bowl of a food processor fitted with the metal blade, with the machine running, drop the garlic clove through the feed tube to mince. Stop the machine and, without removing the garlic, add the potato and onion to the work bowl and process to chop. Remove the vegetables to a large microwavable bowl and replace the metal blade with the 4mm slicing disk. Cut the zucchini to fit the feeding tube and slice.

Add the zucchini to the other vegetables along with 1½ cups of the chicken broth, salt, basil, and Tabasco sauce. Cover and microwave on high power until the vegetables are tender, 15 to 20 minutes.

Purée the mixture in the work bowl of a food processor fitted with the metal blade until smooth (solids first, then adding some of the liquid). Pour into a large bowl and stir in the remaining excess liquid and the remaining 2 cups of chicken broth to the desired consistency. Serve hot or chill before serving topped with a dollop of yogurt.

Variation: Substitute fresh tarragon for the basil.

Steamed Corn on the Cob

Yield: 6 ears corn

Everyone has his or her opinion on the subject of cooking sweet corn. On a hot summer day (when sweet corn is in season) you might not want to heat up the kitchen with a cauldron of boiling water. Try this microwave version. It will save you preparation time—you don't have to be very careful about removing every last bit of corn silk because it sticks to the moist inside of the plastic bag in which it cooks.

6 EARS OF CORN, HUSKED AND SILK REMOVED

2 TABLESPOONS WATER

Place the corn in a gallon-sized zippered plastic bag. Add the water and partially close the bag, leaving a 2-inch opening. Microwave on high power for 6 minutes. Beware of the steam when removing the corn from the bag. Serve immediately.

Asparagus à la Microwave

Yield: 4 to 6 side dish servings

Yes, I know it looks too good to be true. It couldn't be easier, and the mustard lemon caper sauce perfectly complements this vegetable.

1 POUND FRESH ASPARAGUS

2 TABLESPOONS WATER

$^1/_3$ CUP DIJON MUSTARD

JUICE OF 1 LEMON

1 TABLESPOON CAPERS (OPTIONAL), DRAINED

If using thick-stalked asparagus, take a small paring knife or vegetable peeler and remove the outer skin up to 1 inch below the tips. Place the asparagus in a heavy-duty, freezer-strength zippered plastic bag and add the water. Seal the top, leaving it open $1^1/_2$ inches at one end. Microwave on high power for 3 minutes. Being very careful to avoid the steam (point the bag opening away from your body), open the bag and remove the asparagus, discarding the water.

Mix the mustard and lemon juice together and pour over the asparagus. Garnish with the capers.

CHUNKY APPLESAUCE

Yield: 6 servings

Although it tastes old-fashioned, this applesauce is made the most modern way I know. It has a freshness that long stewing cannot achieve. I like to make extra and freeze it in plastic containers. I also like to cook my apples with the skins on, puréeing the skins as well as the fruit. It gives the applesauce a beautiful rosy color and a firmer texture.

2 MCINTOSH APPLES

2 GRANNY SMITH OR OTHER TART APPLES

1 CUP WATER

JUICE OF $^1\!/_2$ LEMON

$^1\!/_2$ CUP GRANULATED SUGAR OR FIRMLY PACKED LIGHT BROWN SUGAR

$^1\!/_2$ TEASPOON GROUND CINNAMON

Halve and core all the apples; peel them if you like. Cut each into 1-inch chunks.

Combine the apples, water, and lemon juice in a deep microwavable 2$^1\!/_2$-quart casserole. Toss the sugar and cinnamon together in a small bowl and stir this into the apple mixture. Cook, uncovered, on high power for 5 minutes. Stir, pressing the apples into the liquid, and return to the microwave. Cook on high power until the apples are soft, another 5 minutes.

In the work bowl of a food processor fitted with the metal blade or in the casserole dish using a handheld blender on high speed, process until the mixture reaches the desired consistency. Allow the applesauce to cool to room temperature, cover, and refrigerate or freeze.

Variation: Substitute 1 to 2 pears for the apples or add a sprinkling of raspberries for apple-raspberry sauce.

Polenta with Pesto and Parmesan

Yield: 6 servings

The combination of yellow cornmeal and red or green pesto makes a festive-looking dish for your holiday buffet table.

3 CUPS WATER

1 CUP MEDIUM-GRIND YELLOW CORNMEAL

2 TEASPOONS KOSHER SALT

3 TABLESPOONS BUTTER

$^1/_8$ TEASPOON FRESHLY GROUND BLACK
    PEPPER

$^1/_4$ CUP FRESHLY GRATED PARMESAN CHEESE

$^1/_3$ CUP PESTO (PAGE 117) OR TOMATO PESTO
    (PAGE 117)

Combine the water, cornmeal, and salt in a microwavable 2-quart soufflé dish. Microwave, uncovered, on high power for 6 minutes. Stir well, cover loosely with waxed paper, and microwave on high power until the cornmeal has absorbed the water and the mixture holds together, about another 6 minutes.

Remove from the microwave. Uncover and stir in the butter, pepper, cheese, and pesto. Let stand for 3 minutes. Serve hot.

Bulgur Pilaf

Yield: 4 to 6 servings

Bulgur is whole wheat berries that have been steamed, then dried and cracked. They have a nuttier flavor than cracked wheat and a softer texture when cooked. This dish makes a wonderful change from the usual potatoes, rice, or pasta. It can also be served cold as the main course of a light lunch or supper.

1 SMALL ONION, FINELY DICED

2 LARGE CLOVES GARLIC, COARSELY CHOPPED

$1^1/_2$ CUPS COARSE BULGUR

2 TABLESPOONS OLIVE OIL

$2^1/_4$ CUPS CHICKEN OR VEGETABLE BROTH

1 MEDIUM-SIZE TOMATO, COARSELY CHOPPED

1 SMALL RED BELL PEPPER, SEEDED AND CUT
    INTO $^1/_4$-INCH DICE

1 MEDIUM-SIZE ZUCCHINI, TRIMMED AND CUT
    INTO $^1/_2$-INCH DICE

2 TABLESPOONS CHOPPED FRESH DILL

½ TEASPOON CHOPPED FRESH OREGANO
LEAVES, OR ¼ TEASPOON DRIED

SALT AND FRESHLY GROUND BLACK PEPPER
TO TASTE

Place the onion, garlic, bulgur, and oil in a large microwavable bowl or deep dish. Stir to mix, then microwave, uncovered, on high power until the onion is soft, about 3 minutes. Stir in the remaining ingredients, cover the dish, and microwave on high power until the bulgur is fluffy and tender, about 13 minutes. Serve hot or chilled.

Variations: Other southern European vegetables, herbs, and spices may be substituted or added. Small pieces of meat, especially meatballs, can also be added.

RISOTTO MILANESE

Yield: 4 to 6 servings

Saffron threads give this risotto its distinctive ocher hue. Be sure to use the best quality Parmesan cheese, such as Reggiano; the taste is worth the extra cost.

1 MEDIUM-SIZE ONION, FINELY CHOPPED

⅓ CUP OLIVE OIL

2 CUPS ARBORIO RICE

½ CUP DRY WHITE WINE

5 CUPS CHICKEN OR VEGETABLE BROTH, AT
ROOM TEMPERATURE

LARGE PINCH OF SAFFRON THREADS

1 TEASPOON SALT

⅓ CUP FRESHLY GRATED PARMESAN CHEESE

Place the onion and olive oil in a large microwavable bowl and microwave, uncovered, on high power until the onion softens, about 3 minutes. Stir in the rice and microwave, uncovered, on high power until the rice begins to turn translucent, about 3 minutes. Stir in the wine, broth, saffron, and salt, cover, and microwave on high power until boiling, about 15 minutes. Remove the cover, stir, and continue to microwave, uncovered, on high power until the rice is cooked through but still chewy, about another 12 minutes. Stir in the cheese and serve immediately.

Speedy Gonzalez

Yield: 8 servings

This superfast, supertasting chili casserole will become a staple at your house.

2 TABLESPOONS VEGETABLE OIL

1 LARGE ONION, DICED

2 CLOVES GARLIC, MINCED

3 POUNDS VERY LEAN GROUND BEEF, CRUMBLED

1 TEASPOON CHILI POWDER

ONE 10-OUNCE BAG FROZEN NIBBLET CORN OR 1 1/2 CUPS FRESH CORN KERNELS

ONE 10-OUNCE CAN COOKED PINTO BEANS

1 1/2 CUPS SALSA, MILD, MEDIUM, OR HOT, TO YOUR TASTE

2 CUPS SLIGHTLY CRUSHED CORN CHIPS

8 OUNCES CHEDDAR CHEESE, SHREDDED

SOUR CREAM OR NONFAT PLAIN YOGURT FOR TOPPING

Place the oil, onion, and garlic in a microwavable 2-quart casserole. Cover and microwave on high power until the onion soften, about 3 minutes. Add the beef, cover, and microwave on high power, stirring once or twice, until the meat is no longer pink, 5 to 7 minutes. Drain off the liquid and stir in the chili powder, corn, beans, and salsa. Microwave, covered, on high power for another 5 minutes. Stir the mixture, then sprinkle with the chips, top with the cheese, cover, and microwave on high power until the cheese melts, about another 2 minutes. To serve, spoon into bowls and top with a dollop of sour cream or yogurt.

Citrus Salmon

Yield: 4 servings

Fish is a popular low-cholesterol entrée, which requires minimal cooking time. Microwave cooking is an ideal method for most fish since it is heated quickly while maintaining its delicate texture and flavor. Overcooking will make the fish tough and dry.

ONE 1-POUND SALMON FILLET, SKIN REMOVED

SALT AND FRESHLY GROUND BLACK PEPPER TO
  TASTE

1 TABLESPOON CORNSTARCH

1 TABLESPOON WATER

2 TABLESPOONS FROZEN ORANGE JUICE
  CONCENTRATE

1 TABLESPOON FRESH LEMON JUICE

1/4 CUP FIRMLY PACKED LIGHT BROWN SUGAR

1 ORANGE, SLICED, FOR GARNISH

CHOPPED FRESH ITALIAN PARSLEY LEAVES FOR
  GARNISH

MICROWAVE

OVEN

Sprinkle both sides of the salmon fillet with salt and pepper. Mix the cornstarch and water together in a small bowl to form a paste. Add the orange juice concentrate, lemon juice, and brown sugar and stir well until all the ingredients are dissolved. Pour half the sauce into the bottom of a microwavable dish. Place the salmon fillet in the dish on top of the sauce. Pour more of the sauce over the salmon. Cover the dish with plastic wrap and poke holes in it to allow steam to escape. Microwave on high power until the fish is completely cooked through, 6 to 8 minutes.

Place the fillet on a serving plate, spoon over the cooking liquid, and garnish with the orange slices and parsley.

CHINESE BAR MITZVAH NOODLES

Yield: 12 to 18 confections

I grew up seeing these rather strange-looking but wonderfully addictive candies on every bar mitzvah dessert table. In retrospect they seemed decidedly rustic next to the polished Dobosh Torts and fancy petits fours. The mix of salty noodles and buttery peanuts held together in an ungainly bird's-nestlike pile remains one of my weaknesses—perhaps it will become one of yours as well.

This recipe suggests the option of adding a handful of dried cranberries, which gives a lovely tartness to the jumble of flavors.

2 CUPS CHOPPED BITTERSWEET OR SEMISWEET
  CHOCOLATE

1 CUP DRY-ROASTED SALTED PEANUTS

1 1/2 CUPS CHINESE CHOW MEIN NOODLES
  BROKEN INTO 1/2- TO 1-INCH PIECES,
  VARYING IN SIZE

1/2 CUP DRIED CRANBERRIES (OPTIONAL FOR
  THE NEW AGE 90S VERSION)

continued

To melt the chocolate in the microwave oven, place it in a 6- or 8-cup microwavable container and microwave on high power, uncovered, at 20-second intervals, stirring with a rubber scraper between each interval, until the chocolate is almost melted. Remove the bowl and stir until the chocolate is completely melted.

Line a large baking sheet with waxed or parchment paper. Place the nuts, noodles, and cranberries in a 4-cup mixing bowl. Pour the melted chocolate into the bowl and mix well to cover as many of the pieces as possible. Use a soup spoon to remove a generous tablespoon at a time and make 12 large or 18 small clumps on the baking sheet. Refrigerate till just set, then remove so they don't get soggy. Store in a covered container at room temperature.

MICROWAVE RUM-CARAMEL SAUCE

Yield: 3 cups

Not that we'd ever get tired of hot fudge sauce, but once in a while something else on my ice cream seems like a good idea. This creamy, rich sauce is also terrific on top of pound cake and French toast. Try it on a slice of toasted Banana Bread (page 213).

$^1/_2$ CUP (1 STICK) UNSALTED BUTTER

1 CUP FIRMLY PACKED LIGHT BROWN SUGAR

$^1/_3$ CUP LIGHT CORN SYRUP

$^1/_4$ TEASPOON SALT

1 CUP HEAVY CREAM

2 TEASPOONS RUM EXTRACT OR $^1/_4$ CUP DARK OR LIGHT RUM

Melt the butter in a covered microwavable 1-quart glass measure on high power for 2 minutes. Stir in the brown sugar, corn syrup, and salt and microwave, uncovered, on high power, stirring twice, until the mixture reaches boiling and 234°F on a candy thermometer, 3 to 5 minutes.

Remove from the heat and whisk in the cream and rum, stirring until smooth. Serve hot or warm over ice cream, fruit, cake, or pancakes.

STRAWBERRY-RHUBARB CRISP

Yield: 6 to 8 servings

On a chilly spring day, when summer seems far away, rhubarb appears in the market—a portent of warm days to come. A quick dessert or midnight snack, this crisp can also be made with frozen rhubarb. Dried strawberries are available in gourmet stores and add a special sweetness to this crumble-type dessert.

2 CUPS DRIED STRAWBERRIES

2 CUPS BOILING WATER

3 TABLESPOONS GRANULATED SUGAR

1 TABLESPOON ALL-PURPOSE FLOUR

2 CUPS ($1/2$-INCH-THICK SLICES) TRIMMED
   RHUBARB

2 TABLESPOONS FINELY CHOPPED CANDIED
   GINGER (OPTIONAL)

For the topping:

$1/2$ CUP FIRMLY PACKED DARK BROWN SUGAR

$1/2$ CUP ALL-PURPOSE FLOUR

$1/2$ CUP QUICK-COOKING OATMEAL

$1/4$ CUP ($1/2$ STICK) COLD BUTTER, CUT INTO
   SMALL PIECES

PLAIN YOGURT OR SOFTLY WHIPPED CREAM
   FOR GARNISH

Soak the dried strawberries in the boiling water in a medium-size bowl until rehydrated, 10 to 12 minutes. Butter a 10-inch microwavable glass pie plate. In a separate bowl, combine the sugar and flour. Drain the strawberries and combine them with the rhubarb and ginger. Toss with the sugar-flour mixture. Spread the fruit in an even layer in the prepared pie plate.

In the work bowl of a food processor fitted with the metal blade, process the topping ingredients together until they resemble coarse crumbs. Sprinkle evenly over the fruit.

Microwave, uncovered, on high power for 8 minutes. Turn the dish a half turn and microwave on high power until the fruit is thickened and bubbly and the top is crisp, another 8 to 9 minutes. Cool slightly before serving topped with yogurt.

SOUR CREAM–CHOCOLATE ICING

Yield: Enough to frost a single-layer 8-inch cake

This simple glaze sets up shiny and smooth, or it can be beaten to form a slightly lighter frosting. It uses just two ingredients and can be prepared in just a few minutes. It lends itself to many uses, including icing cupcakes, piping onto dessert waffles, or filling between cookies. Try a dab on top of Devil's Food Crepes (page 345) or spread between crepes in a stack to form a crepe-torte.

8 OUNCES SEMISWEET CHOCOLATE, CHOPPED   **$^1/_2$ CUP SOUR CREAM**

Place the chocolate in a microwavable medium-large glass bowl and microwave, uncovered, on high power at 20-second intervals, stirring with a rubber scraper between intervals, until the chocolate has almost melted. Remove the bowl from the microwave and stir until smooth. Stir in the sour cream. If you want a smooth, shiny glaze, then mix only until smooth. For a lighter frosting, use a hand mixer fitted with the beater attachment set on medium speed to continue beating until aerated. Use immediately.

MIXER,

HAND

The hand mixer was the first kitchen appliance my children learned how to use. I'm not quite sure how that relates to the fact that two of them are in the restaurant business. One could assume that this handy kitchen appliance was a successful introduction to cooking. The boys, seduced by the dizzying array of accessories, attachments, and gleaming razor-sharp blades and disks, were, of course, dying to go right to the food processor. I told them that when they were older they could play with the more lethal equipment. Meanwhile, the hand mixer was the best way to make their favorite peanut butter and chocolate chip cookies. Today they both own industrial-sized food processors and floor model mixers, but when they cook at home for their own kids, they still make those peanut butter and chocolate chip cookies the way their Mom taught them—with the hand mixer.

GENERAL DESCRIPTION

WHAT DOES IT DO? • Hand mixers can be thought of as supercharged egg beaters. A hand mixer is used to combine ingredients and to aerate liquids or soft solid foods at a variety of speeds. Unlike their bigger cousins, the stand mixers, hand mixers are designed to be portable, giving the flexibility to move them to precisely where the mixing is done, whether in a favorite mixing bowl held in your lap, or in a saucepan on a burner of your stove top. They are especially good for small kitchens and the occasional or physically challenged cook since they are light and portable and thus maneuverable.

WHY DO I NEED THIS? • Generally, hand mixes are best used with sauces and dips, medium to thick pancake and waffle batters, cake mixes, and frostings. Some newer models with increased power can handle heavy cookie dough with ease, and those with very slow speeds can be used to mix dry ingredients together without creating a dust cloud. It is impossible to make a 7-minute frosting without a hand mixer.

HOW DOES IT WORK? • A multiple-speed motor—some with 3 speeds, some with as many as 9 speeds—when turned on by means of a switch, turns a shaft with a gear at the end of it. The gear meshes with another gear at a ninety-degree angle to the first one, bending the rotational motor downward from its original forward-pointing orientation. The rotary motion usually turns a pair of balloon-shaped metal beaters in opposing directions.

Some models also have a bigger single beater for beating egg whites and whipping cream. If given the option to select which hole to use for a single beater, choose the one that makes the beater move in the direction that is most comfortable. Right-handed cooks probably will use the hole that turns the beater counterclockwise, whereas left-handed cooks will probably choose the hole that turns the beater clockwise.

The beaters are made out of metal, and on newer models the metal is shaped into wires like a whisk. Older models have beaters that have been formed out of metal strips. Most of the older beaters have a post running down the center, but newer beaters do not, which makes them easier to clean (and less challenging to lick). When two beaters are used, they typically mesh without touching one another, which is why it is important that they be attached to the beater properly.

Once the beaters are placed in food, the mixer is turned on with the switch. By selecting the appropriate speed, the beaters turn and create a wake in the food, which indicates that it is being mixed according to the hand mixer's intended purpose.

Start mixing at a slower speed and adjust upward during mixing. Take care not to set the speed too high at first to avoid making a mess. Once the beaters are turning, move the bowl and the mixer around in the batter in a circular motion, which is the beauty of a hand mixer, and adjust the speed to ensure that the food is mixed thoroughly. Avoid the temptation to let the beaters rest on the bottom of the bowl while in motion; the bowl might break or the beaters might get bent. If unmixed food clings to the sides of the mixing bowl, scrape it down with a rubber scraper.

When the mixer is turned off, leave the beaters in the food until they stop turning completely to avoid splattering food all over the kitchen.

CARE AND MAINTENANCE • After unplugging the hand mixer, proceed to clean it. Most hand mixers now have a beater release button that ejects the beaters where you want them to be ejected, like a kitchen sink full of soapy water. Most beaters are dishwasher safe; the mixer housing is not. Wipe down the metal or plastic housing with a damp cloth or sponge.

Pay close attention to how the beaters are attached to the mixer. Sometimes it matters which beater goes into which hole. Also, if using beaters made out of wires, do not hold the beaters by the wires when you attach or detach them, or you risk bending them out of shape.

WHICH IS RIGHT FOR ME? • When buying a new hand mixer, consider purchasing one that has a range of speeds that matches your cooking needs. Very slow speeds are needed to mix dry ingredients together, and very fast speeds are needed for aerating. If you are going to be making stiff cookie dough, you should consider a slightly more powerful motor. Consider also the kinds of beaters that are available. For beating egg whites or whipping cream, a balloon whip is required.

Lift all candidate hand mixers to judge if they are light enough with a comfortable handle. Standing over a stove for 7 minutes can make even the lightest of hand mixers seem too heavy.

Make sure that the cord does not attach to the motor at an inconvenient place that will get in your way.

COMMENTS • A safety tip with hand mixers is to always mind the power cord lest you get it tangled in the beaters.

HAND MIXER TIPS

- *Choose a deep enough mixing bowl to accommodate expanding ingredients such as whipped cream.*

- *When done mixing, rest the mixer on its heel, letting the beaters hang over the bowl right over the batter. Scrape the excess batter off of the beaters directly into the bowl.*

- *Make sure to store the mixer, beaters, and power cord together in one place. Wrap a rubber band around the whole thing to keep the pieces together.*

- *Don't store the beaters in the unit as the blades can easily be bent out of shape. Store them in the box or in a heavy-duty plastic bag in a drawer. This will keep them clean and protect them from bending.*

RECIPES

MUFFIN MIX

Yield: Mix makes 4 batches of muffins; each batch makes 12 muffins

When Ellie created the brownie mix on page 215 she was on a roll. When you taste these, you'll be glad she didn't stop with dessert. Add liquid and eggs and presto! Really great-tasting corn muffins hot from your oven. Store the dry mixture in heavy-duty zippered plastic bags in the freezer for up to six months.

For the mix (for each batch of muffins, use 2¹⁄₂ cups less 1 tablespoon of this mix):

7³⁄₄ CUPS ALL-PURPOSE FLOUR

¹⁄₄ CUP YELLOW CORNMEAL (FINE OR REGULAR GRIND; FOR REALLY CRUNCHY, USE COARSE GRIND)

2 TABLESPOONS PLUS 2 TEASPOONS BAKING POWDER

2 TABLESPOONS BAKING SODA

2 TEASPOONS SALT

1¹⁄₃ CUPS SUGAR

For each batch of muffins add:

$^1/_2$ CUP VEGETABLE OIL

2 LARGE EGGS

$^1/_2$ TEASPOON PURE VANILLA EXTRACT

$^3/_4$ CUP PLAIN YOGURT, SOUR CREAM, OR BUTTERMILK (LOW-FAT VERSIONS ARE OKAY)

For the muffin mix, combine all the ingredients in a large heavy-duty zippered plastic bag. Shake well to blend and store in the freezer.

To make a batch of muffins, preheat the oven to 400°F with the rack in the center position. Grease, spray with nonstick vegetable spray, or line a 12-cup muffin pan with fluted papers. Combine the muffin mix with the oil, eggs, vanilla, and yogurt in a 2-quart bowl with a hand mixer fitted with the beater attachment on medium speed, taking care to stop when just combined (overbeating results in tough muffins).

Fill each muffin cup three-quarters full and bake until the tops are golden, 18 to 20 minutes. Remove the muffins from the pan and cool on a wire rack before serving or storing.

Variations: Nectarine or peach muffins: Add 2 peeled, pitted, and chopped nectarines or peaches; $^1/_2$ teaspoon grated lemon zest; and $^1/_8$ teaspoon ground nutmeg.

Blueberry muffins: Add 1 cup blueberries and $^1/_2$ teaspoon grated lemon zest.

Dried fruit muffins: Steep 1 cup chopped dried fruit in boiling water to cover for 15 minutes and drain well. Add to the mix along with $^1/_2$ teaspoon grated lemon zest.

Banana muffins: Add 2 mashed bananas and $^1/_2$ teaspoon grated lemon zest.

Chocolate chip muffins: Add 1 cup chocolate chips.

FEATHERLIGHT BRAN MUFFINS

Yield: 1 dozen muffins

Are you tired of those supermarket bran muffins dripping with molasses and the texture of a golf ball? If so, these lightened-up muffins will make you look forward to breakfast.

continued

1²/₃ CUPS 100% BRAN CEREAL (LIKE ALL-
BRAN)

¹/₂ CUP VEGETABLE OIL

2 LARGE EGGS

¹/₃ CUP FIRMLY PACKED LIGHT OR DARK
BROWN SUGAR

1 CUP LOW-FAT MILK

1 TEASPOON PURE VANILLA EXTRACT

¹/₂ CUP RAISINS

1¹/₄ CUPS UNBLEACHED ALL-PURPOSE FLOUR

1 TABLESPOON BAKING POWDER

1 TEASPOON BAKING SODA

¹/₂ TEASPOON SALT

Preheat the oven to 400°F with the rack in the center position. Generously grease a 12-cup muffin pan.

In a large bowl, combine the cereal with the oil, eggs, brown sugar, milk, vanilla, and raisins using a hand mixer fitted with the beater attachment on medium speed to thoroughly mix. Let stand for at least 10 minutes. (This can be done the night before baking. Just cover the bowl and store in the refrigerator.)

In a small bowl, combine the flour, baking powder, baking soda, and salt and stir with a spoon to mix. Add to the wet mixture and, using the hand mixer on medium speed, combine the ingredients just until mixed. Be careful not to overmix, or your muffins will be tough. Pour the batter into the prepared muffin pan, filling each cup only three-quarters full. Bake until the muffin tops spring back when touched lightly with a finger, 18 to 20 minutes.

Variations: In addition to the raisins, add ¹/₂ cup chopped walnuts or pecans. Or instead of the raisins, use chopped dates; dried apricots; or 1 peeled, cored, and chopped apple.

CORN BREAD AND CORN BREAD MUFFINS

Yield: 10 muffins or 8-inch square pan

You can use this recipe to make corn muffins or easily adapt it for corn bread.

²/₃ CUP MEDIUM OR FINELY GROUND YELLOW
CORNMEAL

1¹/₃ CUPS ALL-PURPOSE FLOUR

4 TEASPOONS BAKING POWDER

3 TABLESPOONS SUGAR

¹/₂ TEASPOON SALT

¹/₄ CUP VEGETABLE OIL

1 LARGE EGG, BEATEN

³/₄ CUP WATER (IF MAKING STUFFING FROM
THE BREAD, INCREASE TO ⁷/₈ CUP)

Preheat the oven to 375°F with the rack in the center position. Grease either an 8-inch square baking pan or two 6-cup muffin pans or line the muffin pans with fluted papers.

Place the dry ingredients in a medium-size bowl and use a hand mixer fitted with the beater attachment on low speed to combine them. Mix the wet ingredients together in a large bowl using the hand mixer on low speed to combine them. Add the dry ingredients to the wet in several additions, using the hand mixer on low speed. Take care not to overmix as this will make the cornbread tough.

Pour and scrape the batter into the prepared pan or fill 10 muffin cups three-quarters full. Bake until the tops are golden brown and a cake tester or toothpick inserted in the center comes out clean and dry, about 30 minutes for the bread and 20 minutes for the muffins. Cool the corn bread slightly before cutting into squares to serve.

Variation: Add ¼ teaspoon Louisiana hot sauce to the wet ingredients.

SMOKED CORN BREAD

Yield: One 9-inch square pan (about 9 servings)

There is nothing quite as satisfying as the aroma of corn bread baking—well, perhaps the taste of hot corn bread. The addition of smoked fresh corn on the cob gives this homey quick bread a whole new dimension. Try serving it with barbecue.

If you don't have any smoked corn on hand, you can substitute fresh or partially defrosted frozen corn.

3 TABLESPOONS BUTTER OR MARGARINE

1 CUP MEDIUM-GRIND YELLOW CORNMEAL

½ CUP ALL-PURPOSE FLOUR

2 TABLESPOONS SUGAR

2 TEASPOONS BAKING POWDER

½ TEASPOON SALT

2 LARGE EGGS

1 CUP MILK

1 CUP GRATED CHEDDAR OR MONTEREY JACK CHEESE

1 CUP SMOKED CORN KERNELS (PAGE 361)

continued

Preheat the oven to 350°F with the rack in the center position. Place the butter in a 9-inch square baking dish or a 10-inch cast-iron skillet. Place the pan in the oven while you prepare the batter.

Place the cornmeal in a large bowl and sift the flour, sugar, baking powder, and salt over it. Use a hand mixer fitted with the beater attachment on the lowest speed to mix the dry ingredients together. With the mixer on low speed, stir in the eggs, milk, cheese, and finally the corn. Do not overbeat; that will make the corn bread tough.

Swirl the melted butter or margarine to coat the bottom and sides of the pan and pour and scrape the batter into it. Bake until the top is golden, about 25 minutes. Cool for 10 minutes in the pan before cutting into squares. Serve hot or at room temperature.

DOUBLE DECADENT BROWNIE TORTE

Yield: One 9-inch single-layer torte

Brownie lovers hale from two camps: those who like their brownies fudgy and those who prefer cakelike treats. This torte will please both groups with its spongy cake and candylike glaze.

For the torte:

1/2 CUP (1 STICK) UNSALTED BUTTER

1/2 CUP LIGHT CORN SYRUP

1 CUP (5 OUNCES) CHOPPED UNSWEETENED CHOCOLATE

1/2 CUP SUGAR

3 EXTRA LARGE EGGS

1 TEASPOON PURE VANILLA EXTRACT

1 CUP ALL-PURPOSE FLOUR

1 CUP FINELY CHOPPED WALNUTS OR PECANS, TOASTED (SEE NOTE, PAGE 131)

For the chocolate glaze:

1/2 CUP (2 1/2 OUNCES) CHOPPED SEMISWEET CHOCOLATE

2 TABLESPOONS BUTTER

1 TABLESPOON LIGHT CORN SYRUP

RASPBERRIES FOR GARNISH

Preheat the oven to 350°F. Butter and flour a 9-inch round cake pan. To make the torte, in a small saucepan over low heat, heat the butter and corn syrup together until the butter is melted. Place the unsweetened chocolate in a medium-size bowl.

Pour the butter-syrup mixture over it and stir until melted using a hand mixer fitted **MIXER,** with the beater attachment set on the lowest speed. Add the sugar and eggs, increase the speed to medium, and blend well. On low speed, stir in the vanilla, flour, and nuts. Pour the batter into the prepared pan. Grasp the edge of the pan and give the bottom a smart smack on the counter to eliminate air bubbles. Bake until the center **HAND** springs back when lightly touched, about 30 minutes. Cool in the pan for 10 minutes before turning out of the pan onto a rack. Cool completely before glazing.

For the glaze, combine the semisweet chocolate, butter, and corn syrup in a small saucepan. Stir over low heat until the chocolate is melted, then remove from the heat. Cool only until the glaze is thick but still flowing and pour over the top of the cake, allowing the drips to run down the sides. Garnish with raspberries just before serving.

BERRY POUND CAKE

Yield: 1 large or 2 smaller cakes

This pretty cake makes a perfect teatime pleasure or a picture-perfect addition to a brunch table. Although the recipe calls for it to be served warm, baked in smaller loaves and cooled it makes a wonderful gift. A recipe for lemon-orange icing follows.

To prepare the pan:

2 TABLESPOONS BUTTER

$^1/_4$ CUP SUGAR

For the cake:

1 CUP (2 STICKS) UNSALTED BUTTER, AT ROOM TEMPERATURE

1 $^2/_3$ CUPS SUGAR

4 EXTRA LARGE EGGS

1 TEASPOON PURE ORANGE EXTRACT

2 $^3/_4$ CUPS SIFTED ALL-PURPOSE FLOUR

1 TEASPOON BAKING POWDER

$^1/_2$ TEASPOON SALT

2 CUPS DRIED CRANBERRIES

Preheat the oven to 325°F with the rack in the center position. Coat a 10-cup bundt pan or two 6-cup loaf pans with the 2 tablespoons butter and sprinkle with the $^1/_4$ cup sugar. Set aside.

Using a hand mixer fitted with the beater attachment on high speed, cream the butter and sugar together in a large bowl until light and fluffy. Add the eggs 1 at a time, then the orange extract. Mix the dry ingredients together in another bowl and gradually add to the egg mixture. Mix well, then fold in the cranberries.

Pour and scrape the batter into the prepared pan and bake until a cake tester or toothpick inserted in the center comes out clean and dry, about 1 hour and 10 minutes. Cool the cake in the pan for 10 minutes before turning out onto a heat-proof platter for frosting.

Variations: Replace the cranberries with dried blueberries or use 1 cup each dried cranberries and dried blueberries.

LEMON-ORANGE ICING

Yield: Enough to glaze 1 cake

1 CUP CONFECTIONERS' SUGAR

1/2 TEASPOON GROUND CINNAMON

1 1/2 TABLESPOONS FRESH LEMON JUICE

1 1/2 TABLESPOONS FRESH ORANGE JUICE

Sift the confectioners' sugar and cinnamon together in a small bowl. Add the juices and, with a hand mixer fitted with the beater attachment on medium-low speed, beat until smooth. Drizzle over the cooled cake.

OLD-FASHIONED VANILLA CAKE WITH BROWN BUTTER PECAN FROSTING

Yield: One 9-inch two-layer cake (8 to 10 servings)

This is an old-fashioned yellow cake that is perfect for a birthday layer cake.

2 1/2 CUPS ALL-PURPOSE FLOUR

2 1/2 TEASPOONS BAKING POWDER

1/2 TEASPOON SALT

3/4 CUP (1 1/2 STICKS) UNSALTED BUTTER, AT ROOM TEMPERATURE

1 2/3 CUPS SUGAR

2 1/2 TEASPOONS PURE VANILLA EXTRACT

3 LARGE EGGS

1 CUP MILK

BROWN BUTTER PECAN FROSTING (PAGE 209)

Preheat the oven to 375°F with the rack in the center position. Grease and flour two 9-inch round cake pans, shaking out any excess flour. In a medium-size bowl, sift together the flour, baking powder, and salt and set aside.

Using a hand mixer fitted with the beater attachment first on low speed, then increasing the speed to medium, cream the butter in a large bowl until fluffy, then add the sugar and vanilla. Next beat in the eggs one at a time. Alternately add the flour mixture and milk, ending with the flour mixture. Mix the batter on medium speed for 30 seconds to make sure all the ingredients are blended.

Pour and scrape the batter into the prepared pans and bake until the tops are golden brown and the sides have just begun to pull away from the pan, about 30 minutes. Allow the cakes to cool in the pans for 10 minutes before turning them out onto wire racks to cool completely before frosting.

BROWN BUTTER PECAN FROSTING

Yield: About 3 cups

¹⁄₄ CUP (¹⁄₂ STICK) UNSALTED BUTTER

8 OUNCES CREAM CHEESE (DO NOT USE WHIPPED CREAM CHEESE), AT ROOM TEMPERATURE

¹⁄₄ CUP HEAVY CREAM

2 CUPS CONFECTIONERS' SUGAR, SIFTED

2 TEASPOONS PURE MAPLE EXTRACT

1 CUP PECANS, TOASTED (SEE NOTE, PAGE 131) AND FINELY CHOPPED

Place the butter in a small saucepan over high heat. Let it melt and then simmer. As soon as the butter begins to brown, remove the pan from the heat and pour the butter into a large bowl. Add the cream cheese and heavy cream and use a hand mixer fitted with the beater attachment on medium speed to beat the mixture until soft and light. On the lowest speed, blend in the sugar, then increase the speed to medium-high and beat until creamy, adding more sugar if a thicker consistency is desired. Blend in the extract, then fold in the pecans and smooth the frosting over the top and sides of the cake.

Pumpkin Cheesecake

Yield: One 9-inch cheesecake (8 servings)

I once spent a wonderful fall traveling around the country making cheesecake as a spokesperson for Philadelphia Cream Cheese. Never were a product and a cook so well matched. It's a testimonial to how much I love Philly to admit that my craving for a slice of cheesecake was as strong at the end of the tour as it was at the beginning. My favorite flavor was and still is pumpkin. It makes a star appearance on my Thanksgiving table every year. Please don't tell my friends and family how easy it is to make—they think I spend hours on it.

TWO 8-OUNCE PACKAGES PHILADELPHIA CREAM CHEESE (REGULAR OR PHILLY FREE—DO NOT USE WHIPPED CREAM CHEESE), AT ROOM TEMPERATURE

$^1/_2$ CUP SUGAR

2 LARGE EGGS

$^1/_2$ TEASPOON GROUND NUTMEG

1 CUP CANNED OR FRESHLY COOKED PUMPKIN PURÉE

$^1/_2$ TEASPOON GROUND CINNAMON

1 CHOCOLATE CRUMB CRUST (STORE BOUGHT OR HOMEMADE, PAGE 128)

Preheat the oven to 350°F with the rack in the center position. Place the cream cheese and sugar in a 2-quart bowl and use a hand mixer fitted with the beater attachment on medium speed to mix until smooth. Add the remaining ingredients, except the crumb crust, and mix only until well combined. Try to avoid beating air into the batter as it will cause the cheesecake to rise during baking, then fall and crack as it cools.

Pour and scrape the batter into the pie shell and smooth the top evenly with a rubber scraper. Bake until the outer edges look dry and shiny and a small damp spot remains in the center, about 30 minutes. Cool on a wire rack for at least 20 minutes before serving or freezing.

The cheesecake can be served immediately, covered with a sheet of plastic wrap and refrigerated for up to 3 days, or wrapped in several layers of plastic wrap and frozen for up to 3 months.

APPLESAUCE-RAISIN CAKE

Yield: One 10-inch tube cake (8 to 10 servings)

You can make this simple cake using store-bought applesauce, or you can try making your own (page 191).

3 CUPS ALL-PURPOSE FLOUR	1½ CUPS GRANULATED SUGAR
2 TEASPOONS BAKING SODA	2 CUPS CHUNKY-STYLE APPLESAUCE
½ TEASPOON SALT	1 TEASPOON PURE VANILLA EXTRACT
1 TEASPOON GROUND CINNAMON	1 CUP RAISINS
1 TEASPOON GROUND NUTMEG	CONFECTIONERS' SUGAR
1 CUP (2 STICKS) BUTTER OR MARGARINE, AT ROOM TEMPERATURE	

Preheat the oven to 325°F with the rack in the center position. Butter and flour a 10-inch tube pan. In a medium-size bowl, sift together the flour, baking soda, salt, cinnamon, and nutmeg. Set aside. In a large bowl, cream together the butter and granulated sugar with a hand mixer fitted with the beater attachment on medium speed until light and fluffy, 5 to 8 minutes. Add the applesauce and vanilla and mix in thoroughly.

Sift the flour mixture over the applesauce mixture. Add the raisins and use a rubber scraper to gently fold everything together until thoroughly blended. Pour and scrape the batter into the prepared pan. Bake until a cake tester or toothpick inserted in the center comes out clean and dry, 70 to 75 minutes. Cool the cake in the pan for 15 minutes before removing to a wire rack to cool completely. Just before serving, dust with confectioners' sugar.

CINNAMON SUGAR–SOUR CREAM COFFEE CAKE

Yield: 8 servings

The hand mixer is the perfect appliance for whipping up this scrumptious coffee cake, which is made by sprinkling a cinnamon sugar filling between layers of batter.

continued

For the filling:

3/4 CUP SUGAR

2 TEASPOONS GROUND CINNAMON

ONE 12-OUNCE BAR SEMISWEET CHOCOLATE, COARSELY CHOPPED

1 CUP WALNUTS, COARSELY CHOPPED

For the batter:

2 3/4 CUPS UNBLEACHED ALL-PURPOSE FLOUR

2 TEASPOONS BAKING POWDER

1/2 TEASPOON BAKING SODA

1 CUP (2 STICKS) UNSALTED BUTTER, AT ROOM TEMPERATURE

1 CUP SUGAR

3 LARGE EGGS, AT ROOM TEMPERATURE

1 1/2 TEASPOONS PURE VANILLA EXTRACT

1 CUP SOUR CREAM, AT ROOM TEMPERATURE

Preheat the oven to 350°F with the rack in the center position. Generously butter the bottom, sides, and center tube of a 10 × 4-inch tube pan. Lightly dust the bottom and sides of the pan with flour and shake out the excess.

To make the filling, combine the sugar and cinnamon in a small bowl. Add the chocolate and walnuts and stir to combine. Set aside.

To make the cake, in a medium-size bowl, sift together the flour, baking powder, and baking soda and set aside. In a large bowl, using a hand mixer fitted with the beater attachment on low speed, beat the butter until creamy, about 30 seconds. Gradually add the sugar and beat on medium speed until light and fluffy, 1 to 2 minutes. Add the eggs 1 at a time, beating well after each addition. Beat in the vanilla in 3 additions, beating at low speed. Mix in the dry ingredients alternately with the sour cream.

Scrape one third of the batter into the prepared pan, spreading it evenly. Cover the batter with one third of the filling. Scrape half the remaining batter over the filling and spread evenly. Cover the batter with half of the remaining filling. Scrape the remaining batter into the pan, spread evenly, and cover with the remaining filling. Bake the coffee cake until a cake tester or toothpick inserted into the center comes out clean and dry, 55 to 65 minutes. Cool in the pan on a wire rack until the chocolate on top starts to harden, about 15 minutes. Run a knife around the edge of the pan to loosen and invert onto a wire rack. Quickly reinvert the cake onto another wire rack and cool completely before serving.

BANANA BREAD

Yield: 1 large loaf, 2 small loaves, or 12 muffins

Don't toss out those leftover ripe bananas! Turn them into this tasty loaf, which is lower in sugar and higher in fiber than most banana breads and has a calcium boost with the addition of both wet and dry low-fat milk. It's just as moist and flavorful as the traditional version.

If you find yourself with an abundance of overripe bananas but not enough time to bake, just peel, slice, and freeze the bananas in a heavy-duty zippered plastic bag. You can defrost them in the microwave and use them in this recipe. The mushy consistency is just right.

2 LARGE VERY RIPE BANANAS, CUT INTO
   1-INCH PIECES

1 TABLESPOON FRESH LEMON JUICE

$1/2$ CUP (1 STICK) BUTTER OR MARGARINE, AT
   ROOM TEMPERATURE

$1/2$ CUP CHOPPED PECANS OR WALNUTS

$3/4$ CUP UNBLEACHED ALL-PURPOSE FLOUR

1 CUP WHOLE WHEAT FLOUR

$1/3$ CUP FIRMLY PACKED DARK BROWN SUGAR

1 LARGE OR EXTRA LARGE EGG

2 LARGE EGG WHITES

$1/3$ CUP LOW-FAT MILK

$1/3$ CUP DRY MILK (NOT RECONSTITUTED)

$1\,1/4$ TEASPOONS BAKING SODA

$3/4$ TEASPOON SALT

$1/2$ TEASPOON GROUND CINNAMON

$1/8$ TEASPOON GROUND NUTMEG

$1/8$ TEASPOON GROUND CLOVES

Preheat the oven to 350°F with the rack in the center position. Grease and flour one 8-cup loaf pan, two 6-cup pans, or a 12-cup muffin pan. Place the bananas and lemon juice in a large bowl and, using a hand mixer fitted with the beater attachment on low speed, mash them together. Mix in the butter, then add the rest of the ingredients and mix on medium speed until well combined. Pour the batter into the prepared pan(s); if making muffins, fill each cup only three-quarters full.

Bake until a cake tester or toothpick inserted in the center comes out clean and dry, 55 to 65 minutes for the 8-cup pan, 40 to 45 minutes for the 6-cup pans, and 15 to 20 minutes for the muffins. Cool for 10 minutes in the pan before unmolding onto a wire rack to cool completely before serving.

PROFITEROLES

Yield: 12 cream puffs

Just the thought of ice-cream-filled, chocolate-sauced cream puffs makes me want to reach for the dessert fork. Profiteroles are easy as can be thanks to the hand mixer.

You can fill these with ice cream and top them with warm Ganache (page 138) or Instant Pastry Cream (page 45). You will need a heavy-duty hand mixer for this job.

6 TABLESPOONS (³⁄₄ STICK) BUTTER	1 ¹⁄₄ CUPS ALL-PURPOSE FLOUR
1 CUP WATER	5 LARGE EGGS, AT ROOM TEMPERATURE,
1 TEASPOON SALT	BROKEN INTO A SPOUTED CUP

Preheat the oven to 400°F with the rack in the center position. Line a heavy-duty baking sheet with parchment paper or aluminum foil.

Place the butter, water, and salt in a small saucepan over high heat. Bring the mixture to a simmer and, when the butter melts, remove the pan from the heat and add the flour. With a hand mixer fitted with the beater attachment on low speed, then increasing to medium speed, mix until smooth.

Return the pan to the stove top and cook over low heat, beating with the mixer on low speed until there are no lumps and the mixture begins to pull away from the sides of the pan. Remove from the heat, increase the mixer speed to medium, and add the eggs one at a time, mixing to combine each before adding the next. The dough should be shiny, smooth, and quite stiff.

Use either a pastry bag fitted with a plain round 1-inch tip or two spoons dipped in water to form 12 mounds 2 inches apart on the prepared sheet. Bake until the tops are golden, about 30 minutes. Remove the sheet from the oven and use a sharp serrated knife to carefully slice off the top third of the cream puff. Scoop out the dough center and discard. Allow the cream puffs to cool on a wire rack before filling with ice cream, whipped cream, or pastry cream.

BROWNIE MIX

Yield: Mix makes 4 batches of brownies; each batch makes a 9 × 13-inch pan of brownies

Ellie had an inspired notion: to create a homemade, shelf-stable brownie mix that can be stored, just ready and waiting for the addition of wet ingredients and the mix-ins of your choice.

Nestlé Choco-Bake is a premelted form of unsweetened chocolate available in the baking section of the supermarket.

For the mix (for each brownie batch, use 2²⁄₃ cups of this mix):

6 CUPS SUGAR

5¹⁄₃ CUPS ALL-PURPOSE FLOUR

1 TEASPOON BAKING POWDER

1 TEASPOON SALT

For each batch of batter add:

4 PACKETS CHOCOBAKE OR 4 SQUARES
   UNSWEETENED CHOCOLATE, MELTED

2 LARGE OR EXTRA LARGE EGGS

¹⁄₂ CUP (1 STICK) BUTTER OR MARGARINE,
   MELTED, OR VEGETABLE OIL

2 TABLESPOONS LIQUID (WATER, COFFEE,
   LIQUEUR, OR LIQUOR OF CHOICE)

Optional additions:

1 CUP COARSELY CHOPPED MACADAMIA NUTS,
   WALNUTS, PECANS; CHOCOLATE CHIPS;
   M&M'S; CHOCOLATE-COVERED ESPRESSO
   BEANS; CHOPPED HEALTH BARS; JUNIOR
   MINTS

Combine all the brownie mix ingredients together. We suggest you divide the mix among four heavy-duty zippered plastic bags, which can be stored at room temperature for up to 1 year.

To make a batch of brownies, preheat the oven to 350°F with the rack in the center position. Grease and flour a 9 × 13-inch baking pan. Place the dry mix in a 2-quart bowl, add the wet ingredients, and mix to combine with a hand mixer fitted with the beater attachment on medium speed. Mix in the optional additions by hand. Pour and scrape the batter into the prepared pan.

Bake until the top is shiny and the sides have just begun to pull away from the pan, 30 to 40 minutes. It is better to underbake these brownies than to overbake them. Cool in the pan before cutting into squares or bars.

DEVIL'S FOOD CAKE

Yield: 1 layer

This moist, chocolatey "birthday" cake can be baked as an 8-inch round single-layer cake, or double the recipe for a two-layer cake. Sour cream–chocolate icing (page 198) is a traditional topping for this cake.

4 OUNCES UNSWEETENED CHOCOLATE, CHOPPED

6 TABLESPOONS BUTTER (³/₄ STICK), SOFTENED

1 CUP FIRMLY PACKED DARK BROWN SUGAR

2 TEASPOONS VANILLA EXTRACT

2 EXTRA LARGE EGGS

¹/₂ CUP STRONG COFFEE OR 1 TABLESPOON INSTANT COFFEE IN ¹/₂ CUP VERY HOT WATER

1 ¹/₂ CUPS ALL-PURPOSE WHITE FLOUR, MEASURED AFTER SIFTING

1 TEASPOON BAKING SODA

¹/₄ TEASPOON SALT

Preheat the oven to 350°F with the rack in the center position. Grease and flour an 8-inch layer pan, knocking out the excess flour. Sift the dry ingredients together and set aside.

Melt the chocolate and butter in the microwave or in a double boiler set over gently simmering water. Using a handheld mixer on medium speed, combine the sugar, vanilla, and egg. Beat until the mixture is smooth. Add the coffee and mix just until blended. On low speed add the chocolate, then finally the dry ingredients and mix, just till well blended.

Bake for 20 to 25 minutes or until a toothpick or cake tester inserted in the center comes out clean. Cool in the pan for 10 minutes before unmolding onto a wire rack to completely cool before frosting.

BUTTERSCOTCH SQUARES

Yield: 12 squares

Even the most ardent brownie fan longs for a change once in a while. These buttery confections will fill the bill.

$^1\!/_4$ CUP ($^1\!/_2$ STICK) BUTTER, AT ROOM TEMPERATURE

1 CUP FIRMLY PACKED LIGHT BROWN SUGAR

1 EXTRA LARGE EGG, BEATEN

1 TEASPOON PURE VANILLA EXTRACT

1 CUP ALL-PURPOSE FLOUR, MEASURED AFTER SIFTING

1 TEASPOON BAKING POWDER

$^1\!/_2$ TEASPOON SALT

$^1\!/_2$ CUP CHOPPED NUTS

$^3\!/_4$ CUP SWEETENED SHREDDED COCONUT (OPTIONAL)

Preheat the oven to 350°F with the rack in the center position. Grease an 8-inch square baking pan. Melt the butter in a microwavable 1-quart bowl in the microwave on high power. Stir in the brown sugar and allow it to cool. With a hand mixer fitted with the beater attachment on low speed, beat in the egg and vanilla, then the dry ingredients, mixing only until combined. Finally, mix in the nuts and if desired, the coconut. Pour the batter into the prepared pan. Bake until the top is dry, 20 to 25 minutes. Cool in the pan, then cut into 12 squares.

ALEX'S BUTTER COOKIES

Yield: About 3 dozen

Ellie's son Alex goes ga-ga over these sugar cookies, especially when they're dipped in chocolate (he is his mother's son, after all). These also make a terrific base for Christmas cookies—get out the decorations, food coloring, and sprinkles and go to town!

1 CUP (2 STICKS) UNSALTED BUTTER, AT ROOM
   TEMPERATURE

$3/4$ CUP SUGAR

1 LARGE OR EXTRA LARGE EGG

$1 1/2$ TEASPOONS PURE VANILLA EXTRACT

$2 1/4$ CUPS SIFTED ALL-PURPOSE FLOUR

$1/2$ TEASPOON SALT

ONE 12-OUNCE PACKAGE SEMISWEET
   CHOCOLATE CHIPS (OPTIONAL)

Preheat the oven to 375°F with the racks dividing the oven into thirds. Grease two heavy-duty baking sheets.

Using a hand mixer fitted with the beater attachment on medium-low speed, cream the butter and sugar together in a large bowl until light and fluffy. Add the egg and vanilla, increase the speed to medium, and beat well. With the mixer on low speed, add the flour and salt and beat until well blended, scraping down the bowl often with a rubber scraper. Wrap the dough with plastic wrap and refrigerate until firm, 2 to 3 hours.

There are several ways you can shape this dough into cookies. One way is to spoon out 1 teaspoon of dough at a time, roll it into a 1-inch ball, flatten it with the palm of your hand, and place it on the prepared baking sheets. Or, you can shape the dough into small logs about $1 1/2$ inches long. Or roll out the dough on a well-floured work surface and cut it with your favorite cookie cutters. The trick is to keep the dough chilled, so only use a portion at a time and keep the rest in the refrigerator until you're ready to use it.

Bake until the edges of the cookies are golden brown, 12 to 15 minutes. Transfer to a wire rack to cool completely.

For decorating, you can sprinkle the unbaked cookies with your favorite sprinkles or colored sugars, or press chocolate chips into the tops. But for a knockout cookie, we like to dip these in chocolate after baking. To melt the chocolate chips, place them in a microwavable bowl and microwave on high power at 20-second intervals, stirring with a rubber scraper between each interval until melted. Either dip one side of each cookie in the chocolate or place a spoonful of chocolate on the underside of half the cookies and sandwich them with the rest of the cookies. Place the dipped and sandwiched cookies on waxed or parchment paper to harden. Store in a tightly closed container.

SOFT AND CHEWY MOLASSES COOKIES

Yield: 30 to 36 cookies

Our local espresso shop sells cookies just like these for a dollar a piece. Now that I have this recipe, I can make my own and spend the money on another latte.

2 CUPS UNBLEACHED ALL-PURPOSE FLOUR, MEASURED AFTER SIFTING

2 TEASPOONS BAKING SODA

1/4 TEASPOON SALT

3/4 TEASPOON GROUND GINGER

1 TEASPOON GROUND CINNAMON

1/2 TEASPOON GROUND CLOVES

1 TEASPOON PURE VANILLA EXTRACT

1 1/4 CUPS (1 1/2 STICKS) BUTTER, AT ROOM TEMPERATURE

1 CUP FIRMLY PACKED DARK BROWN SUGAR

1 LARGE EGG

1/4 CUP MOLASSES

Preheat the oven to 350°F with the rack in the center position. Line two heavy-duty baking sheets with parchment paper or butter the baking sheets and dust with flour, shaking out the excess.

Use a hand mixer fitted with the beater attachment on low speed to combine the first six ingredients. Add the remaining ingredients, increase the speed to medium, and beat for 2 minutes, scraping down the sides of the bowl as necessary. Wrap the dough in plastic wrap and refrigerate for 1 hour.

Roll the chilled dough into walnut-sized balls and place them 2 inches apart on the prepared cookie sheet. Bake until the tops are dry, 12 to 15 minutes. Cool on wire racks.

Stabilized Whipped Cream

Yield: About 4 cups

If you add softened gelatin to whipped cream, the cream will stay whipped longer, although the consistency will be slightly different. This is useful when you have to fill or frost desserts ahead of time. The whipped cream will hold its shape for about 4 hours but should be refrigerated until the decorated dessert is ready to serve.

1 ENVELOPE UNFLAVORED GELATIN

2 TABLESPOONS COLD WATER

1/4 CUP BOILING WATER

2 CUPS HEAVY CREAM

1/2 CUP CONFECTIONERS' SUGAR, OR TO YOUR TASTE

2 TEASPOONS PURE VANILLA EXTRACT, OR TO YOUR TASTE

Sprinkle the gelatin over the cold water in a small bowl. Let stand for 1 minute to soften. Add the boiling water and stir until the gelatin is completely dissolved. Cool the gelatin mixture until tepid, 10 to 15 minutes.

Meanwhile, in a large bowl, whip the heavy cream with a hand mixer fitted with the beater or whip attachment on high speed until it starts to hold its shape. The cream should start to thicken, but *not* peak. Fold the sugar into the cream until blended. Add the vanilla and continue to beat until soft peaks form. Transfer 1 cup of the cream to a small bowl and stir in the tepid gelatin mixture. Fold this mixture back into the rest of the cream and beat until stiff peaks form. Refrigerate about 15 minutes to set.

Broiled Coconut Frosting

Yield: About 2 cups (enough to frost an 8-inch two-layer cake)

Try this on your favorite layer cake or on the Berry Pound Cake on page 207.

2/3 CUP FIRMLY PACKED LIGHT BROWN SUGAR

1/3 CUP BUTTER, MELTED

1/4 CUP LIGHT CREAM

1 1/3 CUPS SWEETENED SHREDDED COCONUT

1 TEASPOON PURE VANILLA EXTRACT

Preheat the broiler with the oven rack in the upper part but not the highest position. Place the cake on an ovenproof platter or tray. Place all the ingredients in a medium-size bowl and use a hand mixer fitted with the beater attachment on low speed to combine them. Increase the speed to medium and beat until smooth, about 1 minute.

Spread the frosting over the warm cake. Place the cake under the broiler and broil just until the top is golden, about 2 minutes. Serve while warm.

MIXER,

HAND

Dark Chocolate–Orange Sauce

Yield: 2 cups

This lovely sauce is the perfect match for a slice of rich chocolate cake. It's also terrific drizzled over fresh fruit, especially berries. If you don't wish to use alcohol, use one of the fruit syrups found in espresso bars to make flavored coffee.

1 CUP HEAVY CREAM

10 OUNCES BEST QUALITY BITTERSWEET CHOCOLATE, BROKEN OR CHOPPED

¼ CUP GRAND MARNIER OR OTHER ORANGE LIQUEUR OR ORANGE SYRUP

Place the cream in a 1½-quart saucepan over medium heat. Bring it to a simmer and add the chocolate. Reduce the heat to low and use a hand mixer fitted with the beater attachment on medium-low to beat until very smooth. Off the heat, blend in the Grand Marnier or syrup. Cool before serving.

If the sauce is stored in the refrigerator, it will firm up. To soften, microwave on high power for 30 to 40 seconds and stir until smooth.

MIXER,

STAND

I started my catering business making meringue mushrooms for Bloomingdale's. The recipe called for 12 jumbo egg whites and 5 cups of granulated sugar to be whipped together for about 40 minutes or until the mixture had acquired the consistency of wet cement. I went through four hand mixers, each one dying a more spectacular death than the next, before I wised up to the fact that any profit I was making in mushrooms was being squandered on replacement mixers.

Buying my first heavy-duty KitchenAid mixer was a big step for me. It was my first major appliance (the usual suspects such as a stove and refrigerator had come with the apartment). This was the Big Mama of mixers—gleaming white and heavier than the air conditioner I gave up in order to buy it, this mixer took up almost all my meager counter space. This was an investment that would take thousands of mushrooms to pay off.

It transformed my kitchen and my cooking. Every time I run my hand over the top and feel its smooth, cool, solid heft, or lift the heavy-duty stainless steel bowl by its handle, or hear the motor engage without hesitation, I feel like a pro. Needless to say, my meringue mushroom production was revolutionized—egg whites whipped into a froth in seconds and sugar was beaten in and dissolved before I could say, "hold stiff peaks."

I bought that mixer in 1972. It has paid for itself a thousand times over and has commanded a place of honor in every kitchen I've had since then. I see that the newer models come in designer colors and offer loads of attachments—sort of like putting a pearl necklace on a draft horse, if you ask me. When you are ready to make the move from "hand" to "stand," go all the way and get the best—you'll never regret it.

MIXER, STAND

GENERAL DESCRIPTION

WHAT DOES IT DO? • Q: How does an existentialist cook order a custom stand mixer? A: Make me one with everything. A stand mixer is closest to being a universal cooking appliance than any other. While food processors can mix batters, they do so without beating air into the mixture. The principle jobs of stand mixers are mixing and aerating, such as for cake batters, egg whites, and whipped cream. The more air combined, the lighter and fluffier batters will be, adding volume to the finished product. Do not use a food processor when you really want to use a mixer.

The motors in stand mixers are more powerful than those of hand mixers and are thus able to work harder. Plus they stand on their own feet and do not need to be held above the food by the strength in the cook's arm. To increase their utility even further, most models have a wide array of auxiliary attachments, including those that turn a stand mixer into a food processor, blender, grain mill, can opener, sausage stuffer, pasta extruder, citrus juicer, and juice extractor.

WHY DO I NEED THIS? • Heavier duty stand mixers are perfect for many jobs, from creaming butter and sugar together and working with mixtures that must have air combined with them, to kneading heavy bread dough. If baking a wide range of things, from bread to chocolate chip cookies to lemon meringue pies, a stand mixer will make life much easier.

HOW DOES IT WORK? • The inside of a stand mixer is a little like a tiny machine shop with a motor turning gears and shafts. As with a hand mixer, when turned on by means of a switch, a multiple speed motor turns a shaft with a gear or several gears at the end of it. The last gear in the train meshes with another gear at a right angle, bending the rotational motion downward from its original forward-pointing orientation. Some models are bigger and stronger versions of a hand mixer and are configured just like them except for their stand. In fact, some of these can be detached from their stands and used as a hand mixer. But others are very different in how they work.

For these devices, the rotary motion usually turns a primary attachment inside a bowl that is affixed to the mixer. The bowls are usually metal or glass and are either fixed in place or can rotate to help with thorough mixing. Standard attachments typically include a paddle, which is usually not one solid piece of metal but rather a lacier though heavy-cast metal device; a balloon whisk; and a dough hook. Because of the gear mechanisms, the attachment does not just turn in a circle but in a more complex pattern. Think of the attachment as the planet Earth. It rotates on its axis just as Earth does to make day and night. Then the revolving attachment spins around in a wider circle as the Earth revolves around the Sun. The multidirectional motion of the beater whips air into the food in the bowl.

The auxiliary attachments connect to the motor shaft directly and are driven from it head-on, or the rotational motion is bent upward by means of another gear mechanism. For a few models, the motion is transferred to another place in the appliance by means of a belt, just like the fan belt turns the fan in your car.

The motor on some stand mixers tilts with the attachment connected, so the contents of the bowl can be more easily tended. Yet others lower the bowl into a position away from the attachments to let you work in it. Whichever way your mixer works, turn it off before you tend to it. For obvious reasons, do not stick your fingers into the bowl of a mixer while it is turned on. Do not be tempted to do this with a rubber scraper or other utensil either. You will destroy the utensil and ruin the mixer.

CARE AND MAINTENANCE • The best way to ensure a heavy-duty stand mixer will last a lifetime is to make sure not to overheat the motor. Feel it with your hand and, if it is getting too warm, turn it off and let it rest for a while. Heat buildup inside a motor can burn the motor out. By the time you can smell it, it is usually too late.

The attachments and work bowl are typically dishwasher safe and the stand and motor housing can be wiped off with a soft damp cloth.

WHICH IS RIGHT FOR ME? • Once you are convinced of the need for a stand mixer, choosing one is the fun part. Know which features are necessary and

which would be good just in case. Larger capacity models might be more attractive if making many loaves of bread at a time or if making wedding cakes from recipes that would not fit smaller capacity models. Some stand mixers have two sizes of mixing bowls. The heavy-duty mixers, however, only have one size bowl per model. If making bread recipes that call for 6 to 8 cups of flour, then a larger mixing bowl is required. If versatility is a key, then find a stand mixer that has lots of auxiliary attachments. The type of attachments needed will influence your decision since not all attachments are available with every mixer. A dough hook is necessary for baking bread.

Next, think about how much power the mixer motor should have. Stiffer batters and doughs require heavier duty motors than lighter recipes. Slower speeds are necessary for mixing dry ingredients without creating fallout all over the kitchen counter, and a wide range of speeds gives added flexibility.

Stand mixers vary in weight, too. Heavier models are hard to carry from place to place, but the weight keeps it from dancing across the counter when you are kneading heavy doughs.

COMMENTS • Belt-driven attachments can be prone to slippage over time, thus decreasing the power delivered from the motor.

STAND MIXER TIPS

- *Before whipping egg whites into a meringue, sprinkle a teaspoon of salt and a tablespoon of vinegar into the work bowl. Scour the inside of the bowl with this mixture and brush out the excess salt with a paper towel, leaving the residue behind. Your egg whites will beat into a more stable foam.*

- *Egg whites and whole eggs should be at room temperature when beaten to get maximum volume.*

- *Chill heavy cream as well as the bowl and whipping attachment before whipping to get maximum volume.*

- *When beating a mixture that will increase in volume, like egg whites or whipping cream, make sure to leave room for expansion in the work bowl.*

- *Using the dough hook to knead heavy yeasted doughs may make your stand mixer walk across the counter. Situate it away from the edge of the counter and keep an eye on it to ensure it does not walk off onto the floor. Heavier stand mixers will be less likely to do this counter waltz.*

- *When mixing heavy doughs, keep one hand on the top of the mixer to steady it and to monitor the amount of heat thrown off by the motor. When the appliance feels hot, turn it off. If you smell a burning odor, turn it off.*

- *Stir dry ingredients at a slow speed. When adding dry ingredients to a mixture in the work bowl, do it at slow speed; the dust cloud can get into the motor and gum up the works.*

- *Start mixing at the slowest speeds and gradually increase to the desired stirring speed.*

- *Clean the appliance and all attachments well after using.*

- *Never attempt to clean ingredients from the beaters while they are in motion.*

- *You can skin toasted hazelnuts by placing them in the mixing bowl and using the flat paddle or regular mixing attachment to move them around the bowl on low speed.*

- *When mixing ingredients that tend to splatter, drape a dishcloth over the top of the machine to protect countertops and walls.*

RECIPES

CHEESE SOUFFLÉ

Yield: 4 servings

While there is an aerobic benefit to whipping egg whites by hand, there is no question that when it comes to whipping egg whites by machine, the stand mixer is king. Once you've got those whites whipped, what better use for them than this lovely cheese soufflé.

$^1/_4$ CUP ($^1/_2$ STICK) BUTTER

3 TABLESPOONS FRESHLY GRATED PARMESAN
CHEESE

$^1/_4$ CUP ALL-PURPOSE FLOUR

1 $^1/_4$ CUPS MILK

6 EXTRA LARGE EGGS, SEPARATED, AT ROOM
TEMPERATURE

1 CUP GRATED SHARP CHEDDAR CHEESE

$^1/_2$ TEASPOON SALT

$^1/_2$ TEASPOON FRESHLY GROUND BLACK
PEPPER

Preheat the oven to 400°F with the rack in the upper third but not the highest position. Use 1 tablespoon of the butter to generously coat the inside of a 10-cup soufflé mold or high-rimmed baking dish. Dust with the grated Parmesan cheese. Set aside.

Melt the remaining 3 tablespoons of butter in a 2-quart saucepan over medium-high heat. Whisk in the flour and cook for 2 minutes, stirring constantly. Whisk in the milk and continue stirring, bringing the mixture to a boil. Cook for 1 minute, then remove from the heat and immediately stir in the egg yolks and Cheddar cheese. Add the salt and pepper.

Beat the egg whites in the bowl of an electric stand mixer fitted with the whisk attachment on high speed until they form stiff but not dry peaks. Fold a third of the whites into the cheese mixture to lighten it, then fold all of the whites in, manipulating the batter as little as possible to avoid deflating the egg whites.

Pour and scrape the mixture evenly into the prepared mold and bake until the top has risen and is browned, about 30 minutes. Serve immediately by spooning onto small plates.

SAVORY CHEESE BISCOTTI

Yield: 60 biscotti

These savory cookies can be served instead of cheese and crackers with a glass of wine or used as an afternoon snack. They also make great picnic fare.

continued

¼ CUP (½ STICK) UNSALTED BUTTER, AT
    ROOM TEMPERATURE

¼ CUP VEGETABLE SHORTENING

2 TABLESPOONS SUGAR

2 TABLESPOONS TOMATO PASTE

1 CUP FRESHLY GRATED PARMESAN CHEESE

1 TO 2 TEASPOONS DRIED ITALIAN HERBS (USE
    A SINGLE HERB OR COMBINATION OF
    ROSEMARY, BASIL, PARSLEY, AND/OR
    OREGANO), TO YOUR TASTE

2 TEASPOONS BAKING POWDER

½ TEASPOON SALT

4 LARGE EGGS

2½ CUPS ALL-PURPOSE FLOUR

1½ CUPS PECAN OR WALNUT HALVES,
    BLANCHED SLIVERED ALMONDS, SKINNED
    HAZELNUTS, PINE NUTS, OR PISTACHIOS,
    TOASTED (SEE NOTE, PAGE 131)

Preheat the oven to 375°F with the rack in the center position. In the large bowl of an electric stand mixer fitted with the flat beater, beat together the butter, shortening, sugar, tomato paste, cheese, herbs, baking powder, and salt on medium-high speed until well combined and fairly smooth. Add the eggs one at a time, beating well after each addition and scraping down the bowl midway through. Mix in the flour until you have a cohesive dough. Add the nuts, mixing until they're well distributed throughout the dough.

Transfer the dough to a lightly floured work surface. Divide it into 3 equal pieces and shape each into a 10-inch-long log. Transfer each log to a parchment-paper-lined or lightly greased heavy-duty baking sheet, spacing them about 3 inches apart; you may need to use two baking sheets. Wet your fingers and pat the logs into smooth-topped rectangles 10 inches long by 2½ inches wide by ⅞ inch thick. Bake until they're beginning to brown around the edges, 20 to 25 minutes.

Remove from the oven and allow to cool for 30 minutes. Lower the oven temperature to 300°F. Gently transfer the logs to a cutting surface and use a serrated knife to cut them on the diagonal into ½-inch-thick slices. Because of the nuts and the nature of the dough, the biscotti at this point are prone to crumbling; just be sure to use a slow, gentle sawing motion and accept the fact that some bits and pieces will break off. Carefully transfer the slices to a parchment-paper-lined (makes cleanup easier) or ungreased baking sheet. Bake for 20 minutes, then remove from the oven, quickly turn them over, and bake until they're very dry and beginning to brown, another 20 minutes. Remove from the oven, cool completely, and store in an airtight container.

ALMOND BISCOTTI

Yield: 84 biscotti

This recipe celebrates the sweet, toasted flavor of almonds in a crisp cookie that was made to be dunked in a cup of coffee.

4 TO 4¹/2 CUPS UNSIFTED ALL-PURPOSE FLOUR

1 TABLESPOON BAKING POWDER

¹/2 TEASPOON SALT

1 CUP (2 STICKS) UNSALTED BUTTER, AT ROOM TEMPERATURE

2 CUPS SUGAR

3 LARGE EGGS PLUS 1 LARGE EGG YOLK

2 TEASPOONS PURE ALMOND EXTRACT

1¹/2 CUPS WHOLE ALMONDS (WITH OR WITHOUT SKINS), TOASTED (PAGE 131)

1 LARGE EGG WHITE BEATEN WITH 2 TABLESPOONS WATER

1 TABLESPOON GROUND CINNAMON MIXED WITH ¹/3 CUP SUGAR

Preheat the oven to 325°F with the rack in the center position. Lightly grease 2 heavy-duty baking sheets or line them with parchment paper. Combine 4 cups of the flour, baking powder, and salt in a medium-size bowl and set aside.

In the bowl of an electric stand mixer fitted with the flat beater, beat the butter and sugar together on medium speed until light and fluffy. Add the whole eggs and egg yolk one at a time, beating well after each addition.

Reduce the mixer speed to low, then gradually add the flour to the butter mixture and beat until well blended. Add the almond and nuts and mix until well blended. If the dough is too soft to shape, stir in some of the remaining ¹/2 cup flour.

Divide the dough into 6 equal pieces. Shape each piece into an 8 × 2-inch roll and place on the prepared baking sheets 2 inches apart. Brush with the egg white glaze and sprinkle generously with the cinnamon sugar. Bake the rolls until firm and golden brown, about 30 minutes.

Transfer the logs from the baking sheet to a cutting board. Reduce the oven temperature to 250°F. Using a serrated knife, with a light sawing motion cut each roll into ¹/2-inch-thick slices on a diagonal. Arrange the slices cut side down on the baking sheets. Bake the slices, turning once, until their tops are dry, about 15 minutes. Cool the slices on a wire rack and store in an airtight container.

Old-fashioned Peanut Butter Cookies

Yield: About 3 dozen cookies

Send these to camp, school, the office, or use them to fill your cookie jar. No matter where you put them, they won't last long.

2¹⁄₂ CUPS ALL-PURPOSE FLOUR

1 TEASPOON BAKING POWDER

SCANT ¹⁄₂ TEASPOON SALT

2 LARGE EGGS

1 CUP (2 STICKS) BUTTER, AT ROOM
    TEMPERATURE

1 CUP CHUNKY PEANUT BUTTER

1 CUP FIRMLY PACKED DARK BROWN SUGAR

1 CUP GRANULATED SUGAR

2 TEASPOONS PURE VANILLA EXTRACT

Preheat the oven to 375°F and position two racks toward the middle of the oven. Line two heavy-duty baking sheets with aluminum foil or parchment paper and apply a light coating of nonstick vegetable spray. Sift together the flour, baking powder, and salt and set aside.

In the bowl of an electric stand mixer fitted with the flat beater, mix the eggs, butter, peanut butter, both sugars, and vanilla on medium speed until well combined. On low speed add the flour and mix until fully combined.

Roll the dough into 1-inch balls and place on the prepared baking sheet 1 inch apart. Indent the tops lightly with the tines of a fork. Bake until the tops are lightly browned, 12 to 14 minutes. Cool the cookies on a wire rack before eating or storing in an airtight container.

Mega-Cookies

Yield: 4¹⁄₂ dozen cookies

These are the kitchen sink of cookies. Kids love them, but grown-ups find them irresistible as well.

1 CUP (2 STICKS) BUTTER OR MARGARINE, AT ROOM TEMPERATURE

1 CUP GRANULATED SUGAR

1 CUP FIRMLY PACKED DARK BROWN SUGAR

2 LARGE EGGS

1 1/2 TEASPOONS PURE VANILLA EXTRACT

1 TABLESPOON PURE MAPLE SYRUP

1 CUP ALL-PURPOSE FLOUR

1/2 CUP WHOLE WHEAT FLOUR

1/2 CUP GRAHAM CRACKER CRUMBS

1 TEASPOON BAKING SODA

1 TEASPOON BAKING POWDER

1/2 TEASPOON SALT

3 CUPS QUICK-COOKING OATS

ONE 12-OUNCE PACKAGE SEMISWEET CHOCOLATE CHIPS

ONE 4-OUNCE BAR MILK CHOCOLATE CANDY, COARSELY CHOPPED

1/2 CUP COARSELY CHOPPED WALNUTS

1/2 CUP COARSELY CHOPPED CASHEWS

1/2 CUP COARSELY CHOPPED PECANS

Preheat the oven to 350°F. Line two heavy-duty baking sheets with parchment paper or aluminum foil and apply a light coating of nonstick vegetable spray. In the bowl of an electric stand mixer fitted with the flat beater, cream the butter on medium-high speed until smooth. Stop and scrape down the bowl. Add the sugars and cream on medium speed for 2 minutes. Stop and scrape down the bowl. Add the eggs, vanilla, and maple syrup and mix on medium speed until combined. Stop and scrape down the bowl. Add the flours, graham cracker crumbs, baking soda and powder, and salt and mix on low speed for 1 minute. Add the oats and mix on low speed until thoroughly blended, 1 to 1 1/2 minutes. Add the chocolate and nuts and mix on low speed just until blended, about 30 seconds.

Drop the cookie dough by the rounded tablespoonfuls onto the prepared sheets 1 inch apart. Bake until the tops look dry, 8 to 10 minutes. Cool completely on wire racks.

COCOA MERINGUE KISSES

Yield: 24 cookies

These melt-in-your-mouth confections are as light as a cloud and a cinch to make. They are dry weather cookies, though, and will tend to be on the sticky side if made in humid conditions. This recipe calls for cocoa that has not been Dutch processed, which tends to burn more easily than regular cocoa. A good brand to use for this is Hershey's.

½ CUP EGG WHITES (ABOUT 4 EXTRA LARGE), AT ROOM TEMPERATURE	3 TABLESPOONS UNSWEETENED COCOA POWDER (NOT DUTCH PROCESSED), SIFTED
PINCH OF CREAM OF TARTAR	1 CUP SEMISWEET CHOCOLATE CHIPS
1 CUP SUGAR	

Preheat the oven to 275°F with the rack in the upper third but not highest position. Line one large or two smaller heavy-duty baking sheets with aluminum foil or parchment paper.

Place the egg whites and cream of tartar in the bowl of an electric stand mixer fitted with the whisk attachment and beat the egg whites on medium-high speed until foamy. Increase the speed to high and gradually add the sugar, beating until the meringue is glossy and holds stiff but not dry peaks. On low speed, add the cocoa, mixing only until combined. Remove the bowl from the mixer and use a rubber scraper to fold in the chocolate chips.

Use a tablespoon to drop the mixture in high mounds about 2 inches across and at least 1 inch apart on the prepared baking sheet(s). Bake the cookies for 1 hour. They should not color; if they begin to brown, reduce the oven temperature to 250°F. At the end of the baking time, turn off the oven and allow the cookies to remain with the oven door shut for another hour.

Lift the kisses off the foil or paper and allow to cool completely. Store in a covered container at room temperature.

COCONUT MACAROONS

Yield: 36 to 40 macaroons

Nothing beats the taste of homemade coconut macaroons. The store-bought kind are always too sweet and made with stuff that looks like, but never tastes like, fresh coconut. Make your own, and you'll be spoiled, just like me. Look in the health food store for unsweetened coconut.

4 EXTRA LARGE EGG WHITES, AT ROOM TEMPERATURE	1 TEASPOON PURE VANILLA EXTRACT
1 1/4 CUPS SUGAR	3 CUPS UNSWEETENED SHREDDED COCONUT
PINCH OF SALT	

Preheat the oven to 375°F with the rack in the center position. Line two heavy-duty baking sheets with parchment paper or aluminum foil and spray them with nonstick vegetable spray.

Place the egg whites, sugar, and salt in the bowl of an electric stand mixer fitted with the whisk attachment and beat on high speed until they form stiff but not dry peaks. On low speed, beat in the vanilla, then remove the bowl from the machine and fold in the coconut by hand.

Use 2 teaspoons dipped in cold water to form the dough into 2-inch mounds and place them about 1 inch apart on the prepared sheets. Bake the sheets one at a time until the cookies are light brown, about 15 minutes. Cool completely on wire racks before serving or storing in airtight containers at room temperature.

BLUEBERRY BUCKLE

Yield: 9 servings

Buckles are an American dessert dating back to Revolutionary days. While they can be made with any berry you choose, my favorite choice is the tiny wild blueberries from Maine.

For the topping:

1/4 CUP GRANULATED SUGAR

1/4 CUP FIRMLY PACKED DARK BROWN SUGAR

1/4 CUP ALL-PURPOSE FLOUR

1/4 CUP (1/2 STICK) BUTTER OR MARGARINE

1/2 TEASPOON GROUND CINNAMON

For the buckle:

2 CUPS ALL-PURPOSE FLOUR

2 TEASPOONS BAKING POWDER

1/2 TEASPOON SALT

3/4 CUP GRANULATED SUGAR

1/4 CUP (1/2 STICK) BUTTER OR MARGARINE, AT ROOM TEMPERATURE

2 LARGE EGGS

1 TEASPOON PURE VANILLA EXTRACT

1/2 CUP BUTTERMILK

2 1/2 CUPS FRESH OR FROZEN BLUEBERRIES (WASHED AND DRIED ON PAPER TOWELS IF FRESH)

continued

Preheat the oven to 375°F with the rack in the center position. Lightly grease a 9-inch square baking pan. With your fingers or a fork mash the topping ingredients together in a small bowl until crumbly. Set aside.

To make the buckle, sift together the flour, baking powder, and salt in a small bowl. Set aside.

In the bowl of an electric stand mixer fitted with the flat beater, beat together the sugar and butter on low speed to combine, then increase the speed to medium-high and beat until smooth and fluffy. Beat in the eggs one at a time, then the vanilla. On low speed, add half the flour mixture, then half the buttermilk, then repeat with the remainder of each, mixing to fully combine each time. Stir in the berries.

Spread the batter evenly in the prepared pan and sprinkle with the topping. Bake until a cake tester or toothpick inserted in the center comes out clean and dry, 25 to 30 minutes. Cool the cake in the pan on a wire rack before cutting into squares.

MY FAVORITE CARROT CAKE

Yield: One 10 × 6-inch cake

Everyone has his or her favorite carrot cake, and this one's mine. Really dense, moist, and slightly chewy, with the carrots sort of hidden so you aren't reminded that what you're really eating is a vegetable concoction for dessert. The cream cheese icing is fun to swirl—you'll feel like Betty Crocker.

For the cake:

2 CUPS ALL-PURPOSE FLOUR, MEASURED AFTER SIFTING

2 TEASPOONS BAKING POWDER

1 1/2 TEASPOONS BAKING SODA

1 TEASPOON SALT

2 TEASPOONS GROUND CINNAMON

1 TEASPOON GROUND GINGER

1/2 TEASPOON GROUND NUTMEG

1/3 CUP FIRMLY PACKED DARK BROWN SUGAR

1 1/2 CUPS VEGETABLE OIL

4 LARGE EGGS, BEATEN

2 CUPS GRATED CARROTS

ONE 8-OUNCE CAN CRUSHED PINEAPPLE, DRAINED

1/2 CUP COARSELY CHOPPED PECANS

For the frosting:

¹/₂ CUP (1 STICK) UNSALTED BUTTER, AT
    ROOM TEMPERATURE

ONE 8-OUNCE PACKAGE CREAM CHEESE (DO
    NOT USE WHIPPED CREAM CHEESE), AT
    ROOM TEMPERATURE

2 TEASPOONS PURE VANILLA EXTRACT

1 POUND CONFECTIONERS' SUGAR, SIFTED

1 CUP SWEETENED SHREDDED COCONUT FOR
    GARNISH (OPTIONAL)

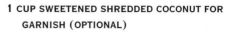

Preheat the oven to 350°F with the rack in the center position. Generously coat a 10-inch tube pan with vegetable shortening or butter. Dust with flour and shake out the excess.

Sift together the flour, baking powder and soda, salt, and spices into a small bowl and set aside.

In the large bowl of an electric stand mixer fitted with the flat beater, beat together the sugar, oil, and eggs on medium speed to combine. On low speed add half the flour mixture and mix to combine, then add the other half and mix. Finally, add the carrots, pineapple, and nuts and continue to mix on low speed only until the ingredients are completely blended.

Pour the mixture into the prepared pan and level off the top with a rubber scraper. Bake until a cake tester or toothpick inserted in the center comes out clean and dry, 50 to 60 minutes. If the cake seems to be browning too quickly, cover it loosely with a piece of aluminum foil. Let the cake cool in the pan for 15 minutes before inverting it onto a wire rack to finish cooling. Cool completely before frosting.

To prepare the frosting, in the large bowl of an electric stand mixer fitted with the flat beater, cream the butter together with the cream cheese and vanilla on medium speed. On low speed add the confectioners' sugar and, when the sugar is moistened, increase the speed to high and beat until light and fluffy, 2 to 3 minutes. Frost the top and sides of the cooled cake with the icing and sprinkle with the coconut.

BROWN SUGAR–CREAM CHEESE POUND CAKE

Yield: One 10-inch tube cake (12 servings)

This is not your average pound cake. Between the cream cheese and brown sugar (which are not your average pound cake ingredients) we have created something mighty special. Yes, this is not diet food, but 1 small slice will feed your sweet tooth.

3 CUPS SIFTED ALL-PURPOSE FLOUR

1 1/2 TEASPOONS BAKING POWDER

1/2 TEASPOON SALT

1 1/2 CUPS (3 STICKS) UNSALTED BUTTER, AT ROOM TEMPERATURE

ONE 8-OUNCE PACKAGE CREAM CHEESE (DO NOT USE WHIPPED CREAM CHEESE), AT ROOM TEMPERATURE

2 CUPS FIRMLY PACKED DARK BROWN SUGAR

2 TEASPOONS PURE VANILLA EXTRACT

6 LARGE OR EXTRA LARGE EGGS

CONFECTIONERS' SUGAR

Preheat the oven to 325°F with the rack in the center position. Coat a 12-cup tube or bundt pan with butter and dust it with flour, shaking out the excess. Sift together the flour, baking powder, and salt in a medium-size bowl and set aside.

Place the butter and cream cheese in the bowl of an electric stand mixer fitted with the flat beater and beat together on medium speed until smooth. On low speed mix in the sugar, then increase the speed to medium-high and beat until the mixture is light and fluffy. Reduce the speed to medium and beat in the vanilla, then the eggs 1 at a time, stopping to scrape down the sides of the bowl. With the mixer on low speed, gradually add the flour mixture, mixing only until combined.

Pour the batter evenly into the prepared pan. Bake until a cake tester or toothpick inserted in the center comes out clean and dry, 70 to 80 minutes. Cool in the pan 10 to 15 minutes, then unmold onto a wire rack to cool completely. Dust lightly with sifted confectioners' sugar.

Variation: Substitute 1/4 teaspoon lemon oil or 1 teaspoon pure lemon extract for the vanilla and add 1/3 cup poppy seeds.

SPONGE CAKE

Yield: One 10-inch tube cake (12 servings)

We serve this simple cake at Passover time when flour and flour products are not allowed in the house. It makes a light and lovely dessert anytime, especially topped with strawberries and a dab of whipped cream.

$\frac{1}{3}$ CUP POTATO STARCH (AVAILABLE IN THE BABY FOOD SECTION OF THE SUPERMARKET)

1 CUP CAKE MEAL (AVAILABLE IN THE KOSHER FOODS SECTION OF THE SUPERMARKET)

12 LARGE OR EXTRA LARGE EGGS, SEPARATED, AT ROOM TEMPERATURE OR SLIGHTLY WARMER

GRATED ZEST OF 1 LEMON

GRATED ZEST OF 1 ORANGE

1$\frac{3}{4}$ CUPS SUGAR

JUICE OF 1 LEMON

JUICE OF 1 ORANGE

Preheat the oven to 350°F with the rack in lower third but not the lowest position. Line the bottom of a 12-cup (10-inch) tube pan with parchment paper. The rest of the pan is ungreased. In a wide mesh strainer set over a small bowl, sift the potato starch together with the cake meal and set aside.

Place the egg yolks, citrus zests, and 1 cup of the sugar in the bowl of an electric stand mixer fitted with the flat beater and beat on low speed until the sugar is thoroughly combined, then increase the speed to high and beat until the mixture is very thick and lemon colored.

In a clean mixer bowl, using the whisk attachment, beat the egg whites on medium speed until foamy. Add the remaining ¾ cup of sugar slowly, then increase the speed to high and beat until the whites form stiff but not dry peaks. Fold the whites into the yolk mixture. Gently fold in the cake meal mixture alternately with the combined juices until you can no longer see any dry areas.

Turn the batter into the prepared cake pan. Bake until a cake tester or toothpick inserted in the center comes out clean and dry, about 1 hour. Cool upside down in the pan before unmolding and serving.

HEAVENLY CHOCOLATE ROLL

Yield: 12 to 16 servings

This is the birthday cake of choice in our household. I love it because it can be made weeks in advance and frozen. Don't panic if the cake splits and cracks while it's being rolled—any blemishes can be artfully disguised with chocolate sauce and whipped cream.

For the cake:

8 OUNCES SEMISWEET CHOCOLATE, CHOPPED

8 EXTRA LARGE EGGS, SEPARATED, AT ROOM TEMPERATURE

1 ½ CUPS SUGAR

¼ CUP ALL-PURPOSE FLOUR

PINCH OF SALT

UNSWEETENED COCOA POWDER

For the filling:

2 PINTS PREMIUM ICE CREAM, SOFTENED IN THE MICROWAVE

For the topping:

HOT FUDGE SAUCE

WHIPPED CREAM

Preheat the oven to 350°F. Grease a 10 × 15-inch jelly roll pan, then line it with parchment paper and grease the paper or spray it with nonstick vegetable oil spray. Set aside. Melt the chocolate either in the microwave oven on high power at 30-second intervals, stirring between each interval, or in the top of a double boiler over gently simmering water. Take care not to burn the chocolate or let water or steam get in it. Cool slightly.

In the bowl of an electric stand mixer fitted with the flat beater on high speed, beat the egg yolks until frothy, then reduce the speed to medium and gradually beat in the sugar until the mixture is very thick and light in color. On low speed mix the melted chocolate into the yolk mixture, then the flour.

Transfer the chocolate mixture to a large bowl. Wash the mixer bowl with hot, soapy water and dry it well. Place the egg whites and salt in the bowl and beat on high speed using the whisk attachment until the whites form stiff but not dry peaks. Carefully fold the whites into the chocolate mixture until there are no white streaks showing.

Pour the mixture into the prepared pan, spreading it evenly with a rubber scraper. Bake until the edges just begin to pull away from the sides of the pan, 15 to 17 minutes.

Set the pan on a wire rack, cover the top of the cake with a slightly damp kitchen towel, and allow to cool to room temperature, at least 1 hour. Sift a layer of cocoa evenly over the top of the cake, then cover with two long overlapping strips of plastic wrap. Cover with another baking sheet and invert. Carefully peel off the parchment. Spread softened ice cream over the chocolate roll, leaving a 1-inch unfilled border around the edges and, using the plastic wrap underneath as a guide, roll the cake like a jelly roll. (Rolling from the long side gives an elegant slender roll that can be cut into 14 to 16 small slices. Rolling from the short side produces a shorter, fatter roll and bigger slices.) Slide seam down onto a board or platter. Wrap in the plastic wrap and a layer of aluminum foil and freeze for several hours.

To serve, use a sharp serrated knife to slice the cake into $1\frac{1}{2}$-inch-thick slices and top with hot fudge sauce and whipped cream.

"FORGET IT" MERINGUE TORTE

Yield: 12 or more servings

The stand mixer, fitted with its whisk attachment, is the perfect appliance for beating air and sugar into egg whites to turn them into fluffy, lighter-than-a-cloud meringue. A squeaky clean bowl and an equally clean beater are the first tricks to getting the most volume out of the whites (any fat or oil residue will coat the egg whites and inhibit the size of the air bubbles). Starting with the egg whites slightly warm (70°F) will also help the sugar melt faster, thus adding to the structure. To this end, before cracking the eggs, dunk them briefly in a pan of hot water just until they no longer feel cold. The third trick to success is to use superfine sugar, which dissolves faster than the regular kind. You can buy superfine sugar or make it in the food processor simply by using the metal blade to grind granulated sugar into a finer powder.

Conversely, whipped cream needs to be very cold to get the proper volume of air into it. This is why it's smart to chill the mixing bowl (preferably metal), the cream, and the beater before making the whipped cream.

This cake is "forgotten" in the oven overnight. If you are forgetful, put a sign on the oven door to make sure you don't preheat the oven for another recipe without removing the cake first.

continued

MELTED BUTTER FOR PREPARING THE PAN

1$\frac{1}{2}$ CUPS EGG WHITES (ABOUT 10 LARGE
    EGGS), AT ROOM TEMPERATURE

$\frac{1}{4}$ TEASPOON CREAM OF TARTAR

2$\frac{1}{2}$ CUPS GRANULATED SUGAR

1 TEASPOON PURE VANILLA EXTRACT

$\frac{1}{2}$ TEASPOON PURE ALMOND EXTRACT

For the raspberry sauce:

THREE 10-OUNCE PACKAGES FROZEN

RASPBERRIES, THAWED

$\frac{1}{2}$ CUP GRANULATED SUGAR

2 TABLESPOONS KIRSCH OR FRAMBOISE
    (OPTIONAL)

To assemble:

2 CUPS COLD HEAVY CREAM

$\frac{1}{3}$ CUP CONFECTIONERS' SUGAR, SIFTED

Preheat the oven to 425°F with the rack in the upper third but not very highest position. Brush the insides and stem of an angel food cake pan with the melted butter.

Add the egg whites to the bowl of an electric stand mixer fitted with the whisk attachment and start beating on medium speed until the whites are frothy. Add the cream of tartar and continue beating. Gradually add the sugar, beating constantly on high speed. Add the vanilla and almond and beat until the mixture is very stiff and has a glossy sheen.

Spoon and scrape the meringue into the prepared pan, packing and smoothing it down as you go. When all the meringue has been added to the pan, smooth over the top. Place the pan in the oven and turn it off. Let the torte stay there overnight. Do not open the door until you are ready to serve the dish.

When the torte in the cake pan is removed, it may—and probably will— look like a caved-in disaster. Not to worry. It will be frosted with whipped cream. Push up on the removable bottom of the pan. Using a knife, slice around the top to cut away the crust. Save all the crumbs. Slide a knife between the bottom of the cake and the tin bottom. Loosen the cake around the cylinder with a small knife. Unmold the cake onto a serving plate.

You can make the raspberry sauce up to 3 days ahead of time and store it in a tightly closed container in the refrigerator. Place the raspberries, sugar, and kirsch in the work bowl of a food processor fitted with the metal blade and process until smooth, then press the mixture through a wire strainer fitted over a bowl to remove the seeds.

Just before serving, beat the heavy cream in the bowl of an electric stand mixer fitted with the whisk attachment on high speed, adding the confectioners' sugar. Beat until firm peaks form. Spoon the whipped cream onto the cake and smooth it over the top and sides. Crumble the reserved crust to make crumbs and sprinkle these around the sides and on top of the cake, pressing gently to make the crumbs adhere. Don't worry about getting it even—it's not supposed to be.

To serve the cake, cut it with a sharp serrated knife. Spoon a generous puddle of the sauce on the bottom of a dessert dish. Gently place a wedge of cake on top, drizzle with a little more sauce, and serve.

CHOCOLATE CLOUD

Yield: 6 servings

This very dark, sophisticated dessert is like a fallen soufflé. Not too sweet and not overly rich, it's perfectly complemented by the kirsch-flavored whipped cream served on the side. Additional good news is that it is made without any fat (other than the small amount of cocoa butter found in the unsweetened cocoa). So if you don't eat the whipped cream, your diet is intact.

7 LARGE EGG WHITES

²/₃ CUP SUPERFINE SUGAR (SEE THE DIRECTIONS BELOW FOR MAKING YOUR OWN SUPERFINE SUGAR)

³/₄ CUP UNSWEETENED COCOA POWDER

1 HEAPING TEASPOON GROUND CINNAMON

1 CUP HEAVY CREAM, WHIPPED TO SOFT PEAKS WITH 1 TO 2 TABLESPOONS KIRSCH AND 2 TABLESPOONS CONFECTIONERS' SUGAR

Preheat the oven to 325°F with the rack in the center position. Butter a 6- or 7-cup mold. The best kind to use is a steamed pudding mold with a central funnel, but a ring mold or kugelhupf will do.

In the bowl of an electric stand mixer fitted with the whisk attachment, whip the egg whites on high speed until they form stiff but not dry peaks. If you overbeat them, it's harder to fold them into the other ingredients. In a small bowl, mix together the sugar, cocoa, and cinnamon, then sprinkle the mixture onto the egg whites. Fold them together gently but thoroughly. A large metal spoon or a wide flexible rubber scraper is the best implement for this operation.

Fill the mold with the prepared mixture. Stand it, uncovered, in a pan filled with hot water to reach halfway up the mold or as close as possible to that height without floating the mold. Bake 45 to 50 minutes; it will be firm, but will still wiggle slightly when moved. Cool completely in the pan (the top will sink a bit) before turning out onto a serving plate. Serve with the flavored whipped cream.

Note: To make your own superfine sugar, you can run regular granulated white sugar through a food processor fitted with the metal blade. Then you can add the cocoa and cinnamon and process to mix.

R I C E

COOKER

Even though my mother is an exceptional cook, I grew up eating Minute Rice. How this substandard faux food ever found its way into her kitchen was a mystery to me—until, as a new bride, I tried cooking rice myself. Perfect rice was a hit-or-miss experience more often than not. Either it was scorched on the bottom, al dente to the point of being unchewable, or overcooked to mush. I rarely served rice for company since it took so much last-minute attention if I hoped to serve it hot. While I never did resort to the instant fix, rice wasn't appearing on our table as often as I would have liked.

That all changed when my eldest son spent his junior year of college in Taipei. He came home with a yen for rice—at every meal. Fortunately he also came home with a rice cooker, explaining that every kitchen in Taiwan had one. We were only slightly ahead of our time; now you'll find rice cookers in many American kitchens—including my mother's. No more Minute Rice for her.

GENERAL DESCRIPTION

WHAT DOES IT DO? • Rice is nice and easy! What Asian home cooks have known for years, the rest of the world is finally beginning to discover. This appliance cooks rice and/or other food in a metal container within a closed environment using moist heat from boiling liquids. Rice cookers are controlled by a device that senses when the rice is done cooking and switches automatically to a lower temperature to keep the rice warm without you watching over it constantly. And the variety of grains that you can cook in this appliance is endless.

WHY DO I NEED THIS? • Cooking quantities of rice and other grains used to take loads of attention on the part of the cook. If you stepped away too soon, the rice would be sticky or burned. This problem led to the creation of instant rice, an abomination that is unfit to eat. With a rice cooker, you can make rice for two to twenty people several hours ahead that is still perfect, hot, and fluffy when it is time to serve. There is no easier way to fulfill the grains segment of the food pyramid than by eating freshly made rice from your rice cooker. Rice cookers are also wonderful ways to make soups and steamed foods as well.

HOW DOES IT WORK? • Typically, these appliances consist of a heating unit set in a metal or plastic housing and a plastic or metal cooking chamber that can hold about 3 quarts. Generally 2 to 11 cups of rice can be cooked at one time. The cooking chamber sits inside the heating chamber. Rice is prepared for cooking by combining it with water directly in the cooking chamber. The amount of water and how quickly the rice absorbs it determines the cooking time. If steaming vegetables or seafood, the food is placed on a metal rack that sits at the bottom of the cooker, separating the food from the boiling water. All of these appliances have lids of either clear glass or metal.

In all cases, either the boiling liquid cooks the food directly, as in the case of rice, or the steam from the boiling liquid cooks the food. Condensation that collects on the lid drips down into a condensation chamber to avoid dripping water on your countertop. When the liquid water is completely boiled off, the temperature of the bottom of the rice cooker rises above 212°F, and the rice cooker knows that the food is done.

Once the appliance senses that the food is done, it will do one of several things. At a minimum, the heating element turns off. Some models make an audible signal and others have a light that turns on when the food is done. Yet other models will automatically switch to a lower warming setting to keep food warm for several hours.

CARE AND MAINTENANCE • Most heating units are not submersible, so do not put them in a sink full of water. Instead, wipe them off with a damp dishcloth when cooled. The cooking chambers are typically dishwasher safe, although if yours has a Teflon surface you run the risk of scratching it. Make sure the lid is dried and the condensation chamber is emptied before storing the rice cooker.

WHICH IS RIGHT FOR ME? • Most rice cookers are flexible in the amount of rice you can make in them, but giant rice cookers have a hard time making only 2 cups of rice at a time. Pick the size of rice cooker that will suit your daily needs and the occasional larger quantity for dinner parties or special occasions. A rice cooker that has some kind of audible indicator that it is done is very handy in a busy kitchen. Also, a unit that keeps the finished rice warm is great for preparing for company.

COMMENTS • Do not open the lid too often or some of the important steam that is needed for cooking will escape. Some units have a cooking chart as part of the heating unit to help you decide how much water to use for which kinds of food.

RICE COOKER TIPS

- *Place the rice pan in the cooker before adding the rice and water.*

- *Do not fill the rice cooker to the brim. Leave head room for the boiling water to have some place to expand.*

- *Generally, more water is needed to cook brown rice and wild rice than white rice.*

- *If your rice cooker pan does not have a nonstick surface, apply a light coating of nonstick vegetable oil spray to it before adding the rice or other ingredients.*

- *Be sure to leave plenty of room on all sides of the rice cooker when it is cooking so air can circulate. Also, make sure the appliance is not directly under kitchen cabinets so the steam does not damage them.*

- *If your rice or other foods are not cooked by the end of the cycle, allow the appliance to cool for several minutes, then restart it. Check after 15 minutes to see if the food is cooked.*

- *Even though most rice cookers have a "keep warm" setting, it's best to use the rice within an hour after it is finished cooking.*

- *Clean the cooker thoroughly after each use. Pay particular attention to the inside of the lid so debris will not collect that could interfere with the seal between the lid and the rice pan.*

- *Do not put the rice pan in the dishwasher or the nonstick coating will flake.*

RECIPES

WHITE RICE

Yield: 4 to 6 servings (3 cups)

There is a dizzying assortment of white rices from which to choose. For success in the rice cooker avoid precooked or instant rice. Choose one of the following: polished long-grain rice (such as Uncle Ben's Converted or Carolina brands) or a short-grain rice such as basmati or jasmine. Reserve Arborio rice for making risotto as it produces a mushier texture not desirable in many conventional rice dishes.

The hardness or softness of the finished rice will depend on the ratio of liquid to rice. This recipe yields a firm but cooked rice. If you like softer rice, increase the liquid by ¼ cup.

1 CUP LONG- OR SHORT-GRAIN RICE (NOT INSTANT), DO NOT RINSE

2 CUPS WATER OR BROTH (CHICKEN, BEEF, OR VEGETABLE), OR 1 CUP HOT WATER INTO WHICH 1 BOUILLON CUBE HAS BEEN DISSOLVED

2 TEASPOONS SALT (OMIT IF YOU ARE USING A BOUILLON CUBE OR SALTED BROTH)

1 TABLESPOON BUTTER OR VEGETABLE OR OLIVE OIL (OPTIONAL)

Place all the ingredients in the rice cooker, cover, program for White Rice, and press Start. The rice cooker will keep the rice warm for several hours until you are ready to serve it.

Stir briefly with a fork and serve.

Variations: Sauté chopped onions in 1 tablespoon butter or oil over medium-high heat until softened and add to the rice before cooking.

Add 1 tablespoon chopped fresh herbs or 1 teaspoon dried to the rice before cooking.

BROWN RICE

Yield: 6 servings

Brown rice is a breeze to make in the rice cooker. Select long-grain brown rice if you like your rice on the fluffier side, although brown rice will never be as fluffy as its white cousin.

1 CUP BROWN RICE, RINSED

1 TEASPOON SALT, OR TO YOUR TASTE

3 CUPS WATER OR VEGETABLE BROTH

Mix the rice and salt together with the water or broth in the rice cooker and let soak for 30 minutes before cooking. Press Start and cook until the grains are fluffy and separate and the liquid is absorbed, 35 to 40 minutes. Check the rice during the last 10 minutes of cooking to ensure that it doesn't overcook or burn. Stir with a fork before serving.

Variation: Add uncooked diced onions and/or other vegetables to the rice and broth before cooking.

CHICKEN-APPLE QUICHE

Yield: Two 9-inch quiches

This unique blend of ingredients yields a savory quiche that can be served hot or at room temperature. Long-grain brown rice will yield fluffy and separate grains while medium- and short-grain rice tends to cling together or become starchy. Rice cookers are one of the best ways to cook brown rice.

1 1/2 CUPS BROWN RICE, RINSED

3 CUPS WATER

1 TEASPOON SALT

1 TEASPOON PLUS 2 TABLESPOONS OLIVE OIL

2 1/2 CUPS APPLE CIDER

3/4 POUND BONELESS, SKINLESS CHICKEN BREASTS

1 LARGE EGG WHITE, LIGHTLY BEATEN

1/4 CUP FRESHLY GRATED PARMESAN CHEESE

1/2 CUP FINELY CHOPPED ONIONS

2 CLOVES GARLIC, MINCED

8 OUNCES MUSHROOMS, SLICED

1 1/2 CUPS PEELED, CORED, AND DICED GRANNY SMITH APPLES

1/2 TEASPOON DRIED TARRAGON

1/4 TEASPOON FRESHLY GROUND BLACK PEPPER

2 TABLESPOONS DRY SHERRY

1 TEASPOON FRESH LEMON JUICE

8 LARGE EGGS, BEATEN

2/3 CUP LOW-FAT MILK

1 CUP GRATED MUENSTER OR MOZZARELLA CHEESE

Place the rice, water, 1/2 teaspoon of the salt, and 1 teaspoon of the olive oil in the rice cooker and let soak for 30 minutes before cooking. Press Start and cook until the grains are fluffy and separate and the liquid is absorbed, 35 to 40 minutes. Check the rice during the last 10 minutes of cooking to ensure that it doesn't over-cook or burn. Remove from the cooker and cool slightly.

Place the cider and chicken in the rice cooker and cook until the chicken is poached, 8 to 10 minutes. Discard the liquid, finely dice the chicken, and set aside.

Preheat the over to 400°F with the rack in the center position. Butter or spray two 9-inch quiche pans with removable bottoms. In a medium-size bowl, mix together the cooked rice, egg white, and Parmesan cheese. Divide the rice mixture between both pans and spread it evenly across the bottom and sides. It should be a thin crust, especially around the sides of the pan. Bake until the crusts are golden brown, 10 to 12 minutes. Let cool.

In an electric or stove top skillet, heat the remaining 2 tablespoons of oil over medium heat. Add the onions and garlic and cook, stirring, until the onions are translucent. Increase the heat to high, add the mushrooms and cook, stirring, 3 to 4 minutes. Add the apples, tarragon, pepper, sherry, and lemon juice and cook another 2 to 3 minutes. Stir in the chicken and mix well. Remove from the heat and set aside.

In a medium-size bowl, beat together the eggs and milk. Place the quiche pans on a heavy-duty baking sheet to guard against leaks. Divide the apple-chicken mixture and spread evenly over both crusts. Sprinkle the Muenster cheese over the apple-chicken mixture. Pour the egg mixture over the top. Bake until the tops are brown and the mixture set, 35 to 40 minutes. Serve hot or at room temperature.

Variation: Substitute diced smoked chicken for the poached chicken breast. Decrease the mushrooms to 4 ounces and add ½ cup seeded and diced red bell pepper.

RICE OLÉ

Yield: 4 to 6 servings

Here's the nineties version of Spanish rice—a version far healthier and livelier than the original.

1 CUP BROWN RICE, RINSED

¼ CUP DRIED LENTILS, RINSED

2 CUPS VEGETABLE BROTH OR WATER

1 LARGE ONION, CHOPPED

3 CLOVES GARLIC, MINCED

ONE 14- TO 15-OUNCE CAN BLACK BEANS, RINSED AND DRAINED

1½ CUPS FRESH, CANNED, OR FROZEN CORN KERNELS

1 CUP SALSA

1 LARGE RED BELL PEPPER, SEEDED AND DICED

1 TEASPOON CHILI POWDER

½ TEASPOON GROUND CUMIN

½ TO 1 TEASPOON JALAPEÑO SAUCE, TO YOUR TASTE

Place the rice, lentils, and broth in a rice cooker, press Start, cook for 15 minutes, then add the remaining ingredients. Continue cooking until the rice and lentils are tender and most of the liquid is absorbed, another 20 to 25 minutes.

Chicken Congee

Yield: 6 to 8 servings (about 12 cups)

Congee is the Chinese equivalent of chicken soup—at least in our house it is. It's a savory porridge much the consistency of thin Cream of Wheat made with rice and either water or stock. It's the ultimate in comfort food and easily made in the rice cooker or slow cooker. Sticky rice is available in stores that specialize in Asian ingredients.

If you have a small rice cooker or slow cooker, you can cut this recipe in half.

1 ½ CUPS STICKY RICE, RINSED

4 QUARTS CHICKEN BROTH

2 LARGE CARROTS, DICED

3 CUPS SHREDDED COOKED CHICKEN

SALT OR SOY SAUCE AND FRESHLY GROUND BLACK PEPPER TO TASTE

Place the rice in the rice cooker, add the broth, press Start, and cook until the rice is completely soft and mushy and the liquid is absorbed to make a thick soup. This will take about three cycles in the rice cooker, 40 to 60 minutes. You will have to restart the rice cooker after each cycle. During the last ½ hour of cooking, add the carrots and chicken. Season with salt or soy sauce and serve hot.

Risotto à la Grecque

Yield: 4 to 6 first course or side dish servings

This risotto is fragrant with flavors of the Mediterranean. Be sure to use Arborio rice (available in gourmet stores and many supermarkets) to get the most authentic taste and texture. Taste the cooked rice before adding seasonings—the feta will make it quite salty.

2 TABLESPOONS OLIVE OIL

2 LARGE SHALLOTS, MINCED

1 LARGE CLOVE GARLIC, MINCED

1 CUP ARBORIO RICE

3 CUPS CHICKEN STOCK OR BROTH

2 TEASPOONS FINELY GRATED LEMON ZEST

3 TABLESPOONS OIL-CURED BLACK OLIVES, PITTED, FINELY CHOPPED

2 TABLESPOONS OIL-PACKED SUN-DRIED TOMATOES, FINELY CHOPPED

¼ CUP CHOPPED FRESH ITALIAN PARSLEY LEAVES

4 OUNCES FETA CHEESE, CRUMBLED

SALT AND FRESHLY GROUND BLACK PEPPER TO TASTE

KALAMATA OLIVES (OPTIONAL)

Place everything except the parsley, feta cheese, salt, pepper, and olives in the rice cooker, press Start, and cook until the rice is tender and most of the liquid is absorbed, 20 to 30 minutes. Add the parsley and feta cheese and toss to combine. Season with salt and pepper. Serve immediately, garnished with kalamata olives, if desired.

WILD RICE

Yield: 6 to 8 servings (about 4 cups)

Forget fear of wild rice—the rice cooker takes all the guesswork out of this sometimes temperamental-to-cook grass that once was known as Indian rice. Slightly crunchy with a heavenly nutty taste, wild rice cries out to be paired with pecans, pumpkin, fresh herbs of all kinds, and, my favorite, wild mushrooms. Adding it to bread dough, waffle and pancake batter, and stuffing yields a wonderful depth of flavor as well as an interesting texture.

1 CUP WILD RICE

3 CUPS WATER OR STOCK (CHICKEN, BEEF, OR VEGETABLE)

2 TEASPOONS SALT

½ TEASPOON FRESHLY GROUND BLACK PEPPER

2 TABLESPOONS BUTTER OR MARGARINE

Place the rice in a strainer and rinse it well to remove any dirt particles. Place all the ingredients in the rice cooker and press Start, programming for Soft, if possible. When the rice is done, it should be slightly crunchy, and 50 percent of the grains should be open, exposing a white interior. Check after 30 minutes, cooking longer if necessary. Drain off any excess liquid and serve hot or use as an ingredient in another recipe.

WILD RICE SALAD

Yield: 6 servings

Everyone is tired of pasta salad, me included. Thanks to the rice cooker, there's a whole new world of possibilities for putting starch on the table. This wild rice salad mixes textures and flavors in a way that will appeal to all. The salad can be made two days ahead and kept in a covered container in the refrigerator; it won't be as crispy, however.

2 STALKS CELERY, CUT INTO $^1/_4$-INCH DICE

2 SMALL, VINE-RIPENED TOMATOES, SEEDED AND CUT INTO $^1/_4$-INCH DICE

$^1/_2$ LARGE CARROT, CUT INTO $^1/_4$-INCH DICE

$^1/_2$ MEDIUM-SIZE RED ONION, FINELY CHOPPED

$^1/_2$ RED BELL PEPPER, SEEDED AND CUT INTO $^1/_4$-INCH DICE

$^1/_2$ GREEN BELL PEPPER, SEEDED AND CUT INTO $^1/_4$-INCH DICE

$^1/_2$ YELLOW BELL PEPPER, SEEDED AND CUT INTO $^1/_4$-INCH DICE

$^1/_2$ CUP SLICED ALMONDS, TOASTED (PAGE 131) UNTIL GOLDEN

$^1/_2$ CUP RAISINS

4 CUPS COOKED WILD RICE (PAGE 251), CHILLED

6 TABLESPOONS BALSAMIC VINEGAR

3 TABLESPOONS VEGETABLE OIL

1 TEASPOON MINCED GARLIC

SALT AND FRESHLY GROUND BLACK PEPPER TO TASTE

In a large bowl, combine the vegetables, almonds, and raisins and toss with the wild rice.

In a small bowl, whisk together the vinegar, oil, and garlic until well combined, then season with the salt and pepper. Pour the dressing over the salad and toss well.

QUINOA WITH VEGETABLES

Yield: 6 servings

The tiny quinoa grain is lighter and more delicately flavored than rice and easily takes on flavorings, such as the tomato in this dish. You can find quinoa in health or natural food stores.

1 1/4 CUPS QUINOA

2 TEASPOONS OLIVE OR VEGETABLE OIL

1/2 CUP FINELY CHOPPED ONIONS

1 MEDIUM-SIZE CLOVE GARLIC, MINCED

1/2 POUND MUSHROOMS, FINELY CHOPPED

2 CUPS CHICKEN STOCK OR BROTH

3/4 CUP TOMATO OR V-8 JUICE

2 TABLESPOONS BALSAMIC OR RED WINE VINEGAR

1/2 TEASPOON SALT

1/4 TEASPOON FRESHLY GROUND BLACK PEPPER

2 MEDIUM-SIZE, RIPE TOMATOES, SEEDED AND FINELY CHOPPED

Place the quinoa in a fine strainer and rinse under cold running water. Drain thoroughly, then blot dry on paper towels. Set aside.

Place the oil, onions, and garlic in a medium-size microwavable bowl. Microwave, covered, on high power for 1½ minutes. Add the mushrooms and microwave another 3 minutes. Place the onion-mushroom mixture and quinoa in the rice cooker and add the stock or broth, tomato juice, vinegar, salt, and pepper. Press Start and cook until the quinoa has popped open and the liquid is absorbed, 30 to 40 minutes. Stir in the tomatoes and serve hot.

VEGETABLE PORRIDGE

Yield: 6 to 8 servings (10 cups)

Vegetarian's heaven! If you want to vary this recipe, you can substitute brown rice for the quinoa and increase the liquid to 4 cups. Take care to wash the dried mushrooms carefully to remove all traces of dirt.

5 TO 6 CUPS COARSELY CHOPPED ASSORTED FRESH VEGETABLES SUCH AS RED AND GREEN BELL PEPPERS, BROCCOLI FLORETS, CAULIFLOWER FLORETS, ONIONS, PEAS, ZUCCHINI, AND/OR YELLOW SQUASH

1 CUP DRIED MUSHROOM PIECES, RINSED VERY WELL

3 TO 4 CUPS VEGETABLE BROTH

1 1/4 CUPS QUINOA (AVAILABLE IN HEALTH AND NATURAL FOOD STORES)

1 TEASPOON SALT

FRESHLY GRATED PARMESAN CHEESE TO TASTE

Place all the ingredients except the cheese in the rice cooker, press Start, and cook until the quinoa is tender and the vegetables are soft, 30 to 40 minutes. To serve, spoon into individual bowls and sprinkle with cheese.

RICE COOKER MASHED POTATOES

Yield: 4 servings (3 to 4 cups)

And you thought it was just for making rice!

3 IDAHO POTATOES, PEELED AND SLICED

WATER, OR CHICKEN OR VEGETABLE STOCK, TO
   COVER

2 TO 3 TABLESPOONS BUTTER, TO YOUR TASTE

$^1/_2$ CUP HEAVY CREAM OR MILK

SALT AND FRESHLY GROUND BLACK PEPPER TO
   TASTE

Put the potatoes in the rice cooker, cover with liquid, press Start, and cook until tender but not mushy, 20 to 30 minutes. Drain off the liquid, add the butter and cream, and mash the potatoes. Season with salt and pepper and serve hot.

CRANBERRY-BOURBON RELISH

Yield: 10 to 12 servings (about 4 cups)

Besides being quite at home alongside turkey, this tangy cranberry relish makes a good accompaniment to any pâté or cold or smoked meat. Its sweet-tart taste is perfect on cold turkey, chicken, or roast beef sandwiches. It will keep several months in a covered container in the refrigerator, so make some for Thanksgiving and Christmas!

1 SMALL ONION, CHOPPED

1 TEASPOON VEGETABLE OIL

1 CUP BOURBON

GRATED ZEST AND JUICE OF 1 ORANGE

ONE 12-OUNCE PACKAGE FRESH
   CRANBERRIES, PICKED OVER

1 CUP SUGAR

$^1/_8$ TEASPOON FRESHLY GROUND BLACK
   PEPPER

Place the onion in a small microwavable bowl with the vegetable oil. Cover and microwave on high power until the onion is translucent, 1 to 1$^1/_2$ minutes.

Put all the ingredients in the rice cooker, press Start, and cook until the cranberries are soft and the liquid is absorbed, about 25 minutes. Transfer to a bowl and let cool to room temperature, about 1 hour. Cover and refrigerate. It will keep at least 3 months.

VEGETABLE STOCK

Yield: 4 to 6 cups

Making your own vegetable stock to use in soups, stews, pasta, and rice dishes is so easy and quick in the rice cooker. This is one time when a large rice cooker comes in handy. If you have a small one, cut the recipe in half or make it in two batches.

1/4 CUP VEGETABLE OIL

2 LARGE ONIONS, CHOPPED

4 CLOVES GARLIC, MASHED

1 LARGE CARROT, CUT INTO 2-INCH-THICK SLICES

2 STALKS CELERY, CUT INTO 2-INCH-THICK SLICES

2 TURNIPS, PEELED AND CUT INTO 2-INCH PIECES

1 LEEK, THOROUGHLY WASHED AND CUT INTO 2-INCH-THICK SLICES

1 BAY LEAF

2 TABLESPOONS CHOPPED FRESH HERBS OF YOUR CHOICE, OR 2 TEASPOONS DRIED

4 TO 6 CUPS WATER

Place the olive oil and onions in a large microwavable bowl, cover, and microwave on high power until softened, 3 to 4 minutes. Add the garlic and microwave another 2 minutes.

Place all the ingredients in the rice cooker and press Start. At the end of the cooking cycle, allow the vegetables to cool in the liquid for 30 minutes, then strain and either use immediately or refrigerate for up to 2 weeks. It can also be frozen for up to 4 months.

Chicken Stock (or Soup)

Yield: 4 to 5 cups

Fowl (a mature hen) makes the most flavorful chicken soup. You can find them in butcher shops, or they can be special ordered in many supermarkets. Do not use boneless, skinless chicken—the result will be far less flavorful.

Making soup in the rice cooker yields chicken that is tender and not over-cooked. Serve the meat along with the vegetables in the soup or turn it into chicken salad.

You'll need a large rice cooker for this recipe, one that makes at least 10 cups of rice.

1 STEWING FOWL, CUT UP, OR 3 POUNDS CHICKEN PIECES

6 CUPS WATER

1 TEASPOON SALT

FRESHLY GROUND BLACK PEPPER TO TASTE

1 LARGE ONION, PEELED AND CUT INTO CHUNKS

2 LARGE CARROTS, PEELED AND CUT INTO CHUNKS

2 STALKS CELERY, CUT INTO CHUNKS

2 SMALL PARSNIPS, PEELED AND SLICED

1/3 CUP CHOPPED FRESH DILL

Place all the ingredients in the rice cooker and press Start. When the cooker turns off, check to see if the chicken is cooked through. If not, cover and press Start again, allowing it to cook another 15 to 20 minutes. Let cool and strain. Either discard the chicken or save for another use.

Chill, then discard the fat, which has risen to the surface of the stock and hardened. If using as stock, you can freeze it in 1-cup servings. Or, boil it down to half the volume, freeze it (it takes up less space in the freezer), and reconstitute the stock with water when using it.

Alternatively, save the chicken (shred when cold), add it to the stock, and serve as chicken soup.

Variation: Add cooked noodles or rice to the chicken soup.

THAI CHICKEN SOUP

Yield: 6 to 8 servings (10 cups)

If you have a hankering for chicken soup with a twist, then try this beloved standard with an Asian air. This fills a 5-cup rice cooker, so if yours is smaller, cut the recipe in half. You can find short-grain jasmine rice (grown in Thailand) in health food and gourmet stores.

1 CUP JASMINE OR OTHER SHORT-GRAIN RICE

TWO 14½-OUNCE CANS CHICKEN BROTH

1 CUP WATER

2½ POUNDS BONELESS, SKINLESS CHICKEN BREASTS OR THIGHS, CUT INTO 1-INCH PIECES

1 MEDIUM-SIZE ONION, COARSELY CHOPPED

2 CLOVES GARLIC, MINCED

1 PIECE FRESH GINGERROOT, ABOUT 1 × 2 INCHES, PEELED AND JULIENNED

⅓ CUP PACKED FRESH CORIANDER (CILANTRO) LEAVES AND STEMS, SNIPPED WITH SCISSORS INTO ½-INCH PIECES

2 STALKS LEMONGRASS, TOUGH OUTER LEAVES PEELED, CUT INTO 4-INCH LENGTHS AND CUT IN HALF LENGTHWISE

2 MEDIUM-SIZE CARROTS, CUT INTO 1-INCH-THICK SLICES

HOT SESAME OIL (OPTIONAL)

Starting with the rice and liquid, place all the ingredients except the sesame oil in the rice cooker. Program for Soft, if possible. If this is not an option, you may have to repeat the cooking cycle at the end of the first cooking time if the rice is too hard and the chicken isn't cooked through. To serve, spoon into large bowls and sprinkle with a few drops of sesame oil.

SMOKED CORN CHOWDER

Yield: 6 to 8 servings (10 cups)

Bet you never looked at your rice maker as a soup maker before! World-class soup in 20 minutes without having to worry about how to keep it warm—the rice cooker does it for you. This soup is the perfect solution for people (like me) who dislike thickening soup with flour.

continued

Corn chowder is a classic New England recipe. This version adds the subtle, sublime taste of smoked corn.

3 LARGE IDAHO POTATOES, PEELED AND CUT INTO ½-INCH CUBES

1 LARGE SPANISH ONION, DICED

6 CUPS CHICKEN BROTH

4 CUPS SMOKED CORN KERNELS (PAGE 361)

2 CUPS LIGHT CREAM, SCALDED

SALT AND FRESHLY GROUND BLACK PEPPER TO TASTE

Place the potatoes, onion, and broth in the rice cooker and press Start. The mixture will come to a boil and should cook until the potatoes are fork-tender, about 15 minutes. Use a handheld blender on high speed to partially purée the mixture, leaving some of the potatoes in pieces. Add the corn and cream, press Start, and allow to cook only until the mixture is hot. Season with salt and pepper. Serve immediately, or use the "keep warm" function to hold the soup until ready to serve.

Variation: If you wish to cut calories, omit the cream. The soup will not have quite the same smooth richness, but will still be quite enjoyable.

SKILLET

& WOK

T he hot wedding present the year I got married (1967) was the super-deluxe Farberware electric skillet. A bunch of my friends pooled their resources and bought me one. Nowadays I suppose I'd say they bought *us* one, but back then husbands didn't cook. I remember unwrapping it and thinking it was a serious kitchen appliance; its unblemished stainless-steel finish gleamed with a just-out-of-the-box virginity that was almost blinding. The cover with its ebony-like handle closed over the pan with a satisfying solidness reminiscent of the door of my uncle's Cadillac. The control unit with its myriad settings had a satisfying heft, and the thick black electric cord looked as if it could conduct all the electricity generated by Niagara Falls right into the skillet. The entire unit required two hands to lift it—it weighed a ton.

That electric skillet was the perfect present for this new bride. Our tiny apartment kitchen had a stone-age stove whose cranky, rusted burners heated just enough so you knew the stove hadn't completely died, but never got hot enough to cook anything. Daily, for five years, I cooked in that skillet everything from scrambled eggs and beef stew to pancakes, fish cakes, and cupcakes. I poached, steamed, boiled, sautéed, pan-fried, deep-fried, and baked. I melted chocolate and warmed baby bottles. When we moved out of the apartment and into a house with a real working stove I was delighted to be able to retire the trusty electric skillet to the basement.

Twenty years later we renovated that house and had to live in two rooms—neither of which was a kitchen. I dragged the electric skillet out of the basement and pressed it back into service. The day before we moved into our new kitchen, the electric skillet gave up the ghost. Nothing dramatic, it just quietly (and coolly) refused to cook that last batch of oatmeal. It was retired with honors and we went out for breakfast.

When I went shopping for this book, I was amazed to see the variety of brands available. Moreover, I was shocked at the seemingly flimsy quality of many of them. They were made of plastic-coated, insubstantial low-grade metal with even cheaper plastic lids, legs, and handles held on by screws applied by someone just learning how to handle a screwdriver. The cords were thin and prone to tangles, and the control units looked like an afterthought. The only thing right about these things was the low price. What the heck, I thought, one of these is good enough for testing recipes. Boy, was I wrong.

Several hundred dollars' worth of ruined ingredients and hours of wasted time later, I returned the wanna-be to the store. The salesperson wasn't at all surprised. "This is fine for reheating stuff and boiling water, but if you're really going to cook, you should buy a Farberware." And that's exactly what I did.

GENERAL DESCRIPTION

WHAT DOES IT DO? • Do you often find yourself short a burner on your stove? Here's a great solution! Electric skillets and woks are metal pans with straight or flared sides that are usually coated with a nonstick material. Using an internal electric heating element, they maintain a set temperature automatically. Electric skillets are generally rectangular, square, or round with flat bottoms while woks are usually bowl-shaped.

WHY DO I NEED THIS? • Pan-frying is easy to do in electric skillets since they are usually deeper than most skillets used on a stove top, which helps to eliminate splatter. They will hold a set temperature to keep the oil at a consistent temperature. They're perfect for pancakes or French toast.

Electric woks heat up quickly and maintain the set temperature throughout the cooking process. If you are preparing a feast for several of your closest friends and need an extra burner, electric skillets and woks are superb supplements to your stove top.

Any buffet table would be lost without an electric skillet to keep hors d'oeuvres and canapés at serving temperature, but only if it can be used without an extension cord or with one that is placed so that it cannot be tripped over or broken.

HOW DOES IT WORK? • Most models of electric skillets and woks are made out of metal with a nonstick coating and have a heating element embedded on their bottoms. Others consist of a special skillet that you sit on top of a burner-like unit. The power is usually connected to the heating element by way of a control unit, which contains a dial knob for setting the temperature by means of a variable bimetallic thermostat, a signal light, a heat-sensing probe, and connectors for the heating element. Always plug the control unit into the skillet or wok before plugging it into the wall outlet. When the skillet or wok is plugged in and the dial is turned to a desired temperature, the heat-sensing probe tells the thermostat that the appliance is not at the correct temperature. So the controller completes a circuit, and the elements get hot to heat up the cooking surface.

For appliances with a separate base unit, the control unit is built into the base unit. An additional switch is embedded in the base unit to disconnect the heating elements when the skillet or wok is not on the base.

When the surface reaches the set cooking temperature, the probe senses the desired temperature and turns off the heating elements. The signal light goes out and the appliance is ready for you to start cooking. During cooking, the light will turn off and on, indicating the appliance is maintaining the set temperature.

Most models come with metal lids that have adjustable vents to allow steam to escape, and others have glass lids that sit ajar to perform this function.

When finished cooking, turn the temperature down to a warm setting to keep food at the correct serving temperature. Some electric skillets look nice enough to unplug and take out to your serving table. On those skillets with separate base units, the skillet or wok can be removed and taken directly to the table if desired.

CARE AND MAINTENANCE • Cool to room temperature before cleaning. Units with embedded heating elements are immersible as long as you disconnect the control unit first since the elements are completely sealed. Skillets and woks with base units can be removed from their bases and washed like regular nonstick skillets. After they have cooled, control units and electronic base units can be cleaned with a damp soft cloth; they should not be immersed.

WHICH IS RIGHT FOR ME? • A variety of sizes of electric skillets and woks is on the market, so pick one that is sized to suit your cooking needs. Skillets made out of heavier gauge metal will last longer, and sturdily attached legs and handles will cause fewer headaches.

COMMENTS • New heating devices can smoke when you first turn them on, so plug them in for a short time to burn off the new smell before you use them. Also, if your skillet or wok has a nonstick coating, make sure to use plastic or wooden utensils and chopsticks, and do not use a harsh cleaning pad when washing the appliance.

SKILLET & WOK TIPS

Think of your electric skillet as a sauté pan connected directly to an extra burner. Almost anything you can make in a deep sauté pan can be made in the electric skillet. With the skillet set on medium-low heat you can simmer soups and stocks as well as reduce sauces. Setting it on the very lowest heat enables you to use it as a chafing dish, keeping foods warm. By adding oil you can use the skillet as a deep fryer. With the cover in place, you can braise, stew, poach, steam, and even bake.

Once your stir-fry skills are honed, you can use your electric wok to cook to order, tableside or on a buffet table.

Be sure to leave plenty of room on all sides of the electric skillet or wok when food is cooking so air can circulate around the appliance. Make sure it is not directly under kitchen cabinets to prevent steam damage.

If you have cooked something with the cover in place, take care not to tilt it when removing it or condensed steam will pour down on top of your food.

If your skillet has a vent, use it to avoid moisture buildup in the lid.

Always turn off the unit, then unplug the outlet end of the cord before unplugging the unit end.

If you have more than one appliance cord stored in a drawer, use a stick-on label to identify which appliance each goes with.

SOURDOUGH–WILD RICE PANCAKES

Yield: 10 pancakes

Oh, boy, these are really good. I had trouble stopping after one serving, and I'll bet you will, too. For breakfast with sweet butter and real maple syrup; at dinnertime as a starch with game or meat; or as a base for scrambled eggs, stew, or a vegetarian entrée; you won't find a more unusual and palate-pleasing morsel.

2 CUPS UNBLEACHED ALL-PURPOSE FLOUR

1 1/2 TEASPOONS SALT

1 TABLESPOON BAKING POWDER

1/2 TEASPOON BAKING SODA

2 TABLESPOONS LORA BRODY'S SOURDOUGH BREAD ENHANCER (AVAILABLE AT GOURMET FOOD STORES)

2 LARGE EGGS

2 TABLESPOONS PURE MAPLE SYRUP

1 1/2 CUPS MILK

FINELY GRATED ZEST OF 1 LARGE ORANGE

1/2 CUP (1 STICK) BUTTER, MELTED AND SLIGHTLY COOLED

1 CUP COOKED WILD RICE

1/2 CUP CHOPPED PECANS

VEGETABLE OIL

Sift the dry ingredients together in a small bowl. In a large bowl, mix together the eggs, maple syrup, milk, orange zest, and butter. Stir the dry ingredients into the wet mixture, mixing just enough to make a smooth batter (overmixing will make the pancakes tough). Stir in the wild rice and pecans.

Heat about 1/8 inch of oil in a large electric skillet set on medium heat (350°F). When hot, drop in 1/4 cupfuls of the wild rice mixture, flattening the cakes with a rubber scraper to spread them out without letting the pancakes touch. Cook until the bottoms are lightly browned and the batter is holding together, about 2 minutes; then turn the pancakes and cook on the other side for a minute or so. Serve immediately.

Variation: Use about half the amount specified above for each pancake, about 2 tablespoons or what will fill a serving spoon. This will produce smaller, crisper pancakes that can be drained on paper towels and served as cocktail hors d'oeuvres.

Soft Tacos with Scrambled Eggs and Green Chilies

Yield: 4 servings

This is great for breakfast, lunch, or a light supper.

8 FLOUR TORTILLAS

4 LARGE EGGS

1 TABLESPOON WATER

$^1/_4$ TEASPOON SALT

$^1/_4$ TEASPOON FRESHLY GROUND BLACK
    PEPPER

1 TABLESPOON BUTTER OR MARGARINE

ONE 4-OUNCE CAN DICED GREEN CHILIES,
    DRAINED

$^1/_2$ MEDIUM-SIZE RED ONION, FINELY CHOPPED

$^1/_2$ CUP PREPARED SALSA

Preheat an electric skillet to medium-low (325°F). Add the tortillas and heat for 2 to 3 minutes.

In the meantime, beat the eggs with the water, salt, and pepper in a medium-size bowl until just mixed.

Remove the tortillas from the skillet and increase the heat to medium-high (375°F). Add the butter; when it is melted and bubbling, add the green chilies and onion and cook on medium heat (350°F), stirring often, until the onion is softened, 3 to 5 minutes. Add the beaten eggs and cook, stirring frequently, until set, about 3 minutes.

Place 2 to 3 tablespoons of the egg filling in the center of each warm tortilla and fold in half. Place 2 filled tortillas on each of four plates and top each serving with 2 tablespoons of salsa.

Frittata

Yield: 6 servings

Think of a frittata as a no-pressure omelet. You don't have to worry about squeezing in the filling or flipping anything over in the pan. You can serve a frittata for breakfast, lunch, or light supper. Hot or at room temperature, it's equally tasty.

1/4 CUP CHICKEN OR VEGETABLE BROTH

2 CLOVES GARLIC, MINCED

1 LARGE SPANISH ONION, CUT INTO THICK
SLICES

1 LARGE IDAHO POTATO, PEELED AND VERY
THINLY SLICED

1 RED BELL PEPPER, SEEDED AND SLICED

1 GREEN BELL PEPPER, SEEDED AND SLICED

6 TO 8 MUSHROOMS, QUARTERED

8 EXTRA LARGE EGGS

1 CUP GRATED MOZZARELLA OR MONTEREY
JACK CHEESE

CHOPPED FRESH ITALIAN PARSLEY LEAVES
FOR GARNISH

Place the broth in an electric skillet set on medium-low heat (325°F) and slowly cook the garlic, onion, potato, and bell peppers until thoroughly tender, stirring occasionally. Add the mushrooms and cook another 2 minutes.

In a large bowl, beat together the eggs and cheese and pour the mixture over the vegetables in the skillet. Shake the pan to coat the vegetables, then cover and cook slowly on medium heat (350°F) for 10 to 15 minutes. Lift one side of the frittata, allowing any uncooked egg mixture to flow underneath. Cook another few minutes, until the eggs are set, then use a plastic or wooden scraper to loosen and slip the frittata onto a large dish. Slice into wedges and serve sprinkled with chopped parsley.

DOUBLE CHICKEN SOUP

Yield: About 8 cups

More like a stew than soup, this hearty, rich dish is a meal in itself when served with rice or noodles. The electric skillet allows you to simmer food gently without having to worry about burning it or having the cooking liquid evaporate. We call this Double Chicken Soup because the recipe calls for chicken broth instead of water as the cooking liquid.

2 BROILING CHICKENS, 5 TO 6 POUNDS TOTAL,
CUT UP

1 LARGE ONION, PEELED AND CUT INTO
CHUNKS

2 CARROTS, PEELED AND CUT INTO CHUNKS

3 STALKS CELERY

1 BAY LEAF

1 SMALL SPRIG FRESH DILL

TWO 14-OUNCE CANS CHICKEN BROTH

SALT AND FRESHLY GROUND BLACK PEPPER TO
TASTE

COOKED EGG NOODLES OR RICE

continued

Place the chicken pieces in an electric skillet, surround them with the vegetables and herbs, and cover with the chicken broth. Cover the skillet and set at medium-high (375°F). When the mixture simmers, reduce the heat to medium-low (325°F) and simmer for 1 hour. Pour the soup and solids into a container and refrigerate.

When the soup is cool enough to touch, remove the fat, which by now should have solidified on the top, and pull the chicken off the bones, discarding the bones and skin and discard the bay leaf.

Return the chicken and soup to the electric skillet set on medium heat (350°F) and bring the mixture to a gentle simmer. Season with the salt and pepper. Spoon cooked egg noodles or rice into soup bowls, add the soup and chicken, and serve immediately.

SKILLET TOMATOES AND ZUCCHINI

Yield: 6 servings

Wondering what to do with the overflowing bounty of the summer's garden? Try this vegetable skillet dish.

2 TABLESPOONS BUTTER OR MARGARINE

2 SMALL ZUCCHINI, SLICED

1 MEDIUM-SIZE ONION, THINLY SLICED

2 MEDIUM-SIZE, RIPE TOMATOES, SLICED

$^1/_4$ TO $^1/_2$ TEASPOON GARLIC SALT, TO YOUR TASTE

$^1/_4$ TEASPOON DRIED BASIL, CRUMBLED

FRESHLY GROUND BLACK PEPPER TO TASTE

4 OUNCES (1 CUP) MOZZARELLA OR CHEDDAR CHEESE, SHREDDED

1 CUP SEASONED CROUTONS

In an electric skillet set on medium heat (350°F), melt the butter. Add the zucchini and onion and cook, stirring, until the zucchini are just tender. Add the tomatoes and seasonings. Cover and cook until the tomatoes are tender, 3 to 5 minutes. Turn off the skillet and sprinkle with the cheese and croutons. Cover and let stand until the cheese melts, 2 to 3 minutes.

Savory Greek Upside-Down Torte

Yield: One 12-inch torte (10 to 12 lunch servings or 20 to 24 appetizer servings)

Feta, spinach, and lemon are combined into a delicious plugged-in electric skillet entrée. Use the rice cooker to make the rice ahead of time and let it cool to room temperature before adding it to the eggs, or they will cook too soon.

3 STRIPS BACON, CUT INTO $^1/_4$-INCH PIECES	3 LARGE EGGS
$^1/_4$ CUP PINE NUTS	2 TABLESPOONS CHOPPED FRESH DILL
4 CLOVES GARLIC, CHOPPED	3 CUPS COOKED RICE, COOLED TO ROOM
2 LARGE ONIONS, COARSELY CHOPPED	TEMPERATURE
5 PACKED CUPS FRESH SPINACH, THOROUGHLY	$^1/_2$ TEASPOON GRATED LEMON ZEST
WASHED AND TRIMMED OF TOUGH STEMS	$^1/_4$ TEASPOON SALT
2 TABLESPOONS FRESH LEMON JUICE	DASH OF FRESHLY GROUND BLACK PEPPER
10 OUNCES FETA CHEESE, CRUMBLED	SPRIGS FRESH DILL FOR GARNISH

Heat the electric skillet to 300°F. Add the bacon and cook, stirring, until crisp. Drain off all but 2 tablespoons of the bacon fat, add the pine nuts, garlic, and onions and cook, stirring, until the onions are softened. Add the spinach and 1 tablespoon of the lemon juice and cook, stirring, until the spinach has wilted. Place the contents of the skillet in a colander and let drain well. Turn off the skillet and allow it to cool while you assemble the rest of the dish.

Distribute the spinach mixture evenly over the bottom of the skillet. Spread the feta cheese evenly over the spinach mixture, then sprinkle with the remaining tablespoon of lemon juice.

In a separate bowl, beat the eggs lightly and stir in the chopped dill. Add the rice, lemon zest, salt, and pepper and stir to combine. Pour the mixture over the feta cheese and use a rubber scraper or wooden spoon to spread it out to the edges of the skillet. With a scraper, push all the layers slightly away from the edge of the skillet. This will make it easier to remove at the end of the cooking time.

Set the skillet temperature to 250°F. Cover and let cook until the eggs are set and the torte registers an internal temperature of 200°F on an instant-read thermometer, about 30 minutes.

Remove the lid without tilting it to avoid dripping the condensed steam into the pan. Turn off the skillet, unplug it from the wall first, and unplug the control unit from the skillet base. Run a knife around the edges to loosen the torte. Place a plate upside down over the skillet and invert. The torte will unmold from the skillet. Garnish with sprigs of fresh dill and serve immediately.

To store, cover with plastic wrap and refrigerate for up to 3 days. Reheat in the microwave oven.

Savory Italian Upside-Down Strata

Yield: 8 entrée servings or 24 appetizer servings

This colorful layered dish has many uses. Served hot it makes a great entrée or served at room temperature and cut in wedges it becomes an easy appetizer.

2 CUPS RICOTTA CHEESE

3 LARGE EGGS

1 TEASPOON EACH DRIED BASIL, THYME, AND OREGANO

²/₃ CUP FRESHLY GRATED PARMESAN CHEESE

1 ¹/₂ TEASPOONS SALT

6 TO 7 TABLESPOONS OLIVE OIL

1 MEDIUM-SIZE ONION, THINLY SLICED

1 RED BELL PEPPER, SEEDED AND CUT INTO 1 ¹/₂-INCH-WIDE STRIPS

1 YELLOW BELL PEPPER, SEEDED AND CUT INTO 1 ¹/₂-INCH-WIDE STRIPS

¹/₂ CUP PITTED SLICED BLACK OLIVES

1 TABLESPOON CAPERS, DRAINED

JUICE OF 1 LEMON

5 CUPS SMALL ITALIAN-FLAVORED CROUTONS

In a medium-size bowl, mix together the ricotta, eggs, herbs, cheese, and salt using a hand mixer fitted with the beater attachment on medium-low speed until smooth. Set aside.

Heat 3 tablespoons of the oil in the electric skillet to 200°F. Add the onion, bell peppers, olives, capers, and lemon juice and cook, stirring, until soft but not mushy, 2 to 4 minutes. Arrange the vegetables evenly over the bottom of the skillet. Pour the ricotta-and-egg mixture over the vegetables. Sprinkle the croutons over the top of the ricotta-and-egg mixture. Drizzle the remaining 3 to 4 tablespoons of olive oil over the croutons. Place a heat-resistant plate over the croutons to weight them down. Cover and cook until the eggs are set, 15 to 20 minutes.

Remove the lid without tilting it to avoid dripping the condensed steam into the pan. Turn off the skillet and let stand 5 to 10 minutes. Remove the plug. Place a large platter upside down over the skillet and invert. Cut and serve while hot or cool to room temperature.

Variation: Add green peppers or zucchini strips.

SKILLET PIZZA

Yield: 1 large pizza (6 to 8 servings)

A quick and easy any-way-you-want-it pizza, for gourmet to eclectic tastes.
1 pound homemade Versatile Pizza Dough (page 63) or 1 package pizza crust mix, prepared according to directions.

1/2 CUP PREPARED PIZZA SAUCE

1 CUP SHREDDED MOZZARELLA CHEESE

For optional toppings:

3/4 CUP SLICED MUSHROOMS, SAUTÉED IN
  OLIVE OIL OR BUTTER UNTIL SOFTENED

1/4 POUND SAUSAGE, CASING REMOVED AND
  COMPLETELY BROWNED

1/4 POUND SLICED PEPPERONI

1/4 POUND SMOKED TURKEY OR CHICKEN,
  DICED

1/4 POUND CANADIAN BACON, SLICED

1 SMALL ONION, DICED

2 TEASPOONS CAPERS, DRAINED

1/4 CUP BLACK OR GREEN OLIVES, SLICED

1/2 RED BELL PEPPER, SEEDED AND DICED

1/4 CUP SHREDDED SMOKED GOUDA

Oil the bottom and sides of a large, heavy-duty electric skillet. Pat the pizza dough in the bottom and slightly up the sides of the pan. Spread on the sauce just as far as the upturned edges. Sprinkle the mozzarella evenly over the top. Complete with the toppings and cheese.

Cover and cook on medium heat (350°F) until the crust is lightly browned, 8 to 10 minutes. Unplug the skillet, slide the pizza out onto a plate, cut, and serve.

Variation: Add 1 tablespoon chopped fresh herbs such as tarragon or basil to the pizza crust mix.

SUN-DRIED TOMATO PASTA SAUCE

Yield: About 3 cups

This tangy, robust tomato sauce is thick enough to adhere to the slipperiest pasta. It makes a great addition to risotto, as well as a sauce to cover chicken breasts or fish. For a heartier sauce, slices of quickly fried pepperoni can be added just before serving.

1/4 CUP OLIVE OIL

1 LARGE YELLOW ONION, CHOPPED

3 STALKS CELERY, MINCED

3 CARROTS, CHOPPED INTO 1-INCH PIECES

3 CLOVES GARLIC, MINCED

1 TEASPOON FENNEL SEEDS

1 SMALL FENNEL BULB, CHOPPED (ABOUT 1 1/2 CUPS)

1 CUP OIL-PACKED SUN-DRIED TOMATOES, UNDRAINED, MINCED

TWO 16-OUNCE CANS CHOPPED TOMATOES

1 CUP DRY WHITE WINE

SALT AND FRESHLY GROUND BLACK PEPPER TO TASTE

1/2 CUP PINE NUTS (OPTIONAL), TOASTED (SEE NOTE, PAGE 131)

Heat the oil in an electric skillet set on medium-high heat (375°F). Add the onion, celery, carrots, garlic, fennel seeds and bulb and cook, stirring, until the vegetables are softened, about 15 minutes.

Stir in both types of tomatoes and the wine and season with the salt and pepper. Simmer on medium-low heat (325°F), uncovered, until the sauce is thick, stirring occasionally, about 1 hour.

Transfer the sauce to the work bowl of a food processor fitted with the metal blade and process with repeated pulses until blended but not smooth; tiny chunks should still remain. Stir in the pine nuts.

Serve the sauce over a hearty pasta, such as thick spaghetti or ziti, with freshly grated Parmesan cheese.

Rigatoni with Tomato and Prosciutto

Yield: 4 servings

A classic Italian dish made quickly and easily in the electric skillet. Omit the prosciutto to make it a vegetarian meal. You can let your creative juices flow by substituting penne or multicolored rotini for the rigatoni.

For the sauce:

¼ CUP (½ STICK) UNSALTED BUTTER

½ CUP CHOPPED ONIONS

½ POUND MUSHROOMS, SLICED

4 OUNCES SLICED PROSCIUTTO, CHOPPED

ONE 28-OUNCE CAN PLUM TOMATOES, COARSELY CHOPPED

1 TABLESPOON CHOPPED FRESH ITALIAN PARSLEY LEAVES

SALT AND FRESHLY GROUND BLACK PEPPER TO TASTE

For the pasta:

1 POUND RIGATONI, COOKED ACCORDING TO THE PACKAGE DIRECTIONS

½ CUP FRESHLY GRATED PARMESAN CHEESE

In an electric skillet set on medium heat (350°F), melt the butter, then add the onions and cook, stirring, until slightly softened. Add the mushrooms and cook, stirring occasionally, until they give up their moisture and are golden brown, 3 to 4 minutes. Add the prosciutto and cook the mixture, stirring, another 2 to 3 minutes. Add the tomatoes and turn up the heat to medium-high (375°F). Add the parsley and bring the sauce to a slow boil. Turn the heat down to maintain a slow simmer. Taste, add the salt, if necessary, and season with pepper. Cover and cook until the sauce thickens slightly, stirring occasionally, 35 to 45 minutes.

Place the cooked and drained pasta in a large serving bowl. Pour the sauce over the pasta and add the Parmesan. Mix well but gently and serve immediately.

Sloppy Joes

Yield: 4 to 6 servings

This hot open sandwich is a real generational crossover dish. Kids love it, and grown-ups eat it and think that they are kids again.

2 TABLESPOONS VEGETABLE OIL

1 SPANISH ONION, QUARTERED

2 STALKS CELERY

2 CLOVES GARLIC, PEELED

½ POUND SHARP CHEDDAR CHEESE

2 POUNDS LEAN GROUND BEEF OR GROUND TURKEY

2 TABLESPOONS FIRMLY PACKED DARK BROWN SUGAR

2 TABLESPOONS RED WINE VINEGAR

1 CUP SALSA (HOMEMADE OR STORE BOUGHT)

1 TABLESPOON WORCESTERSHIRE SAUCE

SALT TO TASTE

ONE 10-OUNCE CAN RED OR BLACK BEANS (OPTIONAL), DRAINED

6 HAMBURGER BUNS

Place the oil in an electric skillet set on medium heat (350°F). In the work bowl of a food processor fitted with the large grating disk, grate the onion, celery, and garlic. Add the vegetables to the skillet and, without washing the food processor, grate the cheese and set it aside. Cook the vegetables, stirring, until the onion is softened, without allowing the garlic to brown. Raise the heat in the skillet to 400°F, add the beef or turkey and cook, uncovered, stirring frequently, until the meat is browned, about 10 minutes. Pour off the liquid, reduce the heat to medium-low (325°F), and stir in the sugar, vinegar, salsa, Worcestershire sauce, salt, and beans. Cook, uncovered, 15 to 20 minutes, then add the cheese and cook until it melts. Spoon the mixture over heated hamburger buns and serve at once.

Beef Stew with Rosemary and Turnips

Yield: 4 servings

The earthy fragrance of this hearty stew will warm your kitchen and invite impatient inquiries of, "When's dinner?" Beef bottom round is an inexpensive cut of meat that benefits from the long, gentle cooking process of the electric skillet or slow cooker.

2 TABLESPOONS OLIVE OIL

2 CLOVES GARLIC, MINCED

2 POUNDS BEEF BOTTOM ROUND, TRIMMED OF FAT AND CUT INTO 1-INCH CUBES

1 CUP BEEF OR VEGETABLE BROTH

1/2 CUP DRY RED WINE

12 SMALL RED POTATOES, SCRUBBED

3 TURNIPS, PEELED, CUT IN HALF LENGTHWISE, AND CUT INTO 2-INCH-THICK SLICES

2 TABLESPOONS FRESH ROSEMARY LEAVES, OR 2 TEASPOONS DRIED

1 BAG FROZEN PEARL ONIONS

SALT AND FRESHLY GROUND BLACK PEPPER TO TASTE

In an electric skillet set on medium heat (350°F), heat the oil and cook the garlic, stirring, until golden but not brown. Remove it, add the beef, and cook until lightly browned on all sides. Return the garlic and the remaining ingredients, except the onions and salt and pepper, to the skillet. Lower the heat to a simmer (225°F), cover, and cook until the meat is very tender, 2 to 3 hours. Add the onions during the last 30 minutes of cooking. Season with the salt and pepper before serving.

MATHEW'S PORK ROAST

Yield: 8 to 10 servings

My friend Mathew is a wonderful cook and loves to entertain. His deservedly famous boneless pork roast with cherries is a hit with company. It's easy to prepare for the novice, but sophisticated enough for the most seasoned palate.

ONE 4- TO 6-POUND BONELESS PORK ROAST

1 TEASPOON SALT

FRESHLY GROUND BLACK PEPPER TO TASTE

4 LARGE ONIONS, THINLY SLICED

2 YAMS, PEELED AND SLICED

1 GENEROUS CUP DRIED CHERRIES (AVAILABLE IN GOURMET STORES AND MANY SUPERMARKETS)

1 CUP APPLE CIDER OR APPLE JUICE

ONE 10-OUNCE JAR CHERRY PRESERVES

2 CUPS DRY WHITE WINE OR CHICKEN BROTH

1/3 CUP CIDER VINEGAR

continued

Sprinkle the roast with the salt and pepper and place it in the electric skillet. Scatter the vegetables and cherries around the roast. Combine the cider, preserves, wine, and vinegar in a small bowl and pour the mixture over the pork. Add a little more wine or water if necessary to make sure there is at least 2 inches of liquid in the bottom of the skillet. Set the thermostat on medium heat (350°F) and cook the roast for 25 minutes per pound, until it has an internal temperature of 175°F measured by an instant-read thermometer.

Let the roast rest for 10 minutes before slicing to allow the juices to settle. Layer the meat slices on a serving platter and arrange the vegetables around them. Place the sauce in a spouted dish and pass separately.

SAUSAGE SKILLET DINNER

Yield: 4 servings

Reggie and Jeff thought this one-pot skillet dinner was the cat's meow. They recommend trying it with green pepper in addition to the apple. The vinegar mixture at the end really gives it a good tang.

12 OUNCES FULLY COOKED SMOKED SAUSAGE, CUT DIAGONALLY INTO 1-INCH-THICK SLICES

2 TABLESPOONS WATER

1 MEDIUM-SIZE ONION, THICKLY SLICED

2 DELICIOUS APPLES, PEELED, CORED, AND CUT INTO EIGHTHS

2 TABLESPOONS BUTTER

2 LARGE IDAHO POTATOES, SCRUBBED AND VERY THINLY SLICED

¹/₄ CUP CIDER VINEGAR

3 TABLESPOONS SUGAR

¹/₂ TEASPOON CARAWAY SEEDS

2 TABLESPOONS CHOPPED FRESH ITALIAN PARSLEY LEAVES

Place the sausage and water in an electric skillet set on medium heat (350°F). Cover and cook until the sausage renders up its fat, stirring occasionally, about 8 minutes. Remove the sausage to a warm platter. Pour off the drippings and add the onion and apple slices and 1 tablespoon of the butter. Cook, stirring, until the apples are just tender, about 4 minutes. Remove to the sausage platter.

Heat the remaining tablespoon of butter, add the potatoes, and cook, covered, on medium-high heat (375°F) until tender, stirring occasionally, about 20 minutes.

Combine the vinegar, sugar, and caraway seeds in a small bowl and mix until the sugar dissolves. Reduce the heat in the skillet to medium (350°F). Return the sausage, apple mixture, and vinegar mixture to the pan and cook, uncovered, until heated through, stirring gently, about 1 minute. Sprinkle with the parsley and serve immediately.

POLLO ALLA TOSCANA

Yield: 2 servings

The combination of sweet and pungent come together in this country-style chicken entrée. While the recipe calls for a whole chicken, split, you certainly may substitute a boned chicken breast. Leave the skin on during cooking as this gives good flavor to this dish.

ONE 2¹⁄₂-POUND BROILER CHICKEN, SPLIT IN
  HALF

1 TEASPOON SALT

¹⁄₂ TEASPOON FRESHLY GROUND BLACK
  PEPPER

2 CLOVES GARLIC, MASHED

2 TABLESPOONS OLIVE OIL

1 LARGE ONION, CUT INTO ¹⁄₂-INCH-THICK
  RINGS

¹⁄₈ CUP PITTED AND COARSELY CHOPPED
  BLACK OLIVES

2 TEASPOONS CAPERS, DRAINED

1 RED BELL PEPPER, SEEDED AND SLICED INTO
  LONG THIN STRIPS

1 TABLESPOON FRESH ROSEMARY LEAVES, OR
  1 TEASPOON DRIED

¹⁄₃ CUP FRESH BASIL LEAVES, RIPPED INTO
  QUARTERS

¹⁄₂ CUP SWEET ITALIAN VERMOUTH

FINELY GRATED ZEST AND JUICE OF 1 LEMON

2 CUPS SLICED MUSHROOMS

¹⁄₄ CUP PACKED FINELY CHOPPED FRESH
  ITALIAN PARSLEY LEAVES

Rub the chicken with the salt, pepper, and garlic. Heat the olive oil in an electric skillet set on medium heat (350°F). Raise the heat to medium-high (375 to 400°F), add the chicken skin side down, and cook, uncovered, until the skin has browned, 7 to 10 minutes. Turn the chicken over and cook another 10 minutes. Remove the chicken from the pan, add the onion rings, and cook, stirring occasionally, until softened and transparent. Add the olives, capers, bell pepper, rosemary, and basil, then stir in the vermouth and lemon zest and juice. Place the chicken back in the skillet and add the mushrooms. Cover and cook on medium-high heat until the chicken juices run clear, about 40 minutes. Sprinkle with the parsley and serve.

CRANBERRY-ORANGE TURKEY BREAST

Yield: 2¹/₂ to 3 servings per pound

This is the all-time winner of the My Favorite Entertaining Recipe Award. New cooks, seasoned cooks, fussy eaters, and cooks-in-a-hurry all rave about this wondrously easy-to-prepare family and crowd-pleasing entrée. Boned, rolled turkey breasts are available in the meat department of almost all grocery stores. You might have to order one in advance, though, so plan ahead.

Be sure that the turkey is fully defrosted before preparing this dish. You will want to cook it with the webbing in place and remove it before slicing.

1 FRESH OR DEFROSTED UNCOOKED WHOLE TURKEY BREAST, WITH THE SKIN ON

2 TEASPOONS SALT

FRESHLY GROUND BLACK PEPPER TO TASTE

4 LARGE ONIONS, CUT IN HALF AND SLICED

4 LARGE CARROTS, CUT INTO ¹/₂-INCH-THICK SLICES

1 CUP DRIED APRICOTS

1 CUP DRIED CRANBERRIES

ONE 6-OUNCE CAN ORANGE JUICE CONCENTRATE, PARTIALLY DEFROSTED

ONE 10- TO 12-OUNCE JAR ORANGE MARMALADE

2 CUPS CANNED CHICKEN BROTH

Rinse the turkey breast and pat the skin dry. Place the breast in an electric skillet and sprinkle with the salt and pepper. Place the vegetables, apricots, and cranberries around the turkey.

Combine the orange juice concentrate, marmalade, and broth, mixing well. Pour the mixture over the vegetables and fruit in the pan. Add a little water if necessary to make sure there is at least 2 inches of liquid in the bottom of the pan. Set the thermostat at medium heat (350°F), cover, and cook until the turkey inserted with an instant-read thermometer has an internal temperature of 185°F at its thickest section, about 2 hours.

Let rest for a few minutes to let the juices settle and slice with an electric knife.

Variations: You can use other types of dried fruit or jams, such as dried cherries or apricot preserves. In addition, white wine may be used instead of chicken broth.

FARMHOUSE SKILLET DINNER

Yield: 4 servings

Here is a down and dirty one-pot-in-a-hurry meal that will appeal to kids and starving grown-ups.

2 TABLESPOONS VEGETABLE OIL

1 1/2 POUNDS GROUND TURKEY

SALT AND FRESHLY GROUND BLACK PEPPER TO TASTE

2 MEDIUM-SIZE ONIONS, CHOPPED

3 CLOVES GARLIC, MINCED

ONE 28-OUNCE CAN WHOLE TOMATOES, UNDRAINED

ONE 12-OUNCE CAN WHOLE KERNEL CORN, UNDRAINED

1 CUP UNCOOKED ELBOW MACARONI

1 TABLESPOON CHILI POWDER OR 1 TEASPOON DRIED THYME OR OREGANO

4 OUNCES CHEDDAR OR MONTEREY JACK, SHREDDED

Preheat an electric skillet to high heat (425°F). Add the oil and brown the turkey, stirring frequently, 5 to 6 minutes. Sprinkle lightly with the salt and pepper. Add the onions, garlic, tomatoes, corn, and macaroni and heat to boiling. Reduce the thermostat to medium heat (350°F), cover, and cook until the macaroni is tender, stirring occasionally, about 20 minutes. Stir in the chili powder or herbs, sprinkle with the shredded cheese, and heat, covered, until the cheese is melted, about 5 minutes. Serve immediately.

SEARED HADDOCK WITH LEMON-HERB CRUST

Yield: 4 servings

This pan-seared haddock has a crust made from parsley, dill, mustard seeds, and lemon. The fish is dipped into butter, then the herb mixture, then fried in the electric skillet.

6 TABLESPOONS (³⁄₄ STICK) UNSALTED
    BUTTER

¹⁄₂ CUP PACKED CHOPPED FRESH ITALIAN
    PARSLEY LEAVES

¹⁄₄ CUP PACKED CHOPPED FRESH DILL

3 TABLESPOONS MUSTARD SEEDS

GRATED ZEST OF 1 LEMON

SALT AND FRESHLY GROUND BLACK PEPPER TO
    TASTE

1 ¹⁄₂ POUNDS SKINLESS HADDOCK FILLETS, CUT
    INTO 4 PIECES

In an electric skillet set on low heat (275°F), melt the butter. Pour the butter into a large, shallow dish.

In the work bowl of a food processor fitted with the metal blade, combine the parsley, dill, mustard seeds, lemon zest, salt, and pepper and pulse the mixture until finely chopped. Transfer the herb mixture to a large, flat plate.

Dip the fish into the butter, coating it well on both sides. Press the fillets into the herb mixture until they are coated all over.

Heat the electric skillet on medium-high (375°F). Carefully place the fish in the skillet and cook for 2 minutes. Turn it over and cook another 2 minutes. Serve immediately.

SHRIMP FRIED RICE

Yield: 2 servings

Because of the rapid cooking time you need to have everything prepared and ready to toss into the electric skillet.

2 TABLESPOONS VEGETABLE OIL

1 TEASPOON MINCED GARLIC

2 LARGE EGGS, LIGHTLY BEATEN

6 SHRIMP, PEELED AND DEVEINED, OR 4
   OUNCES RAW CHICKEN, CUT INTO CHUNKS

2 TABLESPOONS CHOPPED ONIONS

2 TEASPOONS THAI FISH SAUCE, SOY SAUCE,
   OR TAMARI SAUCE

$\frac{1}{2}$ TEASPOON SUGAR

1 $\frac{1}{2}$ CUPS COOKED LONG-GRAIN RICE

1 TABLESPOON FRESH PEAS OR 10 SUGAR
   SNAP PEA PODS, CUT INTO PIECES

$\frac{1}{4}$ RIPE TOMATO, PEELED, SEEDED, AND
   CHOPPED

1 TABLESPOON THINLY SLICED SCALLIONS

Heat the oil in an electric skillet set on medium heat (350°F). Add the garlic and cook, stirring, until light golden, 3 to 5 minutes. Add the eggs and stir-fry for 10 seconds. Add the shrimp, onions, fish sauce, and sugar and stir until the shrimp turn pink, about 2 minutes. Add the rice, peas, tomato, and scallions and stir-fry a few more seconds to blend the flavors. Remove from the heat and serve immediately.

EASY CARAMEL POPCORN

Yield: About 6 cups

This caramel recipe can also be used over apples or to make caramel popcorn balls.

$\frac{1}{2}$ CUP (1 STICK) BUTTER OR MARGARINE

$\frac{1}{2}$ CUP FIRMLY PACKED DARK BROWN SUGAR

7 LARGE MARSHMALLOWS

4 CUPS POPCORN ($\frac{1}{2}$ CUP POPCORN KERNELS,

POPPED EITHER IN A HOT AIR POPPER OR IN
A TRADITIONAL POPPER WITH 2 TO 3
TABLESPOONS VEGETABLE OIL)

In an electric skillet set on medium-high heat (375°F), combine the butter, brown sugar, and marshmallows. Cook and stir over medium heat (350°F) until the mixture bubbles. Spoon the caramel mixture over the popped corn in a large bowl, making sure all the corn is covered. Cool and serve as is, or form into balls by pressing the warm mixture together and letting dry on waxed paper.

Reggibars

Yield: About 12 bars

For a true chocoholic, this is a little square of heaven on Earth. You don't need an oven to make decadent treats. If you live in a dormitory or small apartment without an oven, this is one dessert that is easy to make in an electric skillet and a snap to clean up.

1 1/2 CUPS CRUSHED GRAHAM CRACKERS OR OTHER COOKIES (ABOUT 14 GRAHAM CRACKERS)

1/2 CUP (1 STICK) BUTTER OR MARGARINE, MELTED

1 CUP CHOPPED PECANS OR WALNUTS

1 1/3 CUPS CHOPPED BITTERSWEET CHOCOLATE

1 1/3 CUPS PACKED SWEETENED SHREDDED COCONUT

ONE 14-OUNCE CAN SWEETENED CONDENSED MILK

Layer the ingredients in a cold electric skillet in the order listed and cover. Set the thermostat to 260°F and cook until the mixture is set, about 25 minutes. At the end of the cooking time, remove the lid without tilting it to avoid dripping the condensed steam into the pan. Let it sit for 20 minutes, uncovered, then slice it into bars.

Cherry Streusel Coffee Cake

Yield: 10 servings

Fresh from the oven, coffee cake is yours in a twinkling thanks to the electric kitchen helpers. Feel free to substitute dried cranberries or blueberries for the cherries in this recipe.

For the streusel topping:

1/2 CUP PECAN PIECES

1/4 CUP ALL-PURPOSE FLOUR

1/3 CUP FIRMLY PACKED LIGHT BROWN SUGAR

1/2 TEASPOON GROUND CINNAMON

3 TABLESPOONS COLD BUTTER OR MARGARINE

For the coffee cake:

5 TABLESPOONS BUTTER OR MARGARINE, AT
    ROOM TEMPERATURE

1 CUP GRANULATED SUGAR

1 LARGE EGG

1 CUP LOW-FAT MILK

2 CUPS ALL-PURPOSE FLOUR

3 TEASPOONS BAKING POWDER

¾ TEASPOON SALT

1 GENEROUS CUP PITTED DRIED CHERRIES
    (AVAILABLE IN GOURMET STORES AND
    MANY SUPERMARKETS)

Oil the bottom and sides of a heavy-duty 12-inch electric skillet and preheat it to to 300°F.

Place the streusel ingredients in the work bowl of a food processor fitted with the metal blade and process until just crumbly, about 10 seconds; set aside.

To make the cake, process the butter, sugar, and egg until combined, about 1 minute. Add the milk and process until smooth, stopping to scrape down the bowl, about 15 seconds. Mix the flour, baking powder, and salt together in a bowl; distribute the mixture over the top of the wet ingredients and pulse 5 or 6 times to combine.

Spread half the batter in the bottom of the electric skillet. Top with half of the cherries, then half of the streusel. Repeat the layering. Cover and bake until a cake tester or toothpick inserted in the center comes out clean and dry, 30 to 35 minutes.

At the end of the baking time, remove the lid without tilting it to avoid dripping the condensed steam into the pan. Cool in the pan 10 minutes, then cut into squares and serve warm.

BANANA UPSIDE-DOWN CAKE

Yield: 8 to 10 servings

You'll need a good quality stainless-steel electric skillet to make this tasty dessert.

continued

9$\frac{1}{2}$ TABLESPOONS BUTTER, AT ROOM
   TEMPERATURE

$\frac{1}{2}$ CUP FIRMLY PACKED DARK BROWN SUGAR

1$\frac{1}{2}$ CUPS GRANULATED SUGAR

1 CUP MASHED BANANAS (ABOUT 2 BANANAS)

2 LARGE EGGS

1 TABLESPOON PURE VANILLA EXTRACT

$\frac{1}{4}$ CUP DARK RUM

2 CUPS ALL-PURPOSE FLOUR

1 TEASPOON BAKING SODA

$\frac{1}{2}$ TEASPOON SALT

1 TEASPOON GROUND CINNAMON

$\frac{1}{4}$ TEASPOON GROUND NUTMEG

$\frac{1}{4}$ TEASPOON GROUND GINGER

$\frac{1}{4}$ CUP SOUR CREAM

2 LARGE UNDERRIPE BANANAS, CUT INTO
   $\frac{1}{3}$-INCH-THICK SLICES

1$\frac{1}{4}$ CUPS BROKEN WALNUTS

In a 10-inch electric skillet set on very low heat (250°F), melt 5$\frac{1}{2}$ tablespoons of the butter with the brown sugar.

     Meanwhile, in a large bowl, cream the remaining 4 tablespoons of butter with the white sugar until light. Add the bananas, eggs, vanilla, and rum and stir. Then stir in the flour, baking soda, salt, and spices; beat in the sour cream. Arrange the banana slices in a pretty pattern in the bottom of the skillet with the brown sugar mixture; top with the walnuts. Pour the batter over all, cover, raise the temperature to 350°F, and bake until a cake tester or toothpick inserted in the center comes out clean and dry, 50 to 60 minutes. At the end of the baking time, remove the lid without tilting it to avoid dropping the condensed steam into the pan. Turn out immediately onto a plate. Serve with vanilla ice cream or frozen yogurt.

BANANAS FOSTER

Yield: 6 servings

I love the taste of caramel, and when you add bananas and vanilla ice cream to this equation I'm just about in heaven.

     If you are daring, you can ignite this flambéed dessert at the table. Make sure to unplug the skillet and remove the control panel before you flambé.

6 TABLESPOONS ($\frac{3}{4}$ STICK) UNSALTED
   BUTTER

$\frac{1}{2}$ CUP FIRMLY PACKED DARK BROWN SUGAR

FINELY GRATED ZEST OF 1 LEMON

$\frac{1}{2}$ TEASPOON GROUND CINNAMON

6 RIPE, FIRM, UNBLEMISHED BANANAS,
   PEELED AND SLICED IN HALF LENGTHWISE

1 PINT BEST QUALITY VANILLA ICE CREAM

²/₃ CUP LIGHT OR DARK RUM

JUICE OF 1 LEMON

In an electric skillet set on medium-high heat (375°F), melt the butter together with the brown sugar. Add the lemon zest and stir to blend. Reduce the heat to low (275°F) and stir in the cinnamon. Add the bananas in a single layer and cook, frequently spooning the sauce over them, until just tender, 5 to 7 minutes, depending on their ripeness.

Just before serving, place a scoop of ice cream into each of six bowls. Pour the rum and lemon juice into a small saucepan and heat it. This can also be done in a Pyrex measure in the microwave: Heat on high power until the liquid is hot to the touch, 40 to 50 seconds. Unplug the skillet and remove the control unit. Pour the hot rum over the bananas and use a long kitchen match to ignite it (take care to keep long sleeves, neck ties, and hanging long hair away from this operation). When the flames die down (which happens once the alcohol is burned off), spoon the bananas and sauce over the ice cream and serve.

CAPE COD BAKED APPLES

Yield: 8 baked apples

I spend the month of August in a wonderful house overlooking Cape Cod Bay. I bring my favorite time-saving electric helpers and use them so that I can spend less time in the kitchen and more time on the beach. This dessert was literally thrown together with ingredients on hand.

8 LARGE, FLAVORFUL, FIRM APPLES, SUCH AS
   GRANNY SMITH

JUICE OF 1 LEMON

¹/₂ CUP (1 STICK) BUTTER OR MARGARINE,
   CUT INTO 16 PIECES

1 CUP FIRMLY PACKED DARK BROWN SUGAR

1 CUP GRANOLA

1 CUP DRY WHITE WINE, APPLE CIDER, OR
   ORANGE JUICE

Slice the bottoms off the apples so that they stand upright. Remove the cores and about 1 inch of peel from the stem ends. Sprinkle the apples with the lemon juice to prevent browning and place one piece of the butter and 2 teaspoons of the brown sugar into the cavity of each. Fill each cavity with 1 to 2 tablespoons of the granola (this should mound slightly) and another pat of butter and sprinkle over the remaining brown sugar.

Place the apples next to each other in an electric skillet and add the wine. Cover and cook on medium-low heat (325°F) until the apples are soft but not collapsed, 25 to 30 minutes. Serve hot or warm with vanilla ice cream or heavy cream.

WOK RECIPES

COCKTAIL SPICED PECANS

Yield: 1 pound

Someone in our school system sells pecans for a fund-raiser each Christmastime. Being a dutiful parent, I buy many bags and end up with a pecan glut. It was a real problem until I was dragged to a Super Bowl party (can you tell I'm not a football fan?). Anyway, the best thing about the party were these addictive morsels. I don't even wait for company to whip up a batch.

6 TABLESPOONS (³/₄ STICK) BUTTER

1 CLOVE GARLIC, FINELY MINCED

¹/₂ TEASPOON TABASCO SAUCE

1 POUND PECAN HALVES OR PIECES

1 TEASPOON WORCESTERSHIRE SAUCE

Preheat an electric wok to 400°F. Add the butter and, when it has melted, the Tabasco, Worcestershire sauce, and garlic and stir to combine. Add the pecans, stir to coat them with the butter, and cook, stirring very frequently until the pecans have turned light brown, about 15 minutes. Spoon the cooked pecans onto a paper towel-lined baking sheet and blot off any excess butter. Serve warm or cold.

Chinese Fried Rice

Yield: 1 serving

Here's the perfect use for leftover white, brown, or wild rice.

2 TABLESPOONS VEGETABLE OIL

2 SCALLIONS, CHOPPED, WHITE AND GREEN
   PARTS SEPARATED

1 LARGE EGG, LIGHTLY BEATEN

2 CUPS LEFTOVER RICE

SOY SAUCE TO TASTE

Heat the oil in an electric wok on high heat (425°F) until a drop of water sizzles when dropped into it. Toss in the scallion whites and stir a few times until softened, then pour in the egg. As soon as it begins to set, stir in the rice and continue stirring for several minutes, until the rice is heated through and any clumps have been broken up.

Remove from the heat and stir in the soy sauce to taste. Transfer the fried rice to a bowl and sprinkle with the scallion greens before serving.

Variations: Just after the scallion whites have softened, add 1 to 1½ cups of any of the following: ground beef, veal, or pork; diced eggplant; or sliced mushrooms. Any of these ingredients can be mixed or, even better, marinated for 1 hour with cayenne pepper, salt, and freshly ground black pepper to taste; 1 tablespoon mild sesame or vegetable oil; and 1 teaspoon ground coriander or cardamom. Stir-fry with the scallions until the beef or other solid ingredients have cooked to your taste, about 3 minutes. Then pour in the egg and proceed with the rest of the recipe.

Stir-fried Wild Rice with Cashews

Yield: 6 servings (3½ cups)

To make this a vegetarian entrée, add 1½ cups of cubed soft tofu with the eggs.

3 TABLESPOONS VEGETABLE OIL

2 CLOVES GARLIC, FINELY MINCED

3 SCALLIONS, CHOPPED

ZEST AND JUICE OF 1 LEMON

3 CUPS COOKED WILD RICE

3 LARGE EGGS, LIGHTLY BEATEN WITH
   2 TABLESPOONS SOY SAUCE

1 CUP CASHEWS, TOASTED (SEE NOTE, PAGE 131)

continued

Heat the oil in an electric wok set on medium-high heat (375°F) and stir-fry the garlic for 2 minutes, not allowing it to brown. Add the scallions, lemon zest and juice, and rice and stir rapidly to heat through, about 3 minutes. Mix in the eggs and continue stirring until the cooked egg whites are visible. Quickly stir in the cashews and serve hot or at room temperature.

STIR-FRY OF TWO CABBAGES

Yield: 6 servings

This is a great seafood companion dish, or the kingpin of a vegetarian meal if served with grains or brown rice. Most of the ingredients can be found in supermarkets or Asian groceries.

2 TABLESPOONS RICE VINEGAR

2 TABLESPOONS SOY SAUCE

1 TABLESPOON SESAME OIL

2 TEASPOONS CORNSTARCH

1 TABLESPOON HONEY

3 CUPS FINELY SHREDDED RED CABBAGE

2 CUPS FINELY SHREDDED GREEN CABBAGE

1 CUP BEAN SPROUTS

3 TABLESPOONS VEGETABLE OIL

3 CLOVES GARLIC, MINCED

1 1/2 TEASPOONS PEELED AND CHOPPED FRESH GINGERROOT

2 TABLESPOONS SESAME SEEDS

3 SCALLIONS, THINLY SLICED

Mix the vinegar, soy sauce, sesame oil, cornstarch, and honey together in a small bowl and set aside.

Combine the cabbages and sprouts in a large bowl.

Heat the vegetable oil in an electric wok set on high heat (425°F). Add the garlic, ginger, and sesame seeds and stir-fry 1 minute. Add the cabbage and sprouts and stir-fry just until wilted and translucent, 4 to 5 minutes. Pour in the reserved soy mixture and cook another minute, tossing to coat the vegetables in the sauce. Sprinkle with the scallions and toss. Serve hot or at room temperature.

SZECHUAN PORK WITH BROCCOLI IN BEAN SAUCE

Yield: 4 servings

If your city has a Chinatown, you will have fun shopping for the ingredients for this Chinese stir-fry dish. Most of the ingredients can also be found in stores that specialize in Asian ingredients.

If you are counting calories, substitute additional chicken broth for the sesame oil and proceed as the recipe directs.

¼ TO ½ TEASPOON CHILI OIL (SESAME OIL IN WHICH CHILIES HAVE BEEN STEEPED), TO YOUR TASTE

2 TABLESPOONS SESAME OIL OR VEGETABLE OIL

1 POUND BONELESS LEAN PORK LOIN, TRIMMED OF FAT AND CUT ACROSS THE GRAIN INTO 4 × ¼ × ¼-INCH STRIPS

¾ CUP CHICKEN BROTH

3 TABLESPOONS SOY SAUCE

2 TABLESPOONS BLACK BEAN SAUCE, SOY BEAN SAUCE, OR BEAN PASTE

1 TABLESPOON CORNSTARCH

1 TEASPOON SUGAR

1 CUP CELERY, SLICED ¼ INCH THICK

1 CUP BROCCOLI FLORETS

¾ CUP MINCED SCALLIONS (BOTH GREEN AND WHITE PART)

1 LARGE CLOVE GARLIC, MINCED

In a medium-size bowl, combine the chili and sesame oils. Add the pork and toss to coat. In a small bowl, combine the chicken broth, soy sauce, black bean sauce, cornstarch, and sugar. Set aside.

Preheat an electric wok to medium-high (375°F) and stir-fry the pork (half at a time) with the oils until it is no longer pink, 2 to 3 minutes. Remove the pork from the wok, leaving 2 tablespoons of the oil. Stir-fry the celery, broccoli, and scallions for 2 minutes, then add the garlic and cook another minute. Return the pork to the wok, add the sauce mixture, toss to coat, and heat through, 1 to 2 minutes. Serve immediately on white rice or noodles.

STIR-FRIED STEAK SALAD

Yield: 4 servings

Hot and cool, this spinach salad is seasoned with an Asian flair. In this main course salad the marinade becomes the cooking liquid as well as the dressing. You can substitute chicken tenders (also called chicken fingers) for the beef, if you wish.

1 POUND BEEF TOP ROUND OR BONELESS TOP SIRLOIN STEAK, CUT ³/₄ INCH THICK, OR FLANK STEAK, TRIMMED OF FAT

3 TABLESPOONS OLIVE OIL

5 TABLESPOONS BALSAMIC VINEGAR

2 CLOVES GARLIC, MASHED

1 TABLESPOON SOY SAUCE, OR TO YOUR TASTE

³/₄ TEASPOON DRIED THYME

¹/₄ TEASPOON FRESHLY GROUND BLACK PEPPER

4 CUPS FRESH SPINACH LEAVES, THOROUGHLY WASHED AND TRIMMED OF TOUGH STEMS

1 CUP FROZEN CORN KERNELS, THAWED

¹/₂ TO 1 CUP THINLY SLICED RED ONIONS, TO YOUR TASTE

¹/₂ CUP SLICED ROASTED RED PEPPERS

Cut the steak lengthwise in half and then crosswise into ¹/₈-inch-thick strips. In a medium-size bowl, whisk together the olive oil, 2 tablespoons of the vinegar, garlic, soy sauce, thyme, and pepper. Add the beef; toss to coat and set aside. Arrange the spinach on a serving platter.

Remove the beef from the marinade; reserve the marinade. In an electric wok set on medium-high heat (375°F), heat 2 tablespoons of the marinade. Add the beef (half at a time) and stir-fry until the outside surface is no longer pink, about 1 minute. Do not overcook or the meat will be tough. Add the corn, onions, and red peppers to the beef and cook another 30 seconds. Spoon the beef onto the salad greens.

In the same wok, combine the reserved marinade and the remaining 3 tablespoons of vinegar; bring to a boil. Spoon over the salad and serve immediately.

BANGKOK BUNDLES

Yield: 4 servings

These nifty packets of stir-fried meat and vegetables are Thailand's version of Chinese moo shu. Here we use large cabbage leaves instead of pancakes to wrap up the filling. These should be served as soon as they are formed.

For the Thai peanut sauce:

1 CLOVE GARLIC, PEELED

1 JALAPEÑO PEPPER

1 TABLESPOON FRESH LEMON JUICE

3 TABLESPOONS SOY SAUCE

2 TABLESPOONS WATER

2 TABLESPOONS PEANUT BUTTER

1 TABLESPOON FIRMLY PACKED DARK BROWN SUGAR

For the bundles:

1 POUND BONELESS, SKINLESS CHICKEN BREASTS, MINCED, OR 1 POUND GROUND TURKEY

¹/₄ CUP SOY SAUCE

2 CLOVES GARLIC, MASHED

¹/₄ CUP FRESH LEMON JUICE

2 TABLESPOONS FIRMLY PACKED DARK BROWN SUGAR

2 TABLESPOONS PEANUT OIL

8 LARGE CHINESE CABBAGE LEAVES

¹/₂ CUP ALFALFA SPROUTS

4 SCALLIONS, MINCED

¹/₄ CUP MINCED FRESH CORIANDER (CILANTRO) LEAVES

2 TABLESPOONS MINCED FRESH MINT LEAVES

Place the garlic and jalapeño pepper in the work bowl of a food processor fitted with the metal blade or a blender and process until smooth. Add the remaining sauce ingredients and process again until smooth.

Combine the chicken, soy sauce, garlic, lemon juice, and sugar in a covered bowl or heavy-duty zippered plastic bag. Shake well to coat and refrigerate at least 4 hours or overnight, turning the meat once or twice. Drain the meat and discard the marinade.

Heat the oil in an electric wok set on high (425°F). Quickly stir-fry the chicken until browned. Divide the cooked meat among the cabbage leaves. Top with the sprouts, scallions, coriander, and mint and drizzle with the peanut sauce. Roll up each leaf like a burrito, folding one end over the chicken and rolling the cabbage around the filling. Pass the extra sauce for dipping.

PAD THAI

Yield: *4 servings*

This popular dish is Thailand's answer to pasta primavera. All the ingredients can be found in gourmet or Asian specialty food shops.

1 POUND THAI RICE NOODLES

1¹/₂ TEASPOONS VEGETABLE OIL

1 LARGE CLOVE GARLIC, MINCED

1 LARGE ONION, DICED

12 MEDIUM-SIZE SHRIMP, PEELED AND DEVEINED

1 TABLESPOON KETCHUP

1 TABLESPOON THAI FISH SAUCE

1 TABLESPOON SUGAR

1 TABLESPOON FRESH LEMON JUICE

1 TABLESPOON WHITE WINE VINEGAR

2 LARGE EGGS, LIGHTLY BEATEN

¹/₄ POUND BEAN SPROUTS

¹/₂ CUP UNSALTED PEANUTS, COARSELY GROUND

For garnish:

¹/₄ POUND BEAN SPROUTS

1 LEMON, CUT INTO WEDGES

¹/₂ CUP UNSALTED PEANUTS, COARSELY GROUND

CHOPPED FRESH CORIANDER (CILANTRO) LEAVES

In a medium-size bowl, cover the noodles with cold water and set aside to soak for 15 minutes. Drain. Return the noodles to the bowl, pour hot water over the noodles, and soak for another 15 minutes. Drain, rinse in cold water, and drain again. Set aside.

Heat the oil in an electric wok set on medium heat (350°F). Add the garlic and onion and stir-fry until the onion is translucent, about 5 minutes. Do not allow the garlic to brown. Add the shrimp and stir-fry until pink, 2 to 3 minutes. Add the ketchup, fish sauce, sugar, lemon juice, and vinegar and stir well. Pour in the beaten eggs and let them set slightly, about 3 minutes. Add the noodles, bean sprouts, and peanuts and mix well.

Transfer the noodles to a large serving platter and place a heap of bean sprouts and lemon wedges to one side. Sprinkle the peanuts and coriander over the noodles and serve.

S L O W

COOKER

If only you were pretty you'd be much more popular. If you were streamlined, sleek, and shiny instead of chintzy and beige, more folks would take you out for the evening. If you weren't so clunky, so squat, so heavy, you could have a place of honor at the dinner table. But for the lack of a little sex appeal, a bit of sophistication, a little glamour, all those closet and back-counter relationships would be made public with pride.

It's a good thing that in my kitchen looks aren't everything. I love the inner you; the you that has dinner ready and waiting without my having to hover. I worship your steadfast refusal to burn, scorch, or shrivel meals. I am in awe of the way the toughest roasts turn tender at your touch. No one does beans with quite the same *je ne sais quoi* or chicken soup with the same perfection. Unlike many of your less stalwart fans, I would never abandon you at a yard sale—I'd be lost without you. Some day your prince (or a smart manufacturer) will wave a magic wand and turn you into a dazzling thing of beauty—I'm willing to wait.

GENERAL DESCRIPTION

WHAT DOES IT DO? • If your watched chicken pot won't boil, try using an appliance that lets you take your eyes off the birdie. Slow cookers cook foods that benefit from long cooking times by maintaining a relatively low temperature in a closed, moist environment. They maintain their heat at a relatively even level by means of a thick, heavy crockery insert and do not need to be watched constantly, since they never reach a temperature on the bottom that could allow the food that is cooking inside to burn.

WHY DO I NEED THIS? • If you like the taste of foods that are cooked slowly and you do not have the time to baby-sit them, then you need a slow cooker. Any food that can benefit from cooking in a moist environment can be made beautifully in a slow cooker. They are great on an informal buffet table for soups and stews. Plus, slow cookers are relatively inexpensive, and the cost/benefit ratio of a slow cooker is very, very low.

HOW DOES IT WORK? • Two basic types of slow cookers are on the market. *Please note, however, that slow cookers that use crockery inserts were the only type tested for this book.* These cookers are commonly called crock-pots, but the term Crock-Pot is a registered trademark of the Rival company. This is the same phenomenon that happened with the terms Xerox and Kleenex, but only Rival makes Crock-Pots.

When you plug in a slow cooker, a heating element warms the contents in its round or oval container. Most slow cookers have multiple heat settings that are adjusted by turning on the appropriate heating element that is set for that temperature. For safe slow cooking, temperatures must reach at least 165°F, so most models typically have a minimum temperature of 200°F.

The containers on slow cookers are made of heavy ceramic, and bigger models require heavy lifting skills. The heating elements are coiled around the sides of the vessel within an enameled metal exterior. The coils actually hug the crockery insert and gently heat it and the food inside. Typically, this configuration yields more even heat since it does not concentrate it on the bottom.

The containers range in size from very small (8 ounces) to a capable 6 quarts. Remember that stoneware is very sensitive to dramatic changes in temperature, so do not put a frozen chicken in a ceramic slow cooker. As the chicken thaws, the cold liquid will drip on the hot ceramic and might crack it.

All slow cookers have lids that beg you to peek inside, but resist the temptation to take the lid off to check on the food. Every time the lid is raised, some of the liquid and the heat in the cooker escapes, reducing the temperature and interrupting the way the slow cooker was intended to work. Clear lids supplement your willpower, but when they are covered with water droplets, it is still difficult to see inside. Glass lids look nicer than plastic ones and clean up better, but they still bead up and fog. If a lid does not fit perfectly on a stoneware cooking vessel, this should not affect operation since the water droplets from the lid tend to seal any cracks between the stoneware and lid.

Some slow cookers have roasting racks or cake pans. In a pinch, it is possible to use your slow cooker as an oven.

CARE AND MAINTENANCE • Slow cookers are easy to clean, particularly if the cooking pot is removable. Clean it well after every use and do not let food stains build up, as these can retain strong flavors. Usually removable containers are dishwasher safe. But the part of the cooker containing the heating element should never be immersed in water. Wipe this part off with a damp sponge and dry it off before plugging it in.

WHICH IS RIGHT FOR ME? • Buy a slow cooker that is the right size for most of your cooking needs. A 6-quart cooker will roast a whole chicken, but if making smaller quantities of chili or stew, a smaller cooker is better suited to the task. Once the usefulness of a slow cooker is understood, you might want two sizes to fit all occasions. If using a slow cooker that has a removable container, it can be filled the night before and refrigerated. Then in the morning, it can be put back into the cooker and turned on.

The mini slow cooker is useful for reconstituting dehydrated fruits and vegetables, especially using wine or liquor as the base liquid.

COMMENTS • Things that affect the temperature of a slow cooker have a great impact on how they work. Temperatures vary from model to model, so recipes may need to be adjusted if not written specifically for your slow cooker. Also, since the voltage in your home can vary, the slow cooker may either be a little hotter or a little cooler than its rated temperature setting, thus affecting cooking times. Ceramic containers tend to hold their temperature better than metal ones once they reach cooking temperature.

When adapting regular recipes for slow cookers, the liquid is usually decreased by half. If substituting liquids in recipes for slow cookers, substitute them equally measure for measure.

Contrary to popular belief, slow cookers heat food hot enough fast enough to avoid spoilage, and it is quite safe to leave them cooking unsupervised—all night long or during the day when you are out and about.

SLOW COOKER TIPS

- *Stoneware is fairly sensitive to dramatic changes in temperature. Don't set a hot crock on a cold surface. Always place a hot pad or towel under it.*

- *If you fill the cooking chamber the night before and put it into the refrigerator, the next morning the crock must be put into a cold base unit. Put a cold crock only in a cold slow cooker.*

- *Slow cookers with crockery inserts are heavy. If an empty crock is too heavy to lift when it is empty, then it will certainly be too heavy to lift when filled with food.*

- *High altitude (greater than 3,500 feet above sea level) cooking requires longer cooking times.*

- *If possible, use leaf or whole herbs and spices, and use half the amount needed. If you use dried or ground herbs and spices, use $1/4$ the amount of fresh and add them during the last hour of cooking.*

- *Most milk-based products tend to break down during slow cooking. If possible, add them during the last hour of cooking.*

- *Fat retains heat more readily than water, so fattier recipes will cook faster than those with less fat. Trim meats and brown them prior to putting them in the slow cooker to reduce this effect. Foods cooked in fat will be more tender than those cooked in stock, water, or vegetable juice.*

- *Use a slow cooker on a buffet table to keep soup or stew hot.*

- *The mini slow cookers are terrific for making sauces, stewing individual pieces of fruit, and melting chocolate.*

- *Clean the ceramic crock in the dishwasher. Soak, then scrub off all cooked-on stains between uses. Abrasive cleanser is fine for this. Don't be tempted to leave food residue on the crock. It will cook off and become part of the next meal—yuk!*

SLOW COOKER OATMEAL

Yield: About 6 cups

This is my favorite winter breakfast dish, especially when I have overnight guests. They wake up to the intoxicating aroma of hot oatmeal perfuming the kitchen and think I've been up since dawn preparing it. Try tossing in a handful of raisins or dried cherries to give a special sweetness to the cereal.

1 CUP OATS, NOT INSTANT OR QUICK COOKING

4 CUPS WATER

2 TEASPOONS SALT

2 TABLESPOONS BUTTER (OPTIONAL)

$^1/_2$ CUP FIRMLY PACKED DARK BROWN SUGAR

$^1/_2$ TO 1 CUP RAISINS OR DRIED CHERRIES (OPTIONAL), TO YOUR TASTE

Place all the ingredients in the slow cooker, cover, and set on low. Cook for at least 4 hours or overnight. Serve with a dab of butter and real maple syrup.

MUSHROOM AND WHITE BEAN SOUP

Yield: 10 servings

Thinking about this cold weather soup somehow makes winter more appealing. Thick and fragrant with the earthy taste of the mushrooms, this soup is truly a meal in itself.

1 POUND DRIED WHITE BEANS

6 CUPS BROTH (VEGETABLE, BEEF, OR CHICKEN)

3 STALKS CELERY, FINELY DICED

4 CLOVES GARLIC, MINCED

1 LARGE ONION, CHOPPED, OR 2 CARAMELIZED ONIONS (PAGE 297)

1 BAY LEAF

2 OUNCES DRIED MUSHROOMS, SOAKED TO RECONSTITUTE, PLUS THE SOAKING LIQUID STRAINED THROUGH A FINE MESH STRAINER OR CHEESECLOTH OR 2 CUPS FRESH MUSHROOMS, STEMS TRIMMED AND CUT INTO $^1/_2$-INCH SLICES

$^1/_2$ POUND SMOKED HAM OR SMOKED TURKEY (OPTIONAL), DICED

SALT AND FRESHLY GROUND BLACK PEPPER TO TASTE

continued

Place all the ingredients except the mushrooms, ham, salt, and pepper in a slow cooker, cover, set on high, and cook until the beans are very tender, 3 to 4 hours. Add the mushrooms and ham, cover, and cook another hour on high. Discard the bay leaf, season with the salt and pepper, and serve hot.

WON'T YOU COME HOME PEARL BARLEY SOUP

Yield: 6 to 8 servings

I named this hearty soup after my parrot, Pearl. She's a very vocal African Grey who kept insisting that she wanted a taste all the while this was cooking. "Smells good!" she screamed over and over. Tastes good as well. I always serve this with a thick slice of black bread spread with sweet butter.

3 CUPS DRIED MUSHROOMS

1 CUP PEARL BARLEY OR 1 1/2 CUPS FOR A
    MORE STEWLIKE CONSISTENCY

1 LARGE SPANISH ONION, DICED

3 STALKS CELERY, CUT INTO 1/2-INCH-THICK
    SLICES

1 BAY LEAF

SALT AND FRESHLY GROUND BLACK PEPPER TO
    TASTE

8 CUPS CHICKEN OR VEGETABLE BROTH

Rinse the mushrooms in several changes of water to get rid of any sand and grit. Place the barley in a fine mesh sieve and rinse well. Put all the ingredients in a slow cooker, cover, set on high, and cook until the barley is soft, 2 to 3 hours. Remove the bay leaf before serving.

To serve, spoon into soup bowls and sprinkle with a generous amount of freshly ground black pepper.

Variation: Use 1 to 3 caramelized Vidalia onions and their juice (see page 297).

SWEET AND SOUR CABBAGE SOUP

Yield: 8 servings

The slow cooker makes this stick-to-your-ribs, one-pot meal a breeze. You can start it in the morning, and its heavenly aroma will welcome you home at the end of the day.

3 TABLESPOONS VEGETABLE OIL

TWO 1- TO 1½-POUND STRIPS FLANKEN (BEEF SHORT RIBS), AVAILABLE IN KOSHER MARKETS

2 TO 3 QUARTS WATER, AS NEEDED

ONE 16-OUNCE CAN WHOLE TOMATOES

2 LARGE ONIONS, COARSELY CHOPPED

1 BAY LEAF

3 CLOVES GARLIC, MINCED

1 MEDIUM-SIZE HEAD CABBAGE, SHREDDED

¼ CUP FIRMLY PACKED DARK BROWN SUGAR

½ CUP RED WINE VINEGAR

1 CUP SAUERKRAUT, UNDRAINED

SALT AND FRESHLY GROUND BLACK PEPPER TO TASTE

Heat the oil in a 6-quart, heavy-bottomed pot over medium-high heat and sear the meat on both sides until browned. Place the meat and the remaining ingredients, except the sauerkraut, salt, and pepper, in a slow cooker, cover, set on high, and cook for 2 hours. Stir in the sauerkraut, cover, and cook on high until all the ingredients are tender, another 30 to 45 minutes. Skim off any fat that has accumulated on the surface. Season with the salt and pepper, remove the bay leaf, and serve hot.

CARAMELIZED ONIONS

Yield: About 5 cups onions and 2 cups liquid

Whenever Vidalia or Sweet Maui onions show up in my local market, I buy a whole case, run home, and get out my slow cooker. I promise that the heavenly aroma of onions gently simmering will make your kitchen the most sought-after room in the house. The addition of these sweet golden brown onions and their cooking liquid will enliven a multitude of dishes in a way you never dreamed possible. Be sure to make extra to freeze—having them safely tucked away is like having extra money in the bank.

6 TO 8 VIDALIA OR OTHER SWEET ONIONS
(APPROXIMATELY 2½ POUNDS), 3 TO 4
INCHES IN DIAMETER, STEM AND ROOT
ENDS REMOVED, PEELED AND LEFT WHOLE

½ CUP (1 STICK) BUTTER OR MARGARINE
ONE 10-OUNCE CAN CHICKEN OR VEGETABLE
BROTH

Place the onions, butter, and broth in a slow cooker set on low and cook until the onions are deep golden brown and very soft, 12 to 24 hours. Different slow cookers will take different amounts of time. It's almost impossible to overcook this, so go for the deepest brown.

Use the onions and liquid to flavor soup, stock, and stews. They make a wonderful addition to risotto, a perfect pasta sauce, and the world's best pizza topping (first drain off the liquid).

Store in zippered plastic bags in the refrigerator up to 2 weeks, or in the freezer up to 1 year.

Variation: Add cloves of peeled elephant garlic or a handful of shallots along with the onions.

CARAMELIZED ONION SOUP

Yield: 6 to 8 servings (about 10 cups)

Real French onion soup just got a whole lot easier to make, thanks to the slow cooker.

3 TO 4 CUPS CARAMELIZED ONIONS (ABOVE),
THICKLY SLICED

3 CUPS ONION COOKING LIQUID

3 CUPS BROTH (CHICKEN, BEEF, OR
VEGETABLE)

SALT AND FRESHLY GROUND BLACK PEPPER TO
TASTE

8 THICK SLICES FRENCH BREAD, TOASTED

GRATED SWISS CHEESE

Combine the onions, cooking liquid, and broth in a large pot over medium heat. Stir occasionally as the soup comes to a simmer. Season with the salt and pepper.

Preheat the broiler to high with the rack in the upper part of the oven. Place eight ovenproof bowls on a heavy-duty baking sheet or rimmed toasting pan. Ladle the hot soup into the bowls and top each with a slice of toast. Sprinkle generously with cheese and broil until the cheese melts and begins to bubble. Serve immediately.

Dal (Split Pea or Lentil Purée)

Yield: 6 cups

These lentils can be used as a side dish or as an addition to soup, stew, or salad.

2 CUPS DRIED YELLOW OR RED LENTILS

4 CUPS WATER

1 TEASPOON GROUND TURMERIC

SALT TO TASTE

1 MEDIUM-SIZE ONION, FINELY CHOPPED

2 TABLESPOONS VEGETABLE OIL

2 CLOVES GARLIC, CHOPPED

1 TEASPOON CUMIN SEEDS

Place all the ingredients in a slow cooker, cover, set on high, and cook for 1 hour, then reduce the heat to low and cook until the beans are very tender, about another 2 hours. The dal should have the consistency of mashed potatoes. If it seems too watery, simmer, uncovered, for part of the cooking time.

Orange Wild Rice

Yield: 6 to 8 servings

The perfect pairing of citrus and nuts just enhances the crunchiness of the wild rice.

1 1/2 CUPS WILD RICE

3 CUPS CHICKEN BROTH

3 TABLESPOONS GRATED ORANGE ZEST OR
   1 TABLESPOON DRIED ORANGE PEEL

2 TABLESPOONS FRESH ORANGE JUICE

1 TEASPOON SALT

1 TABLESPOON UNSALTED BUTTER

1/2 TO 3/4 CUP CHOPPED PECANS, TO YOUR
   TASTE, TOASTED (SEE NOTE, PAGE 131)

1/4 CUP CHOPPED SCALLIONS

1/4 CUP PACKED CHOPPED FRESH ITALIAN
   PARSLEY LEAVES

continued

Rinse the wild rice in a strainer under cold running water. In a slow cooker, combine the rice, broth, orange zest and juice, salt, and butter. Cover, set on high, and cook until the kernels are open and tender but not mushy, 2 to 3 hours. Stir in the pecans, scallions, and parsley and serve.

SAVORY BREAD PUDDING

Yield: 12 to 14 servings

Looking for an appetizing alternative to potatoes, rice, or noodles? Here's a whole new take on a vegetarian or side dish—savory bread pudding made from corn muffins (or you can use packaged corn bread stuffing). The slow cooker makes it unnecessary to baby-sit this tasty treat; it cooks while you go about your business. You'll need a large slow cooker to make this.

2 TABLESPOONS BUTTER

1/2 CUP (1 STICK) BUTTER, MELTED

5 LARGE EGGS, BEATEN

2 CUPS HEAVY CREAM

3 1/2 CUPS MILK

1 CUP FROZEN CORN KERNELS (NO NEED TO THAW BEFORE USING)

1 SMALL CAN JALAPEÑO CHILIES, OR LESS TO TASTE, DRAINED

ABOUT 14 CORN MUFFINS, CUT INTO 1 1/2-INCH CUBES, OR 12 CUPS PACKAGED CORN BREAD STUFFING

2 CUPS SHREDDED MONTEREY JACK CHEESE

Grease the ceramic insert of a slow cooker with the unmelted butter. In a large bowl, combine the melted butter, eggs, cream, milk, corn, and chilies.

Divide the muffin cubes or stuffing evenly into 3 piles and, beginning with the muffins, layer alternately with the egg mixture into the slow cooker, ending with the egg mixture. You'll have 3 bread layers and 3 egg layers. Sprinkle the cheese over the top. Cover, set on high, and cook for 1 hour, then turn to low and cook until the top is set and an instant-read thermometer inserted in the center registers 190°F or a cake tester or toothpick inserted in the center comes out clean and dry, another 2 to 3 hours. Serve hot or warm as a side dish.

VEGETABLES PROVENCE

Yield: 6 servings

So, you've invited your vegetarian friends to dinner. This will make them glad they came.

3 LARGE SPANISH ONIONS, CUT INTO ¹⁄₂-INCH-
   THICK SLICES

4 CLOVES GARLIC, MASHED

¹⁄₄ CUP OLIVE OIL

2 TABLESPOONS FRESH THYME LEAVES

2 CLOVES GARLIC, MINCED

1 MEDIUM-SIZE EGGPLANT, CUT INTO
   ¹⁄₂-INCH-THICK SLICES

4 MEDIUM-SIZE ZUCCHINI, CUT INTO ¹⁄₂-
   TO ³⁄₄-INCH-THICK SLICES

1 POUND RIPE TOMATOES, CUT INTO
   ¹⁄₂- TO ³⁄₄-INCH-THICK SLICES

SALT AND FRESHLY GROUND BLACK PEPPER TO
   TASTE

1 CUP SMOKED GOUDA OR MOZZARELLA
   CHEESE CUBES

¹⁄₄ CUP FRESHLY GRATED PARMESAN CHEESE

Place everything except the salt, pepper, and 2 cheeses in a slow cooker, cover, set on high, and cook until the vegetables are extremely tender and soft, about 2 hours.

   Half an hour before serving, season with salt and pepper, then stir in the smoked cheese and allow it to melt. Just before serving, transfer to a broiler-proof casserole and sprinkle on the Parmesan cheese. Place the dish under a preheated broiler just long enough for the cheese to brown. Serve hot.

BEEF RAGOUT

Yield: 6 servings

This is a wonderful recipe that takes full advantage of slow cooking. It is a Flemish adaptation of a French stew using dark beer as one of the ingredients.

continued

½ CUP ALL-PURPOSE FLOUR

½ TEASPOON SALT

2 POUNDS LEAN BEEF CHUCK, TRIMMED OF FAT
AND CUT INTO 1-INCH CUBES

¼ CUP VEGETABLE OIL

3 CLOVES GARLIC, MINCED

¼ CUP FIRMLY PACKED DARK BROWN SUGAR

½ CUP PACKED CHOPPED FRESH ITALIAN
PARSLEY LEAVES

1½ CUPS BEEF BROTH

ONE 12-OUNCE BOTTLE BEER

1 BAY LEAF

1 LARGE SPANISH ONION, THINLY SLICED

1 TEASPOON WORCESTERSHIRE SAUCE

1 TABLESPOON RED WINE VINEGAR

SALT AND FRESHLY GROUND BLACK PEPPER TO
TASTE

HOT EGG NOODLES OR WILD RICE

In a medium-size bowl, mix together the flour and salt. Dredge the beef cubes in the flour, shaking off any excess.

In either an electric skillet set at 300°F or a large skillet over medium heat, heat the oil and brown the cubes of beef on all sides. Remove the beef to a slow cooker. Reduce the heat of the electric skillet to low (150°F). Add the garlic to the skillet and cook, stirring, until golden but not brown. Add the brown sugar, parsley, beef broth, and beer to the skillet, stir to loosen the browned bits from the bottom, then pour the mixture over the meat in the slow cooker. Add the bay leaf and place the onion slices on top of the beef. Cover, set on low, and cook for 6 hours, stirring the onion into the mixture after 2 to 3 hours. Stir in the Worcestershire sauce and vinegar during the last 15 minutes of cooking time.

Remove the bay leaf, season with salt and pepper, and serve over hot noodles or wild rice.

CHILI MOLE

Yield: 8 to 10 servings

Mole in Mexican cooking is a flavorful sauce made with spices, chilies, and sometimes even chocolate. This recipe brings together the traditional flavors of mole, simmered to perfection in a slow cooker.

1½ POUNDS LEAN GROUND BEEF, CRUMBLED

2 TABLESPOONS GARLIC OIL (AVAILABLE IN
SUPERMARKETS AND GOURMET STORES)

2 MEDIUM-SIZE ONIONS, CHOPPED

1 LARGE GREEN BELL PEPPER, SEEDED AND
CHOPPED

ONE 28-OUNCE CAN WHOLE TOMATOES

ONE 15-OUNCE CAN BLACK BEANS, DRAINED

1 OUNCE UNSWEETENED CHOCOLATE, CHOPPED

1 TABLESPOON FINELY CHOPPED CANNED
   CHIPOTLE CHILIES, OR MORE TO YOUR
   TASTE

1 TEASPOON SALT

1/2 TEASPOON GROUND CINNAMON

1/4 TEASPOON GROUND CLOVES

1 TEASPOON DRIED OREGANO

1 TABLESPOON CHILI POWDER

1 TEASPOON GROUND CUMIN

1/4 CUP KAHLÚA (OPTIONAL)

HOT WHITE RICE

S L O W

C O O K E R

Place the beef in a microwavable glass bowl, cover, and microwave on high power until browned, stirring once during the cooking time, 5 to 7 minutes. Drain off the liquid and remove the meat to a slow cooker. Without washing the bowl, add the oil and onions, cover, and microwave on high power until wilted, 4 to 5 minutes. Add all the ingredients, except the rice, to the slow cooker, cover, set on low, and cook 4 to 6 hours or overnight. Serve over rice.

MOCK MOUSSAKA

Yield: A mess of moussaka, about three-quarters of a slow cooker full

Moussaka is usually a very beautiful layered Greek dish. This recipe lets you enjoy all the flavor of moussaka without all of the work.

ABOUT 3 POUNDS EGGPLANT, PEELED AND CUT
   INTO 1/4-INCH-THICK SLICES

1 1/2 POUNDS GROUND BEEF, LAMB, OR TURKEY

1 LARGE ONION, CHOPPED

3 CLOVES GARLIC, MINCED

For the sauce:

2 TABLESPOONS OLIVE OIL

ONE 28-OUNCE CAN CRUSHED TOMATOES

ONE 6-OUNCE CAN TOMATO PASTE

1/3 CUP PITTED AND CHOPPED BLACK OR
   GREEN OLIVES (KALAMATAS ARE DELICIOUS
   IN THIS RECIPE)

3 TABLESPOONS CHOPPED FRESH BASIL
   LEAVES

1/2 CUP PACKED CHOPPED FRESH ITALIAN
   PARSLEY LEAVES

1/2 TEASPOON DRIED OREGANO

1 1/2 TEASPOONS SUGAR

For the topping:

2 TO 3 OUNCES FETA CHEESE, TO YOUR TASTE,
   CRUMBLED

3 SPRIGS FRESH DILL, CHOPPED

continued

To prepare the eggplant, salt both sides of each piece and place in a colander in a single layer for about 1 hour to drain. Rinse, pat dry, and set aside.

Brown the beef in a medium-size skillet over medium heat. Drain off the fat and liquid and remove the meat to a bowl or plate. Using the same skillet (you needn't thoroughly clean it), cook the onion and garlic, stirring, over medium heat until softened. To make the sauce, add the rest of the ingredients, except the feta cheese and dill, and simmer until hot and slightly thickened, 15 to 20 minutes.

Layer in the slow cooker in this order: sauce, eggplant, beef, sauce, eggplant, beef, sauce. Sprinkle the feta cheese on top and the dill on top of that. Cover, set on low, and cook for 7 to 9 hours or set on high and cook for 2 to 3 hours.

LASAGNE

Yield: 10 to 12 servings

Who knew you could make great lasagne in the slow cooker? The secret, we discovered, is *not* to precook the noodles, and to double layer them to keep them from getting mushy.

1 1/2 POUNDS GROUND BEEF

2 TABLESPOONS OLIVE OIL

1 MEDIUM-SIZE ONION, CHOPPED

2 CLOVES GARLIC, MINCED

ONE 28-OUNCE CAN WHOLE TOMATOES, UNDRAINED

ONE 6-OUNCE CAN TOMATO PASTE

ONE 12-OUNCE CAN TOMATO SAUCE

1/2 CUP TOMATO PESTO (PAGE 117)

1 1/2 TEASPOONS SALT

1 1/2 TABLESPOONS SUGAR

1 TABLESPOON CHOPPED FRESH OREGANO LEAVES, OR 1 TEASPOON DRIED

3 TABLESPOONS CHOPPED FRESH BASIL LEAVES, OR 1 TABLESPOON DRIED

12 OUNCES RICOTTA CHEESE

1/2 CUP FRESHLY GRATED PARMESAN CHEESE

8 TO 12 LASAGNA NOODLES (DO *NOT* PRECOOK)

12 OUNCES MOZZARELLA CHEESE, SHREDDED

In a large skillet, brown the beef completely over medium-high heat, then drain in a colander and set aside. In the same skillet, heat the olive oil over medium-high heat and cook the onion and garlic, stirring, until softened. Add the meat, tomatoes with their juice, tomato paste, tomato sauce, pesto, salt, sugar, and herbs and heat through.

In a large bowl, mix the ricotta and Parmesan cheeses together. Layer the ingredients in a slow cooker as follows: meat sauce, a double layer of noodles (broken to fit the cooker), ricotta mixture, and mozzarella. Repeat the order of layers again, ending with sauce on top. Cover, set on low, and cook for 6 to 8 hours or set on high and cook for 2 hours.

Variation: Use green pesto (page 117) instead of the tomato pesto.

LAMB VINDALOO

Yield: 4 to 6 servings

Typical Indian spices combine to make both a marinade and a cooking base for this savory classic. It's traditionally served with rice, but I prefer throwing in some sliced potatoes 1 hour before serving. Either way, its aromatic essence will perfume your kitchen.

1 LARGE ONION, QUARTERED

ONE 1-INCH PIECE FRESH GINGERROOT, PEELED

2 CLOVES GARLIC, MINCED

$^1/_3$ CUP RED WINE VINEGAR

2 TABLESPOONS DRY MUSTARD

1 TABLESPOON GROUND CORIANDER

1 TABLESPOON GROUND CUMIN

1 TABLESPOON TURMERIC

1 TEASPOON SALT

$^1/_2$ TEASPOON CAYENNE PEPPER

3 POUNDS BONELESS LAMB SHOULDER, TRIMMED OF FAT AND CUT INTO 2-INCH PIECES

3 MEDIUM-SIZE CARROTS, PEELED AND CUT INTO THICK SLICES

1 CUP WATER

3 IDAHO POTATOES (OPTIONAL), PEELED, HALVED, AND CUT INTO 1-INCH-THICK SLICES

HOT WHITE RICE (OPTIONAL)

In the work bowl of a food processor fitted with the metal blade, process the onion, ginger, and garlic together until finely chopped. Add the vinegar, mustard, coriander, cumin, turmeric, salt, and cayenne pepper and process until the mixture forms a smooth paste. Transfer the paste to a $3^1/_2$-quart slow cooker crockery insert. Add the lamb and toss to coat well with the paste. Cover with plastic wrap and refrigerate at least 4 hours or overnight.

continued

Place the insert in the slow cooker, add the carrots and water, cover, set on low, and cook until the lamb is tender, 6 to 7 hours. Add the potatoes 1 hour before the cooking is completed, or plan to serve the stew over rice.

Transfer the lamb and cooking juices to a large saucepan and cook over medium-high heat, stirring often, until all the liquid has evaporated and the lamb is sizzling, about 20 minutes. Reduce the heat to low and continue cooking, stirring often, until the spice coating turns light brown, about another 5 minutes. Serve immediately.

Coq au Vin

Yield: 10 servings

This French classic made easy with the help of a slow cooker and an electric skillet makes great party fare. It can be made ahead and frozen up to three months, then defrosted and reheated in the microwave.

1 POUND LEAN SLICED BACON

3 TABLESPOONS OLIVE OIL

4 POUNDS SKINLESS BONELESS CHICKEN BREASTS, CUT INTO BITE-SIZE PIECES

1 LARGE ONION, CHOPPED

24 SMALL WHITE ONIONS, PEELED AND LEFT WHOLE

2 CLOVES GARLIC, MINCED

¼ CUP ALL-PURPOSE FLOUR

1 CUP BURGUNDY WINE

3 CUPS BEEF BROTH

2 BAY LEAVES

1 TEASPOON DRIED THYME

1 TEASPOON DRIED BASIL

8 OUNCES MUSHROOMS, SLICED

SALT AND FRESHLY GROUND BLACK PEPPER TO TASTE

To finish and garnish:

1 CUP PEELED, SEEDED, AND DICED RIPE TOMATOES

¼ CUP COGNAC OR BRANDY

2 TO 3 TABLESPOONS CHOPPED FRESH ITALIAN PARSLEY LEAVES, TO YOUR TASTE

2 TABLESPOONS CORNSTARCH MIXED WITH 4 TO 5 TABLESPOONS WATER, IF NEEDED

In an electric skillet set on medium heat (350°F) or in a large skillet over medium heat, fry the bacon until crisp. Remove the bacon to paper towels to drain and discard all but 2 to 3 tablespoons of the fat from the pan. Add the olive oil and increase the heat to medium-high (375°F). Add the chicken and brown on all sides.

Tear the bacon into bite-sized pieces and divide them into two portions, setting aside one portion for garnish.

Place the other half of the bacon, the browned chicken, and the remaining ingredients, except the garnishes, in a slow cooker, cover, set on high, and cook until the onions and chicken are thoroughly cooked, 3½ to 4 hours.

Prepare the garnish ingredients and set aside. At the end of the cooking time the sauce should coat the back of a spoon. If it does not, quickly stir the cornstarch mixture into the slow cooker and cook on low until thick, another 10 to 15 minutes. Discard the bay leaf, stir in the garnish ingredients (remember the reserved bacon!), and serve.

JERK CHICKEN

Yield: 4 servings

Think of coming home from a long work day to a slow cooker full of one of the best chicken dishes you've ever had. You can adjust the heat of this dish by adding fewer chilies. If you go full throttle, make sure you have some rice handy to cool down the fire.

1 LARGE ONION, CUT INTO 8 PIECES

1 GENEROUS TABLESPOON CANDIED GINGER

1½ TABLESPOONS MINCED CANNED CHIPOTLE CHILIES, OR MORE TO YOUR TASTE

½ TEASPOON GROUND ALLSPICE

2 TABLESPOONS DRY MUSTARD

1 TEASPOON FRESHLY GROUND BLACK PEPPER

2 TABLESPOONS BALSAMIC VINEGAR

2 TABLESPOONS SOY SAUCE

2 TABLESPOONS GARLIC OIL (AVAILABLE IN SUPERMARKETS AND GOURMET STORES)

ONE 3½ POUND CHICKEN, SKIN REMOVED AND CUT INTO 8 PIECES, OR 3½ POUNDS CHICKEN TENDERS (FINGERS)

To prepare the sauce, place the onions and ginger in the work bowl of a food processor fitted with the metal blade and process to chop into very fine pieces. Add everything but the chicken and pulse to combine.

Place the chicken in a slow cooker and coat with the sauce. Cover, set on low, and cook for 6 to 8 hours or set on high and cook until the chicken is tender, 2 to 3 hours.

CASSOULET

Yield: 8 servings

This is baked beans, French style. The recipe for confit (preserved duck or goose) can be found below. If you cannot find herbes de Provence, you can make your own by combining equal amounts of dried tarragon, rosemary, chervil, basil, and thyme.

1 RECIPE DUCK OR GOOSE CONFIT, BONES, SKIN, AND COOKING FAT REMOVED AND MEAT SHREDDED

1 POUND DRIED FRENCH WHITE BEANS (LIMA BEANS ARE ALSO FINE)

3 STALKS CELERY, CUT INTO 2-INCH LENGTHS

3 LARGE CARROTS, CUT INTO 1-INCH-THICK SLICES

4 CLOVES GARLIC, MASHED

3 CUPS CARAMELIZED ONIONS (PAGE 297), SLICED, PLUS 1 CUP OF THEIR COOKING LIQUID, OR 2 LARGE SPANISH ONIONS, CUT INTO THICK SLICES

1 BAY LEAF

4 TO 5 CUPS BEEF OR CHICKEN BROTH

1 TABLESPOON DRIED HERBES DE PROVENCE

SALT AND FRESHLY GROUND BLACK PEPPER TO TASTE

Place all the ingredients in a slow cooker, cover, and set on high. Cook until the mixture starts to simmer, about 1 hour. Reduce the heat to low and cook until the beans are very soft, another 2 to 3 hours. Remove the bay leaf before serving.

DUCK CONFIT

Yield: 1½ pounds

Confit is an age-old method of preserving goose or other meats for winter consumption. The goose is salted and slowly simmered in its own fat. In this way most of the heavy fat under the skin is removed and all of the moisture is evaporated. After the process is completed, the meat is put in crocks and sealed with fat for storage.

Modern refrigeration and freezers have changed the need for the confit tradition. The taste and the unique tenderness that result from this cooking technique are what we're after here, and the slow cooker is the perfect vehicle for delivering it. Duck lends itself readily to this recipe as does the traditional goose. I like to serve this with white beans that have been stewed in chicken broth and tarragon.

- 1 1/2 POUNDS RENDERED GOOSE FAT OR CHICKEN FAT (SEE NOTE BELOW)
- 1 DUCK (ABOUT 2 1/2 POUNDS), PLUS NECK, QUARTERED
- 6 CLOVES GARLIC, PEELED
- 1 LARGE SHALLOT, COARSELY CHOPPED
- 1 TABLESPOON KOSHER SALT
- 2 TEASPOONS FRESHLY GROUND BLACK PEPPER
- 1 TABLESPOON DRIED HERBS DE PROVENCE

Place the duck pieces in a slow cooker and add the remaining ingredients. Cover, set on high, and cook for 1 hour, then reduce the heat to low and cook until very, very tender, at least 4 hours or up to 8 hours. Use a slotted spoon to remove the duck from the fat, which can be frozen and reused. Serve the duck hot or at room temperature. The duck can also be combined into a cassoulet, the French version of baked beans (page 308).

Note: You can buy chicken fat from most butchers and in all kosher meat markets. Canned goose fat is available in gourmet food shops. You can also skim the fat off the surface of chicken soup and store it in a plastic container in the freezer until ready to use.

ALL-AMERICAN BARBECUE SAUCE

Yield: 2 pints

Try marinating your ribs or steak in this sweet/tangy sauce, as well as using it to baste chicken and game when you grill.

- 1 TABLESPOON VEGETABLE OIL
- 2 LARGE YELLOW ONIONS, ROUGHLY CHOPPED
- ONE 16-OUNCE CAN TOMATO PURÉE
- THREE 24-OUNCE CANS WHOLE TOMATOES
- 1 1/4 CUPS WHITE VINEGAR
- 1/4 CUP FIRMLY PACKED DARK BROWN SUGAR
- 3 TABLESPOONS MOLASSES
- 2 TEASPOONS SALT
- 1 TABLESPOON FRESHLY GROUND BLACK PEPPER
- 1 TABLESPOON SWEET PAPRIKA
- 1 TABLESPOON CHILI POWDER
- 1/2 CUP ORANGE JUICE
- 1/4 CUP DIJON MUSTARD

continued

Place all the ingredients in a slow cooker, cover, set on low, and cook until the sauce is somewhat thickened, 4 to 6 hours. This will keep up to 4 months in a tightly sealed container in the refrigerator.

Variations: Mexican style: Add 1 teaspoon ground cumin, an additional 1 teaspoon chili powder, juice of 2 limes, and 1 tablespoon coarsely chopped fresh coriander (cilantro) leaves.

Asian style: Add 2 teaspoons peeled and minced fresh ginger or 1 teaspoon ground ginger, ¼ cup soy sauce, ¼ cup rice wine vinegar, 2 tablespoons granulated sugar, and 1 tablespoon sesame oil.

Caribbean style: Add an additional 1 tablespoon firmly packed dark brown sugar, ¼ cup pineapple juice, ¼ cup light or dark rum, ¼ cup Caribbean-style hot sauce, juice of 1 orange, and a generous pinch of ground allspice.

Mediterranean style: Add ¼ cup balsamic vinegar, 2 tablespoons minced garlic, 2 tablespoons olive oil, 1 small ripe diced tomato, juice of 1 lemon, and ½ cup packed coarsely chopped fresh basil leaves.

APPLE CIDER SYRUP

Yield: 1½ cups

Here's one for you apple lovers out there! Try this sauce on your morning waffles or pancakes, use it to dress up chicken breasts, or drizzle it on vanilla cheesecake. Although you can make this with apple juice, it's the cider that packs the flavor punch.

¾ CUP APPLE CIDER

½ CUP FIRMLY PACKED DARK BROWN SUGAR

½ CUP LIGHT CORN SYRUP

2 TABLESPOONS UNSALTED BUTTER OR MARGARINE

PINCH OF FRESHLY GRATED NUTMEG

PINCH OF GROUND CINNAMON

½ TEASPOON FRESH LEMON JUICE

Place all the ingredients in a medium-size bowl and stir to combine. Pour into a mini slow cooker, cover, set on low, and cook until slightly thickened, about 2 hours. Serve hot, warm, or at room temperature. Store in a tightly covered container in the refrigerator for up to 4 weeks.

FANTASY CHERRY SAUCE

Yield: 2 cups

Serve this on ice cream, pound cake, oatmeal (page 295), fresh fruit, or on Rum-Croissant Bread Pudding (page 316).

1 CUP PACKED DRIED BING CHERRIES   3^1/4 CUP KIRSCH OR OTHER CHERRY LIQUEUR

^{1}/4 CUP WATER

Place the cherries, water, and kirsch in a mini slow cooker, cover, set on low, and cook until the cherries are completely soft, about 2 hours. Serve hot, warm, or at room temperature. Store in a tightly covered container in the refrigerator for up to 6 months.

SOUSED STRAWBERRY SAUCE

Yield: 1 cup

We layered this luscious sauce with chunks of rehydrated sun-dried strawberries over frozen vanilla yogurt to make a parfait. It also makes a lovely topping on toast and muffins.

1 CUP DRIED STRAWBERRIES (AVAILABLE IN ^{1}/2 CUP ORANGE JUICE
  SUPERMARKETS AND GOURMET STORES)

^{1}/2 CUP GRAND MARNIER OR OTHER ORANGE
  LIQUEUR

Place all the ingredients in a mini slow cooker, cover, and cook until the strawberries are completely soft, about 2 hours.

CANDIED GINGER

Yield: About 1¹/₂ cups

This recipe makes either crystallized ginger or stem ginger in thick syrup.

2 OR 3 VERY LARGE PIECES (THEY'RE EASIER
TO PEEL) FRESH GINGERROOT (ABOUT
1 CUP PEELED AND SLICED)

2 CUPS WATER

2 CUPS SUGAR PLUS EXTRA FOR COATING

¹/₄ CUP LIGHT CORN SYRUP

Peel the gingerroot with a small sharp knife. Slice lengthwise into ¹/₄-inch-thick pieces.

Place the water, sugar, and corn syrup in a slow cooker and stir to mix. Add the gingerroot, cover, and set on high until the liquid begins to simmer. Reduce the heat to low and cook until the ginger is tender and the syrup deep golden brown, about 24 hours.

Cool the ginger in the syrup. Roll the pieces in the extra sugar and use the syrup as a sauce or topping, or store the unsugared ginger in the syrup. Store the sugared pieces in a plastic bag at room temperature for up to 6 months. Store the syrup (and ginger in the syrup) in a tightly covered container in the refrigerator for up to 1 year.

CHOCOLATE-COVERED STRAWBERRIES

Yield: 12 to 16 large berries

Recently I have seen enormous strawberries with their stems attached for sale in the market. These fairly cry out to be dipped in chocolate (although if you can't find them there's no reason not to use regular-sized, stemless berries). Be sure to use the best quality real chocolate (made with cocoa butter, not palm kernel oil) for this treat.

Once the berries are dipped, they really should be eaten within 8 hours, and they taste much better if not refrigerated.

2 CUPS FINELY CHOPPED BITTERSWEET
   CHOCOLATE

LARGE UNBLEMISHED RIPE STRAWBERRIES
   WITH STEMS ATTACHED

FLUTED PAPER CUPS BIG ENOUGH TO
ACCOMMODATE THE STRAWBERRIES

Make sure everything is assembled before starting. If you don't want to use paper cups, have a baking sheet lined with parchment or waxed paper at hand.

Place the chocolate in a mini slow cooker, cover, set on low, and allow to melt until there are just a few pieces left whole. Unplug the unit and stir to melt the remaining chocolate. If you have waited too long and all the chocolate is melted, add another unmelted piece and stir until it melts. This is to "seed" the chocolate so that the cocoa butter won't separate and rise to the top.

Make sure the strawberries are absolutely dry. Leaving the stems on the strawberries, dip them bottom first into the chocolate, covering about two thirds of the strawberry—it looks pretty to have some of the berry showing. Place in a paper cup or on the baking sheet. Repeat with the remaining strawberries. Chill in the refrigerator only until the chocolate is set, then store at room temperature until ready to serve.

MIXED FRUIT COMPOTE

Yield: About 10 cups

This lovely, fragrant mélange of stewed dried fruit is wonderful to have on hand. It can be served as a topping on hot or cold cereal, with yogurt, or on toast for breakfast. It can be used as a fruit condiment when serving game or pork. It's great on ice cream and on pound cake and, finally, it's wonderful all by itself served in a pretty dish.

If you can't find exactly the fruits listed here, substitute your own favorites. Take care that the pits have been removed. While you can certainly serve the compote as soon as it's cool enough to eat, I find that it tastes even better if refrigerated a day or so to allow the juices to thicken and the flavors to combine.

continued   313

1 CUP GOLDEN RAISINS

1 1/2 CUPS DRIED SWEET CHERRIES

2 CUPS DRIED TART CHERRIES

2 1/2 CUPS PITTED PRUNES

1 CUP DRIED APPLE RING HALVES

1 CUP DRIED APRICOTS

4 CUPS ORANGE JUICE

2 LARGE NAVEL ORANGES, CUT INTO 1/2-INCH-
THICK SLICES

4 CUPS WATER

2 OUNCES MEDIUM SWEET KOSHER RED WINE
OR GRAPE JUICE

1 CINNAMON STICK

Place all the ingredients in a slow cooker, cover, set on high, and cook until the liquid is almost absorbed and the fruit is soft, 2 to 3 hours. The compote will keep for several months if stored in a covered container in the refrigerator.

Pears in Caramel Syrup

Yield: 8 servings

The combination of caramelized sugar and ripe pears is irresistible.

8 FIRM, UNBLEMISHED, RIPE COMICE OR
ANJOU PEARS

JUICE OF 1 LEMON

3 CUPS WATER

2 CUPS SUGAR

1/3 CUP PEAR BRANDY

WHIPPED CREAM (OPTIONAL)

Peel the pears, leaving the stems on. As each pear is peeled, sprinkle it with lemon juice to prevent browning. Place the water and 1 cup of the sugar in a slow cooker. Add the pears, stems upright. Cover, set on high, and cook the pears in the liquid, turning them gently several times, until they are firm but tender, 1 1/2 to 2 hours. Carefully remove the pears and reserve the syrup. Arrange the pears on a serving dish or in individual bowls.

Pour 1 cup of the reserved syrup into a saucepan, add the remaining cup of sugar and the brandy, and bring the mixture to a boil. Let it continue to boil until the syrup starts to deepen in color, 10 to 15 minutes, shaking the skillet in a circular fashion. Don't let the syrup burn! Carefully spoon the caramel syrup over the pears. Cool slightly and serve with whipped cream.

Variation: Substitute apples for the pears.

PLUGGED-IN ORANGE MARMALADE

Yield: About 4 cups

Wait until thick-skinned navel oranges are in season to make this fabulous marmalade. The cooking time will depend on your slow cooker—some are hotter than others.

4 TO 5 VERY LARGE NAVEL ORANGES (3¹/₂ TO 4 POUNDS TOTAL)

2¹/₂ CUPS SUGAR

1 CUP WATER OR ORANGE JUICE

Trim off the stems and navel ends of the oranges, cut in half, and slice either by hand or in the work bowl of a food processor fitted with the 4mm blade into ¹/₈-inch-thick pieces. Place the oranges, sugar, and water or juice in a slow cooker and try to push the oranges down so they are covered as much as possible by the liquid (don't leave any clinging to the sides or they will burn). Cover, set on high, and cook for 8 hours. Remove the lid, reduce the heat, to low, and cook, uncovered, until the syrup is thick, another 2 to 3 hours. Cool slightly, then spoon into jars, cover, and refrigerate. It will keep for up to 6 months.

GRAPE-NUTS PUDDING

Yield: 5 servings

Comfort food at its best, with low-fat options. Don't forget the scoop of vanilla ice cream or frozen yogurt melting on top.

3 LARGE EGGS OR ³/₄ CUP EGG SUBSTITUTE

2 CUPS MILK

¹/₂ CUP SUGAR

1 TEASPOON PURE VANILLA EXTRACT

1 TEASPOON GROUND CINNAMON

1 CUP GRAPE-NUTS CEREAL

HOT MILK OR HEAVY CREAM, OR A SCOOP OF VANILLA ICE CREAM OR FROZEN YOGURT FOR GARNISH (OPTIONAL)

With a hand mixer or whisk in a medium-size bowl, beat the eggs, then beat in the milk, sugar, vanilla, and cinnamon. Stir in the Grape-Nuts, then pour and scrape the mixture into a slow cooker, cover, set on low, and cook until the pudding is firm and no longer jiggles, about 2 hours. Serve hot, warm, or at room temperature with the garnish of your choice.

Variation: Add ¼ to ½ cup dried apricots, plumped in boiling water for 15 to 20 minutes, then well drained.

RUM-CROISSANT BREAD PUDDING

Yield: 10 to 12 servings

If you are looking for an indulgent dish to serve a crowd, you've come to the right place. This bread pudding not only makes a gorgeous centerpiece, it will satisfy the sweet tooth of every dessert lover you know. Leaving the croissants out overnight uncovered will get them stale enough for this recipe.

Since different slow cookers cook at different temperatures, the best way to judge when this is done is to use an instant-read thermometer. You'll need a large slow cooker to make this.

2 TABLESPOONS BUTTER

2 CUPS WHOLE MILK

2 CUPS HEAVY CREAM

4 LARGE EGGS

½ CUP FIRMLY PACKED DARK BROWN SUGAR

⅓ CUP DARK OR LIGHT RUM

1½ TEASPOONS PURE VANILLA EXTRACT

½ CUP PECAN HALVES

5 LARGE STALE CROISSANTS, CUT INTO THIRDS HORIZONTALLY

FANTASY CHERRY SAUCE (PAGE 311)

Grease the crockery insert of a slow cooker generously with the butter. Combine the milk, cream, eggs, sugar, rum, vanilla, and pecans in a large bowl and stir well to combine.

Divide the croissant slices evenly into four piles. Place one pile in an overlapping fashion in the bottom of the slow cooker. Pour in one third of the milk mixture. Add another layer of croissants, then another third of the liquid. Repeat one more time, finishing with a layer of croissants. Cover, set on high, and cook for 1 hour, then reduce the heat to low and cook until the custard is set and an instant-read thermometer inserted in the center registers 190°F, about 3 hours. Serve hot or at room temperature with the cherry sauce.

TRIPLE APPLE MULLED CIDER

Yield: 8 servings

During the fall and the height of the apple harvest, get yourself hard cider to make this. You may have to buy regular cider and leave it out for a day or so before it "turns." To make this a nonalcoholic beverage, substitute apple cider for the hard cider and leave out the Calvados.

¹⁄₂ ORANGE	1 CUP GINGER ALE
¹⁄₂ LEMON	1 CUP DICED DRIED APPLES
2 CINNAMON STICKS	¹⁄₂ CUP FIRMLY PACKED DARK BROWN SUGAR, OR MORE TO TASTE
5 CLOVES	
3 ALLSPICE BERRIES	¹⁄₈ TEASPOON GROUND MACE
4 CUPS APPLE CIDER	1 CUP CALVADOS (APPLE BRANDY) OR APPLEJACK
2 CUPS HARD CIDER OR APPLE CIDER	

Using a vegetable peeler, remove the zest (the colored part only, leaving behind the white pith) in strips from the orange and lemon halves. Place the zests, cinnamon, cloves, and allspice berries on a cheesecloth square, tie it securely closed, and place it in a slow cooker. Add both ciders, the ginger ale, apples, brown sugar, and mace. Squeeze the juice from the orange and lemon halves into the cider mixture, cover, set on high, and cook for 1 hour or set on low and cook for 2 hours, to thoroughly heat and allow the flavors to blend. Skim off any foam that rises to the surface at the end of the cooking time. Remove the cheesecloth bundle. Taste the cider; add more brown sugar, if desired.

To serve, pour 2 tablespoons of Calvados into each mug, then ladle the cider into the mugs.

STEAMER,

ELECTRIC

A re you looking to cut calories and fat without cutting flavor? Then look no further than the electric steamer. This lightweight, easy-to-use appliance cooks quickly and efficiently, and in small kitchens it can almost take the place of a burner.

GENERAL DESCRIPTION

WHAT DOES IT DO? • These appliances will not clean your carpet or press your pleats, but they will steam your food to perfection. In a plastic tray or basket within a closed environment using moist heat from boiling liquids, your food is transformed to precisely the desired level of doneness. Plus, it retains its fresh flavor and color and is always moist and tender.

WHY DO I NEED THIS? • If steaming vegetables or fish, it is possible to set the timer and walk away, carefree, knowing that the meal will be ready when the timer rings and will not burn.

HOW DOES IT WORK? • These appliances consist of a plastic heating unit and a plastic cooking chamber that can hold about 2 cups of vegetables or fish. Water is placed in a reservoir in the heating unit to an indicated level, and the cook-

ing chamber is placed on top of the heating unit. For these steamers, a plastic bowl is provided for cooking rice and a plastic steaming basket for steaming other foods. Some manufacturers of these units say that keeping the cooking water separate from the liquids that leach from the food provides an advantage. When the timer is moved off zero, a heating element in the reservoir boils the water, and the steam surrounds the food in the cooking chamber, cooking the food.

You control the amount of cooking by the amount of time set on the timer. When the timer runs out, the heating element turns off. It is important to take the food out of the cooking chamber right away, because if it is left in the cooking chamber, heat from the residual steam will continue to cook the food.

CARE AND MAINTENANCE • Most heating units are not submersible, so do not put them in a sink full of water. In the case where water is in direct contact with a heating element, mineral deposits can build up, so the chamber should be cleaned with a solution of vinegar and water. The cooking chambers are typically dishwasher safe.

WHICH IS RIGHT FOR ME? • Make sure the steamer will handle the amount of food typically cooked at one time. If it is too large, you will spend time waiting for the water to boil before cooking begins. Also, some timers are more accurate than others. Check the timer before buying a steamer so you understand exactly how it works and whether or not it is calibrated properly.

COMMENTS • Beware of hot steam. It is very easy to get a steam burn when removing the lid from a steamer. Tilt the lid away from you to let the steam escape away from your face and hands. Do not open the lid too often or some of the important steam and heat that is needed for cooking will escape. Some units have a cooking chart as part of the heating unit to help determine how much water to use for which kinds of food.

STEAMER TIPS

● *Leave plenty of room around the steamer to allow air to circulate. Do not place the appliance under cabinets, to avoid steam and heat damage.*

● *Be extremely careful to avoid steam burns. Use oven mitts and open the lid away from you.*

- *Steam condenses into water that collects in the steamer basket or elsewhere. This water is hot, so extreme caution should be heeded.*

- *When cooking for extended periods of time, check to see if the liquid should be replenished and add if necessary.*

- *When steaming frozen vegetables, break them up into smaller blocks so they fit in the steaming bowl.*

- *Cook most foods until they are slightly underdone. Residual heat from the steam will continue to cook the foods for a time when they are removed from the steamer.*

- *Keep a list of how long your favorite dishes take to cook and refer to it when you need to steam them.*

RECIPES

ARTICHOKES WITH TAHINI VINAIGRETTE

Yield: 4 artichokes, which, for friendly people who enjoy sharing, is enough for 8; for hungry people or those who aren't into eating off a group plate, this serves 4

Artichokes are such fun to eat, for those of us who enjoy eating finger food, anyway. They take a while to eat, what with pulling off and sucking each leaf, so they make great sharing food, too. The Tahini Vinaigrette is a wonderful dipping sauce for the artichokes and goes beautifully with steamed green beans or Brussels sprouts.

A tiny warning note, however. Steamers vary in size, so check yours to see how many artichokes it can handle.

4 MEDIUM-SIZE ($\frac{1}{2}$ TO $\frac{3}{4}$ POUND) ARTICHOKES

For the Tahini Vinaigrette:

$\frac{1}{3}$ CUP OLIVE OIL

1 $\frac{1}{2}$ TABLESPOONS TAHINI (AVAILABLE IN SUPERMARKETS AND HEALTH FOOD STORES)

1 TABLESPOON SESAME SEEDS

1 $\frac{1}{2}$ TABLESPOONS FRESH LEMON JUICE

1 TABLESPOON RED WINE VINEGAR

1 TEASPOON SOY SAUCE

2 TEASPOONS HONEY

SALT AND FRESHLY GROUND BLACK PEPPER TO TASTE

Cut the bottom ½ inch off the stems of the artichokes. With the artichokes on their sides, cut off the top third. Place the artichokes in a single layer in the steaming basket and steam according to the manufacturer's directions until the stem ends are tender when pierced with a fork or knife, 30 to 45 minutes.

Meanwhile, prepare the vinaigrette. Place all of the vinaigrette ingredients in a small bowl and combine, using a handheld blender or a whisk.

To serve, place the vinaigrette in a small bowl and use it as a dipping sauce for the steamed artichokes.

VEGGIE WONTON BUNDLES

Yield: 8 to 10 servings (30 to 40 wontons)

This is an impressive-looking dish. It takes a little time to make, mainly for stuffing the wontons; but the skins are quite easy to work with, and these little gems will be the hit of your menu.

1½ POUNDS VEGETABLES OF YOUR CHOICE (I USED EQUAL AMOUNTS OF CARROTS, SWEET POTATOES, AND WINTER SQUASH)

⅓ CUP SOY SAUCE

⅓ CUP HOISIN SAUCE

1 TABLESPOON CORNSTARCH

1 PACKAGE SMALL WONTON SKINS (ABOUT 3 INCHES SQUARE, FOUND IN THE PRODUCE SECTION OF THE SUPERMARKET)

To make the filling, shred the vegetables in the work bowl of a food processor fitted with the shredding disk and place them in a large bowl. In a small bowl, combine the soy sauce, hoisin sauce, and cornstarch and stir thoroughly. Mix the sauce into the vegetables.

To make the bundles, place a wonton square on a plate and place about 1 tablespoon of the vegetable mixture in the center. Keeping a small bowl of cold water at hand, use your finger to moisten the perimeter of the square with the water. Bring the four corners up above the center and press the sides together. The water helps the sides to stick.

To steam, place as many wontons as can fit in a single layer in the steamer basket without touching one another. (Once cooked, they can stick together. Also, they can stick to the steamer basket, but spraying your favorite nonstick vegetable oil spray on the basket before filling it takes care of this problem.) Steam according to the manufacturer's directions for 10 minutes. You may need to steam 3 to 4 batches to complete the recipe. They can be reheated in the microwave by placing them in a single layer in a microwave dish, covering with a double layer of damp paper towels, and microwaving on high power for 30 to 40 seconds. Serve with soy sauce or the dipping sauce of your choice.

SHRIMP AND RICE DUMPLINGS

Yield: 6 to 8 servings (about 40 small dumplings)

Wonton wrappers are now available in almost every supermarket. Look for them in the produce section. Chinese five-spice powder is available in gourmet stores.

1 TABLESPOON CORNSTARCH

1/4 CUP DRY SHERRY

1/2 CUP WATER CHESTNUTS, DRAINED AND COARSELY CHOPPED

1 TABLESPOON SESAME OIL

3 TABLESPOONS SOY SAUCE, PLUS EXTRA FOR DIPPING THE STEAMED DUMPLINGS

1 TABLESPOON PEELED AND GRATED FRESH GINGERROOT

1/2 TEASPOON CHINESE FIVE-SPICE POWDER

3/4 TEASPOON SALT

1 SCALLION, CHOPPED

1/2 OUNCE DRIED SHIITAKE MUSHROOMS, STEEPED IN BOILING WATER TO COVER FOR AT LEAST 30 MINUTES, DRAINED, TOUGH PARTS DISCARDED, AND TENDER PARTS CHOPPED, OR 3 OUNCES FRESH MUSHROOMS, RINSED AND CHOPPED

1/2 POUND LARGE RAW SHRIMP, PEELED AND DEVEINED

1/2 CUP SMALL FROZEN PEAS

2 CUPS COOKED RICE

40 SMALL WONTON SKINS

In a medium-size bowl, combine the cornstarch and sherry. Add the remaining ingredients, except the wonton skins, and stir well. Place 1 generous tablespoon of filling in the center of each wonton skin. Keeping a small bowl of cold water at hand, use your finger to moisten the perimeter of the square with water. Bring the four points up above the center and press the sides together. The water helps the sides to stick.

Place as many dumplings as can fit in a single layer in the steamer basket without touching one another. (Once cooked, they can stick together. Also, they can stick to the steamer basket, but spraying your favorite nonstick vegetable oil spray on the basket before filling it takes care of this problem.) Steam according to the manufacturer's directions for 10 minutes, then remove and repeat with the next batch of dumplings until they have all been steamed. They can be reheated in the microwave by placing them in a single layer in a microwave dish, covering with several damp paper towels, and microwaving on high power for 30 to 40 seconds. Serve with a bowl of soy sauce for dipping.

Variation: Use ground turkey or chicken instead of the shrimp.

BLUE-EYED PAUL'S SHRIMP

Yield: 6 to 8 appetizer servings; 2 to 3 entrée servings

It doesn't take a genius to figure out how this dish got its name. While Paul Newman probably won't become a staple in your house, I promise these shrimp will—as long as they last. Try serving them cold as an appetizer or hot as a first or even main course.

1 POUND SHRIMP (WHICHEVER SIZE YOU LIKE), PEELED AND DEVEINED

⅓ CUP BEST QUALITY ITALIAN SALAD DRESSING (WE LOVE PAUL NEWMAN'S OWN)

Combine the shrimp and dressing in a bowl. Cover and refrigerate for at least 30 minutes or up to 1 day to marinate.

Remove the shrimp from the marinade and place in a single layer in the steamer basket. If they don't all fit, cook them in 2 batches. Steam according to the manufacturer's directions until the shrimp turn pink, 8 to 10 minutes. These are best served chilled.

CARROTS WITH BROWN SUGAR AND CINNAMON

Yield: 4 servings

Here is a vegetable that kids (as well as adults) will love. A little butter and brown sugar goes a long way. The rum mildly flavors the carrots and provides an accent that distinguishes them from your average candied carrots.

1 1/2 POUNDS BABY CARROTS

1 1/2 TABLESPOONS UNSALTED BUTTER, CUT INTO SMALL PIECES

1/2 TEASPOON GROUND CINNAMON

2 TABLESPOONS FIRMLY PACKED LIGHT OR DARK BROWN SUGAR

1/4 TEASPOON GRATED LEMON ZEST (DEHYDRATED LEMON PEEL FROM THE SPICE SECTION IS FINE)

1/2 TEASPOON SALT

1 TO 2 TABLESPOONS RUM (OPTIONAL), TO YOUR TASTE

Wash the carrots and place them in the steamer basket. Steam according to the manufacturer's directions until tender, about 20 minutes. Drain the carrots well, then place them, still warm, in a bowl with the rest of the ingredients and stir gently to mix. Serve warm or at room temperature.

GARLIC RED POTATOES

Yield: 4 to 6 servings

Easy yet classy. Delicious to boot. What more can you ask for? Try to find small red potatoes that don't need to be cut into smaller pieces.

1 1/4 TO 1 1/2 POUNDS SMALL RED POTATOES

3 CLOVES GARLIC, MINCED

2 TABLESPOONS CHOPPED FRESH ITALIAN PARSLEY LEAVES

2 TABLESPOONS BUTTER

SALT AND FRESHLY GROUND BLACK PEPPER TO TASTE

Wash the potatoes and, using a paring knife, remove a small (1/4- to 1/2-inch-wide) strip from each potato (like removing the equator from a globe). Rub each potato with the garlic and place in the steamer basket. Steam according to the manufacturer's directions until tender, 25 to 30 minutes. Place in a bowl with the rest of the ingredients and stir gently to mix. Serve warm.

LIGHTNING BRUSSELS SPROUTS

Yield: 4 to 6 servings

Welcome to the secret life of Brussels sprouts. So, you thought they had no personality. Well, this dish will light your fire!

1 POUND BRUSSELS SPROUTS, ALL ABOUT THE
    SAME SIZE (SMALLER IS BETTER)

For the sauce:

2 TEASPOONS DIJON MUSTARD

2 TABLESPOONS MAYONNAISE

1 TABLESPOON SOY SAUCE

1 TABLESPOON FIRMLY PACKED DARK BROWN
    SUGAR

1 TEASPOON MILD SESAME OIL

5 TO 8 DROPS TABASCO SAUCE, TO YOUR
    TASTE

Remove the outer leaves from the Brussels sprouts and trim off the bottoms. Use a small paring knife to cut a shallow "X" in the bottom of each (this will keep the leaves from coming off). Place them in the steamer basket and steam according to the manufacturer's directions just until tender, 6 to 8 minutes.

      While they are steaming, whisk together the sauce ingredients. Drain the hot Brussels sprouts, toss with the sauce in a serving bowl, and serve immediately.

MINTY SUGAR SNAP PEAS

Yield: 6 servings

Sugar snap peas are a great favorite in my house. While some of us can't resist eating them right out of the grocery bag, this teamed preparation is almost as wonderful—the fresh crispness remains, and the mint brings out the brightness and sweetness of the peas.

1 TO 1¼ POUNDS SUGAR SNAP PEAS, ENDS TRIMMED AND STRINGS REMOVED, IF NECESSARY

1 SMALL ONION, CHOPPED

½ CUP PACKED CHOPPED FRESH MINT LEAVES

1 TEASPOON HONEY

1 TO 2 TABLESPOONS UNSALTED BUTTER, TO YOUR TASTE

SALT AND FRESHLY GROUND BLACK PEPPER TO TASTE

Place the sugar snap peas with the onion in the steamer basket and steam according to the manufacturer's directions until the color of the pea pods brightens, 5 to 10 minutes.

Remove the peas and onions from the steamer and combine them with the rest of the ingredients in a serving bowl, stirring thoroughly. Serve immediately.

GREEN BEANS AND ONIONS VINAIGRETTE

Yield: 2 servings

Thanks to the steamer, the beans stay firm and flavorful in this salad, which can be served warm, at room temperature, or chilled.

½ POUND GREEN BEANS

For the dressing:

1 TABLESPOON FINELY CHOPPED FRESH ITALIAN PARSLEY LEAVES

2 TEASPOONS RED WINE VINEGAR

1 TEASPOON DIJON MUSTARD

2 TABLESPOONS OLIVE OIL

SALT AND FRESHLY GROUND BLACK PEPPER TO TASTE

1 SMALL RED ONION, CUT INTO THIN RINGS FOR GARNISH

Trim or snap off the ends of the beans. If the beans have "strings," pull them off. Otherwise, leave the beans whole. Place in the steamer basket and steam according to the manufacturer's directions until crisp-tender, 4 to 6 minutes. Rinse the beans briefly under cold running water; stop while the beans are still warm.

To make the dressing, place the parsley, vinegar, and mustard in the work bowl of a food processor fitted with the metal or plastic blade or in a blender. Add the olive oil, season with the salt and pepper, and process briefly.

Arrange the beans on a serving platter, top with the red onion rings and dressing, and serve.

LEMON-SESAME SPINACH

Yield: 3 servings

This is a really flavorful and healthy dish. Try serving it under the Steamed Scallops with Dill (page 328).

10 OUNCES SPINACH, THOROUGHLY WASHED AND TRIMMED OF TOUGH STEMS

1 SMALL ONION, CHOPPED

1 CLOVE GARLIC, CHOPPED

1/2 CUP SLICED WATER CHESTNUTS, DRAINED

1 TABLESPOON FRESH LEMON JUICE

1 1/2 TABLESPOONS SOY SAUCE

1 TEASPOON HONEY

1 TABLESPOON SESAME SEEDS

Place the spinach, onion, garlic, and water chestnuts in the steamer basket and steam according to the manufacturer's directions until the spinach wilts, 5 to 7 minutes. Combine this mixture in a serving bowl with the rest of the ingredients, mix thoroughly, and serve immediately.

MUSSELS MARINIÈRE

Yield: 2 to 3 servings

The steamer is the perfect place to gently cook shellfish. If you allow mussels or clams to steam just until the shells open, they will be tender and succulent.

2 POUNDS MUSSELS, SCRUBBED AND DEBEARDED

4 CLOVES GARLIC, CHOPPED

1/2 CUP BOTTLED CLAM JUICE

1/4 CUP (1/2 STICK) BUTTER, MELTED

3 TABLESPOONS CHOPPED FRESH ITALIAN PARSLEY LEAVES

SALT AND FRESHLY GROUND BLACK PEPPER TO TASTE

continued

To steam the mussels, place them with the garlic in the steamer basket and steam according to the manufacturer's directions until the shells open, about 15 minutes. Discard any that remain unopened.

Place the mussels in a large serving bowl, combine with the remaining ingredients, and serve.

STEAMED SCALLOPS WITH DILL

Yield: 3 to 4 servings

This is the world's best low-calorie indulgence entrée. Serve the scallops over a bed of Lemon-Sesame Spinach (page 327), add a couple of drops of soy sauce instead of the salt, and you've got yourself a quick, easy, and supremely delicious dinner for two. You can also refrigerate them to serve cold.

1 POUND SCALLOPS, TOUGH SIDE MUSCLES REMOVED	SALT AND FRESHLY GROUND BLACK PEPPER TO TASTE
JUICE OF 1 LEMON	COOKED RICE OR PASTA
3 TABLESPOONS CHOPPED FRESH DILL	

Sprinkle the scallops with the lemon juice and dill and place them in the steamer basket in a single layer. Cover and steam according to the manufacturer's directions until firm to the touch, 10 to 15 minutes. Season with the salt and pepper and serve immediately over rice or pasta.

SWORDFISH CHUNKS WITH LIME AND FETA CHEESE

Yield: 3 servings

This dish was inspired by my fishmonger who just happened to be having a sale on swordfish chunks. Look for them—they're a real bargain, especially when compared to the steaks. They are the perfect thing to make in the steamer.

1 POUND SWORDFISH CHUNKS

2 TABLESPOONS FRESH LIME JUICE

¹/₄ CUP OLIVE OIL

3 TABLESPOONS CRUMBLED FETA CHEESE

FRESHLY GROUND BLACK PEPPER TO TASTE

COOKED RICE OR BOILED RED POTATOES

Place the swordfish chunks in the steamer basket and steam according to the manufacturer's directions until still a bit rare in the center, 10 to 12 minutes. Set the covered basket on a plate and let it stand for a few minutes to let the fish finish cooking. Sprinkle the fish with the lime juice and olive oil and crumble the feta cheese over the top. Season with pepper and serve hot over rice or boiled red potatoes.

BARBECUED BABY BACK RIBS

Yield: 4 servings; 1 rack of ribs (15 to 20 small ribs)

Here we use steam to remove almost all the fat from the ribs before they are grilled. Steaming leaves them moist and tender as well. What a great way to make ribs without a lot of excess fat!

1 RACK PORK BABY BACK RIBS (ABOUT
2 POUNDS)

BARBECUE SAUCE OR SPICE RUB OF YOUR
CHOICE

Cut the rack of ribs into individual pieces and place them in the steaming basket. Steam according to the manufacturer's directions until the meat is tender and most of the fat rendered, about 1¹/₂ hours. Check the basin a few times during the steaming time to see if the liquid needs pouring off.

Let the ribs cool enough to handle (or you can refrigerate them at this point and continue with the preparation later), then coat them with the barbecue sauce. Grill until glazed, 10 to 15 minutes. If you don't have a grill, bake them in a preheated 450°F oven for 10 to 15 minutes.

STEAMED PEARS WITH RASPBERRY SAUCE

Yield: 4 to 6 servings

This dessert makes a stunning presentation. The bright red sauce perfectly complements the pale pears. If you chill the pears in the raspberry sauce, the pears get rosy, which also makes quite a gorgeous sight. And it's light and delicious, too.

Keep this raspberry sauce recipe in mind for other uses. It makes a fabulous foil for a rich chocolate dessert, such as the Bête Noire on page 125.

4 RIPE PEARS, PEELED, CORED, AND HALVED (CHECK YOUR STEAMER TO SEE IF IT CAN ACCOMMODATE THIS MANY; YOU MAY NEED TO USE 1 OR 2 FEWER HALVES)

2 TABLESPOONS SUGAR, OR TO YOUR TASTE

2 TABLESPOONS FRAMBOISE (RASPBERRY LIQUEUR) OR YOUR FAVORITE BERRY LIQUEUR (OPTIONAL)

For the raspberry sauce:

ONE 10-OUNCE PACKAGE FROZEN SWEETENED RASPBERRIES, THAWED

For garnish:

PAPER-THIN LEMON SLICES OR SPRIGS FRESH MINT

Place the pears in a single layer cored side down in the steaming basket and steam according to the manufacturer's directions until tender when pierced with a knife, about 10 minutes. Place the pears in a covered container and chill in the refrigerator.

To make the sauce, cook the sauce ingredients together in a medium-size nonreactive saucepan over medium heat until the mixture looks glossy and the berries have broken down, about 10 minutes. Let cool. Using a fine mesh strainer set over a large bowl, strain out and discard the seeds. Chill the sauce.

To serve, place 1 or 2 pear halves on a plate and spoon the sauce over, or puddle the sauce on the plate with the pear placed on top of the sauce. Garnish with a slice of lemon, twisted once, or with a sprig of mint.

BANANAS AMARETTO

Yield: 4 servings

This is one of those rare desserts that merits the dual descriptions of "down home" yet "elegant." Cooked bananas are a comfort food extraordinaire, but the amaretto and pecans dress this up enough to serve at a fancy dinner party. The amaretto gives only a mild kick and had my guests at a party guessing the identity of the "mystery ingredient." They go well with butter cookies or vanilla (or better yet, butter pecan or praline) ice cream.

3 BANANAS, PEELED AND CUT ON THE DIAGONAL INTO ¹/₂- TO 1-INCH-THICK SLICES

1¹/₂ TABLESPOONS FIRMLY PACKED DARK BROWN SUGAR

2 TABLESPOONS AMARETTO

1 TEASPOON PURE MAPLE EXTRACT

1¹/₂ TABLESPOONS UNSALTED BUTTER, CUT INTO PIECES

¹/₄ CUP CHOPPED PECANS

1 PINT PREMIUM VANILLA ICE CREAM

Cut a 12 × 16-inch piece of aluminum foil and place the bananas in its center. Top with the rest of the ingredients, except the ice cream. Bring 2 opposite sides of the foil together and fold the edges over 3 times in ¹/₄-inch folds to seal. Fold together the other 2 sides the same way. Place the package in the steaming basket and steam according to the manufacturer's directions for about 10 minutes.

Spoon the ice cream into bowls. Remove the packet from the steamer, cut the foil open with scissors or knife, and spoon the bananas and sauce over the ice cream.

Variation: Use a different liqueur or extract, or variety of nuts.

PUMPKIN PUDDING WITH WHISKEY SAUCE

Yield: 6 servings

Here's just the dessert for a small Thanksgiving dinner and a nice change of pace from traditional pumpkin pie. Although it tastes best made with fresh pumpkin, substitute canned pumpkin to simplify the recipe. If using prespiced canned pumpkin, do not add the cinnamon, allspice, and nutmeg.

For the pudding:

ONE 8-OUNCE CAN UNSWEETENED CRUSHED PINEAPPLE, UNDRAINED

$^1/_2$ CUP DRIED CRANBERRIES

$^1/_2$ CUP FIRMLY PACKED DARK BROWN SUGAR

2 TABLESPOONS CHILLED BUTTER OR MARGARINE, CUT INTO PIECES

2 LARGE EGGS PLUS 1 LARGE EGG WHITE

1 CUP MASHED COOKED PUMPKIN (CANNED IS FINE)

1 CUP ALL-PURPOSE FLOUR

$^1/_2$ CUP SOFT FRESH BREAD CRUMBS

1 TEASPOON BAKING POWDER

1 TEASPOON GROUND CINNAMON

$^1/_2$ TEASPOON GROUND ALLSPICE

$^1/_2$ TEASPOON GROUND NUTMEG

$^1/_2$ TEASPOON SALT

$^1/_4$ TEASPOON CHOPPED PECANS

For the whiskey sauce:

$^1/_2$ CUP APPLE JUICE

$^1/_4$ CUP FIRMLY PACKED DARK BROWN SUGAR

$^1/_4$ CUP BOURBON

2 TABLESPOONS BUTTER OR MARGARINE

$^1/_8$ TEASPOON GROUND CINNAMON

$^2/_3$ CUP WATER

$2^1/_2$ TEASPOONS CORNSTARCH

For the pudding, drain the pineapple, reserving $^1/_4$ cup of the liquid; set the pineapple aside. Combine the pineapple liquid with the dried cranberries in a small microwavable glass bowl; microwave on high power until softened, about 1 minute and 15 seconds. Set aside.

Place the sugar, butter, whole eggs, and egg white in the work bowl of a food processor fitted with the metal blade and process until blended, about 1 minute. Add the pumpkin and process until smooth. Add the flour, bread crumbs, baking powder, spices, and salt and process until blended, pulsing about 7 times. Add the pineapple and pecans and pulse 4 times to combine. Add the soaked cranberries and pulse 2 times. Spoon into a buttered 6-cup steamed pudding mold or the rice bowl that comes with the steamer and cover with a lid or a sheet of aluminum foil. Steam according to the manufacturer's directions until a cake tester or toothpick inserted in the center comes out almost clean, $1^1/_2$ to 2 hours, even though the top may still look wet. Cool on a wire rack for 10 minutes, then unmold.

While the pudding is cooling, make the sauce. Combine the apple juice, sugar, bourbon, butter, and cinnamon in a small nonreactive saucepan over medium heat, stirring frequently, until the sugar dissolves. Combine the water and cornstarch, stir well to make a slurry, and add to the apple juice mixture. Bring to a boil and cook until thickened, stirring constantly, about 1 minute. Serve warm over the warm pudding.

CRÈME BRÛLÉE WITH DRIED CHERRIES AND KIRSCH

Yield: 2 servings

Looking for a great and indulgent dessert for just the two of you? Well, here it is. Sweet dark cherries buried in a meltingly smooth and heavenly rich custard, topped off with a thin, crisp sugar crust. It doesn't get much better than this.

¼ CUP DRIED SWEET CHERRIES (AVAILABLE IN SUPERMARKETS AND GOURMET STORES)

¼ CUP KIRSCH OR OTHER CHERRY LIQUEUR

2 LARGE EGGS

3 TABLESPOONS PLUS 2 TEASPOONS FIRMLY PACKED DARK BROWN SUGAR

⅔ CUP HALF-AND-HALF

½ TEASPOON PURE VANILLA EXTRACT

Combine the dried cherries and kirsch in a small microwavable bowl, cover, and microwave on high power until the cherries have begun to absorb the kirsch, about 1 minute and 15 seconds. Set aside.

Using a whisk or handheld blender, combine the eggs, 3 tablespoons of the brown sugar, half-and-half, and vanilla in a small bowl. Stir in the cherry mixture. Pour into 2 buttered custard cups or ramekins (first making sure that they can fit together into the steamer basket and are safe to place under the broiler). Place in the steamer and steam according to the manufacturer's directions until barely set and the center jiggles just slightly, 18 to 25 minutes.

Remove from the steamer and sprinkle 1 teaspoon of the remaining brown sugar on top of each, spreading it so it covers the entire surface. Preheat the broiler to high with the rack in the upper position. Broil until the sugar begins to bubble and is almost completely melted, about 2 minutes. Allow the sugar to harden before serving.

Variation: Use a different dried fruit and liqueur; for instance, cranberries and cranberry liqueur, or apricots and Cointreau or Grand Marnier.

CHOCOLATE CUSTARD

Yield: 2 servings

Since this recipe makes only enough for two, plan either to serve this to someone very special at the end of a romantic dinner, or don't tell anyone you're making it and eat both portions yourself. This has a delectable texture, a very thick pudding with a deep, dark taste. It's chocolate heaven.

3 OUNCES SEMISWEET OR BITTERSWEET
    CHOCOLATE, CHOPPED

2/3 CUP HALF-AND-HALF

1 TEASPOON FREEZE-DRIED "INSTANT"
    COFFEE OR ESPRESSO

2 EXTRA LARGE EGGS

2 TABLESPOONS SUGAR

Place the chocolate, half-and-half, and coffee together in a microwavable bowl, cover, and microwave on high power until the chocolate is melted, 1½ to 2 minutes. You may need to mix it a bit to get the chocolate melted; take care not to let it burn.

    Using a whisk or a handheld blender, add the eggs and sugar to the chocolate mixture and blend well. Pour into two buttered custard cups or ramekins (first making sure that they will fit into the steaming basket together). Cover the ramekins with a sheet of aluminum foil, place in the steamer, and steam according to the manufacturer's directions until barely set and the center jiggles just slightly, 18 to 25 minutes. Let cool, then chill in the refrigerator. Serve chilled.

Variation: The coffee can be omitted.

TORTILLA

PRESS

I had so much fun using the tortilla press that there was a serious danger that my fixation on it would mean nothing else got tested. Wait until you see all the swell things you can do with this nifty appliance. If you're going to spring for one, make sure to get the electric model; it heats and cooks much more evenly than the stove top type.

GENERAL DESCRIPTION

WHAT DOES IT DO? • When I was a kid, I was mesmerized by the clamshell steam presses in the laundry down the street from our house. A pair of pants would be placed precisely on the bottom half of the press, and the top half would be brought down to flatten them. Lots of steam would escape from between the two halves of the press, and when they were opened up a nicely creased pair of pants awaited their hanger. A tortilla press reminds me of these clamshell presses since it flattens dough balls into circles and allows lots of steam to escape from between the two halves of the press. But you get to eat the baked tortillas instead of wearing the pants to Grandma's house on Sunday afternoon.

WHY DO I NEED THIS? • Fresh is best, and this applies to flatbreads of every variety. With a tortilla press, fresh nutritious flour tortillas, masa harina corn chips, moo shu pancakes, and crepes are made out of ingredients you select, whenever the need for them arises.

HOW DOES IT WORK? • Think of a waffle iron without the grooves. A tortilla press consists of two metal grill plates set within metal housings that are hinged together on one side. The grill plates are typically treated with a nonstick coating and are round and perfectly flat. Behind the grill plates are heating elements. When you plug in the tortilla press and, on some models, turn on the power switch, the elements get hot and heat up the grill plates. The temperature is maintained by a thermostat.

Once the tortilla press reaches cooking temperature, indicated on some models by lighting or extinguishing a signal light, a round lump of dough is placed on the bottom plate and the top plate is closed over it, pressing down to form the tortilla. The weight of the top plate helps to distribute the dough on the bottom grill plate, and the heat browns it. Once the tortilla is shaped, the press is opened and the tortilla finishes baking on the bottom grill plate. The tortilla is flipped over at least once during baking to get an even browning. On models with signal lights, the light will turn off and on during cooking. This typically means that the thermostat is turning the power on and off to the heating elements, maintaining the proper cooking temperature.

When the tortilla is done, it is removed with a utensil that will not damage the grill plate.

CARE AND MAINTENANCE • When finished making tortillas, leave the press open and turn it off or unplug it. Then let it cool to room temperature before cleaning it. On some models, it is possible to remove the grill plates and wash them in the sink. But most models must be cleaned with a soft damp cloth and should not be immersed. Also, if the tortilla press has a nonstick coating, make sure to use plastic or wooden utensils and do not use a harsh cleaning pad when washing the appliance.

COMMENTS • Sometimes a nonstick vegetable oil spray is necessary, especially for sticky corn tortillas dough, but you usually do not need to coat the surface with oil or fat. New heating devices can smoke when you first turn them on, so plug in a new press for a short time to burn off the new smell before using it.

TORTILLA PRESS TIPS

- *Dough should be placed slightly off center, about a third of the way from the hinge toward the handle. Turn flour-based tortillas a quarter turn for several turns while flattening. Leave the plates open when they are cooking and turn them over from time to time to ensure both sides are browned.*

- *Almost any batter or dough can be used in the tortilla press. Experiment with your favorites—you'll be delighted with the results.*

- *When making corn tortillas, press them once and open the plates quickly or the residual steam will cause the tortilla to become lacy and difficult to handle.*

RECIPES

BLACK BEAN TORTILLAS

Yield: 6 to 7 servings (12 to 15 tortillas)

The tortilla press is one of my unexpected successes. The following recipe for soft bean tortillas can be made ahead and refrigerated or frozen—ready to pull out and stuff with your favorite fillings. Use these in place of bread for sandwiches or to make the Easy Fajitas on page 339.

3 CUPS ALL-PURPOSE FLOUR

1/2 TEASPOON SALT

1 CUP CANNED BLACK BEANS, DRAINED

1/3 CUP CANOLA OR VEGETABLE OIL

2/3 CUP WARM WATER

Place the flour, salt, black beans, and oil in the work bowl of a food processor fitted with the metal blade and process for a few seconds to blend. Slowly pour in the water until the dough forms a ball.

Divide the dough into 12 to 15 equal pieces, roll them into balls, cover with plastic wrap, and let rest at least 30 minutes at room temperature. Serve filled with stuffing of your choice.

continued   337

Spray a tortilla press with nonstick vegetable oil spray and preheat it according to the manufacturer's directions. Place 1 ball at a time on the press and gently close the lid, but only press hard enough to flatten the dough. Lift and lower the lid, rotating the tortilla as necessary until it is cooked. Remove to a wire rack to cool and repeat with the remaining dough balls.

CHILI-CHEESE FLOUR TORTILLAS

Yield: 6 to 7 servings (12 to 15 tortillas)

Another innovative use for the tortilla press: Try these filled with sliced smoked turkey, sliced avocado, and chopped red onions.

3 CUPS ALL-PURPOSE FLOUR

1/2 TEASPOON SALT

1 TEASPOON CHILI POWDER

2 TABLESPOONS FRESHLY GRATED PARMESAN
   CHEESE

1/2 CUP VEGETABLE SHORTENING

1 CUP WARM WATER

Place the flour, salt, chili powder, and cheese in the work bowl of a food processor fitted with the metal blade. Add the shortening and process for about 3 seconds. With the machine running, pour the water through the feed tube in a steady stream. Let the machine run until the dough forms a ball. The dough should have a medium-stiff consistency. If the dough is too stiff, add a little more water.

Divide the dough into 12 to 15 equal pieces, roll them into balls, cover with plastic wrap, and let rest at least 30 minutes at room temperature.

Spray a tortilla press with nonstick vegetable oil spray and preheat it according to the manufacturer's directions. Place 1 ball at a time on the press and gently close the lid, but only press hard enough to flatten the dough. Lift and lower the lid, rotating the tortilla as necessary until it is cooked. Remove to a wire rack to cool and repeat with the remaining dough balls.

Variation: Omit the chili powder and Parmesan cheese for plain flour tortillas.

Easy Fajitas

Yield: 4 servings

Here's the perfect thing to whip up for supper when time is limited and your family is starving.

2 TABLESPOONS OLIVE OR VEGETABLE OIL

1 POUND SKINLESS, BONELESS CHICKEN BREASTS, CUT INTO THIN STRIPS

1 MEDIUM-SIZE ONION, CUT INTO THIN SLICES

1 MEDIUM-SIZE BELL PEPPER, SEEDED AND CUT INTO THIN STRIPS

2 TABLESPOONS FRESH LIME JUICE

1 TEASPOON CRUSHED DRIED OREGANO

2 TEASPOONS CHILI POWDER

$^1/_2$ TEASPOON GARLIC POWDER OR 1 CLOVE GARLIC, FINELY MINCED

1 TEASPOON SOY SAUCE

SALT AND FRESHLY GROUND BLACK PEPPER TO TASTE

4 WARM FLOUR TORTILLAS

SALSA OF YOUR CHOICE

SOUR CREAM

In a large skillet, heat the oil over medium-high heat, then add the chicken, onion, and bell pepper and cook, stirring, until the chicken is no longer pink, about 5 minutes.

Mix together the lime juice, oregano, chili powder, garlic, and soy sauce in a small bowl and season with salt and pepper. Stir well and add to the chicken mixture, still over medium-high heat. Cook another 5 minutes, stirring.

Place one quarter of the mixture in the center of each warm tortilla. Top with salsa and sour cream, roll up, and serve.

Variations: Use strips of beef sirloin instead, or a chicken-and-beef combination.

Quesadillas

Yield: 6 servings

Now that you've made your own tortillas, here is the perfect filling!

continued

ONE 7-OUNCE CAN CALIFORNIA GREEN
  CHILIES, SEEDS AND STEMS REMOVED

1 POUND MONTEREY JACK CHEESE, CUT INTO
  1 × 4 × 2-INCH STICKS

12 FLOUR TORTILLAS

BUTTER, LARD, OR VEGETABLE OIL FOR FRYING
  (OPTIONAL)

To make each quesadilla, place about half a chili and a stick of the cheese in the center of each tortilla. Fold the tortilla over the cheese and pin shut with a small wooden skewer.

Heat 1½ inches of oil in a large skillet or electric skillet to 360°F. Fry the rolled tortillas in the hot oil 4 at a time, turning occasionally, until crisp and the cheese has melted. Drain on paper towels and repeat with the remaining tortilla rolls. Or you may heat and soften the cheese-stuffed tortillas on a tortilla press.

Variations: Use shredded cheese mixed with chopped chilies to fill the tortillas. Or you may use sliced green chilies and shredded cheese on top of a flat tortilla and heat in a preheated 350°F oven or under the broiler until the cheese melts, 5 to 10 minutes.

Try different kinds of chilies. Or, add cilantro; chopped ripe tomatoes; minced cooked meat, chicken, or flaked crabmeat for additional variation.

MANDARIN PANCAKES

Yield: 6 to 8 servings (24 pancakes)

Use these for moo shu pork or any recipe that calls for egg roll wrappers, wontons, or pot sticker skins.

2 CUPS ALL-PURPOSE FLOUR

¾ CUP BOILING WATER

1 TO 2 TABLESPOONS SESAME OR VEGETABLE
  OIL TO BRUSH THE DOUGH

Place the flour in the work bowl of a food processor fitted with the plastic blade. With the machine running, add the boiling water slowly through the feed tube until the dough forms a ball. Cover the ball with plastic wrap and let it rest at least 30 minutes at room temperature.

Spray a tortilla press with nonstick vegetable oil spray and preheat according to the manufacturer's directions. Meanwhile, with your hands, roll the dough into a 15-inch-long log and cut it into 24 equal pieces. Work with 1 piece at a time, and keep the remaining dough covered with plastic wrap. Roll each piece of dough into a ball and flatten to about a 2-inch diameter. Brush one side of each round evenly to the edges with some of the oil; place the oiled surfaces of two rounds together and press firmly. Place each double round on the preheated tortilla maker, close, and press down the lever quickly, then open. Bake for a few seconds, then turn over and bake another few seconds. Do not overcook. Pull the 2 halves of the pancake apart after cooking. Stack on a plate and keep covered with a clean kitchen cloth to keep warm.

Stuff with the filling of your choice or see the recipe for Mandarin Pancake Cannelloni below.

MANDARIN PANCAKE CANNELLONI

Yield: 6 servings

The tortilla press is not just for Mexican food, as this luscious cannelloni recipe illustrates. Using the Mandarin Pancakes recipe above, you make wrappers that get filled with a traditional cannelloni stuffing.

6 OUNCES SAUSAGE, CASING REMOVED, CRUMBLED

ONE 10-OUNCE PACKAGE FROZEN CHOPPED SPINACH, THAWED AND SQUEEZED DRY

1 CUP RICOTTA CHEESE

1 LARGE EGG, SLIGHTLY BEATEN

1/2 CUP FRESHLY GRATED PARMESAN CHEESE

1/2 TEASPOON DRIED OREGANO

1/8 TEASPOON FRESHLY GROUND BLACK PEPPER

12 MANDARIN PANCAKES (ABOVE)

3 CUPS MARINARA SAUCE OF YOUR CHOICE

1/2 POUND MONTEREY JACK CHEESE, SHREDDED

Preheat the oven to 400°F with the rack in the center position. In a small skillet, brown the sausage over medium heat. Drain and discard any excess fat.

In a large bowl, combine the sausage, spinach, ricotta cheese, egg,

Parmesan cheese, oregano, and pepper and mix well. Spread ¼ cup of the filling along one edge of each pancake, then roll to enclose the filling.

Spread half of the marinara sauce in a shallow baking dish. Place the filled pancakes seam side down in the sauce. Spoon the remaining sauce over the cannelloni and top with the Monterey Jack cheese. Bake, uncovered, until the sauce bubbles and the cheese has melted, about 30 minutes.

PIZZA-DOUGH TORTILLAS

Yield: 8 to 10 servings (about 30 tortillas)

We had some pizza dough left over and the tortilla press was hot, so we decided to see what happened to pizza dough when it was pressed and steamed. To our delight the result was a crisp, wafer-thin flatbread. Dipping the dough in grated cheese added a sparkle to an already swell idea. Then we tried dipping the dough in butter and next in a cinnamon sugar mixture. A flatbread version of churros (sweet fried dough) was the result.

1 RECIPE VERSATILE PIZZA DOUGH (PAGE 63) OR ANY QUANTITY LEFTOVER PIZZA DOUGH

½ CUP GRATED CHEESE (PARMESAN, CHEDDAR, OR MONTEREY JACK), OR 2 TABLESPOONS BUTTER, MELTED, AND 2 TEASPOONS GROUND CINNAMON MIXED WITH ⅓ CUP SUGAR

Spray a tortilla press with nonstick vegetable oil spray and preheat according to the manufacturer's directions. Cut off a piece of dough about the size of a walnut. Flatten it slightly in the palm of your hand and either roll it in the grated cheese or dip it in butter and then in the cinnamon sugar. Lay it on the tortilla press and close and open the press several times to flatten the dough. Then allow the dough to cook with the press open, turning it over several times until the inside is cooked. The thinner you press the dough, the crisper it will be. If you wish the dough to bubble, do not press it quite as thin. Serve hot or at room temperature.

Socca (Chickpea Pizza)

Yield: About 8 small loaves

Chickpea flour is the main ingredient in this crisp flatbread from the south of France, and you can find it in your local health food store or shops that specialize in Middle Eastern ingredients. You can cook these either on the tortilla press or a griddle. I like to serve them with tuna salad or black olives and goat cheese.

²/₃ CUP OLIVE OIL

1 LARGE CLOVE GARLIC, PEELED

2 CUPS WATER

¹/₄ TEASPOON DRIED THYME

¹/₄ TEASPOON DRIED TARRAGON

1 TEASPOON SALT

¹/₂ TEASPOON FRESHLY GROUND BLACK PEPPER

1 ¹/₂ CUPS CHICKPEA FLOUR

Place the oil and garlic in a blender and process until the garlic is completely pulverized. Add the remaining ingredients and blend to make a batter, scraping down the sides of the blender to combine all the ingredients. Allow the batter to rest at room temperature for 30 minutes.

Preheat the tortilla press according to the manufacturer's directions. Coat the surfaces with a thin layer of olive oil. Use a ¹/₄-cup measure to pour a small puddle of batter in the center of the hot surface. With the tortilla press open, cook until the underside is dry and slightly browned, then turn and cook the other side. Cool slightly on wire rack, then pile them on top of each other. Serve hot or at room temperature, either whole or in wedges.

Sweet Potato Crepes

Yield: 8 to 10 servings (about 24 crepes)

These are easily made from Thanksgiving leftovers: Use candied yams in the crepes, then layer with leftover turkey and cranberry sauce to make a crepe torte. Or wrap these soft, fragrant crepes around the filling of your choice. Try spreading them with Spiced Nut Butter (page 97) and a slice of smoked turkey, then rolling them up. Arrange on a platter and serve with Trouble in Tahiti salsa (page 98) for an elegant lunch or brunch dish.

You can use either fresh or canned cooked sweet potatoes for this recipe. If you choose fresh, scrub them well and cube them; it's not necessary to peel them.

1 CUP COOKED SWEET POTATOES

2 EXTRA LARGE EGGS

$1/2$ CUP (1 STICK) BUTTER, AT ROOM
  TEMPERATURE

FINELY GRATED ZEST AND JUICE OF 1 LEMON

1 TEASPOON SALT

$1/2$ TEASPOON FRESHLY GROUND BLACK
  PEPPER

1 TEASPOON GROUND CINNAMON

$1/4$ TEASPOON GROUND NUTMEG

1 TEASPOON GROUND GINGER OR 1
  TABLESPOON CHOPPED CANDIED GINGER

2 CUPS ALL-PURPOSE FLOUR

2 TEASPOONS BAKING POWDER

2 CUPS WHOLE MILK

2 TABLESPOONS PURE MAPLE SYRUP

Place the sweet potatoes, eggs, butter, lemon zest and juice, salt, pepper, and spices in a 2-quart bowl. Mix well with a handheld blender fitted with the puréeing disk or mash together until smooth.

Place the flour and baking powder in a small bowl and stir with a fork to combine. Add the milk and maple syrup to a spouted 2-cup glass measure. Add the dry ingredients to the sweet potato mixture in three additions alternately with the milk mixture, blending to combine. The mixture should have the consistency of thick cream and should flow.

Before starting to cook, set several wire racks nearby. Spray a tortilla press with nonstick vegetable oil spray and preheat according to the manufacturer's directions. Use a $1/4$-cup measure or ladle to pour a 3-inch puddle of batter in the center of the tortilla press. Use the bottom of the cup or ladle to spread the batter to within 1 inch of the edge of the surface. Cook with the lid open for 15 seconds, then gently lower the lid to rest on top of the crepe but do not press down. Cook until the underside is deep golden brown (the top, or nonpublic, side will not brown much at all). Use tongs to remove the crepes to the wire racks to cool. You can pile them with plastic wrap between each crepe.

Variations: Use white potatoes mashed with garlic oil or caramelized onions and omit the cinnamon, nutmeg, and ginger.

DEVIL'S FOOD CREPES

Yield: 8 to 10 crepes or 1 crepe torte to serve 10

Here's your choice of two truly smashing desserts custom-made for the chocophile. Both are based on Devil's Food cake batter, which is then made into crepes using the tortilla press. One dessert is cream-filled rolled crepes, and the other is a crepe torte.

1 RECIPE DEVIL'S FOOD CAKE BATTER FOR A
   SINGLE LAYER (PAGE 216)

For the filling:

1 POUND WHOLE MILK RICOTTA CHEESE

1 CUP HEAVY CREAM, WHIPPED WITH 3
   TABLESPOONS GRANULATED SUGAR TO
   FIRM PEAKS

FINELY GRATED ZEST OF 1 LARGE ORANGE

3 TABLESPOONS ORANGE LIQUEUR (OPTIONAL)

For the topping:

1 RECIPE GANACHE GLAZE (PAGE 138)

CONFECTIONERS' SUGAR

To make the crepes, spray a tortilla press with nonstick vegetable oil spray and preheat according to the manufacturer's directions. Use a ¼-cup measure to pour a 2-inch puddle of the batter in the center of the press. Gently close the lid, but only press hard enough to spread the batter. Lift and lower the lid, rotating the crepe as necessary until it is cooked. Remove the crepe to a wire rack to cool completely, and repeat with the remaining batter. You can pile them with plastic wrap between each crepe.

To make the filling, spoon the ricotta into a medium-size bowl and stir it slightly. Fold in the whipped cream, zest, and liqueur.

To assemble the crepes, spoon ⅓ cup of the filling in the center of each crepe and fold the sides over to form a roll. Place the roll seam side down on a serving dish. When all the crepes have been filled, drizzle the glaze over them, dust with confectioners' sugar, and serve.

To make a crepe torte, select a flat serving plate. Spread each crepe evenly with about 2 tablespoons of the filling. Pile them on top of each other and use any remaining filling to frost the top. Drizzle the ganache glaze decoratively over the top, or allow it to chill and use it to frost the sides. Dust the top with confectioners' sugar and cut into wedges to serve.

GINGERBREAD CREPES

Yield: 8 servings (20 crepes)

Wow! This amazing batter is magic! Take your choice of delectable gingerbread waffles (page 352) or these delicate, wafer-thin crepes. Serve them with the traditional dollop of whipped cream or maple syrup and use the Cinnamon Ice Cream to fill the crepes.

2 CUPS ALL-PURPOSE FLOUR

1/2 TEASPOON SALT

2 TEASPOONS BAKING POWDER

1 TEASPOON GROUND GINGER

1 TEASPOON GROUND CINNAMON

1 1/2 CUPS MILK

2 TEASPOONS PURE VANILLA EXTRACT

3 TEASPOONS FINELY GRATED LEMON ZEST OR
1 TEASPOON DRIED LEMON PEEL

4 LARGE EGGS, LIGHTLY BEATEN

1/3 CUP FIRMLY PACKED DARK BROWN SUGAR

2 TABLESPOONS VEGETABLE OIL

CINNAMON ICE CREAM (PAGE 167)

Sift the flour, salt, baking powder, and spices together in a small bowl and set aside. Mix together the milk, vanilla, and lemon zest and set aside.

Place the eggs and sugar in a large bowl and use a hand mixer fitted with the beater attachment on medium speed to beat the mixture for 3 minutes. Mix in the oil, then on low speed mix in the flour alternately with the milk mixture. Mix only until the batter is smooth.

Preheat the tortilla press according to the manufacturer's directions. Lightly spray each side with nonstick vegetable oil spray (you may have to repeat this between each crepe). Pour about 1/4 cup of the batter in the center of the press, hold the top down 15 seconds to spread the crepe, then, with the top open, cook the crepe until it is almost dry but still flexible. Cool the crepes on a wire rack completely before filling with Cinnamon Ice Cream.

WAFFLE

MAKER

My recipe tester par excellence, Ellie Nelson, wants you to know this: The waffle maker gives you the opportunity to take very everyday ingredients plus leftovers and, with minimal effort, turn them into something that even the finickiest kids will consume with gusto. Ellie should know; she has three finicky eaters—all boys and all the same age (seven years old)—yes, you guessed it, triplets! Here is an abridged list of the things they won't eat: food that is touching other food, food that has unfamiliar ingredients, anything mushy, anything hard to chew (except pizza), anything spicy, anything between two pieces of bread, anything with green specks, anything with sauce (especially sauce with lumps), and anything that resembles stew. And just when you think you've found something they like, they won't eat that either. Or one will go on strike and the others gaily follow. They like their food dry and crisp and easy to chew.

Waffle maker to the rescue. The triplets are fascinated by its power to transform food into something they might consider putting in their mouths—something crispy and dry, which can be smothered in maple syrup (something they do eat). When your child rejects something, it's a blow to the ego, but think about getting three times as much stuff rejected—and throwing away three times as much food. Imagine how many ways these smart guys can yell, "Do you really expect me to eat this?"

Waffle maker to the rescue. Check out the following recipes, and you'll be amazed at how you can use it to tame the fussy eaters in your house.

GENERAL DESCRIPTION

WHAT DOES IT DO? • Waffle makers heat up and cook batters, constraining the puffing batter while forming it into one of several traditional or nontraditional decorative shapes.

WHY DO I NEED THIS? • Fresh sweet or savory waffles can be at your fingertips whenever you are in the mood. And you can control what goes in and on them.

HOW DOES IT WORK? • Like the tortilla press, waffle makers consist of two metal grill plates set within metal enclosures that are hinged together on one side. The grill plates are typically treated with a nonstick coating and are formed in a decorative pattern, the most popular of which are regular waffles and Belgian waffles. Behind the grill plates are heating elements. When the waffle maker is plugged in and, on some models, the power switch is turned on, the elements get hot and heat up the grill plates. Electric waffle makers are better than stove top models because the proper cooking temperature is maintained automatically. On most models, the temperature is maintained by a thermostat, but on some a control knob allows the level at which the temperature is held steady to be adjusted.

Once the waffle maker reaches cooking temperature, indicated on some models by lighting or extinguishing a signal light, about ½ cup of batter is poured over the bottom plate and the top plate is closed over it. The weight of the top plate helps to distribute the batter throughout the pattern on the grill plate, and the heat cooks the batter. Because the batter typically contains some sort of leavening, and because water in the batter turns to steam, the waffle puffs up between the pattern on both grill plates and cooks.

On models with signal lights, the light might turn off and on during cooking. This typically means that the thermostat is turning the power to the heating elements on and off, maintaining the proper cooking temperature.

When the waffle is done, lift the top plate and remove the waffle with a utensil that will not damage the grill plate.

CARE AND MAINTENANCE • Most manufacturers recommend that, when finished making waffles, you leave the waffle maker open and turn it off or unplug it. Then let it cool to room temperature before cleaning it. On some models, it is pos-

sible to remove the grill plates and wash them in the sink. But most models must be
cleaned with a soft damp cloth and should not be immersed. We believe it is better
to strike while the waffle maker is hot. Unplug it while the grill plates are still hot
and slightly dampen several thicknesses of paper towels. Place them on the grill
plates and close the waffle maker. When the steam stops, open it and remove the
paper towels. Your waffle maker will be as clean as a whistle.

Cleaning up any mishaps is very important with an electric waffle maker. If a
waffle sticks to the grill plate all debris must be removed before making another
waffle. Otherwise, the mess will just keep compounding, and the waffle maker will
be ruined.

If the waffle maker has a nonstick coating, make sure to use plastic or wooden
utensils and do not use a harsh cleaning pad when washing the appliance.

WHICH IS RIGHT FOR ME? • A wide variety of decorative patterns is available on new waffle makers. When purchasing a waffle maker, make sure the pattern is something that suits your needs for as long as you make waffles.

COMMENTS • New heating devices can smoke when you first turn them
on, so plug in a new waffle maker for a short time to burn off the new smell before
using it.

WAFFLE MAKER TIPS

● *It's very important to either coat the waffle maker lightly with nonstick
vegetable oil spray or use a paper towel to apply a thin coating of vegetable oil before you heat it to prevent sticking. Take care not to allow a
buildup of oil as this will affect the taste of the waffles and your ability to
remove them from the waffle maker.*

● *Adding fat in the form of butter, margarine, or vegetable oil to the waffle
batter will help prevent sticking.*

● *When pouring batter into the waffle maker, allow for expansion and
spread. Overfilling will cause the batter to leak out and make a mess.*

● *Generally speaking, the waffle is done when steam has stopped escaping
and the surface of the waffle is browned, crisp, and dry.*

> *Waffles containing little or no sugar, fat, or diary products will not brown or crisp very much. These can be placed on a heavy-duty baking sheet and "toasted" in a preheated 350°F oven for 10 minutes or placed in the toaster oven to crisp.*
>
> *Waffles should be completely cold before being wrapped and frozen.*

RECIPES

BLUE CORN–BUTTERMILK WAFFLES IN HONOR OF JULIA

Yield: 8 servings, (about 16 waffles, depending on the size of your waffle maker)

Rose Mary created this splendid dish when Julia Child came for dinner to meet the *Plugged In* crew. We watched her feverishly throwing ingredients into a mixing bowl and were delighted with the outcome. We served this topped with some Duck Confit (page 308). They'd also be swell topped with a slice of smoked salmon (page 367) and a schmear of mascarpone cheese.

2 CUPS BLUE OR YELLOW CORNMEAL

2 CUPS ALL-PURPOSE FLOUR

1 CUP SUGAR

1 1/2 TEASPOONS SALT

2 TABLESPOONS BAKING POWDER

2 CUPS BUTTERMILK

1/2 CUP VEGETABLE OIL

4 EXTRA LARGE EGGS

1 1/2 CUPS GRATED SHARP CHEDDAR CHEESE

1/3 CUP FRESHLY GRATED PARMESAN CHEESE

1 TABLESPOON PLUS 1 TEASPOON CANNED CHIPOTLE PEPPER, OR

1 TABLESPOON HOT SAUCE

Place all the ingredients in a 2-quart bowl and use either a handheld blender or hand mixer to blend the ingredients until just combined. You can also use the blender to make this batter. Do not overbeat or your waffles will be tough.

Preheat the waffle maker according to the manufacturer's directions. Coat both sides with nonstick vegetable oil spray, then use a 1-cup measure to ladle about 1/3 cup of the batter into each waffle section. Close the lid and cook until there is no more steam—check for doneness after 2 minutes; the waffles should be puffy and light golden colored. If the lid is sticking, lower it and cook another minute or so before checking again.

Variations: Add ½ cup smoked corn (page 361) or pecans to the batter.

FRENCH TOAST WAFFLES

Yield: 4 to 6 servings (8 waffles)

This is the recipe that convinced me to write this book. If something as simple as a slice of bread could be transformed with a little electricity into something my family raved about, imagine the potential for using appliances in other unusual ways.

Whether you use homemade bread or the best quality store bought, you'll find that these waffles will become a staple at your breakfast (or even supper) table.

3 LARGE EGGS OR EGG SUBSTITUTE

1 ½ CUPS MILK (WHOLE OR LOW FAT)

2 TEASPOONS SUGAR (OPTIONAL)

1 TEASPOON SALT

2 TABLESPOONS BUTTER OR MARGARINE,
    MELTED

8 THICK SLICES OF BREAD (WHITE, WHOLE
    WHEAT, RYE, MULTIGRAIN, RAISIN, OR
    SOURDOUGH)

Coat both sides of a waffle maker with nonstick vegetable oil spray and preheat it according to the manufacturer's directions. In a shallow 9-inch pan, mix together the eggs, milk, sugar, salt, and butter. Dip the slices of bread in the egg mixture, allowing it to soak in, but removing before the bread falls apart. Place each slice on the waffle maker, close the lid, and cook until there is no more steam and the waffles are golden brown. Serve with the traditional maple syrup or fresh fruit.

Variations: Omit the sugar and use a savory kind of bread for the waffles, then serve it with salsa; or use the waffles as the bread part of a hot sandwich containing smoked turkey, ham, or cheese.

Gingerbread Waffles

Yield: 4 to 6 servings (8 waffles)

This is a wonderfully spicy waffle with an intricate blend of spices and crystallized ginger. Top it with syrup or whipped cream for breakfast or use the batter to make crepes for brunch or dessert.

2 CUPS ALL-PURPOSE FLOUR, MEASURED
AFTER SIFTING

$^1/_2$ TEASPOON SALT

2 TEASPOONS BAKING POWDER

1 TEASPOON GROUND GINGER

1 TEASPOON GROUND CINNAMON

4 LARGE EGGS, LIGHTLY BEATEN

2 TABLESPOONS VEGETABLE OIL

$4^1/_2$ TABLESPOONS FIRMLY PACKED DARK
BROWN SUGAR

$1^1/_2$ CUPS MILK

2 TEASPOONS PURE VANILLA EXTRACT

1 TABLESPOON FINELY GRATED LEMON ZEST

2 TABLESPOONS MINCED CRYSTALLIZED
GINGER

Coat both sides of a waffle maker with nonstick vegetable oil spray and preheat according to the manufacturer's directions.

In a large bowl, stir together the flour, salt, baking powder, and spices and set aside.

In a medium-size bowl, lightly beat the eggs, then mix in the oil, brown sugar, milk, vanilla, zest, and ginger.

Add the liquid ingredients to the dry and blend just until moistened (don't overmix or your waffles will be tough). Pour $^1/_4$ cup of batter into each waffles section. Close the lid and cook until there is no more steam and the waffles are puffy and light golden colored, 2 to 3 minutes.

Sweet Potato Waffles

Yield: 6 to 8 servings (about 12 waffles, depending on the size of the waffle maker)

Waffles take on a whole meaning in this recipe—soft and moist and flavorful. The mix of flavors traditionally associated with fall in New England—cinnamon, nutmeg, ginger, and sweet potatoes—combine to give these a place on your breakfast, brunch, or even dinner table. The batter can be made up to 12 hours ahead and stored in a covered container in the refrigerator. Store the finished waffles in zippered plastic bags in the refrigerater for 2 days, or layer in waxed paper in zippered plastic bags once completely cooled and freeze.

1 RECIPE SWEET POTATO CREPES BATTER
 (PAGE 343)

If you are planning to serve the waffles immediately, preheat the oven to 200°F with a heavy-duty baking sheet positioned on the center rack. If you are making the waffles to serve at another time, arrange several wire racks nearby.

Generously coat both sides of a waffle maker with nonstick vegetable oil spray and preheat according to the manufacturer's directions. Pour ¼ cup of the batter into each waffle section, close the lid, and cook until there is no more steam. The waffles are done when the bottoms are nicely browned and crisp and the tops are dry and lightly browned, 2 to 3 minutes. Do not undercook as the insides will be soggy. Use a fork to loosen the waffles and tongs to remove them from the waffle maker. If you are making the waffles to eat immediately, transfer them to the baking sheet. If not, transfer to the rack and allow to cool before refrigerating or freezing.

HAM AND CHEESE WAFFLES

Yield: 4 to 6 servings (twelve 3-inch biscuits)

If you want an extremely versatile savory bread substitute, this is an excellent one to try. It can be used as an appetizer or for a brunch or lunch.

2 CUPS ALL-PURPOSE FLOUR

1 TABLESPOON BAKING POWDER

¼ TEASPOON SALT

1 TEASPOON SUGAR

1 TEASPOON BUTTER

½ RED BELL PEPPER, SEEDED AND DICED

½ SMALL ONION, FINELY CHOPPED

½ CUP (1 STICK) BUTTER, MELTED

¾ CUP BUTTERMILK

¼ POUND SLICED HAM, DICED

½ CUP GRATED CHEDDAR CHEESE

continued

Coat both sides of a waffle maker with nonstick vegetable oil spray and preheat according to the manufacturer's directions.

In a large bowl, sift together the flour, baking powder, salt, and sugar and set aside.

In a small skillet, melt the teaspoon of butter over medium heat, then cook the bell pepper and onion, stirring, until softened.

Add the melted butter, buttermilk, pepper and onion, ham, and cheese to the batter and mix until just blended (don't overmix or your waffles will be tough). Pour about ¼ cup of batter in each waffle section and close the lid. Cook until there is no more steam and the waffles are puffy and light golden colored, 2 to 3 minutes.

SMOKED TURKEY—CHEDDAR WAFFLES

Yield: 8 servings (30 to 40 small waffles)

These waffles are sensational! Don't think of them as breakfast food—offer them at dinner, lunch, or better yet, brunch! Substitute your favorite cheese and meat and create a totally different taste. We loved the Roquefort and hard salami version, as well as the one with Brie and smoked salmon. Serve them as is or use them as a base for other ingredients; or cut them into small pieces to serve as canapés with mustard dipping sauce.

2 CUPS ALL-PURPOSE FLOUR

1 TABLESPOON BAKING POWDER

¼ TEASPOON BAKING SODA

¼ TEASPOON SALT

1 TEASPOON DRIED THYME

1 TEASPOON SUGAR

½ CUP (1 STICK) PLUS 1 TABLESPOON BUTTER, MELTED

¾ CUP BUTTERMILK

½ CUP DICED SMOKED TURKEY

½ CUP SHREDDED CHEDDAR CHEESE

Coat both sides of a waffle maker with nonstick vegetable oil spray and preheat according to the manufacturer's directions. In a large bowl mix together the flour, baking powder and soda, salt, thyme, and sugar. Add the butter, buttermilk, turkey, and cheese and mix until just blended (don't overmix or your waffles will be tough).

Pour about 2 tablespoons batter in each waffle section, close the lid, and cook until there is no more steam and the waffles are puffy and light golden colored, 2 to 3 minutes.

Variations: Substitute ham for the turkey, or Monterey Jack or jalapeño cheese for the Cheddar. Add a few diced sun-dried tomatoes.

QUICK AND EASY FILLED WAFFLES

Yield: 6 servings (12 waffles)

Stuck home with the kids screaming for lunch and you're fresh out of peanut butter and jelly? Poke around in the back of your freezer, and chances are you'll come up with a can of crescent rolls you bought sometime last year with the thought that you'd turn them into some dish now long forgotten. Well, here's that something. It's quick and easy and, thanks to the waffle maker, a lot more interesting than rolls.

1 CAN FROZEN CRESCENT ROLL DOUGH

FILLING OF YOUR CHOICE:

CHEESE (A HARD TYPE IS BEST, SUCH AS
    CHEDDAR OR SWISS), CUT INTO 2 × 2 ×
    ¹/₄-INCH-THICK SLICES

SLICED HAM, TURKEY, CHICKEN, BOLOGNA,
    AND/OR SALAMI, OR A COMBINATION OF
    BOTH CHEESE AND MEAT

Thaw the dough according to the package directions. Coat both sides of the waffle maker with nonstick vegetable oil spray and preheat according to the manufacturer's directions.

Unroll the dough and lay each piece flat on a work surface. Wrap each piece of dough around a piece of cheese or slice of meat, completely covering the filling. Place in the waffle maker, figuring on 1 piece for each waffle section. Close the lid and check in 2 minutes to see if it looks golden. The cheese that leaks out can be scooped out of the iron with a spoon and served on top of the waffle. These should take 2 to 4 minutes to cook, depending on your waffle maker. Serve hot.

Variations: Try different doughs and cheeses. How about Monterey Jack with a bit of salsa?

WATER SMOKER,

ELECTRIC

Before I started this book I had a mental list of the appliances I thought would make the Big Twenty. The electric water smoker was not on it. Truth be told, it never even crossed my mind until I had the good fortune to meet Cheryl and Bill Jamison in Sante Fe, New Mexico. Authors of *Sublime Smoke* and *Smoke & Spice* (Harvard Common Press, 1994 and 1996), they lit my interest if not my fire when they said I should at least take a look at the smoker before I wrote it off.

Buying the model specified by the Jamisons was not as simple as going to my local barbecue store. This baby had to be mail-ordered. The fact that it was delivered in a box that contained parts and directions for assembly did not start me off on the right foot. However, an hour with a screwdriver and a pair of pliers found me with smoker intact with no pieces left over.

"This is cute—it looks like R2D2," said one of my kids. It did look sort of friendly—I just hoped it was user-friendly. I decided to use the flank steak and some ripe tomatoes I had in my refrigerator to take it out for a test drive. Loading the food and starting the smoker seemed much too easy to be right. I read the directions a couple of times: "Put the steak (spread with barbecue sauce, if desired) on one rack and the tomatoes on another. Place water in the pan, wet chips on the bottom, plug it in, and Bob's Your Uncle." We had about an hour to test some margaritas in the blender while we waited for the results.

I was hooked by the seductive aroma even before I had my first bite of steak. A subtle sweet smokiness had gently infused the tender, succulent meat, leaving it perfectly pink on the inside with a lovely brown surface. The tomatoes were magnificent—the smoke balanced the acid in much the way olive oil does vinegar. Suddenly every sort of food in the house became a potential for my new, best appliance. "Told you so," said Bill and Cheryl.

GENERAL DESCRIPTION

WHAT DOES IT DO? • Electric water smokers cook meat, fish, and vegetables using steam that is flavored with smoke from aromatic wood chips. The moisture keeps the food from drying out while it cooks food to succulent perfection. Wood chips from several kinds of trees such as hickory, cherry, and maple are commercially available, as are wood chips that have been soaked in a variety of liquids ranging from bourbon to Tabasco sauce. The variety of wood chips adds a new dimension of creativity for the cook who's really smokin'!

WHY DO I NEED THIS? • Cooking food with smoky steam imparts a deep flavor without masking the natural flavors of the food.

HOW DOES IT WORK? • An electric water smoker consists of several parts. The metal housing has feet to keep it up off the surface on which it is sitting and a lid to keep the moist smoke in. At the bottom of the smoker is an electric heating element. The wood chips are soaked in water and placed so they are touching the heating element. Above the heating element is a basin into which is poured about a quart of water. Above the water basin are one or two metal racks that hold the food.

The heating element is connected to a control unit, which is then plugged into the electrical outlet. When the knob on the control unit is set to the desired temperature, the heating element gets hot and causes the wet wood chips to smoke and the water in the basin to begin to steam. The hot smoke combines with steam from the water and surrounds the food, cooking it and imparting a sweet, smoked flavor to it. Any fat that drips from the food will drop into the water basin and will not cause grease fires from dripping on the heating element directly.

When the food has finished cooking, remove it from the smoker and turn off the control unit. Then unplug the smoker and allow it to cool.

CARE AND MAINTENANCE • The food racks should be cleaned after every use and then stored in the smoker. Ashes from the wood chips should be brushed out once they have cooled, and the water basin should be washed with soap and water.

WHICH IS RIGHT FOR ME? • Smokers can be purchased in a variety of sizes, and for a wide range of prices. Choose one that will accommodate the amount of smoked foods you need to prepare at one time. A 2-foot-diameter smoker with one rack will comfortably smoke 2 small fish and 2 ears of corn. Larger smokers will smoke more food.

ELECTRIC WATER SMOKER TIPS

- *Aromatic wood chips should be soaked in liquid before using, and can be soaked in anything from plain water to cheap whiskey.*

- *Wood must be aged and dried before you can use it for smoking food, so plan on storing those apple branches for at least a year before using them. Not all wood is suitable for smoking—pine, for example, has too much resin and will ruin the food.*

- *Never use charcoal, lighter fluid, or fuel or any kind other than dried wood specifically prepared for the smoker.*

- *Be careful how you dispose of wood chips—they may contain live ash.*

- *You can alter the amount of smoked flavor by the amount of wood chips you use during the smoking process.*

- *Make sure the top fits tightly, and keep children and pets away from the smoker—it will not look as hot as it really is.*

- *Be careful when lifting the dome—smoke and hot air will pour into your eyes.*

- *Place the smoker on a level, noncombustible surface.*

- *Do not attempt to move the smoker when it is on or when the water pan is full.*

- *If there is a flare-up in the smoker, do not attempt to put it out with water. Simply close the lid to eliminate the oxygen. The fire will extinguish itself.*

- *Stock up on disposable foil pans to use in the smoker when not cooking food directly on the rack.*

- *Line the water pan with aluminum foil before pouring water in it, making cleanup a snap.*

- *Monitor the water level in the pan and unplug the smoker before adding more water.*

- *To prevent rusting of the smoker interior, apply a thin coating of nonstick vegetable oil spray to all areas except where the heating element is housed.*

- *Bring food to room temperature before smoking.*

- *Marinating meats helps to break down the cellular structure and generally reduces cooking time.*

- *Brush poultry, lean meats, and vegetables with oil or butter before smoking.*

- *It is not necessary to baste foods while they are smoking; the smoker is self-basting. Repeatedly opening the top of the smoker reduces the heat and lengthens the cooking time.*

- *On the model we tested, the thermostat really had nothing to do with the inside temperature of the smoker. We used cooking time and an instant-read thermometer rather than degree of heat to determine doneness.*

- *Make sure to remove the control panel and cord and store them inside when you're done. If you store your smoker outdoors, wipe away any moisture that may have accumulated before inserting the supply cord.*

- *If your smoker contains lava rocks, they can be cleaned periodically with a solution of baking soda and water.*

- *Do not use an electric smoker in the rain.*

- *Smokers must be located where they can be shielded from the wind.*

- *Smokers used outside on a cold day will take much longer to cook food than on a warm day—plan accordingly.*

- *If you plan on storing the smoker outside on a deck or patio year round, invest in the smoker cover that fits it. The cover is typically an accessory that can be purchased from the same place you bought the smoker.*

SMOKED BUTTERNUT SQUASH

Yield: 3 cups as a side dish or 6 cups as a soup

Supermarkets make it so easy to use butternut squash; they have it all peeled, saving you an arduous, boring task. Here it's placed in the electric water smoker, then microwaved until soft. This delicately smoked, sage-scented preparation can take the place of mashed potatoes or rice at your dinner table. Or you can thin it out with broth and have a hearty soup.

1 POUND BUTTERNUT SQUASH, PEELED AND
   CUT INTO 1-INCH CHUNKS

3 TABLESPOONS WATER

¹⁄₄ CUP (¹⁄₂ STICK) BUTTER, CUT INTO SMALL
   PIECES

8 FRESH SAGE LEAVES, VERY FINELY MINCED

1 CUP CANNED CHICKEN OR VEGETABLE STOCK
   (FOR SOUP, ADD 3 CUPS)

2 TABLESPOONS BOURBON (OPTIONAL)

1 TEASPOON SALT

FRESHLY GROUND BLACK PEPPER TO TASTE

3 TO 4 DROPS TABASCO SAUCE, TO YOUR
   TASTE

Place the squash chunks in a disposable pan and add the water to the bottom of the pan. Dot with the butter. Smoke according to the manufacturer's directions for 1 hour and 15 minutes.

     Cut the squash into cubes and place along with the cooking liquid, sage, and broth in a large microwavable bowl. Cover and microwave on high power until the squash is very soft, about 8 minutes.

     With a handheld blender, purée the squash and its liquid, adding the bourbon, salt, pepper, and Tabasco sauce.

SMOKED CORN–CRAWFISH SALAD

Yield: 8 servings (about 6 cups)

While you can certainly substitute smoked shrimp, scallops, or mussels in this recipe, the delicately sweet, nutty taste of crawfish is sublime. You can often find frozen crawfish tails in high-end supermarkets or you can order them by mail directly from Louisiana.

1/2 CUP MAYONNAISE

JUICE OF 1 LEMON

2 TABLESPOONS SOY SAUCE

3 CUPS SMOKED CORN (PAGE 361)

1 POUND COOKED CRAWFISH TAILS

1 MEDIUM-SIZE BERMUDA ONION, DICED

1 RED BELL PEPPER, SEEDED AND DICED

Combine the mayonnaise, lemon juice, and soy sauce in the bottom of a large bowl. Add the remaining ingredients, toss until they are coated with the dressing, and serve.

SMOKED CORN ON THE COB

Yield: 6 cups kernels

If you have ever entertained the thought of buying an electric water smoker, here's a simple recipe to push you over the edge. The delicate sweetness of fresh corn perfumed with the dusky essence of smoked hickory or apple chips is something that dreams are made of.

Smoked corn can be the basis of dozens of recipes, from Smoked Corn Chowder (page 257), Smoked Corn Relish (page 362), and Smoked Corn–Crawfish Salad (page 360) to your favorite salsa recipe or the one for Roasted Red Pepper Salsa on page 97. Be sure to try the Smoked Corn Bread (page 205). You can go on a smoking binge when corn is in season, freeze the kernels, and pull them out when you want a taste of summertime.

6 EARS FRESHLY PICKED CORN

2 TABLESPOONS BUTTER

SALT AND FRESHLY GROUND BLACK PEPPER TO TASTE

Soak hickory or apple chips (or use your own personal favorite) for 20 minutes in water. Prepare an electric water smoker according to the manufacturer's directions. Peel the corn and arrange the ears in a single layer on the smoking rack. Smoke for 1 hour. Cool, then use a sharp knife to cut the kernels off the corn. Toss with the butter and season to taste.

Variation: To serve cold, mix with 1/2 cup mayonnaise; 1 red bell pepper, seeded and minced; and 3 scallions, thinly sliced.

SMOKED CORN RELISH

Yield: About 2 cups

Yet another great use for those smoked corn kernels.

1¹/₂ CUPS SMOKED CORN KERNELS (PAGE 361)

1 SMALL RED ONION, FINELY MINCED

1 SMALL RED BELL PEPPER, SEEDED AND DICED

3 TABLESPOONS HONEY

3 TABLESPOONS CIDER VINEGAR

1 TEASPOON DIJON MUSTARD

¹/₄ TEASPOON DILL SEEDS

SALT AND FRESHLY GROUND BLACK PEPPER TO TASTE

Combine all the ingredients in a mixing bowl and stir. Store the relish in a covered container in the refrigerator at least 48 hours before serving.

SMOKED DUCK

Yield: 4 main-course servings or 6 to 8 salad servings

Hot or cold, by itself or in a salad or sandwich, home-smoked duck is a heavenly taste delight. You might want to make extra and freeze the leftovers and add them to a stew or soup.

For the marinade:

¹/₄ CUP GARLIC OIL

¹/₄ CUP RED WINE VINEGAR

3 TABLESPOONS SOY SAUCE

1 TABLESPOON GREEN PEPPERCORNS IN BRINE, DRAINED

2 TABLESPOONS PREPARED MUSTARD

2 TABLESPOONS HONEY

To smoke:

2 WHOLE BONELESS DUCK BREASTS, SKINNED

Combine the marinade ingredients in a bowl and mix well. Pour into a shallow non-reactive pan or heavy-duty zippered plastic bag placed in a roasting pan. Add the duck breasts and marinate for at least 1 hour or up to 24 hours in the refrigerator.

Prepare an electric water smoker according to manufacturer's directions and smoke the duck until its internal temperature is 120°F, 40 minutes to 1 hour. Cool for 10 minutes before slicing thinly against the grain.

SMOKED FLANK STEAK

Yield: 6 servings (2 1/2 pounds)

Flank steak made an appearance once a week at our dinner table. Because my father insisted that all meats be cooked to the far side of well done, it wasn't until I grew up that I learned how tasty flank steak can be when it is marinated before cooking and served rare. Taking it one delicious step further, here is a recipe for marinating and then smoking the flank steak—an improvement on something already almost perfect.

1 SMALL ONION, CHOPPED

1 SMALL CARROT, SLICED

1/2 STALK CELERY, SLICED

2 CLOVES GARLIC, CHOPPED

1 TEASPOON PEELED AND CHOPPED FRESH
    GINGERROOT

1/3 CUP RICE WINE VINEGAR

1/4 CUP SESAME OIL

1/2 TEASPOON TABASCO SAUCE

2 TABLESPOONS SOY SAUCE

2 TABLESPOONS FIRMLY PACKED DARK BROWN
    SUGAR

2 TABLESPOONS PURE MAPLE SYRUP

2 1/2 POUNDS FLANK STEAK, TRIMMED OF FAT

Place the onion, carrot, celery, garlic, and ginger in the work bowl of a food processor (or blender) fitted with the metal blade and process (or blend) to a smooth paste. Add the vinegar, oil, Tabasco sauce, soy sauce, brown sugar, and maple syrup and process (or blend) another minute.

    Lightly score both sides of the steak in a crosshatch pattern with a sharp knife. Place it in a large, heavy-duty zippered plastic bag. Add the marinade and close the bag (it helps to put the bag in a roasting pan or rimmed baking sheet for support). Refrigerate for at least 2 hours or overnight.

    Prepare an electric water smoker with cedar chips according to the manufacturer's directions. Smoke the steak until the outside is lightly browned and the center still quite pink, and the thickest part registers at least 120°F on an instant-read thermometer, about 1 hour. Cool for 15 minutes, then slice against the grain with an electric knife.

SMOKED PORCINI MUSHROOMS

Yield: ¹/₂ pound mushrooms

I suppose you could call this the ultimate indulgent vegetable. I prefer to think of it as yet another fine example of why everyone should own a smoker. Serve these hot, at room temperature, cold in a salad, or use them in the Mushroom and White Bean Soup (page 295).

¹/₄ CUP PORCINI MUSHROOM OIL, IF
    AVAILABLE, OR OLIVE OIL

2 TABLESPOONS SOY SAUCE

3 TABLESPOONS BALSAMIC VINEGAR

2 TABLESPOONS PURE MAPLE SYRUP

¹/₂ POUND PORTABELLO MUSHROOM CAPS,
    WIPED CLEAN AND CUT INTO ¹/₂-INCH-THICK
    SLICES

In a medium-size bowl, combine the oil, soy sauce, vinegar, and maple syrup and mix to blend. Add the mushrooms and let soak at least ¹/₂ hour at room temperature.

Prepare an electric water smoker according to the manufacturer's directions and smoke the mushrooms for 30 minutes.

SMOKED RIBS

Yield: 3 to 4 servings (2 pounds)

Now that barbecue places are springing up on every corner it's time to see that your homemade version is just as good as the "pros"—and less expensive as well.

¹/₂ CUP A.1. STEAK SAUCE

¹/₄ CUP KETCHUP

¹/₄ CUP PREPARED MUSTARD

10 DROPS TABASCO SAUCE

¹/₄ CUP RED WINE VINEGAR

¹/₄ CUP PURE MAPLE SYRUP

To smoke:

2 POUNDS PORK RIBS, CUT APART

Combine the marinade ingredients, pour over the ribs in a shallow nonreactive pan, cover with plastic wrap, and marinate in the refrigerator for at least 1 hour or overnight.

Prepare an electric water smoker according to the manufacturer's directions and smoke the ribs to an internal temperature of 170 to 180°F, until they are no longer pink, 45 minutes to 1 hour. Serve immediately.

SMOKED SWEET POTATO SALAD WITH BACON AND CHIVES

Yield: 6 servings (6 cups)

Here's a whole new way of looking at potato salad! You can make this with sweet potatoes or yams.

4 LARGE SWEET POTATOES

VEGETABLE OIL

For the dressing:

1/2 CUP MAYONNAISE

1 TABLESPOON FIRMLY PACKED DARK BROWN SUGAR

1 TABLESPOON DIJON MUSTARD

1 TABLESPOON SOY SAUCE

4 STRIPS BACON, COOKED UNTIL CRISP, CRUMBLED

1/4 CUP CHOPPED FRESH CHIVES

Prepare an electric water smoker according to the manufacturer's directions. Peel the potatoes and cut them into 2-inch chunks. Place them in a disposable metal dish and drizzle with the oil, turning to coat. Smoke until they are soft, 1 to 1½ hours.

This salad can be made and served when the potatoes are either hot or cold. Mix together the dressing ingredients, add the potatoes, and toss well.

SMOKED TOMATOES

Yield: About 6 cups

If I had to pick a favorite vegetable dish/ingredient that was generated from this entire project, this would be it. I started using smoked tomatoes in so many recipes that the team threatened to revoke my license to smoke. I had to limit myself to the following brainstorms: Smoked Tomato Ketchup (page 96), Smoked Tomato Salad (page 366), Smoked Tomato Sauce (page 24), and Smoky Joe Bloody Mary (page 31). Use it in place of regular tomatoes in the Seafood Gazpacho on page 110. You are not obligated to hold back—use these smoky/sweet morsels in anything that rings your bells.

12 LARGE, VERY FLAVORFUL RIPE TOMATOES   2 TEASPOONS SALT
    OR 24 PLUM TOMATOES

3 TABLESPOONS OLIVE OIL

Remove the stems and cut the tomatoes in half lengthwise. Drizzle olive oil on top of each tomato and sprinkle generously with salt. Allow the tomatoes to sit at room temperature about 10 minutes.

Prepare an electric water smoker according to the manufacturer's directions. Smoke the tomatoes 1 hour and 15 minutes. The tomatoes can be used right away, stored in a sealed container in the refrigerator for 1 week, or frozen up to 6 months.

SMOKED TOMATO SALAD

Yield: 4 servings (about 4 cups)

This recipe is so simple, yet its flavors and textures are complex and truly delectable. If possible, use vine-ripe tomatoes in season.

1/2 RECIPE SMOKED TOMATOES (PAGE 365)   1 SMALL PURPLE ONION, FINELY DICED
    OR 10 PLUM TOMATOES

    SALT AND FRESHLY GROUND BLACK PEPPER TO

3 TABLESPOONS RED WINE VINEGAR   TASTE

1/3 CUP OLIVE OIL

2 STALKS CELERY WITH LEAVES, FINELY
    MINCED

Chop the tomatoes into 2-inch pieces and place on a platter or on individual salad plates. Sprinkle with vinegar and oil, scatter the celery and onion on top, and season with salt and pepper.

KODIAK SMOKED SALMON

Yield: 6 to 8 servings (one 3-pound salmon fillet)

Thanks to the electric water smoker, home-smoked salmon is yours at a fraction of the price and three times the taste of any you can buy in the store (unless you live in the Pacific Northwest). So, for those of you stranded on the East Coast and hinterlands, here's a recipe that will satisfy your craving as well as your budget.

For the marinade:

1/2 CUP FIRMLY PACKED DARK BROWN SUGAR

2 TABLESPOONS DIJON MUSTARD

1/4 CUP SOY SAUCE

2 TABLESPOONS SHERRY VINEGAR

2 TABLESPOON OLIVE OIL

5 TO 6 DROPS TABASCO SAUCE, TO YOUR TASTE

To smoke:

1 LARGE SALMON FILLET (ABOUT 3 POUNDS), SKIN REMOVED

Combine the marinade ingredients in a large heavy-duty zippered plastic bag. Add the salmon, seal the bag, and refrigerate for at least 2 hours or up to 12 hours.

Prepare an electric smoker according to the manufacturer's directions. Remove the salmon from the marinade and smoke until the edges are brown and slightly crusty and the interior is pink and soft and flakes easily, 1 to 1 1/2 hours (depending on the thickness of the fillet).

PLUGGED IN

AND ON-LINE

COMPUTERS, THE INTERNET, AND THE KITCHEN

Writing is a lonely business: long, solitary hours hunkered down over the computer keyboard, trying to pin down thoughts and ideas that are at times as illusive as a fresh truffle and as difficult to mold into shape as a collapsed soufflé. After all my day's work is done, though, it's my keyboard that connects me to the outside world. I have an extraordinary group of cooking friends I have met on the Internet. They are among the most generous, compassionate, creative, humorous, resilient, and accommodating cast of characters you could ever imagine. There is something liberating about corresponding by E-mail (no one seems to care about spelling, punctuation, or complete sentences), and as people reveal themselves it's interesting to learn what has brought them to "cook" on the Internet.

One of my favorite stories comes from Liz Waters (many of you may know her as EBWATERS, host of the Cooking Club):

It is likely that I have been cooking online about as long as anyone. I started trading recipes for access to local bulletin boards in the early 1980's. We had purchased our first computer, an Apple IIe, in 1983 so that our son, Brian, who has Duchenne's muscular dystrophy, could become familiar with the technology. At 13, he already was dependent on a wheelchair for mobility, and it seemed to me a good bet that he would be using computers in the years ahead. I set out to master personal computers in order to teach Brian, and I have been banging away at keyboards ever since. I spent a year as assistant editor at a weekly newspaper earning starvation wages in order to use the computer equipment in the office and learn first hand what would be right for Brian from what was available. One of my jobs there was editing the cooking column, and even ghost writing it when the column didn't arrive in time. It was a good experience for me, and I had pretty much learned all I needed to pick out an Apple IIe when the pay-checks started bouncing and I left to stay home where I was more accessible to Brian.

My love-hate relationship with that first computer led me to join a local Apple User's Group, so I could get new programs the members had developed for Brian. The members were kind and generous to a fault—sending me home with piles of disks and instructions on how to run the magical programs they contained. What fun to unravel the mysterious convolutions necessary to get programs to run, and how frustrating. I discovered that while I had little talent for programming, I could make most of the pro-grams work if I managed to hold my temper long enough. But I had nothing to give in return. But even if I couldn't program, I could cook, so I started bringing brownies and cookies to the meetings. This evolved into my trading downloadable recipes for access to local bulletin boards for Brian and for me.

It was in the back of an Apple computer newsletter that I found the ad for volun-teers to participate in the testing of a "top secret project" using modems. Always intrigued by a secret, I signed right up and discovered that I was testing a new online system for Apple and a company called Quantum. During the testing, I did what I have always done—started talking recipes and cooking, and when the test was drawing to a close, proposed a Cooking Club for the new online community when the system was launched. That system eventually became America Online as we know it today, and the Cooking Club has been growing up with the system.

The centerpiece of the Cooking Club is our massive cookbook with over 25,000 recipes contributed by America Online members. We have always invited members to leave a favorite recipe when they take one of ours to add to their collections, and the members have been generous, from the rather exotic jellied moose nose from the Alaskan wilderness to the quite ordinary Southern cornbread in several different versions. It is a huge collection of family favorite foods and an unprecedented representation of culi-

nary diversity. We have real time visiting in the kitchen online, too, where members from all over the country gather at a virtual table in a virtual kitchen and trade recipes and ideas and just visit with one another. If you want to figure out what to substitute for an ingredient you are missing, raise the question in the kitchen. Someone will know what works, and if they don't, someone will look it up for you. In the kitchen, I have discussed politics with writer Tom Clancy, recipes with actor Harry Anderson, and talked food with a White House chef. In the Cooking Club auditorium, I had the honor of introducing Julia Child, Paul Prudhomme, and writer Diane Mott Davidson to the online world with their first online interviews. And as we grow, we have discovered that online instruction and reference are great tools for the home cook. Gosh, I even met Lora Brody up close and personal online.

As we continue to grow, I look forward to putting video instructions online for everything from basic biscuit baking to advanced gourmet techniques in the Cooking Club. As they say in the plugged-in-online world of cookery, the best is yet to come.

To get to the Cooking Club: Log on to the America Online Community and from the opening screen select Channels. Then, from the Channels screen, select the box called Lifestyles and Interests. From the Lifestyles and Interests top screen select the Cooking Club from the alphabetically arranged listbox on the right side of the screen. The main Cooking Club screen will give you a choice of options, so you can start exploring right away.

COMPUTERS have maneuvered their way into virtually every aspect of modern living, and kitchen appliances are certainly no exception to this trend. Bread machines, microwave ovens, and rice cookers are some of the appliances that have microelectronic computerized brains that tell them when to do that voodoo that they do so well. Personal computers are essential tools to running households and businesses, from entertaining and educating children, to providing financial organization, balancing checkbooks, and sharing information electronically. In this section, the variety of ways personal computers can help in the kitchen will be described. Their power to help organize recipes, find information on the latest electric kitchen appliances before they hit the market, and share tips and tricks with cooks around the world will be revealed. If you are not convinced that computers can make cooking life more interesting, then read on and be amazed.

What are computers and how do they work? Computers consist of two kinds of components: hardware and software. Computer hardware simply consists of the boxes that are sitting on the desk and the electronics inside of them that make them work together. People "talk" to the computer through the keyboard and mouse, and the computer "talks" back through the monitor, printer, and speakers. Inside the computer box, different contraptions allow the computer to "read" information on floppy disks or CD-ROMs or to store information electronically for later retrieval on a permanent hard disk or a floppy. Other devices connect everything together and allow electronic signals to be passed to the "brain" of the computer, the CPU or central processing unit. Some computers "talk" with other computers directly through network connections, or indirectly over the telephone through a modem.

To get all the pieces of equipment doing something useful, the computer follows sets of step-by-step instructions. A set of instructions that turns the computer into a functional device is called a *program*, and collectively these programs are called software. Software enables a computer to check spelling, plan a budget, print homework, play mah-jongg, and organize life.

The advent of culinary software has meant an end to boxes and boxes of recipe cards and newspaper clippings lost between the pages of your favorite cookbooks. These programs have been targeted primarily for storing recipes. They have standard ways of entering ingredients and recipe instructions, and recipes can be searched in several different ways. For instance, if you have leeks on hand and you need to use them, you can use your computer to find the recipes in your file that use leeks. Or if you want to build a soup and you have a few extra porcini mushrooms and sun-dried tomatoes on hand, you can search the file for all soups that use these ingredients. All of these programs allow you to store your favorite recipes, and many of them can be purchased with several recipes already loaded. Some of them also calculate nutritional information for a recipe, will scale the recipe up or down, and even create a shopping list based on a selected menu. One particular program includes video clips of famous chefs who present audio and video commentary on recipes and techniques. Are you amazed yet? Stand back. . . .

If two heads are better than one, then connecting to more than one computer should be outrageous! In fact, it is. Once a computer has access to the Internet, the global network of connected computers, through either a major service like America Online, Prodigy, or CompuServe, or any one of several other Internet service providers, also known as ISPs, the world is your oyster. Send and receive electronic mail messages, or E-mail, with anyone on or orbiting the planet—a friend recently sent E-mail to an astronaut on the space shuttle when it was in flight—as long as they have an E-mail address. The telltale sign of an E-mail address is the "at" sign (@) used as one of its symbols. Share tips and comments on things culinary or otherwise, trade recipes and sources for ingredients, and brag about baking successes all for the price of connect time on an ISP.

Several unwritten rules about appropriate behavior have evolved with the advent of electronic information sharing, and it is in everyone's best interest that these rules be followed. These rules of etiquette when applied to computer networks is appropriately called netiquette. One of the principal rules of netiquette is that words typed in all capital letters are to be read as if the writer were SCREAMING them, so avoid typing in all caps unless you mean it. Another rule of netiquette is not to clog up the works with junk mail (called spam by those of us who get far too much of it). The capacity of the Internet is not infinite, and it is a shared resource. Some ISPs enforce a limit on the size of message that can be sent through their service and the number of copies of messages that can be sent simultaneously. Generally, the golden rule applies.

Standard acronyms, such as IMHO for "in my humble opinion," and groupings of symbols have evolved over the years to help convey elaborate messages in very short spaces. Some shortcuts even try to add the inflection missing from the electronic word that would be present when spoken by using "smiley faces" or "smileys" that are combinations of standard keyboard characters: :-) is a smiling face when viewed sideways and usually indicates a tongue-in-cheek or sarcastic remark; :-(is a frown and ;-) is a wink. Many others exist. You can find a glossary of smiley faces on the Internet.

Once E-mail is mastered, then the next step in one's coming-of-age on the Internet is to subscribe to mailing lists. Messages that are related to a particular topic are collected and distributed electronically to E-mail addresses of people who subscribe to a mailing list. Typically, a message is sent to a list server requesting a subscription to a particular list and, when accepted, any message that is sent to the mailing list is automatically re-sent to all subscribers of the list. Sometimes these messages are collected and re-sent automatically, and other times people who are called list owners receive the messages, massage them, and then send the messages out in a digest format to all subscribers. Mailing lists and digests are a great way to share information on topics with people of mutual interests, and food-related lists exist on topics ranging from baking bread to living a vegetarian life.

A more public forum for sharing information is that of newsgroups, also known as bulletin boards or bboards (read "BEE-boards"). Some ISPs provide a service called USENET, which is a collection of electronic repositories for announcements or commentaries on particular subjects. Like mailing lists, they are organized by topic. But, unlike mailing lists, messages are not sent directly to subscribers. Rather, messages are posted to a central location and readers scan the list of posted messages, selecting those items that they wish to read and ignoring the rest. Just like a physical bulletin board, if the subject line of a posted item is not of interest, simply choose not to read the item. Some newsgroups are more active than others, so read those that fit your personal style and interests. Usually, subscribing and unsubscribing to newsgroups is very simple, so it is easy to tailor reading to exactly your areas of interest. Some newsgroups cover broad topic areas, such as creative cooking, kitchen design, or nutrition, and others have a narrower focus, such as chocolate, bakeware, or southern Italian cooking.

This computing repast has presented E-mail as the appetizer, mailing lists for the soup course, and newsgroups as the salad. Now it's time for the main course. The World Wide Web, also known as known as the Web or WWW, is a group of many, many computers across the globe that are connected to one another and share access to information stored on them. Take a minute to fathom the possibilities and be astounded. Access to the Web is by means of a program called a Web browser. The Web browser connects to a Web server, a computer running software to connect to the Web, and from there any computer that is running a Web server, or a Web site, is available to peer into or to connect to other Web sites. Individuals, corporations, and organizations create series of documents, called Web pages, on these computers that provide personal, product, or general information. Each Web server designates one page as its primary page, called a home page, which usually has a menu of services you can use to learn more. It is also possible to request information be sent to your E-mail address, as is sending the owner, or Webmaster, of that particular site a message about how you like or dislike their pages. Each site is identified by a unique code, called a universal resource locator, or URL, that typically begins with a prefix such as http://. Many commercial businesses have realized the power of the Web and announce their URL in their TV and magazine advertisements.

Many food-related Web sites exist. Appliance manufacturers, professional culinary organizations, cooking magazines, television cooking shows, epicurean hobbyists, kitchen designers and suppliers, ingredient retailers, and cookbook publishers are just a few of the types of Web sites that are accessible over the Web. Ask friends for the URL of their favorite Web sites or "surf" the Web using one of a variety of search tools that are accessible on the Web.

A note of caution is in order. Many Web sites allow the purchase of items over the Web and require submission of a credit card number electronically. As a kitchen appliance addict, it is very tempting to make culinary purchases over the Web. But at the time this section was written, no mechanism has been widely incorporated to ensure that information on the Web cannot be stolen and used indiscreetly. By its very nature, the Web is information that is accessible, so it is really not safe to send information about yourself or your credit cards that you would not want to be public knowledge by electronic means. Protect yourself; do not send a credit card number over the Web or via E-mail and submit only information about yourself over the Web that you would not mind being used for purposes other than that for which it was originally intended.

Below is a list of some interesting electronic cooking resources on the information supermarket. They are organized by type, starting with our E-mail address, then a list of culinary mailing lists, followed by food-related newsgroups, and URLs for several Web sites for cooks. We are presenting these with the caveat that electronic resources are powerful because they are flexible, and at any time this information may change, sometimes without warning. But, during the writing of this section, these resources were active, and we thought you might appreciate the diversity.

ELECTRONIC MAIL ADDRESS: Requires E-mail

Lora Brody Blanche007@aol.com

MAILING LISTS: Require E-mail

Bread Baker's Digest To subscribe, send an electronic message to: *bread-bakers-request@lists.best.com* and include in the body of the message only the word *SUBSCRIBE*.

Fat Free Digest To subscribe, send an electronic message to: *fatfree-request@hustle.rahul.net* and include in the subject of the message the words *ADD DIGEST*.

Jewish Food List To subscribe, send an electronic message to: *listproc@eskimo.com* and include in the body of the message the words *SUBSCRIBEjewish-food* followed by your *first name* then your *last name*.

Vegetarian Food List To subscribe, send an electronic message to: *listproc@cadserv.cadlab.vt.edu* and include in the body of the message the word *SUBSCRIBEVEGFOOD* followed by your *first name* then your *last name*.

Chocolate List To subscribe, send an electronic message to: *majordomo@apk.net* and include in the body of the message the words *SUBSCRIBE CHOCO.*

Other lists can be found on the mailing lists Web site in the final part of this section.

NEWSGROUPS: Require USENET access

BAKING	rec.food.baking	**FOOD INDUSTRY**	clari.biz.industry.food
BARBECUE	alt.food.barbecue		clari.biz.industry.
BEVERAGES	alt.beer		food.cbd
	alt.food.wine		clari.biz.industry.
	rec.crafts.winemaking		food.releases
	rec.food.drink		clari.biz.industry.
	rec.food.drink.beer		food.retail.releases
	rec.food.drink.coffee	**FOR SALE**	rec.food.marketplace
	rec.food.drink.tea	**FRUIT**	sci.agriculture.fruit
BUFFALO WINGS	alt.food.bw3	**GENERAL**	
CEREAL	alt.cereal	**COOKING**	alt.cooking-chat
CHOCOLATE	alt.food.chocolate		rec.food.cooking
	rec.food.chocolate	**GOURMANDS**	alt.creative-cook
COFFEE	alt.coffee		alt.creative-cooking
COOKBOOKS	rec.arts.books		alt.gourmand
	rec.arts.books.	**GRITS**	alt.food.grits
	marketplace	**HISTORIC FOOD**	rec.food.historic
		ICE CREAM	alt.food.ice-cream
EQUIPMENT	rec.food.equipment	**POULTRY**	sci.agriculture.poultry
	rec.food.bakeware	**PRESERVING**	rec.food.preserving

RECIPES	rec.food.recipes	**SOURDOUGH BAKING**	rec.food.sourdough
REDUCED-FAT COOKING	alt.food.fat-free	**VEGETARIAN LIVING**	rec.food.veg
	alt.food.low-fat		rec.food.veg.cooking
RESTAURANTS	rec.food.restaurants		

WEB SITES: Require a Web browser and Internet access

AMERICAN INSTITUTE OF BAKING	http://;www.aibonline.org/
APPLIANCE MAGAZINE	http://www.appliance.com/
BAKERY-NET	http://bakery-net.com/rdocs/option12.html
BLACK & DECKER	http://www.blackanddecker.com/
BREAD BAKERS GUILD OF AMERICA	http://www.bbga.org/
BREAD DIGEST RECIPE ARCHIVE	ftp://ftp.best.com/pub/reggie/archives/bread/
CUISINART	http://www.cuisinart.com/
EPICURIOUS FOOD & TRAVEL	http://www.epicurious.com/
FOOD DAY AND THE ELECTRONIC GOURMET GUIDE	http://www.foodwine.com/
FOODNET	http://www.foodnet.com/
FOODPLEX	http://www.gigaplex.com/food/index.htm
FOODSERVICE WORLD	http://www.foodserviceworld.com/
FOODTV	http://www.foodtv.com/
GOURMET FARE	http://ceo-online.com/gourmet/
HAMILTON BEACH/ PROCTOR-SILEX	http://www.hambeach.com/
INTERNATIONAL ASSOCIATION OF CULINARY PROFESSIONALS	http://iacp-online.org/
INTERNET KITCHEN	http://www.your-kitchen.com/
JULIA CHILD UNCENSORED	http://www-personal.washtenaw.cc.mi.us/~ssusnick/julia/
KING ARTHUR FLOUR	http://home.kingarthurflour.com/
KITCHENAID	http://www.kitchenaid.com/index.shtml
KITCHEN LINK	http://www.kitchenlink.com/
LINK CULINAIRE	http://users.why.net/ftp/users/chefnet/

MIMI'S CYBER KITCHEN	http://www.cyber-kitchen.com/
NATIONAL BAKING CENTER	http://www.dunwoody.tec.mn.us/NBC.htm
NATIONAL RESTAURANT ASSOCIATION	http://206.65.85.86/index.htm
SALLY'S PLACE	http://www.bpe.com/
THE BLUE DIRECTORY OF FOOD & BEVERAGE BUSINESS	http://www.pvo.com/pvo-plus/Food-Bev/ Business.shtml
VAN NOSTRAND REINHOLD CULINARY ARTS BOOKS	http://www.thomson.com/vnr/cahome.html
VILLAGE BAKERY	http://countrylife.net/bread/
WHAT ARE YEASTS?	http://stout.Stanford.EDU/Saccharomyces/ VL-what __are__yeast.html
WHIRLPOOL CORPORATION	http://www.whirlpool.com/
LIST OF MAILING LISTS	http://catalog.com/vivien/interest-group-search. html

RESOURCES

Buying kitchen electrics by catalog can be a rewarding and time-saving experience when you choose those that are staffed by knowledgeable sales personnel. Here are my favorite resources:

WILLIAMS-SONOMA: (800) 541-2233—equipment and ingredients and Lora Brody's Bread Dough Enhancers

CHEF'S CATALOG: (800) 338-3232—equipment and ingredients and Lora Brody's Bread Dough Enhancers

KING ARTHUR FLOUR BAKER'S CATALOG: (800) 827-6836—equipment and ingredients and Lora Brody's Bread Dough Enhancers

KITCHEN AND HOME CATALOG: (800) 414-5544

BROOKSTONE: (800) 351-7222

And if your Cuisinart blade should take that one-way trip down the garbage disposal:
Replacement parts:

CULINARY PARTS: (800) 543-7549
EUROPEAN KITCHEN BAZAAR: (800) 243-8540

The best guide we've found to finding food sources and sites on the Internet is called *Food and Wine On-Line: A Guide to Culinary On-line Services,* by Gary Holleman (Van Nostrand Reinhold, 1995). You can even order it and lots of other wonderful food related books on-line from Amazon at Amazon.com.

INDEX